ADAMS FAMILY

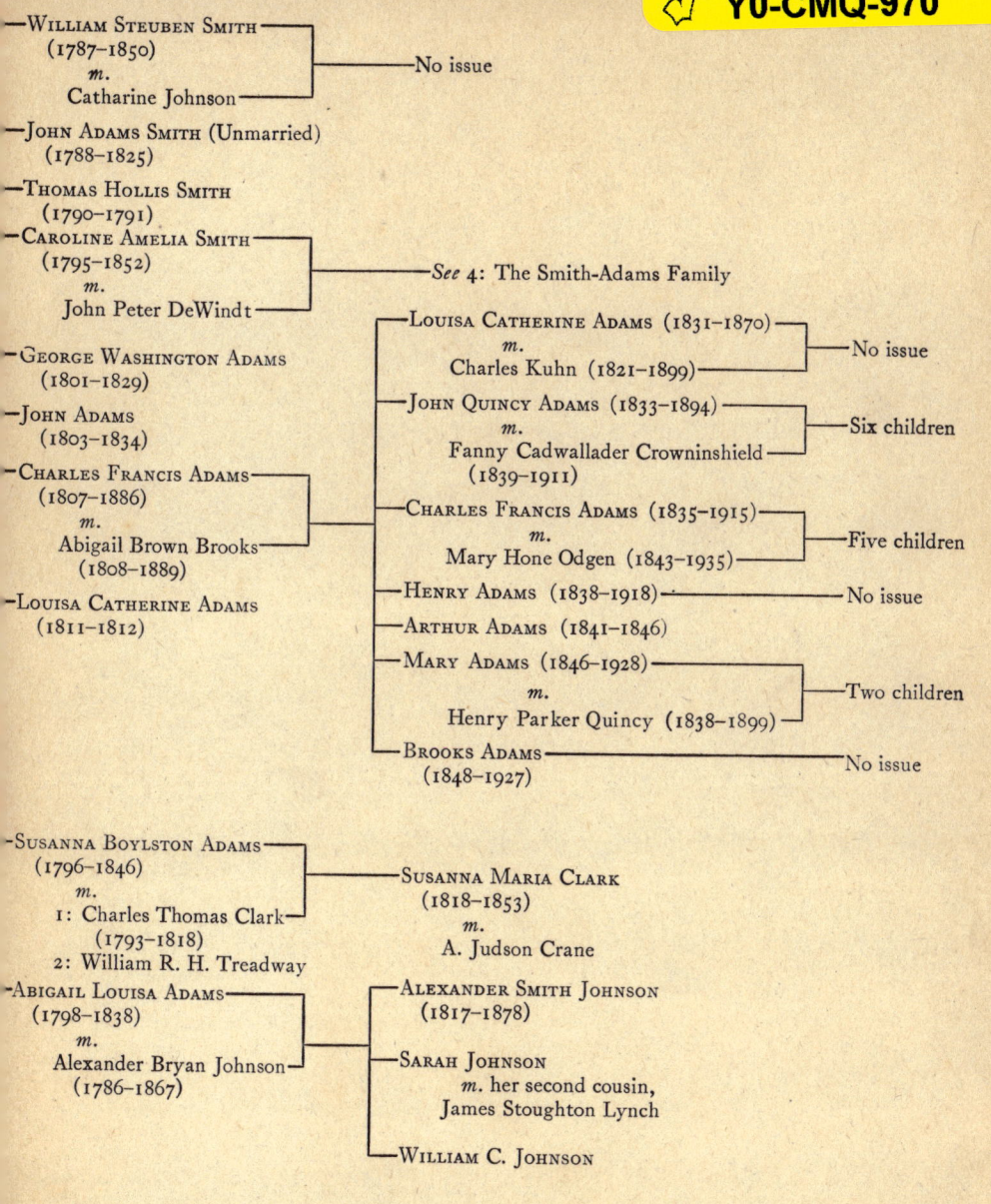

- William Steuben Smith (1787–1850) m. Catharine Johnson — No issue
- John Adams Smith (Unmarried) (1788–1825)
- Thomas Hollis Smith (1790–1791)
- Caroline Amelia Smith (1795–1852) m. John Peter DeWindt — *See 4: The Smith-Adams Family*
- George Washington Adams (1801–1829)
- John Adams (1803–1834)
- Charles Francis Adams (1807–1886) m. Abigail Brown Brooks (1808–1889)
  - Louisa Catherine Adams (1831–1870) m. Charles Kuhn (1821–1899) — No issue
  - John Quincy Adams (1833–1894) m. Fanny Cadwallader Crowninshield (1839–1911) — Six children
  - Charles Francis Adams (1835–1915) m. Mary Hone Odgen (1843–1935) — Five children
  - Henry Adams (1838–1918) — No issue
  - Arthur Adams (1841–1846)
  - Mary Adams (1846–1928) m. Henry Parker Quincy (1838–1899) — Two children
  - Brooks Adams (1848–1927) — No issue
- Louisa Catherine Adams (1811–1812)

- Susanna Boylston Adams (1796–1846) m. 1: Charles Thomas Clark (1793–1818); 2: William R. H. Treadway
  - Susanna Maria Clark (1818–1853) m. A. Judson Crane
- Abigail Louisa Adams (1798–1838) m. Alexander Bryan Johnson (1786–1867)
  - Alexander Smith Johnson (1817–1878)
  - Sarah Johnson m. her second cousin, James Stoughton Lynch
  - William C. Johnson

- Four sons and Three daughters — No issue

- Four daughters

New Letters of Abigail Adams

ABIGAIL ADAMS   *Gilbert Stuart*

New Letters
of
Abigail Adams
1788-1801

EDITED
WITH AN INTRODUCTION
BY
Stewart Mitchell

HOUGHTON MIFFLIN COMPANY · BOSTON
The Riverside Press Cambridge
1947

None of these letters, or any part of these letters, may be reproduced, with the exception of short passages for the purpose of review, without permission in writing from the Director of the American Antiquarian Society, Worcester, Massachusetts

Copyright 1947, by the American Antiquarian Society

PRINTED IN THE U.S.A.

R. D. C.
(1909-1939)

Γῆς ἐπέβην γυμνός, γυμνός θ' ὑπὸ γαῖαν ἄπειμι,
καὶ τί μάτην μοχθῶ, γυμνὸν ὁρῶν τὸ τέλος;

Palladas

"My letters to you are first thoughts, without correction"
Abigail Adams to Mary Cranch, May 26, 1798.

ACKNOWLEDGMENTS

In preparing these letters for publication, the editor has received generous and invaluable assistance from a great number of people, in particular, from the late Allyn B. Forbes, Director of the Massachusetts Historical Society, and also the members of its staff; as well as Clarence S. Brigham and Clifford K. Shipton, Director and Librarian, respectively, of the American Antiquarian Society; Robert W. G. Vail, Director of the New York Historical Society; and Nicholas B. Wainwright, Assistant Librarian of the Historical Society of Pennsylvania. He is indebted, moreover, to members of the staff of the Harvard College Library and the Fogg Art Museum, to Miss Dorothy S. Manks, Librarian of the Massachusetts Horticultural Society, and to Miss Dorothy C. Barck, Librarian of the New York Historical Society.

He is under obligation, also, to Mrs. Henry D. Holmes and Miss Frances Holmes, of Montpelier, Vermont; to Heyliger DeWindt, of Boston; to John Kieran, of "Information Please"; and to the late Albert Matthews, former Editor of the Colonial Society of Massachusetts. From first to last, the services of his secretary, Miss Marjorie M. Bruce, were continuous and faithful, and without them this work could not have been carried to completion.

Stewart Mitchell

ILLUSTRATIONS

ABIGAIL ADAMS	*Gilbert Stuart*	Frontispiece
MRS. WILLIAM STEPHENS SMITH, 1787 . . .	*J. S. Copley*	16
RICHMOND HILL, NEW YORK CITY, 1790		
BUSH HILL, PHILADELPHIA, 1787	*J. P. Malcom*	32
THE ADAMS MANSION, QUINCY, 1787 . . .	*E. Malcolm*	80
THE EXECUTIVE MANSION, PHILADELPHIA, 1790		
THE MORRIS HOUSES, PHILADELPHIA, 1790		96
WILLIAM STEPHENS SMITH, 1786 . . .	*Mather Brown*	128
JOHN ADAMS, 1789	*John Trumbull*	144
LETTER OF ABIGAIL ADAMS, 1800		240

CONTENTS

Calendar of Letters xv

Introduction xxiii

Letters of Abigail Adams 3

Bibliography 267

Genealogical Charts 268

Additions and Corrections 270

Index 271

Calendar of Letters

1788

Jamaica, [New York,] November 24: Birth of John Adams Smith. Colonel Smith's home at Jamaica 3

Jamaica, December 15–18: Recovery of Mrs. William Stephens Smith. Mother and sisters of Colonel Smith. Anxiety for Susanna (Boylston) [Adams] Hall . . 4

1789

"Richmond Hill," [New York,] January 24: Visit of William Smith. Social life as wife of Vice-President 7

Providence, [Rhode Island,] June 19: Journey from Braintree and social life in Rhode Island 9

"Richmond Hill," [New York,] June 28: Pleasant visits in Providence and Newport. Voyage from Newport to New York. George and Martha Washington, and social life in New York 11

"Richmond Hill," July 12: Intense heat. Character and habits of George Washington. Sentiments and politics of Congress. Anxiety for Mrs. Richard Cranch, and future of her son. Correspondence between Mercy (Otis) Warren and Elbridge Gerry. Description of "Richmond Hill" 14

"Richmond Hill," August 9: Burden of social duties. Form of reception by President and Mrs. Washington. Indolence and drunkenness of servants in New York. Political criticism of Washington and Adams. Household at "Richmond Hill" 18

"Richmond Hill," September 1: Funding the national debt. Proposal to move capital to Philadelphia. Edward Church's libel against Adams 22

"Richmond Hill," October 4: Superiority of Massachusetts preachers to those of New York. Adjournment of Congress and disappointment at inability to visit Braintree. Advantages of private over public life. "Bedlamites" in Congress 26

"Richmond Hill," October 11: Departure of Adams for Braintree. President Washington's tour of New England. Visit to "Prince's Gardens." Trouble with poor servants 29

"Richmond Hill," November 1: Inoculation for small-pox. Second marriage of Dr. Cotton Tufts. Hopes for early return of John Adams. Supplies of food from Braintree and Boston 31

"Richmond Hill," November 3: Pleasure and expense of living at "Richmond Hill." Trouble with servants. Plans for J. Q. and T. B. Adams 33

1790

"Richmond Hill," January 5–10: Dutch New Year's in New York. President's reception. Character of Washington. Plans for future of her three sons. Character of her grandsons 34

"Richmond Hill," February 20: Death of Mrs. Palmer. Hamilton's proposal for funding debt. John Gardiner a madman 36

xv

New York, February 28: Illness of T. B. Adams. John Gardiner 39

New York, March 15: Plans for Joseph Cranch. New babies amongst relatives. Health of T. B. Adams. Consumption in Boston 40

New York, March 21: Future of Joseph Cranch. Marriages and births. Financial burden of large family 42

New York, April 3: A new grand-nephew. Satisfaction with Mrs. Smith's children. Beauty of spring at "Richmond Hill." Plans for Joseph Cranch. Thomas Jefferson. Poor preachers in New York 43

"Richmond Hill," April 21: Advice for recovery from childbirth. Henry Knox and advancement for Joseph Cranch. William Steuben Smith 45

"Richmond Hill," April 28: Attack of rheumatism and general illness in household. Trouble with servants, except for slaves. Polly Tailor 46

New York, May 30: Washington's illness. Beauty of "Richmond Hill" . . . 48

"Richmond Hill," June 9: Influenza in New York. Furniture for "Richmond Hill" 50

New York, June 13: Possibility of moving capital to Baltimore. Excursion with Mrs. Washington 51

New York, June 27: New tenant for house in Braintree. Another grandson by Mrs. Smith 52

New York, July 4: Reopening of Dutch church. Picture of "Richmond Hill." Sedentary duties of John Adams 53

"Richmond Hill," July 27: Harvard Commencement. Tenant for house at Braintree. Scandalous Boston gossip about New York 54

New York, August 8: Birth of Thomas Hollis Smith. Visit of McGillivray and Creek Indians 56

New York, August 29: Farewell to Mrs. Washington. Philadelphia the new national capital. Careers of T. B. Adams and Joseph Cranch 57

New York, October 3: Moving to Philadelphia. Inoculation for small-pox . . . 59

New York, October 10: Sorrow at leaving New York for Philadelphia. Tenant for house at Braintree. Clothing for cold weather 60

New York, October 17: Departure from "Richmond Hill" for New York City. Gift of wine to Cranches. Illness of John Adams 62

New York, October 25: Serious illness. Shipping furniture to Philadelphia. Cure for pleurisy 63

New York, November 7: Recovery from illness. Farewell to Mrs. William S. Smith. Treatment of small-pox 64

Philadelphia, December 12–14: Journey to Philadelphia. Illness in Adams household. Dr. Benjamin Rush. Departure of Colonel Smith for England . . 65

1791

Philadelphia, January 9: Philadelphia compared with New York. Loneliness for daughter. Indolent and drunken servants. Future of T. B. Adams . . . 67

Bush Hill, [Pennsylvania,] March 12: Remarks on Colonel Smith. Plans for future of

her three sons. Servant problems. Domestic affairs at Braintree. Washington's southern tour 69
Bush Hill, April 18: Supplies for garden and house at Braintree 72
New York, May 6: Visit with Mrs. William Stephens Smith. Supplies for house at Braintree 72
Philadelphia, October 30: Trip from Braintree to Philadelphia. New house in city. Domestic affairs in Braintree 73
Philadelphia, December 18: Social life and expenses at Philadelphia. Illness of John Adams. St. Clair's Defeat. Domestic affairs at Braintree. 74

1792

Philadelphia, February 5: Visit of Smiths and Charles Adams. Proposed trip of Smiths to England. Social life in Philadelphia. Unpopularity of Indian war 77
Philadelphia, March 20–21: Long illness. Plans for returning to Quincy. Provisions for household 78
Philadelphia, March 25–29: Impatience at long confinement. Supplies for Quincy. Reapportionment of House of Representatives. Mania for speculation. "Republican" hostility to Hamilton. Washington's head on coins 80
Philadelphia, April 20: Continued illness. Supplies for house at Quincy. Financial panic. Newspaper campaign against Knox and Hamilton 81
New York, April 29: Results of panic in New York. Plans for reaching Quincy . . 84

1795

New York, June 25: Providing for poor relations. Jay's Treaty. William Cranch, James Greenleaf, and the North American Land Company 84

1797

Springfield, [Massachusetts,] April 30: Braintree to Springfield. Responsibilities as wife of President. Death of mother of John Adams 86
East Chester, [New York,] May 5: Visit with Mrs. William Stephens Smith. Farm at Quincy 88
Philadelphia, May 16: Colonel William Stephens Smith. Charles Adams and family. New York to Philadelphia. "Splendid misery" as wife of President . . . 89
Philadelphia, May 24: Domestic and social routine. Decline in public character and morals. France and American Jacobins. Food from Boston 91
Philadelphia, June 3: Unseasonably cold weather. President's speech. "XYZ Mission." Violence of newspapers. Transfer of J. Q. Adams from Netherlands to Prussia. Bache and "Peter Porcupine" 93
Philadelphia, June 6–8: Trouble in town meeting. Adams eager to return to Quincy. Falsehoods of Anti-Federalist press. Ruin of Greenleaf and Morris 96
Philadelphia, June 23: Good news of house and farm at Quincy. Entertaining Congress at dinner. Expense of celebrating Fourth of July. Gerry for "XYZ Mission." Washington's approval of Adams. Fenno's *Gazette* 98

Philadelphia, July 6 (with enclosure): Fourth of July. Senator William Blount. Opposition to President leaving Philadelphia. Future of William Cranch. Gerry and "XYZ Mission" 100

Philadelphia, July 11: Gifts for family. Hopes for news from Quincy 103

Philadelphia, July 19: Preparations for returning to Quincy. Heat and dysentery in Philadelphia 104

Philadelphia, July [21]: Suffocating heat. Plans for two nephews, and care of niece 104

East Chester, [New York,] July [24]: Fatiguing trip from Philadelphia to New York 105

East Chester, July 29: Plans for departure for Quincy. Supplies for household. Care of Smith grandsons 106

Worcester, Massachusetts, October 5: Trip from Quincy to Worcester, on way to Philadelphia 107

East Chester, October 22: Visit with Mrs. William Stephens Smith. Lack of news from Smith grandsons. Long absence of Colonel Smith. Loneliness and desolation of daughter 108

East Chester, October 31: Low spirits of daughter. Letters from sons in London. Marriage of J. Q. Adams 109

Philadelphia, November 15: Disciplining John Adams. Long absence of Colonel Smith. Assistant clergyman for Quincy. Bache's abuse of Adams 110

Philadelphia, November 28–29: Troubles of Colonel Smith and family. Congress and the President's speech. French Directory a scourge to the world. Supplies of food from Quincy 113

Philadelphia, December 12, (with enclosure): Assistant clergyman for Quincy. Death of Mr. and Mrs. Hall. Letter from T. B. Adams. Sermon of Bishop of Norwich. Jefferson to dinner. Calvinism in Philadelphia. Criticism of Bache 115

Philadelphia, December 26: Dislike of Calvinism. Serious illness. Loneliness of daughter, and anxiety for Smith grandsons. Care of Hall orphan daughter. President and wife as "Darby and Joan" 119

1798

Philadelphia, January 5: Death of Halls, and care of their daughter. Death of nephew of Mrs. Adams. News of peace between Austria and France . . . 121

Philadelphia, January 20: Denunciation of French Directory and its American supporters. Assistant clergyman for Quincy 124

Philadelphia, February [1–5]: Dismissal of Tench Coxe. Venality in Pickering's office. News of J. Q. Adams in Prussia 126

Philadelphia, February 6: Financial troubles of Colonel Smith. Letters from sons in Prussia 130

Philadelphia, February 15: Brawl between Griswold and Lyon. Bad manners of Philadelphians, and discourteous proposal to celebrate Washington's birthday 132

Philadelphia, February 21: Illness of Mrs. Adams. Financial troubles of Greenleaf and Morris. Failure of effort to expel Lyon. Anxiety for her brother . . . 134

Philadelphia, February 28: Failure of ball in honor of George Washington . . . 136

Philadelphia, March 3: Letters from Berlin. Death of King of Prussia. Foreign Intercourse Bill 138

Philadelphia, March 5: Mrs. Thomas Law. Superiority of New Englanders to people of Philadelphia. Failure of mission to France. Domestic affairs at Quincy 139

Philadelphia, March 13: Business difficulties of William Cranch. Tense relations with France. "Peter Porcupine" and Bache. Anxiety for J. Q. Adams . . 142

Philadelphia, March 14: Disputes over policy toward France. Latest styles in female attire. Visit of Indian kings 144

Philadelphia, March 20: Secrecy as to news from France. Bache's attack on Adams 146

Philadelphia, March 27: Vanity and vexation of life. Perverse wickedness of Directory. Division of American opinion over France. Foreign Intercourse Bill . . 147

Philadelphia, March 31: Bad manners of Virginians in regard to Foreign Intercourse Bill. Bache's ridicule of John Adams 149

Philadelphia, April 4: Failure of "XYZ Mission." Character and conduct of Talleyrand 150

Philadelphia, April 7: Publication of dispatches from envoys to France. Jacobin sympathy with France in the United States. Anxiety for personal safety of envoys 153

Philadelphia, April 13: Liberation of Greenleaf from prison. Letters from Berlin: friendly conduct of Frederick William III. Insolence of Directory towards the United States 155

Philadelphia, April 21: Trip of J. Q. Adams from London to Berlin. French bureaucracy under Directory. Malice and falsehood of Bache 157

Philadelphia, April 22: Work on house in Quincy. Jesuit Gallatin and Jacobins in Congress. Patriotic addresses to John Adams. French depredations. Care of Hall orphan 160

Philadelphia, April 26: First singing of "Hail Columbia." Sedition Bill. Bache's false report 164

Philadelphia, April 28: Alterations to house in Quincy. Demonstrations of loyalty in Philadelphia 167

Philadelphia, May 7: Mrs. Thrale's Dialogue on Death. French Revolution a scourge to all nations. Patriotic parades in Philadelphia. Financial difficulties of Greenleaf. Work on house at Quincy 168

Philadelphia, May 10: A French conspiracy in Philadelphia. Popular support of John Adams. Bache and his Jacobin slanders. Alien and Sedition Bill . . 170

Philadelphia, May 13: Fatigue of President Adams from answering public addresses 172

Philadelphia, May 13, to Mrs. John Greenleaf: Present for her daughter. Death of Mary Carter Smith 173

Philadelphia, May 18: Patriotic demonstrations in Philadelphia. Volunteer Corps. Anxiety for "XYZ Mission" 174

Philadelphia, May 20–21: Patriotic tension and false rumors. Danger of war with France. News from William Vans Murray. Exhaustion of President Adams . 176

Philadelphia, May 26: Alien and Sedition Bill. Volunteer Corps. Robison's book on Freemasons. Victor Du Pont arrives in Philadelphia. Burke's opinion of French Republic 179

Philadelphia, May 29: Visit to frigate *United States*. Benjamin Russell's *Columbian Centinel* 182

Philadelphia, June 1: Financial difficulties caused by failure of Greenleaf. Work on house at Quincy 183

Philadelphia, June 4: Assistant for Anthony Wibird, and new secretary for J. Q. Adams. Alarm for American envoys to France. England only barrier to French domination of Europe 184

Philadelphia, June 8: Visit to "Belmont," Pennsylvania. Relations with France. Edward Church and John Adams 187

Philadelphia, June 13: News from J. Q. Adams. French invasion of Switzerland and Gerry's decision to remain in France 190

Philadelphia, June 19: Breaking up of "XYZ Mission" and villainy of Talleyrand. Alarm over Gerry 193

Philadelphia, June 23: Heat and disease in Philadelphia. Dilatory tactics of Congress. Hard work and homesickness of John Adams. Sedition Act for Massachusetts 194

Philadelphia, June 25: Depressing heat. Reception for Marshall on return from France. Invitation to visit "Mount Vernon" 196

Philadelphia, June 27: Reflections on the death of Jeremy Belknap and John Clarke 197

Philadelphia, July 3: Exhausting heat. Washington named commander-in-chief . 199

Philadelphia, July 9: Capture of French privateer. Arrest of Bache and Burk. Absent treatment by Benjamin Rush. Unwillingness of Congress to declare war on France. Universal confidence in Washington 199

Philadelphia, July 12: Advice for William Smith Shaw, future secretary to President Adams 202

Philadelphia, July 13: Legal business of William Cranch in Washington. Benjamin Stoddert, first Secretary of Navy. Nomination of officers for Army. Disappointment at missing Harvard Commencement 202

Philadelphia, July 17: Senate waits word from "Mount Vernon." Gerry, and rumors of peace with France. Supplies for house at Quincy. Secretary McHenry returns with Washington's acceptance. Nomination of officers for Army . . 205

1799

New York, January 17: Early and dangerous spring. News from J. Q. Adams at Dresden. Outburst of John Randolph of Roanoke 208

Brookfield, Massachusetts, October 13: Stay with Thomas Marshall and family at Weston. Worry over President's cold 208

East Chester, New York, October 20: Yellow fever in New York and Philadelphia. Work on house at Quincy 209

East Chester, October 31: Domestic illnesses. John Adams at Trenton, New Jersey. Family of Charles Adams, and his intemperance. Anxiety for J. Q. Adams 210

xx

[East Chester, November 1–3]: Impending departure for Philadelphia. Envoys to France ready to sail. Attack of Thomas Cooper 212

Philadelphia, November 15: Trip from New York to Philadelphia. Visit to camp at Plainfield, New Jersey. Social duties at Philadelphia. Celebration of the President's birthday. French fashions in America 213

Philadelphia, November 26: Theory of the good life. Political violence of Thomas Cooper and his friends. News from J. Q. Adams. Stormy session of Congress anticipated 215

Philadelphia, December 4: President's address to Congress. Eagerness for news from France. Domestic matters in Quincy. Dana as successor to Governor Sumner 217

Philadelphia, December 11: Assistant clergyman for Quincy. Melancholy visit to Mrs. Robert Morris. President's speech to Congress. Popular reaction to peace with France. Disloyalty of Timothy Pickering 219

Philadelphia, December 22–23: Death of George Washington. His character and conduct. Squabbles over new assistant clergyman for Quincy. Benjamin Rush and "Peter Porcupine" 222

Philadelphia, December 30–31: Letter from Talleyrand to President Adams. Hamilton's prediction of imminent restoration of Bourbons. Mourning for Washington at Philadelphia. Danger lest Washington be praised beyond his deserts 224

1800

Philadelphia, January 7: Assistant clergyman for Quincy. Blunders of Boston printers. William Smith Shaw's visit to "Mount Vernon." Business troubles of James Greenleaf. General Lee's oration on Washington 226

Philadelphia, January 28: Indiscreet praise of Washington: Messinger's oration. Bonaparte an adventurer. Letter of John Randolph of Roanoke. Alterations to house at Quincy 228

Philadelphia, January 30: Burden of social duties as wife of the President . . . 231

Philadelphia, February 12: William Cranch's candidacy for clerk of Supreme Court 232

Philadelphia, February 27: Reverend Peter Whitney colleague to Anthony Wibird. Delightful weather at Philadelphia. Unpleasant prospect of removing to Washington. William Jackson's oration on George Washington. Improvement in health 234

Philadelphia, March 5: Surrender of Thomas Nash to British. Danger of frequent popular elections. Public feeling as to George Washington 236

Philadelphia, March 15–18: Dilatory tactics of Congress. A broken engagement. House for the Reverend Peter Whitney. Character of James Greenleaf. Immodest dress of women 238

Philadelphia, March 22: Providing for the Porters in Quincy 242

Philadelphia, April 7: Success of William Cranch in Washington. Beauty of spring in Philadelphia. Major and Mrs. Tousard 244

Philadelphia, April 15: Alterations to house in Quincy 245

xxi

Philadelphia, April 17: Domestic details of removal to Quincy for summer, and Washington for winter 246

Philadelphia, April 24–26: Illness and success of William Cranch in Washington. Mrs. Joshua Johnson and social life. Indecent dress of young ladies. Preparations for return to Quincy. Arrival of Christopher Gore from England . . 246

Philadelphia, [May 3]: Character of Reverend Anthony Wibird. Last Drawing-Room at Philadelphia 249

[Philadelphia, May 5]: Alterations to house at Quincy. Importance of New York in coming election. Scurrilous attacks on Adams. Sectional animosity . . . 250

Norwalk, Connecticut, May 26: Visit to Scotch Plains. Character and conduct of Colonel Smith. Bitter campaign for President, and disgust with world . . 252

New Haven, Connecticut, November 2: Impending departure for Philadelphia and Washington. Adams on his way to Washington 254

Philadelphia, November 10: Deathbed of Charles Adams. Election letter of Hamilton 254

Washington, November 21: Stay with Snowdens at "Montpelier," Maryland. Arrival at Georgetown. Adams's birthday at Quincy. Hamilton in disgrace. Adams's speech to Congress. The President's House in Washington . . . 256

Washington, December 1: Sickness in family. Election of 1800 260

Washington, December 8: Death of Charles Adams 261

1801

Washington, January 15: Poor health in Washington. Dignified defeat better than resignation for Adams. Norton Quincy. Adams determined to leave public life 262

Washington, February 7: Public excitement over tie between Burr and Jefferson. Danger of popular government. Character of Burr and Jefferson. Prospect of hard journey back to Quincy 264

Introduction

I

THE LETTERS

IN 1942 there came into the possession of the American Antiquarian Society, of Worcester, Massachusetts, a collection of about two hundred and fifty letters which Abigail (Smith) Adams, the wife of President John Adams, wrote to her elder sister, Mary Cranch, who was married to Richard Cranch, of Braintree. These letters came from the estate of William George Arthur Turner (1858–1936), who was the husband of Mary Greenleaf Dawes (1861–1934), the great-great-granddaughter of the lady to whom most of them were addressed. Only sixteen of these letters had ever been published, having been included in the various collections of her correspondence edited by her grandson, Charles Francis Adams, from 1840 to 1876.

For this volume 141 hitherto unpublished letters were selected from the whole Cranch-Dawes-Turner Collection. These 141 letters were written over a period of fourteen years, and from all three capitals of the United States—New York (1789–1790), Philadelphia (1790–1800), and Washington (1800–1801). By far the greatest number of them are dated during the first vice-presidency of John Adams and his single term as President. For the years 1793–1796 only one letter exists. Mrs. Adams spent most of that time at home, in the neighborhood of her elder, and favorite, sister, and had no reason to write to her. On the other hand, no fewer than ninety-five of these letters were composed while "Her Majesty" Abigail Adams was First Lady of the Land. These reflect the political and military anxieties, much of the growing factional rancor of the period, and the worries connected with our strained and stormy relations with France.

This is the first time that any considerable number of the letters of Abigail Adams have been printed precisely and completely as she wrote them.[1] The different editions prepared by Charles Francis Adams must be used with great caution, for Abigail's grandson not only modernized her spelling, but took unindicated liberties with the texts. As an editor he was excessively cautious in his care not to publish anything which would offend even the descendants of the contemporaries of John Adams. Proof of this glacial discretion is to be found in a comparison of the sixteen letters as printed by Mr. Adams from 1840 to 1876 with the originals of these letters now in Worcester. Abigail Adams observed of herself: "My pen is always freer than my tongue. I have written many things to you that I suppose I never could have talked."[2]

Although no time and trouble have been spared to preserve the flavor of Abigail's phonetic spelling, and even her punctuation and the use of capitals, these are, after all, of trifling importance. Samuel Johnson established orthodox spelling in England when he brought out his *Dictionary* in 1755; about half a century later Noah Webster did much the same thing for the United States. Tampering with the contents of letters, however, is dangerous business, especially when it is prompted by consideration for the feelings not only of others but of ourselves. Family pride has held back the course of history time and again; yet sooner or later these dams are always broken, and the truth bursts through. Any "family," of course, is simply a convenient social fiction, undue regard for which can sink to absurd superstition. "Families" blend one into another in hopeless, interlocking confusion. Children, to be sure, wear the last names of their fathers; that

---

[1] Twenty-five letters, written by Abigail Adams to Mercy Warren between 1773 and 1814, appeared in the *Warren-Adams Letters: 1743–1777*, Boston, 1917–1925. In 1942, twelve letters written by Abigail Adams between 1786 and 1811 were published in the sixty-sixth volume of the *Proceedings* of the Massachusetts Historical Society. The originals of these thirty-seven letters are in the Warren Papers and the DeWindt Collection in the Society. Two of the letters included in this volume, those of June 19 and June 28, 1789, were printed in *Rhode Island History*, October, 1942.

[2] *Familiar Letters of John Adams and His Wife Abigail Adams, During the Revolution*, Charles Francis Adams, Editor, New York, 1876, p. 115.

this custom determines their character, and thus decides their fate, is nothing more than amiable nonsense. No matter whose feelings are involved, and how, it is high time to lift all censorship from the papers of persons who lived and died one hundred years ago. Here for the first time, at last, we have intimate details of the domestic life and troubles of the tribe of Adams.

There is still another respect in which these letters are significant. Abigail Adams enjoys a good, if not great, reputation as a correspondent. In the days of her youth it was fashionable for young ladies writing to one another to adopt classical pen-names; so Abigail chose "Diana"; subsequent to her marriage, she signed herself, more appropriately, "Portia." These young ladies seem to have worked hard over their compositions. Thus, when Abigail wrote to her top-flight friends and to literary people her usual practice was to prepare rough drafts, and then make copies of these with such corrections as she thought fitting. Sometimes one of her sons would work out the final version for her. Not so with these letters to her sister Mary—all those in this volume were composed hastily, and posted promptly. "My letters to you," she wrote on May 26, 1798, "are first thoughts, without correction." The style, of course, is more intimate and easy, and the comments more familiar, even if some of the domestic details may seem trivial to persons not greatly interested in social history.

They are full of references to current politics, many of them tart and partisan, for Abigail became an ardent Federalist. Most of her opinions probably reflect the private thoughts and feelings of her husband. This correspondence is filled with information as to conditions of life, especially in New York City and Philadelphia, at the close of the eighteenth century. We get glimpses of how people lived, in spite of sudden and serious sickness, and recurrent epidemics of smallpox and yellow fever. Keeping house was no simple matter, for servants were not only incompetent, but frequently drunkards, rogues, and thieves, and the fluctuating value of money in those days of inflation was an unpredictable mystery. People suffered cruelly from poor food and bad water, and quinine seems to have been the common cure for every ailment, apart from the barbarous and dangerous practice of blistering and bleeding.

In addition to all the trials and tribulations of public life, and the hardships of living away from home, Abigail suffered severely from her generous sense of responsibility for poor relations and indigent friends. Her courage and good nature, her unfailing kindness, even under the stress of sickness, disappointment, and misfortune, make a pleasant contrast to the unhappy circumstances of some of these fourteen years. The first letter was written from Jamaica, Long Island, whither Mrs. Adams had gone to greet her daughter, Mrs. William Stephens Smith, who had just recently returned from England, on the eve of giving birth to her second son, John Adams Smith. The last letter was written from the brand-new White House, not long before Abigail Adams left Washington forever.

In editing these letters, every effort has been made to identify persons and quotations, and to explain references to places and to circumstances. Not all these efforts were successful, for some of the friends and neighbors of Mrs. Cranch and Mrs. Adams were utterly obscure. Although the footnotes were designed to help, rather than to distract readers, complete discretion in this matter is difficult. It is not always easy to determine what readers know, or remember—or care to be told. All canceled words, and all editorial additions to the text are enclosed in square brackets. Often these have been employed to avoid the use of footnotes.

The genealogical charts were prepared in the hope that they might assist readers in unraveling the complicated relation and descent of persons frequently referred to. Marriage among cousins, the use of only Christian names, and the frequent recurrence of the surname Smith make accurate identification doubtful in some cases. The chart of the John Adams Family has an additional interest, for it proves that the greatest proportion of ability appeared among the children of Charles Francis Adams (1807–1886). Each of the Adams Presidents had one distinguished son—but one only.

II
Abigail Adams

Abigail Smith (1744–1818), who became the wife of John Adams, was the second of four children of the Reverend William Smith (1707–1783), of Weymouth, who married Elizabeth Quincy (1722–1775). She had two sisters, Mary and Elizabeth, and a brother, William, a captain of the militia, who settled in Lincoln and seems to have been a person of slight significance. Only son of a parson, he did not even go to Harvard—though not everyone did, in those days. Abigail was descended from some of the most distinguished men and women of New England. Her maternal grandfather was Colonel John Quincy (1689–1767), Speaker of the House of Representatives, and a member of the Council, who married Elizabeth Norton (1696–1769), the daughter of John Norton, the second minister of Hingham. The mother of this John Norton was the daughter of Thomas Shepard, first of that name, and minister of Charlestown.

Abigail, who was delicate, never went to school a day in her life. The greatest influence on her character and education seems to have been that of her maternal grandmother, with whom she spent much of her youth, in seclusion at Mount Wollaston. This remarkable old lady died when Abigail was twenty-five, and already (1764) married to John Adams. Her affection and regard for this Mrs. Quincy and for the mother of her husband, Susanna Boylston (1709–1797), is noticeable and touching. All three women seem to have been exceptional persons. There is a bit of mystery about Susanna Boylston, even though it is often said that she it was who brought the "brains" into the House of Adams—two sisters, it will be observed, married two brothers. The father of President John died in 1761, and about 1775, at the age of sixty-six, Susanna took a second husband, a Lieutenant John Hall, who predeceased her by many years. It is practically impossible to find out anything about this man. Somebody did not like this second marriage. No mention of it appears on the old lady's tombstone, but the notice of her death as published in the *Columbian Centinel* of May 3, 1797, described her as "Mrs.

Susannah Hall, the venerable mother of John Adams, President of the United States of America."

Although she had no formal education, Abigail Adams became a literate young lady, and a well-read woman. She quotes frequently, if always freely, from the Bible and Shakespeare, and from popular eighteenth-century authors like Swift, Sterne, and Burke, and that lively, loving, literary lady, Mrs. Hester Lynch (Salusbury) [Thrale] Piozzi. She married John Adams when she was not quite twenty, and bore him five children: two daughters, one of whom died as an infant, and three sons—John Quincy, Charles, and Thomas Boylston. Only one of these children achieved distinction. After ten years of happy married life as the wife of a provincial lawyer, Abigail found her household broken up by the American Revolution. For the next ten years she had not only the care of four children on her hands, but the farm at Quincy to look after, for public business kept her husband away from home much of that time.

In 1784 she finally joined John Adams in Europe, to spend eight months in Paris and then three years in London. Many of her most delightful letters date from this period. In 1787 the Adamses returned to the United States, and there Abigail spent the rest of her life. In spite of delicate health and attacks of serious illness, she seems to have been of a cheerful disposition, and a companionable, popular person. The political opponents of her husband probably exaggerated her influence over him: Albert Gallatin called her "Mrs. President not of the United States, but of a faction." Charles Francis Adams argues otherwise, and at some length—for him, perhaps, the perfect wife was no more than the moon to the sunlight of her husband.

If Abigail Adams was not a perfect wife, she was a very good one, who managed financial matters so well as to protect the second President from the dangerous indigence of old age. As an affectionate mother, however, she cannot quite be cleared of the suspicion of having spoiled two of her children—her pretty daughter, Mrs. Smith, who seems to have complained much of the man whom she had deigned to accept as her husband; and her second son, Charles, who met an early and a very unhappy death. This son was a cause of constant worry to his parents. Born in 1770, he was graduated from Harvard College in 1789, and moved to New York City, where he married the sister of his sister's husband, Sarah Smith (1769–1828), and had two daughters. He planned to practise law, but he could not stick to anything. He was popular, gregarious, and unstable; he lived high, and he took to drink. Two of his mother's letters, those of November 10 and December 8, 1800, contain painful descriptions of his last illness and pitiable death in New York City on Sunday, November 30, 1800.

The tragic end of this attractive son is often referred to as the reason for the last-minute departure of John Adams from Washington just before the arrival of Thomas Jefferson, for his inauguration. Adams drove off at sunrise on March 4, 1801; yet the troublesome son (whom he had not even stopped off to see when he passed through New York on his way to Washington in the autumn of 1800) had been dead and buried all of three months when the second President climbed into his coach that winter morning. His grandson knew what was uppermost in the mind of John Adams, deftly as he tried to cover it with a web of words.

To them, then, as well as to Mr. Jefferson's followers he was to be made a spectacle, if he should stay to be a part of the pageant. No. His proud spirit would not endure it. He would not consent to enact the captive chief in the triumphant procession of the victor to the capitol.[3]

Colonel William Stephens Smith, the handsome, gallant, and spoiled son of a rich merchant of New York, lived longer, and caused even more trouble for Abigail Adams, her husband, and their daughter. Smith had served well and bravely during the Revolution; so Washington, whose aide he had been, sent him to London, as secretary to the first legation. There he met and married the daughter of the American minister, although he has been coldly described as "a stranger to the family." As late as 1798, John Adams lectured him in a letter complaining of his "pride and ostentation." The colonel had expensive tastes; so he cheerfully planned to make himself a fortune by speculating

---

[3] John Quincy Adams and Charles Francis Adams, *The Life of John Adams*, Philadelphia, 1871, vol. 2, p. 353.

in land. His scheme was attractively simple: he would buy land low on credit, and sell it high for cash. He acquired large areas in central New York State, and promptly became bankrupt in the crash of 1797. Even Alexander Hamilton interceded for him with the swarms of his creditors. The unpleasant story of Smith's treatment of one of these, Lieutenant-Colonel William W. Burrows, first commandant of the United States Marine Corps, came to light in 1800 at the time of the outcry over Colonel Smith's appointment by his father-in-law as surveyor-general of the Port of New York.[4] There is reason to suspect that the greatest influence of Abigail on President John was this unfortunate, if gentle, pressure to keep needy members of the family in funds by putting them on the public pay rolls. Enemies of Adams who accused him of nepotism were not wholly unjust.

Abigail's first report of this son-in-law is precisely what one would expect of her cheerful and generous nature. In 1786, immediately prior to the marriage of her daughter, Mrs. Adams wrote from London to her sister, Mrs. Cranch:

> Your niece is engaged to a gentleman worthy of her; one whom you will be proud to take by the hand and own as a nephew. With regard to his person, he is tall, slender, and a good figure; a complexion naturally dark, but made still more so by seven years' service in the field. He appears a gentleman in every thought, word, and action.[5]

But Colonel Smith liked punch, and loved to consort with his convivial brothers. The letters which follow show that he was frequently absent from home for protracted periods, during which time no news of him reached his lonely, anxious wife. Abigail Adams was blunt but not far wrong when she told the mother of the colonel that she had "been too indulgent to her sons." So much for the domestic tribulations of Abigail Adams.

Her social and public worries stemmed from the fact that Abigail was a Yankee, born and bred, and really never felt at home anywhere in the world except in her beloved New England. The preachers of New York were ranting bores; the dress and

[4] Massachusetts Historical Society: Pickering Manuscripts, vol. 51: misc. 2: William W. Burrows to Gouverneur Morris, February 4, 1801.
[5] *New York Genealogical and Biographical Record*, vol. 25 (1894), p. 160.

manners of the "Republican Court" in Philadelphia were loose and offensive; the so-called courtly ladies and gentlemen from Virginia did not seem even polite to her. The growth of faction, especially after George Washington withdrew to Mount Vernon, tempted her tongue to be a trifle too tart at the expense of the opponents of her hot-tempered husband. Devious Thomas Jefferson, it is amusing to notice, was diplomatic enough to make her call him companionable. Her distress at an obscure radical like John Gardiner, of Boston, was so unduly violent as to lead her to denounce him as a "madman" (February 20, 1790).

Her vexation at partisan journalists like Bache seems excessive. She was strongly in favor of the Alien and Sedition Bills—that rash legislation which helped to bring about the ruin of her hasty husband. The letter of May 26, 1798, supplies an odd instance of her lapses into gullibility. Unfortunately for her, Abigail somehow got hold of a bad book by a good man—John Robison's sensational and silly attack on the Freemasons. This volume was published in Edinburgh in 1797, and reprinted in New York in 1798. It sold well—like most stories of conspiracies against the world. Mrs. Adams swallowed it, hook, line, bait, and sinker, and sent a copy to Jeremy Belknap. What the founder of the Massachusetts Historical Society thought of this "lasting monument of fatuous credulity" does not appear.

Then there was revolutionary France, and Abigail was an ardent disciple of Edmund Burke. The dress of the Directory displeased her no less distinctly than its diplomacy. In April, 1800, her son, Thomas Boylston Adams, persuaded her to permit an impromptu dance in the home of the President, in Philadelphia. "Her Majesty" did not like all she saw. Worse still, the indecently dressed, if divine, young lady, Elizabeth Mason, hailed from the best of Boston!

Just before I rose from table, Thomas [Boylston Adams] came round to me and whisperd me, have you any objection to my having a dance this Evening? None in the world, provided it comes thus accidental. The company soon came up to the drawing Room to Tea, and in an hours time, the tables were removed, the lights light & the Room all in order. At 8 the dancing commenced. At 12, it finishd. More pleasure, ease and enjoyment I have rarely witnessd. The President went down about an hour & then retired. I tarried it out, but was obliged to go to Bed at 8 oclock last night in concequence. Several of the company declared that they should always remember the Evening as one of the pleasentesst of their lives—Amongst the company was Miss B. M. with manners perfectly affable, polite and agreable, without affectation, or any haughtyness of demeanour, but really fassinating. I could not but lament, that the uncoverd bosom should display, what ought to have been veild, or that the well turnd, and finely proportiond form, should not have been less conspicuous in the dance, from the thin drapery which coverd it. I wishd that more had been left to the imagination, and less to the Eye. She dances elegantly. "Grace was in all her steps."

There were blank spots in the brains of Puritans, just as there was a bleak aspect to the age in which they had to live. Abigail's droll comments on the sweetest, if not the greatest, satirist Europe has produced are completely in character:

I send with this the 1 volm of Molière and should be glad of your oppinion of them. I cannot be brought to like them. There seems to me to be a general want of Spirit, at the close of every one I have felt dissapointed. There are no characters but what appear unfinished and he seems to have ridiculed Vice without engageing us to Virtue; and tho he sometimes makes us laugh, yet tis a Smile of indignation. There is one Negative Virtue of which he is possess'd, I mean that of Decency. His Cit, turnd Gentleman, among many others has met with approbation. Tho I can readily acknowledg that the cit by acting so contrary to his real character has displayed a stupid vanity justly deserving ridicule, yet the fine Gentleman who defrauds and tricks him is as much the baser character as his advantages are superior to the others. Molière is said to have been an Honest Man, but Sure he has not coppied from his own Heart. Tho he has drawn many pictures of real life, yet all pictures of life are not fit to be exibited upon the Stage. I fear I shall incur the charge of vanity by thus criticising upon an Author who has met with so much applause. You, Madam, I hope will forgive me.[6]

Yet writers and readers of satire are not likely to be resolute persons, or given to being brave or gay. One of the favorite quotations of Abigail Adams was something she remembered from *Proverbs*, "A merry heart doeth good like a medicine." This spirit

---

[6] *See* Warren Papers: Abigail Adams to Mercy Warren, December 11, 1773, in the Massachusetts Historical Society. "Cit" was a cant term of the eighteenth century for a climber. Mrs. Adams refers to M. Jourdain, of "Le Bourgeois Gentilhomme."

carried her safely over a sea of troubles. In 1813 she lost her daughter; three years later the troublesome Colonel Smith followed his wife. She was old and often ill. Perhaps it is best to take leave of this noble lady by quoting three very different persons, men who knew her in her lifetime. When her faithful and successful son, then Secretary of State, got the news that she was gone forever, he made this gentle entry in his grim journal:

Had she lived to the age of the Patriarchs, every day of her life would have been filled with clouds of goodness and of love. There is not a virtue that can abide in the female heart but it was the ornament of hers. She had been fifty-four years the delight of my father's heart, the sweetener of all his toils, the comforter of all his sorrows, the sharer and heightener of all his joys. It was but the last time when I saw my father that he told me, with an ejaculation of gratitude to the Giver of every good and every perfect gift, that in all the vicissitudes of his fortunes, through all the good report and evil report of the world, in all his struggles and in all his sorrows, the affectionate participation and cheering encouragement of his wife had been his never-failing support, without which he was sure he should never have lived through them.[7]

That stubborn Republican-Democrat, the Reverend William Bentley, a stranger in the strange land of stiff-necked Salem, learning of her death on October 30, 1818, wrote in his diary:

We have had notice of the death of Abigail, wife of the late President John Adams, who is still living at his home in Quincy.... The first time I ever saw Madam was at her own house shelling her beans for a family dinner at which without any ceremony or apology she invited me but from engagements I did not accept. I saw her repeatedly at her own house without any impression unfavourable to her person or manners. I found a freedom in conversation which took its familiar topics. When at my own house in Salem she left the kind opinion of a respect for herself adapted to make her courtesy and conversation more valuable and agreeable. She was in appearance of middle size, in the dress of the matrons who were in New England in my youth. The black bonnet, the short cloak, the gown open before, and quilted petticoat, and the high heeled shoe, as worn universally in that day. Everything the best but nothing different from our wealthy and modest citizens. She was possessed of the history of our country and of the great occurrences in it. She had a distinct view of our public men and measures and had her own

[7] *Memoirs of John Quincy Adams*, Charles Francis Adams, Editor, Philadelphia, 1875, vol. 4, p. 157.

opinions which she was free to disclose but not eager to defend in public circles. She had the vigour of a firm constitution and seemed designed for great old age. Her children are of disproportioned genius, but the Secretary of State would be an honour to any family. Mr. Adams always appeared in full confidence, but that of an equal and friend who had lived himself into one with the wife of his bosom.[8]

Long afterward, Josiah Quincy recalled his pleasant visits to the quiet home of old President John and Abigail when he was a little boy:

With Mrs. Adams there was . . . a consciousness of age and dignity, which was often somewhat oppressive, [but] customary with old people of that day in the presence of the young. Something of this Mrs. Adams certainly had, though it wore off or came to be disregarded by me, for in the end I was strongly attached to her. She always dressed handsomely, and her rich silks and laces seemed appropriate to a lady of her dignified position in the town. If there was a little savor of patronage in the generous hospitality she exercised among her simple neighbors, it was never regarded as more than a natural emphasis of her undoubted claims to precedence.[9]

Gilbert Stuart painted Abigail Adams about the time of "Mr. Madison's War"—the portrait which is the original of the frontispiece of this volume. A description of that picture sticks in the memory, for clothing, and the color of it, are often close to character:

She is shown, three-quarters right, seated in a yellow Empire armchair upholstered in figured satin of brownish-yellow, with her brown eyes directed to the spectator. Only a few ringlets of her brown hair show on her forehead beneath the white lace of her beribboned cap. She wears a mulberry-colored silk dress with the low neck filled in with a white muslin yoke, and long sleeves with lace at the wrists. Around her neck is a white lace collar in two folds. A thin white lace shawl is thrown over her shoulders and falls onto her lap, in which her right hand lies; the left hand is not shown. The background is plain and of warm grays and browns.[10]

A stately lady, yet a lovely one.

[8] *The Diary of William Bentley, D.D., 1784–1819*, Salem, 1905–1914, vol. 4, pp. 556–7.
[9] Josiah Quincy, *Figures of the Past*, Boston, 1883, p. 61.
[10] *Gilbert Stuart: An Illustrated Descriptive List of his Works*, Compiled by Lawrence Park, New York, 1926, vol. 1, p. 93.

III

The Fall of John Adams

When John Adams became President of the United States in 1797, he was already sixty-one years of age. For more than twenty years he had been continuously in the service of the American people, in the Old World or the New, and on poor, uncertain pay. He had first gone to Europe in 1778, in circumstances of great danger, to begin his years of wrangling with Franklin and Vergennes. The utter incapacity of Adams to get on with the one and only great American who was a man of the world, is extremely significant. Then for three years (1785–1788) he had filled the ugly office of first American minister to King George. Writing of the financial worries of the founders of our nation, Edward Channing observes: "They gave their lives, their properties, and their reputations to their country." At one time Adams had earned his living as a lawyer, but he had had to neglect his personal affairs, and he would have suffered a penniless old age except for the care which Doctor Cotton Tufts and Abigail took of the family property at Quincy. And when he left Washington forever in March, 1801, he had more than a quarter of a century yet to live.

In one respect, our first Vice-President was the most distinguished of them all. During his eight years in that office, Adams presided over a Senate that was frequently divided by tie votes; so he used his casting ballot more often than any of his successors. His decision to give the President the power to remove officials without the consent of the Senate was of immense importance. His enemies accused him of acting so as to build up the power of the office of chief executive merely because he hoped to inherit it from Washington. Whatever his motive, he succeeded in preventing our Presidents from being creatures of Congress. Then Washington retired, and Hamilton let Adams have first place by three votes!

The initial act of Adams as President was a great mistake—or so it seems to those who are lucky enough to be able to look back on the consequences of it. Just why John Adams kept the Cabinet of Washington in office is not easy to say; certainly the event was not successful. Perhaps he hoped to build up a government of national union in the face of rival factions at home, and the increasing confusion in Europe. There is, indeed, a striking parallel between his problems and those of the American Presidents who have had to deal with the two great wars of the twentieth century. By 1797, Great Britain stood alone against a France which seemed likely to conquer the whole Continent. The Coriscan was coming to the fore from the shock and bloodshed of the Revolution. It looks as if John Adams hoped at one time to enlist the aid of some leading Republicans. He called to them, in fact, but the only one who came was Elbridge Gerry. The Jeffersonians were closing ranks against the Federalists.

France and England went to war in 1793—a war which ended only at Waterloo, more than twenty-two years later. In 1794, Washington sent John Jay to London to negotiate the famous treaty known by his name. While Jay was busy bargaining with the British, it was Alexander Hamilton who hinted to Hammond, the British minister to the United States, that Jay's demands on behalf of their own country should not be taken too seriously.[11] The treaty was ratified in 1795, much to the rage and indignation of the French, who rather dishonestly denounced it as a betrayal of the alliance which the Americans had made with a Bourbon king! Thereafter, relations between the two republics became increasingly tense, for French ministers were indiscreet and arrogant, and French generals were victorious. Washington had replaced aristocratic Gouverneur Morris at Paris with James Monroe; later, Pickering persuaded him to recall Monroe and send Charles Cotesworth Pinckney in his place. In 1797 Adams put the office in commission by sending over Marshall and Gerry to join Pinckney in Paris.

The purpose of Adams was obvious and honest. Although the Franco-British War had opened great opportunities for American commerce on the Atlantic, the rival fleets of England and France seemed likely to sweep American vessels from the sea. Adams

[11] S. F. Bemis, *Jay's Treaty*, New York, 1923, pp. 246–7. Mr. Bemis uses the word "amazing" in describing Hamilton's second interview with George Hammond, when Jay was already in London.

hoped that his commissioners could win from France some sort of understanding such as Jay had got in London. Pinckney, Marshall, and Gerry faced not only a truculent Directory, but one of the most adroit diplomats in all history—perhaps the last great statesman of Europe to look on Europe as a whole—Talleyrand. The three Americans waited in Paris and argued one with another. Then came mysterious, indirect suggestions as to loans—and, worse still, bribes. Gerry and Marshall roomed and boarded at the home of a Madame de Villette, a formidable woman who had once passed for the adopted daughter of Voltaire, and was now a lady friend of Talleyrand! Madame de Villette became the connecting link between the American ministers and Messrs. "X," "Y," and "Z." "X" was Jean-Conrad Hottinguer (1764–1841), of Zurich, who settled in Paris and made a malodorous fortune financing the French armies. Hottinguer had traveled extensively in the United States, and subsequently became a financial intimate of John Jacob Astor.[12] "Y" was a Mr. Bellamy, an American banker living in Hamburg, whose first name is not known. "Z" was Lucien Hauteval, another fly-by-night Switzer.

The American uproar over the proposal to pay Talleyrand £50,000 was not only partisan but hypocritical. Hamilton and his "high Federalists" were eager for a declaration of war against France, and made the most of the angry messages from the American ministers. More important yet, however, the administrations of both Washington and Adams, it ought to be remembered, had regularly paid annual bribes to both the American Indians and the Mediterranean pirates—as M. Hottinguer impolitely pointed out. Why should not the French be bought off, too? Nobody got anywhere, even though the amiable Beaumarchais intervened in the negotiations to promise that if his lawyer, John Marshall, were to win his suit for land against Virginia, he himself would pay off Talleyrand out of his profits. Eventually the mission broke up—Marshall returned in "triumph" to the United States; Pinckney took his sick daughter to the south

[12] See E. Wilson Lyon, "The Directory and the United States," *American Historical Review*, vol. 53 (1938), pp. 514–532; Samuel E. Morison, "Elbridge Gerry, Gentleman-Democrat, " *New England Quarterly*, vol. 2 (1929), pp. 6–33; and Thomas A. Bailey, *A Diplomatic History of the American People*, New York, 1946, pp. 71–89.

of France, and Gerry remained a hostage in the hands of Talleyrand, and the object of unmerited abuse from excited Americans.

The United States had been "insulted," and a declaration of war seemed certain, until the wily Jefferson slipped in behind the scenes. The Vice-President talked to Victor Du Pont, the French consul at Charleston, who had come to Philadelphia, warning him that Talleyrand was in great danger of overestimating the strength of American sympathy for France. To go to war would be to fall into the trap of William Pitt and Alexander Hamilton. Du Pont sailed for Bordeaux promptly and hastened on to Paris to report to Talleyrand. Within a week the offending French decrees of spoliation had been negatived, and the Directory was feeling for new negotiations by way of Holland. In the meantime, President Adams was in direct communication with William Vans Murray, the American minister to the Netherlands, and Richard Codman, a Boston speculator resident in Paris, both of whom had good reasons for assuring him that France did not want to go to war with the United States. To the rage of the Hamiltonians, Adams suddenly made Murray minister to France, and then sent Chief-Justice Oliver Ellsworth and William Richardson Davie to join him there to keep the peace in Paris. The Convention of Mortefontaine, September 30, 1800, is a lasting monument to the courage of Adams and the consummate wisdom of Talleyrand.[13]

Adams smashed his party, but he saved his country. Twelve years later, Madison, in similar circumstances, stumbled into the mistake which Adams avoided, stabbing Britain in the back for Henry Clay's promise of a quick conquest of Canada! Success abroad came too late, however, to save Adams at home. The outcry over the publication of the "X Y Z" dispatches led to the harsh Alien and Sedition Acts, and the Jeffersonians responded with the Virginia and the Kentucky Resolutions, defying federal encroachment on the sovereign people. Then, suddenly, George Washington died at Mount Vernon, and John Adams was lost. His one tie with Hamilton was broken.

Within two weeks of the death of Washington, the two rivals

[13] Samuel E. Morison, "Du Pont, Talleyrand, and the French Spoliations," *Proc. Mass. Hist. Soc.*, vol. 49 (1916), pp. 63–79.

met at Trenton, where Adams was staying because of a plague of yellow fever in Philadelphia. Hamilton came over from New York to urge him not to trust France. The account of their interview, as given by Abigail Adams on December 30, 1799, is an amazing revelation of the wishful thinking of the one man and the foresight of the other.

He [Hamilton] made the President a visit at Trenton, and was perfectly sanguine in the opinion that the Stateholder would be reinstated before Christmass and Louis the 18th upon the Throne of France. I should as soon expect, replied the President, that the sun, moon & stars will fall from their orbits, as events of that kind take place in any such period, but suppose such an event possible, can it be any injury to our Country to have envoys there? It will be only necessary for them to wait for new commissions. And if France is disposed to accommodate our differences, will she be less so under a Royall than a Directorial Government?

John Adams was often accused of being jealous of George Washington—a pardonable weakness! Two of the letters in this volume reveal the vanity and want of tact which cost him the political success he desired and really deserved. In 1798, when it was proposed to celebrate Washington's birthday in Philadelphia, John Adams and his wife felt that the plan was a studied insult to the New England successor to the great Virginian. The letter of February 15 is loaded with detailed indignation at what Abigail thought was the outrageous plan for a grand celebration; that of February 28 tells Mrs. Cranch how completely the obvious displeasure of the President and his wife had thrown a wet blanket over the whole business. Even after his death, Washington was praised far beyond their belief as to what was fitting and proper (January 28, 1800). Yet one of the most pleasant aspects of the early letters of this volume is the intimate description of Washington and his wife—the stately courtesy and nobility of the gentleman from Virginia, and the kindness of his gracious lady. Thought of this mighty man to whom fate and a physician gave not three years of the peace and quiet of Mount Vernon after a long, hard life in the service of his people, puts out of mind all memory of our Jeffersons and Jacksons, our Lincolns and our

Wilsons, even of our Roosevelts, "just as the sun, rising in heaven, extinguishes the stars."

Three men—beside himself—deprived John Adams of a second term as President. The first of these was Jefferson, who had deftly been gathering into his own hands all the threads of opposition to the Federalists. Never thereafter, it should be remembered, were the President and the Vice-President leaders of opposing parties. Yet it was Aaron Burr who won the election of 1800 for the Republicans, for he carried the electoral vote of New York, and, without New York, Jefferson would not have replaced Adams in the White House. And had Burr lifted so much as his little finger, it is extremely doubtful if the House of Representatives would have chosen Jefferson for President in 1801. The bad reputation of Burr with American historians is no puzzle if we remember that he was so brave—or rash—as to make deadly enemies of both Federalists and Republicans. Because he was sneered at as nothing but a "politician" no life of him was allowed in the *American Statesmen*—that series which includes a biography of Thaddeus Stevens! Just why Edward Channing wrote that Burr kept "the most disgraceful journal in existence" will never be known. Hated by Hamilton and Jefferson alike, Aaron Burr was always more sinned against than sinning. And so is he, to this day.

It was Alexander the great Hamilton, however, who made the defeat of Adams certain—Hamilton, "the brain" of their party! After the sudden death of Washington in December, 1799, Hamilton seems to have looked at himself as the leader of the Federalists, with the President as his puppet. For Adams to usurp that leadership, as in dismissing Pickering, was too much for his pride and consuming desire for power. In this sense, the death of Washington was decisive, for it broke the one and only tie between the President and the vindictive New Yorker whom he liked to call an "alien," or the "bastard brat of a Scotch pedlar"! When Tench Coxe, whom Adams had ousted from office in 1797, published an indiscreet letter which Adams had written to him in 1792 implying that Hamilton was under British influence, Hamilton, after two of his letters of enquiry to the President had gone unanswered, prepared his untimely, intemperate, and notorious indictment of Adams in October, 1800. Hamilton intended this outburst to circulate secretly among the leaders of the Federalist Party, but a copy of it came into the hands of Aaron Burr, who promptly took care to see that it was published and spread abroad. This sealed the doom of John Adams.

The bitter truth is that Burr and Hamilton were two peas out of one pod—ridiculous as zealous partisans of each have made themselves in trying to deny this obvious resemblance. Each was able and ambitious; each was sinuous and ardent; each was utterly charming—drunk or sober. Each was an adventurer, and each was loyal, first and last, to himself alone. Greek met Greek on the dueling ground at Weehawken. Yet it is not wise to be too hasty with the presently unpopular politics of Hamilton. We who live later may live late enough at last to learn, perhaps, that possibly "your people" is "a great beast" and that government had better belong to the "rich and to the well-born."

All the great Presidents of the United States save one have been politicians to the tips of their fingers. Nor was Adams: moreover, he was vain—like most men of small stature—he wanted tact, and he was hot-tempered. Hamilton thought that his outburts of rage approached insanity. Not so: John Adams was simply one of the last Puritans, if not the last, in American politics, and a Puritan must make it his business to rove about in search of righteousness. Take Abigail's opinion of Jefferson, written on the eve of his inauguration. Her judgment is probably nothing more than an echo of the angry Mr. Adams.

Have we any claim to the favour or protection of Providence, when we have against warning admonition and advise Chosen as our chief Majestrate a man who makes no pretentions to the belief of an all wise and suprem Governour of the World, ordering or directing or overruling the events which take place in it? I do not mean that he is an Atheist, for I do not think that he is—but he believes Religion only usefull as it may be made a political Engine, and that the outward forms are only, as I once heard him express himself—mere Mummery. In short, he is not a believer in the Christian system.

And again. In 1807 Napoleon Bonaparte was at the peak of his power. Pitt, the Winston Churchill of those days, was dead of drink and despair; the Treaty of Tilsit was in the offing; the

Corsican had yet to take the road to Russia and to ruin—though Talleyrand quietly quit him at the very crest. That year Mercy Warren wrote to Abigail Adams to ask her to find out just what her husband thought of him whom foolish men still call "the great emperor." The answer speaks volumes:

You inquire what does Mr. Adams think of Napoleon? If you had asked Mrs. Adams, she would have replied to you in the words of Pope,
    If plagues and earthquakes brake not heavens design
    Why then a Borgia or a Napoline?
I am authorized to replie to your question, What does Mr. Adams think Napoleon was made for? "My answer shall be as prompt and frank as her question. Napoleon's Maker alone can tell all he was made for. In general Napoleon was, I will not say made, but permitted for a cat-o'nine-tails, to inflict ten thousand lashes upon the back of Europe as divine vengeance for the Atheism, Infidelity, Fornications, Adulteries, Incests, and Sodomies, as well as Briberies, Robberies, Murders, Thefts, Intrigues, and fraudelent speculations of her inhabitants, and if we are far enough advanced in the career, and certainly we have progressd very rapidly, to whip us for the same crimes, and after he has answerd the end he was made, or permitted for, to be thrown into the fire."[14]

Here, in a nutshell, is the hideous Puritan doctrine that the consequences of the mistakes of men—even their misfortunes—are nothing more than just punishments for their "sins."

In 1815, however, at the end of "Mr. Madison's War," when Bonaparte was bottled up, for the moment, in Elba, the old President recovered his sense of proportion long enough to write proudly:

I will defend my missions to France, as long as I have an eye to direct my hand, or a finger to hold my pen. They were the most disinterested and meritorious actions of my life. I reflect upon them with so much satisfaction, that I desire no other inscription over my gravestone than: "Here lies John Adams, who took upon himself the responsibility of the peace with France in the year 1800."[15]

This was John Adams at his bravest and his best. Yet he had made so many enemies in life, that his noblest deed in office drove him out of it forever.   STEWART MITCHELL

[14] *Warren-Adams Letters*, vol. 2, p. 353.
[15] Bailey, *Diplomatic History of the American People*, p. 89.

New Letters of Abigail Adams

New Letters of Abigail Adams

Jamaica [Long Island, New York], Novbr. 24, 1788

MY DEAR SISTER:

I know you will rejoice with me that all was happily over & Mrs. Smith safely abed before I reachd her. She thought she should do as she did before, so told no one that she was unwell, untill Mr. Smiths Mamma & sister could scarcly reach her, and a Negro woman whom she has was obliged to officiate for her. Happily she had on some former occasions assisted some of her own coulour, but all were teribly frightned. However no one sufferd, but Mrs. Smith & my young Grandson are as well as usual at this period. Master William is the very Image of his Mamma at the same age, except that he has a great share of vivacity & sprightlyness, the merest little Trunchion that you ever saw, very pleasent & good humourd.[1]

I find this place a very retired one, Rural & delightfull in the summer. Mr. Smith has a large connection of Sisters & Brothers who as well as his Mamma appear very fond of their sister & her daughter & Grandsons.[2] Belinda who keeps chiefly here, is very pleasing & soft in her manners, much like my Friend Mrs. Rogers. I was so short a Time at New York that I saw nothing of it, and I feel as if I ought to return to my Family again, as soon as Mrs. Smith gets about, but it is a long journey, & the

---

[1] Abigail (1765–1813), the only surviving daughter of John and Abigail (Smith) Adams, became the wife, in London, June 12, 1786, of Colonel William Stephens Smith (1755–1816). Colonel Smith was born in New York City, the son of John, a wealthy merchant, and Margaret (Stephens) Smith, whose relatives were Loyalists; he was graduated from Princeton in 1774, enlisted at the outbreak of the Revolution, and served brilliantly under Sullivan and Putnam. Later on, he became an aide to George Washington. In 1785, he was appointed secretary of the legation in London, where he met the daughter of John Adams, the American minister. Colonel and Mrs. Smith had four children: William Steuben (1787), John Adams (1788), Thomas Hollis (1790), and Caroline Amelia (1795), who married John Peter DeWindt. For portraits of Colonel and Mrs. Smith, see *Old-Time New England:* The *Bulletin* of the Society for the Preservation of New England Antiquities, vol. 19, No. 3 (January, 1929).

For a blunt letter (1798) from John Adams to this son-in-law, criticizing his "pride and ostentation," see John Adams, *Works*, vol. 8, Boston, 1853, pp. 617–8.

[2] John Smith and Margaret (Stephens) Smith had ten children: four sons and six daughters. For a description of the daughters, see the following letter.

stages I find are very inconvenient for a Lady & wholy improper on many accounts for me. They are not hung upon springs & they drive very Rapidly over very bad road. I hope you will write me and give me some account of my Family, about which I am anxious. You will learn from Esther how she makes out. I wish to know whether she is able to take the care which is upon her. I also want to know how Mr. J. Q. A.'s health is. I know you will feel a care for all of them in my absence. Mr. Adams will Frank your Letters which please to direct under cover to Col. Smith.

My Love to my dear Neices and tell Betsy I design to be at Home to [her] wedding.[3] Mrs. Smith joins me in affectionate Regard to you & Family. I am, my dear Sister,

Affectionately yours
A. ADAMS

I wish my dear Sister if it will not dissapoint Cousin Betsy that you would write a line to the chair maker at Milton to send the half dozen to Mr. Smiths store in Boston put up so as to send safely on Board the first vessel which shall sail for New York, & let him know that I will pay him on my return. Pray Mr. Smith to address them to Mr. Daniel Macormick, New York.[4]

Jamaica [Long Island], December 15, 1788

MY DEAR SISTER:

I thank you for your kind Letter of Novbr. 30th Decbr. 2nd. You judgd rightly I was almost melancholy to be a Month from Home, and not to hear once from Home in all that Time, but the post is long in comeing. I am Eleven miles from [New] York with a great Ferry between, and you are ten from Boston so that we do not always get our Letters ready for post day. I wrote you the day after I arrived here &

---

[3] Elizabeth, daughter of Mary (Smith) Cranch and Richard Cranch (1726–1811), who married the Reverend Jacob Norton, Harvard, 1786.

[4] Of William Smith, only son of the Reverend William Smith, and younger brother of Mrs. John Adams, very little is known. He was born in 1746, and seems to have married three times. Several of his children were reared by their relatives. The date of his death has not been found. His first wife was probably Catherine Louisa Salmon (married January 3, 1779); his second wife, Hannah Carter (married May 16, 1787); and his third wife, Martha White (b. 1755), daughter of Daniel and Sarah (Turner) White, by whom he had at least one child, Daniel White Smith (b. 1796). See *Records of Braintree* and *Boston Marriages: 1752–1809*.

Thus, in the letters which follow, "Mrs. Smith" may refer to any one of three, or possibly five women: the daughter of Mrs. John Adams, Mrs. William Stephens Smith; the mother-in-law of that daughter, Mrs. John Smith or, thirdly, one of the three wives of William Smith, the brother of Mrs. Adams.

trust you have long ago got the Letter. Your Neice is very well, except weak, & very free with her Mamma as I can instance to you, for [I] having written a Letter to her Pappa & seald it, she comes in & says O, Mamma what, is the Letter seald, why I must see it, and very cordially opens it to read. The little Boy grows finely, but I dont feel so fond of him yet as I do of William. Whether it is because he was Born in our own House, or the first or the best temperd child I cannot determine.

Dec'br. 18th, [1788]

Mrs. Smith has had several of her Neighbours to visit her since I have been here. They appear to be Geenteel people, but all the acquaintance she has upon the Island are of the ceremonious kind. In their own Family are four young Ladies, all of them agreeable, sensible, well behaved women. Peggy the oldest is tall, agreeable rather than handsome, and the most particularly attentive to her manners without discovering any affectation of any Lady I have met with. Belinda the second daughter has less of person to boast of than her Elder Sister, but she has that Interesting countanance & openness of manners that Interests you at first sight, nor are you dissapointed upon a further acquaintance. Her temper and disposition appear perfectly amiable, accommodating and kind. I have more acquaintance with her than with either of the others. I found [her] here when I came, taking charge of Mrs. Smiths Family during her confinement. This she performd with much ease and tender sisterly affection. At Home their Mamma has used them to the care of her Family by Turns. Each take it a week at a Time. Charity is the third daughter, and if it was not for the loss of one Eye which she was deprived of at two years old I think she would be the Bel of the Family. She has been absent till last Sunday ever since I came. I have seen her but once. She is more social, has read more and appears to have the greatest turn for literature of either. She has a taste for drawing, for musick &c. The fine arts seem to be the objects of her attention, and as she has a most inquisitive mind, she would shine with brightness if she had Books to direct her and masters to instruct her. She dresses with neatness but great simplicity, rather in the Quaker stile, avoids all publick company, assemblies &c but is strongly attachd to her Friends. I take from Mrs. Smith part of her History for, as I observd before, I have seen her but once. Sally is the fourth daughter, about 17, tall as Mrs. Guile, a fine figure & a pretty Face, unaffected and artless in her manners, modest and composed. She wants only a little more animation to render her truly Interesting. She has dignity, & that you know is inconsistant with a gay, playfull, humour.[1] This Belinda has. They are four fine women and well educated for wives as well as daughters. There are two young ones, Betsy & Nancy, one of ten & the other seven years old. Daughters so agreeable must have a worthy Mother, and this is universally her character. Mrs. Smith is a Large, tall woman, not unlike Mrs. Gray. She is about 50 years old and has been a very Handsome woman, tenderly attachd to all her children. She has I tell her been too indulgent to her sons, of whom she has four, but of them an other Time.[2] She is really a Charming woman as far as I have been able to form an acquaintance with her, and she has been here a good deal & I have visited her. We have had company several Times from N[ew] York and I have had many & repeated requests to go there, but my Trunk is, I know not where. I have only one morning gown & a green sattin which I very fortunatly had in my small Trunk or I should not have been able to have seen any body. I have no shoes but the pr I wear, no Bonnet, very little Linnen & only my calimanco Skirt, and there are very few things of Mrs. Smiths that I can wear.[3] I am sadly of. We had yesterday a cold snow storm, hardly enough to cover the ground, but it has cleard up very cold. I think of my poor dear & pitty him. I long to get back to my Family, but must wait for snow as the roads are too bad to Travel without. I regret daily the distance, but Mrs. Smith comforts herself with thinking that I shall very soon be nearer to her, but I fear I shall not have much comfort if that should happen. Tis only on plain ground that one walks easily. Up hill or down is painfull. I am afraid J. Jr. will turn Hermit, if business does not soon call him into the World, but how much better is this, than having no given object, no persuit. I had rather a son of mine should follow any mechanical trade whatever than be a gentleman at large without any occupation.

I am sorry to hear my good Mother had met with such an accident.[4] It is one source of my anxiety to get home, that I have thought for some

[1] This Sally, or Sarah Smith (1769–1828), married Charles Adams (1770–1800), and became the mother of two daughters: Susanna Boylston (1796–1846) and Abigail Louisa (1798–1838).

[2] The four sons, and eldest children, of John and Margaret (Stephens) Smith were William Stephens, John, James, and Justus.

[3] "Calimanco," obsolete for "calamanco." A woollen stuff of Flanders, glossy on the surface, and woven with a satin twill and chequered in the warp, so that the checks are seen on one side only; much used in the eighteenth century. *Oxford English Dictionary.*

[4] Abigail Adams refers to her mother-in-law, Susanna (Boylston) [Adams] Hall (1709–1797), who married again after the death of the father of John Adams.

months that she would not Live through the winter. Pray present my duty to her and tell her that her grandchildren & great grandchildren talk of comeing to see her. My Love to my [your?] two daughters. Tell Betsy she must not steal a march upon me. If she waits an other month Mrs. Smith will come & be Bride[s]maid. Present me kindly to Brother Cranch & go as often as you can & see my good Gentleman.[5] Tell Esther she must write to me & let me know how she makes out. My fingers are so cold I can scarcly hold a pen. Adieu my dear Sister. Write as often as you can. Mrs. Smith desires me to present her duty & Love. She will write soon.

Yours most tenderly
A. ADAMS

Richmond Hill [New York], Janry 24, 1789[1]

MY DEAR SISTER:

I embrace this opportunity By my Brother to write you a few lines tho it is only to tell you what you would have learnt from him, Namely that we are all well. He is come in persuit of Betsy Crosby. How well the child might have been provided for if the Dr. had lived, I cannot pretend to say, but two thirds of her property is already consumed, every minutia being charged to her as the account will show. However this is no concern of mine.[2] I am not without hopes my dear Sister of comeing to Braintree and spending several months with you during the next recess of congress. How long they will set this Session I cannot pretend to say, but rather think they will rise early in the Spring. I think it would be a pleasure to me to have a small Family, and be able when I returnd to visit my Friends a little more than I have done. I never rode so little as I have done since I resided here. There are no pleasant rides, no variety of scenes round New York, unless you cross ferrys over to long Island or to the Jerseys. I have however enjoyd a greater share of Health than I

[5] John Adams did not come down to New York until April 20, 1789. See footnote 8 to the enclosure with the letter of December 12, 1797.

[1] The manor house of "Richmond Hill" stood near what is now Macdougal Street, in Greenwich Village, New York City. Its original proprietor was Abraham Mortier; at the time John Adams and his wife occupied it, "Richmond Hill" was the property of a Mrs. Jephson. Aaron Burr bought it on June 17, 1797. It was subsequently removed to a new site, was turned into a theatre, and demolished in 1849. For a picture of the house, see the *New-York Magazine* (June, 1790), where it is described as the residence of Vice-President Adams. I. N. Phelps Stokes, *The Iconography of Manhattan Island*, New York, 1915–1928, vol. 3, p. 951; vol. 5, pp. 1254–5, 1274, and 1304; also, vol. 1, plate 55A, and pp. 416–7.

[2] Dr. Ebenezer Crosby, Harvard, 1777, Yale, 1782, died in New York City in 1788. William S. Pattee, *A History of Old Braintree and Quincy*, Quincy, 1878.

have for some years past & been less afflicted with the Complaint which used to allarm as well as distress me.

How is my Neice Mrs. Norton?[3] Give my Love to her & tell her I hope to find her with a fine Girl in her Arms when I return to Braintree. Tell Lucy she is quite as usefull as if she was married.[4] I want to see her much as well as the rest of my dear Friends. To many of them I owe Letters, but I really hate to touch a pen. I am ashamed to say how laizy I am grown in that respect.

I could give an account of visiting and receiving visits, but in that there is so little variety that one Letter only might contain the whole History. For Instance on Monday Evenings Mrs. Adams Receives company. That is her Rooms are lighted & put in order. Servants & Gentlemen and Ladies, as many as inclination, curiosity or Fashion tempts, come out to make their Bow & Curtzy, take coffe & Tea, chat an half hour, or longer, and then return to Town again. On Tuesday the same Ceremony is performed at Lady Temple's,[5] on Wednesday at Mrs. Knox's,[6] on Thursdays at Mrs. Jays[7] and on Fryday at Mrs. Washingtons, so that if any person has so little to employ themselves in as to want an amusement five Evenings in a week, they may find it at one or other of these places. To Mrs. Washingtons I usually go as often as once a fortnight, and to the others occasionally.

So I learn that my Young Friend Nancy[8] is seriously thinking of

[3] Elizabeth (Cranch) Norton, to whom sons were born in 1790 and 1791. See the letter of February 5, 1792.

[4] Lucy Cranch (1767–1846), who married her first cousin, John Greenleaf (1763–1848).

[5] "Lady" Temple, so called, was Elizabeth Bowdoin (1750–1809), daughter of James Bowdoin (1726–1790), one of the richest and most influential men in the Province of Massachusetts, and subsequently Governor of the state of Massachusetts (1785–1787), during Shays's Rebellion. Elizabeth married John Temple (1730–1798), a native of Massachusetts, and surveyor-general of the customs under George III. After November 11, 1786, this John Temple called himself "Sir" John Temple, claiming succession to the baronetcy of Stowe, in Buckinghamshire, but this claim was never proved or acknowledged. *Burke's Peerage*, London, 1938, "Temple of Stowe," pp. 2393–4. Temple was British consul-general at New York from 1788 to 1798. On June 17, 1797, he bought Aaron Burr's mansion-house, "Richmond Hill." Portraits of "Sir" John and "Lady" Temple are in the Massachusetts Historical Society. They had two children, "Sir" Grenville Temple (1768–1829) and Elizabeth Bowdoin Temple (1769–1825), the wife of Thomas Lindall Winthrop, father of Robert C. Winthrop (1809–1894), Speaker of the House of Representatives (1847–1849).

[6] Lucy (Flucker) Knox, wife of Henry Knox (1750–1806), first Secretary of War, 1789–1795.

[7] Sarah Van Brugh (Livingston) Jay, wife of John Jay (1745–1829), first Chief Justice, and daughter of William Livingston (1723–1790), first Governor of New Jersey.

[8] Anna (Nancy) Greenleaf (1772–1843) married William Cranch (1769–1855), whom John Adams (February 27, 1801) appointed judge of the United States Circuit Court of the District of Columbia.

becomeing the Madam of a parish. Be sure to tell her, that I like it much as it will be so fine a half way House to call at when I go & come From N[ew] York to Braintree. But laying selfish considerations aside, I hope she is like to be setled to the mind of herself & Family.

My best Regards to Mrs. Quincy[9] and all other Friends.

Brother says you wrote to me by Mrs. Cushing.[10] She is not yet arrived. Adieu.

Yours most tenderly
A. ADAMS

Providence, [Rhode Island], June 19, 1789[1]

MY DEAR SISTER:

This day is the Aniversary of my Landing in Boston and Tomorrow that of my departure from it. Many are the mercies I have to be thankfull for through all my Perigrinations. All the painfull scenes I have past through, has been the temporary seperation from my Friends. Fatigue either of Body or Mind I scarcly name amongst them for I have my pleasures and gratifications which I set down as a balance to them. Cousin Lucy[2] has told you that I left Home about 8 oclock. We proceeded to Man's Inn[3] in Wrentham before we stop'd, 27 miles, where we dinned upon roast veal, roast chickings, sallad &c. West India sweet meats I ought not to forget in the desert. It is really a very good Inn. We sat off at three oclock and reachd Attleboroug[h] about five where we Rested. I met with Mr. and Mrs. Mason & Miss Powel going to Newport. We past an agreeable Hour together. At six we renewed our journey and reachd Providence at half after seven. We put up at Daggets Inn[4] just at the entrance of the Town situated upon a Hill opposite the State House[5] commanding a fine view of the River & the

---

[9] The wife of Norton Quincy (1716–1801), Harvard, 1736, the uncle of Abigail (Smith) Adams and Mary (Smith) Cranch.

[10] Hannah (Phillips) Cushing (1754–1834), wife of William Cushing (1732–1810), justice of the Supreme Court (1789–1810). Cushing refused the office of Chief Justice in 1796.

[1] Footnotes for this and the following letter are chiefly drawn from *Rhode Island History*, vol. 1, no. 4 (October, 1942), pp. 97–104.

[2] Lucy Cranch (1767–1846), daughter of Richard Cranch (1726–1811) and Mary (Smith) Cranch (1741–1811), who married John Greenleaf (1763–1848).

[3] David Man kept an inn at Wrentham as early as 1724.

[4] Daggett's Inn was the Mansion House, sometimes called the Golden Ball Inn. It was situated on Benefit Street, opposite the Old State House, which was pulled down in 1941.

[5] This State House is still standing on North Main Street, and is now the Sixth District Court.

whole Town. We are tolerably well accommodated, but should have been much better if the Governour[6] had not taken the best Chamber before I came, (the court being now in Session) and he has not had the politeness either to offer to give it up or to make me a visit, tho he has had much conversation with Polly[7] and now & then takes a peep at me from [the] entry. My first inquiry was after a packet. I found only [Captain] Browns here. He came & I like him. He has a very good packet & Bears a good character himself, but says he cannot be ready to sail till Saturday morning. The wind to day is directly against us.

In about an hour after my arrival I received the visits of the following persons. Mr. & Mrs. Arnold, the Gentleman was one of the Committe who came to Mr. Adams, from the Towns of Newport & Providence. Mr. & Mrs. Francis, this Lady is the daughter of Mr. John Brown of this Town, so celebrated for his wealth.[8] Miss Bowen the sister to the late Governour.[9] Colonel Peck, Mr. Robins, Tutor to the Colledge & Mr. Shrimpton Hutchinson and Mrs. Nightingale, all of whom in the Name of many other Gentlemen & Ladies regreeted [sic] that I had dissapointed them in not letting it be known when I should be here as they had agreed to meet me several miles out of Town. Mr. & Mrs. Francis invited me to take up my abode with them. I excused myself, but have promised to take Tea & spend the Evening if I do not go out of Town. This morning I am to take a ride with them to see the Town & to return my visits, if I am not prevented by company, but my wish is not to be detained a moment. Pray write me & let me know by the next post whether my furniture is all on Board Barnard & when he will sail. I should be glad to hear how Mrs. Brisler is.[10] I left her in great affliction.

[6] John Collins, of Newport (1717–1795), third Governor of the state of Rhode Island (1786–1790). Collins cast the deciding vote in the State Senate (January 17, 1790) which led to the calling of the convention by which Rhode Island entered the Union, May 29, 1790.

[7] Polly Tailor, the maid of Mrs. Adams. For further reference to Polly Tailor, see letters of October 11 and November 3, 1789, and April 28, 1790.

[8] John Brown (1736–1803), son of James and Hope (Power) Brown, was the third of four brothers, Nicholas, Joseph, John, and Moses, of the mercantile firm of Nicholas Brown & Company, of Providence. In 1787, he became a partner in Brown & Francis, and in December of that year the *General Washington* cleared for the East, the first ship in the beginning of trade that brought fortune to Rhode Island for more than half a century. John Brown married Sarah, daughter of Daniel and Dorcas (Harris) Smith. Abby Brown, his daughter, married John Francis.

[9] Miss Mary Bowen, sister of Lieutenant-Governor Jabez Bowen, who was graduated from Yale in 1757 and died in 1815. Bowen also had two half-sisters, Elizabeth (Betsy) and Nancy.

[10] Mrs. Briesler was the wife of John Briesler, major-domo to John Adams.

I feel the want of Mrs. Brisler as a Hair dresser. On other accounts Polly does very well. Matilda[11] is well, & her finger much better. Let Mrs. Storer know if you please.[12] My best Regards to all my dear Friends. It grieved me to see you so dull. You used to keep up your Spirits better. Do not let them flagg. A merry Heart does good like a medicine.[13] We shall hear often from one an other, and the seperation be renderd less painfull by that means.

This moment a Card is brought me from Mr. Brown & Lady with an invitation to dine with them to day & that they will visit me at ten. I accept it, as [Captain] Brown cannot go till tomorrow. Adieu my dear Sister.

Most affectionatly yours
ABIGAIL ADAMS

Richmond Hill, June 28th, 1789

MY DEAR SISTER:

I wrote you from Providence some account of my polite reception there & closed my Letter just as I had accepted an invitation to dine with Mr. Brown & Lady. The forenoon was pass't in receiving visits from all the principal Gentlemen and Ladies of the Town, who seemed to vie with each other, to convince me that tho they were inhabitants of an Antifederal State, they were themselves totally against the measures persued by it, and that they entertaind the highest Regard and Respect for the Character with which I was so intimately connected, altho to their great mortification they had been prevented the Honour of having any share in placing him in His respected Station.[1]

Mr. Brown sent his Carriage & son to conduct me [to] his House which is one of the grandest I have seen in this Country. Every thing in and about it, wore the marks of magnificence & taste. Mrs. Brown met me at the door & with the most obliging smile accosted me with, "Friend I am glad to see the here." The simplicity of her manners & dress with the openness of her countanance & the friendlyness of her behavior charmed me beyond all the studied politeness of European manners. They had collected between 22 persons to dine with me tho the notice was so short, & gave an elegant entertainment upon a service of Plate.

[11] Matilda was a kind of companion to Mrs. Adams.

[12] Hannah (Quincy) Storer (1736–1826), daughter of Josiah Quincy, who married as her second husband Ebenezer Storer. John Adams courted Hannah Quincy before he married Abigail Smith.

[13] *Proverbs*, XVII, 22.

[1] Rhode Island refused to ratify the Constitution and join the Union until May 29, 1790, and then only by the close convention vote of thirty-four to thirty-two.

Towards evening I made a Tour round the Town, & drank Tea & spent the Evening with Mr. & Mrs. Francis whom I mentioned to you before. Then the company was much enlarged, & many persons introduced to me who had no opportunity before of visiting me. Amongst those Ladies with whom I was most pleased was the Lady & two Sisters of Governour Bowen. About Eleven I returnd to my lodgings and the next morning went on Board the Hancock packet. We had contrary wind all day, by which means we did not reach Newport untill seven oclock. I had been only a few moments arrived when Mr. Merchant came on Board and insisted that I with my whole Family should go on shore & Lodge at his House.[2] He would take no refusal. He sent his daughter down to receive & accompany my Neice, & came himself in a few moments with a carriage to attend me.[3] At his House I was kindly & Hospitably Treated by his Lady & daughters. We slept there & the next morning were early summond on Board the packet. Captain Brown had very civily taken his wife to attend upon me, & accomodate me during my passage. I found her a very well Bred Geenteel [sic] woman, but neither civility attention or politeness could remedy the sea sickness or give me a fair wind or dispell the Thunder Gusts which attended us both night and day. In short I resolved upon what I have frequently before, that I would never again embark upon the water, but this resolution I presume will be kept as my former ones have been. We were five days upon the water. Heat, want of rest, sea sickness & terror, for I had my share of that, all contributed to fatigue me, and I felt upon my arrival quite tame & spiritless. Louisa was very sick, but behaved like a Heroine. Matilda had her share but when she was a little recoverd she was the life of us all. Polly was half dead all the passage & sufferd more from sea sickness than any of us. Charl[e]s eat & slept without any inconvenience.[4] When we came to the wharff, I desired the Captain to go to our Friend Mr. Macormick and inform him of my arrival, if he was not to be found to go to the Senate Chamber & inform Mr. A[dams], who from the hour of the day I knew must be there. Mr. Otis[5] the Secretary came to me with a

[2] Henry Marchant (1741–1796), a prominent attorney of Newport, one of the signers of the Articles of Confederation, member of the Continental Congress (1777–1780 and 1783–1784), and federal judge (1790–1796).

[3] This niece was Louisa Smith, who made her home with John and Abigail Adams, and is frequently mentioned in the letters which follow. Louisa was the daughter of William Smith, the brother of Mrs. Adams.

[4] The three sons of John and Abigail Adams were John Quincy (1767–1848), Charles (1770–1800), and Thomas Boylston (1772–1832).

[5] Samuel Allyne Otis (1740–1814), brother of James and Mercy (Otis) Warren, and father of Harrison Gray Otis (1765–1848). Samuel A. Otis was chosen Secretary of the United States Senate in 1789 and served until his death, April 22, 1814.

Carriage & I reach'd Richmond Hill on Thursday one oclock to my no small joy. I found Mr. Adams in better Health than I feard, Mr. & Mrs. Smith quite well & everything so well arranged that Beds & a few other articles seem only necessary towards keeping House with comfort, and I begin to think that my furniture will be troublesome to me, some part of it I mean, whilst Mrs. Smith remains with me. Master John was grown out of my knowledge. William is still at Jamaica. Our House has been a mere Levee ever since I arrived morning & evening. I took the earliest opportunity (the morning after my arrival) to go & pay my respects to Mrs. Washington. Mrs. Smith accompanied me. She received me with great ease & politeness. She is plain in her dress, but that plainness is the best of every article. She is in mourning. Her Hair is white, her Teeth beautifull, her person rather short than otherways, hardly so large as my Ladyship, and if I was to speak sincerly, I think she is a much better figure. Her manners are modest and unassuming, dignified and femenine [sic], not the Tincture of ha'ture about her. *His Majesty* was ill & confined to his Room. I had not the pleasure of a presentation to him, but the satisfaction of hearing that he regreted it equally with myself. Col. Humphries,[6] who had paid his compliments to me in the morning & Breakfasted with me, attended Mrs. Washington & Mr. Lear,[7] the Private Secretary, was the introducer. Thus you have an account of my first appearence. The Principal Ladies who have visited me are the Lady & daughter of the Governour,[8] Lady Temple, the Countess de Brehim[9], Mrs. Knox & 25 other Ladies, many of the Senators, all their Ladies, all the Foreign ministers & some of the Rep[resentative]s.

[6] David Humphreys (1752–1818), youngest son of the Reverend Daniel Humphrey [sic] and Sarah (Riggs) Bowers, widow of John Bowers. Colonel Humphreys, Yale, 1771, was aide-de-camp to George Washington.

[7] Tobias Lear (1762–1816), born at Portsmouth, New Hampshire, and graduated from Harvard College in 1783. Lear was private secretary to George Washington from 1785 to 1793.

[8] George Clinton (1739–1812), first Governor of New York (1777–1795 and 1801–1804), elected Vice-President of the United States in 1804 and 1808.

[9] The comtesse de Brehan arrived at Philadelphia on February 26, 1788, with her brother, Eleonore-François-Elie, comte de Moustier (1751–1817), French minister to the United States from 1787 to 1790. Madame de Brehan, eccentric both in appearance and deportment, was a painter, and made several miniatures of George Washington. G. A. Eisen, *Portraits of Washington*, New York, 1932, pp. 454–6 and 669. A letter which she wrote to Jefferson on September 3, 1787, from Brest, on her way to America, thanking him for the loan of his book, *Notes on the State of Virginia*, Paris, 1784–5, will be found in the Jefferson Papers, in the Coolidge Collection, at the Massachusetts Historical Society. This letter is written in English, but with obvious effort. See, also, Katharine M. Roof, *Colonel William Smith and Lady*, Boston, 1929, p. 196.

We are most delightfully situated. The prospect all around is Beautifull in the highest degree. It is a mixture of the sublime & Beautifull. Amidst it all I sigh for many of my dear Friends and connections. I can make no domestick arrangment till Brisler arrives. Remember me affectionatly to all my Friends particularly my aged parent,[10] to my children to whom I cannot write as yet, to my dear Lucy & worthy Dr. Tufts,[11] in short to all whom I love.

Yours most tenderly
A. ADAMS

Richmond Hill, July 12th, 1789

MY DEAR SISTER:

I received your kind Letter by Mr. Brisler who reachd here on the 4th of July, since which you will easily suppose I have been very buisily engaged in arranging my Family affairs. This added to the intence heat of the season, some company (tho for three days I was *fashionably* not at Home,) and some visiting which was indispensable, having more than fifty upon my list, my Time has been so wholy occupied that I have not taken a pen. Yet my thoughts have not been so occupied, but that they have frequently visited you, and my other Friends in the Neighbourhood, and tho I have here, as to situation one of the most delightfull spots I have seen in this country, yet I find the want of some of my particular connection's, but an all wise Providence has seen fit to curtail our wishes and to limit our enjoyments, that we may not be unmindfull of our dependance or forget the Hand from whence they flow. I have a favour to request of all my near and intimate Friends. It is to desire them to watch over my conduct and if at any time they perceive any alteration in me with respect to them, arising as they may suppose from my situation in Life, I beg they would with the utmost freedom acquaint me with it. I do not feel within myself the least disposition of the kind, but I

---

[10] The Reverend William Smith died in 1783, and his wife in 1775. "Aged parent" refers to the mother of John Adams, Susanna (Boylston) [Adams] Hall (1709-1797). For a diary of the Reverend William Smith, see 3 *Proc. Mass. Hist. Soc.*, vol. 42.

[11] Cotton Tufts (1732-1815) of Weymouth, an uncle of Mrs. Adams by marriage, and nephew of John Tufts (1689-1752). Like his father, Simon, Cotton Tufts became a physician. He had full charge of the private affairs of John Adams during the latter's absence from home: John Adams, *Life and Works*, Boston, 1850-1856, vol. 9, p. 548n. Cotton Tufts first married Lucy Quincy (died 1785), daughter of John Quincy. His second wife (October 22, 1789) was Mrs. Susannah Warner, of Gloucester. See letters of November 1, 1789, and March 21, 1790; and for reference to his first wife, that of May 16, 1797. For a diary of Dr. Cotton Tufts, see 3 *Proc. Mass. Hist. Soc.*, vol. 42.

know mankind are prone to decieve themselves, and some are disposed to misconstrue the conduct of those whom they conceive placed above them.

Our August Pressident [*sic*] is a singular example of modesty and diffidence. He has a dignity which forbids Familiarity mixed with an easy affibility which creates Love and Reverence. The fever which he had terminated in an absess, so that he cannot sit up. Upon my second visit to Mrs. Washington he sent for me into his Chamber. He was laying [*sic*] upon a settee and half raising himself up, beggd me to excuse his receiving me in that posture, congratulated me upon my arrival in N[ew] York and asked me how I could Relish the simple manners of America after having been accustomed to those of Europe. I replied to him that where I found simple manners I esteemed them, but that I thought we approachd much nearer to the Luxury and manners of Europe according to our ability, than most persons were sensible of, and that we had our full share of taste and fondness for them. The President has a Bed put into his Carriage and rides out in that way, allways with six Horses in his Carriage & four attendants. Mrs. Washington accompanies him. I requested him to make Richmond Hill his resting place, and the next day he did so, but he found walking up stairs so difficult, that he has done it but once. Mrs. Washington is one of those unassuming characters which create Love & Esteem. A most becoming pleasentness sits upon her countanance & an unaffected deportment which renders her the object of veneration and Respect. With all these feelings and Sensations I found myself much more deeply impressd than I ever did before their Majesties of Britain.

You ask me concerning politicks. Upon my word I hear less of them here, than I did in in [*sic*] Massa'ts. The two Houses are very buisy upon very important Bill's, the judiciary, and the Collecting Bills. The Senate is composed of many men of great abilities, who appear to be liberal in their sentiments and candid towards each other. The House is composed of some men of equal talants. Others, the debates will give you the best Idea of them, but there is not a member whose sentiment clash more with my Ideas of things than Mr. G[err]y.[1] He certainly does not comprehend the Great National System which must Render us respectable abroad & energetick at Home and will assuredly find himself lost amidst Rocks & sands.

My dear Sister some parts of your Letter made me melancholy. Are

[1] Elbridge Gerry (1744–1814), signer of the Declaration of Independence, who helped to make the Constitution and then refused to urge its ratification; Anti-Federalist member of the House of Representatives (1789–1793).

you in any difficulties unknown to me? I know very well that a small Farm must afford you a scanty support and that you are a sufferer from being obliged to receive pay in paper but I know your prudence & occonomy has carried you along, tho not in affluence, yet with decency and comfort, and I hope you will still be able to live so. You have one daughter comfortably situated. Your son will from his merit & abilities soon get into some buisness. Your other daughter, you have every reason to be satisfied with. Do not look upon the gloomy side only. How easily might your situation be changed for the worse. Even if you were in possession of Riches yet there is a competancy which is so desirable that one cannot avoid an anxiety for it. I have a request to make you. Desire Mr. Cranch[2] to make out his account which he has against Mr. A[dams]. I gave Cousin Lucy a memmorandum. Let the balance be drawn and inclose to me, and I will send you a Receit in full. This I consider myself at full liberty to do, because the little sum Lent you was my own pocket money. Put the Letter under cover to Mrs. Smith. It will then fall into no hands but my own. But cover the whole for a frank to Mr. A[dams]—Do not talk of oblagations [sic]. Reverse the matter & then ask yourself if you would not do as much for me?

I wish it was in Mr. A.'s power to help Mr. Cranch to some office at Home which would assist him. Mr. A. exprest the same wish to me, but at present he does not see any, tho a certain Lady in the full assurance of hope, wrote him that he now had it in his power to establish his own Family & successfully help his Friends and that she is sure of his patronage for certain purposes, to which Mr. A. replied, "that he has no patronage but if he had, neither her children or his own could be sure of it beyond his own clear conviction of the publick Good, that he should bely the whole course of his publick and private conduct, and all the maxims of his Life, if he should ever consider publick Authority entrusted to him, to be made subservient to his private views, or those of his Family and Friends." You cannot mistake who the Lady was. I know no other equally ambitious, but I presume her pretentions & those of her Family will fail, as I think they ought to if one quarter part is true which has been reported of them. I fancy a constant correspondence is kept up between Mrs. W[arre]n[3] & Mr. G[err]y and like enough with several

[2] Richard Cranch (1726–1811), husband of Mary (Smith) Cranch (1741–1811), the woman to whom these letters are addressed. "Cousin Lucy" was their daughter.

[3] Mercy (Otis) Warren (1728–1814), historian, poet, and dramatist, and sister of the famous James Otis. Although Mrs. Warren was a friend of Abigail Adams, the publication of her *History . . . of the American Revolution* (1805) led to a sad quarrel with John Adams.

Mrs. William Stephens Smith, 1787   *J. S. Copley*

other jealous Partizans, but I hope they will never have sufficient interest to disturb the Government. I really believe Mr. G[err]y to be an honest Man. The other has been gravely misled, and I do soberly think by the unbridled ambition of all she told me upon her last visit, that she did not perceive any alteration in *Mr. A's* conduct towards them. I am sure she must have told what was not true if she had said there was none in mine, for I feel it, and I cannot deceive. With regard to Mr. A. he has dealt by them like a sincere Friend, and an honest Man and their own Hearts must approve his conduct, however grating to their feelings. I am most sincerely sorry for the cause. They were my old and dear Friend's for whom I once entertaind the highest respect.

Col. Mrs. Smith, Charles & little Jack are gone this week to Jamaica to get out of the Bustle at home and are not yet returnd. C[harles][4] will not go into any company but such as his Father or Col. Smith introduces him to. He appears steady and sedate & I hope will continue so. Time and example will prevail over youthfull folly I trust. My Love to Mrs. Norton. How does she do? Louisa appears very happy, but I am obliged to keep her a mere prisoner on account of the small pox of which there is always danger in N[ew] York. As soon as the weather will permit [I] shall have her innoculated. I find as many servants necessary here as in England, but not half as well calculated for their buisness. The distance from Town requires one or two extra as they are obliged to go & come always four, & frequently six times a day. We have to send constantly to market in addition, but notwithstanding all this I would not change this situation for any I know of in Town. Richmond Hill is situated upon the North River which communicates with Albany. Pauls hook[5] as it is calld is in full sight & the Jersy shore. Vessels are constantly passing up & down. The House is situated upon a high Hill which commands a most extensive prospect. On one side we have a view of the city & of Long Island, the river in Front, Jersy and the adjasant country on the other side. You turn a little from the Road and enter a Gate. A winding Road with trees in clumps leads you to the House, and all round the House, it looks wild and Rural as uncultivated Nature. The House is convenient for one family, but much too small for more. You enter under

[4] Charles Adams (1770–1800), who was preparing to practise law in New York. See footnote 1 to the letter of May 16, 1797.
[5] Paulus Hook was also spelled "Pauls" and "Powles" Hook, and is the present Jersey City, the site of which was originally called Communipaw. Stokes, *Iconography of Manhattan Island*, vol. 6, pp. 453–4. Paulus Hook was the scene of one of the most brilliant actions of the Revolution, when "Light Horse Harry" Lee attacked and captured the British garrison there on July 19, 1779.

a piazza into a Hall & turning to the right Hand ascend a stair case which lands you in an other of equal dimensions of which I make a drawing Room. It has a Glass door which opens into a gallery the whole Front of the house which is exceeding pleasant. The Chambers are on each side. The House is not in good repair, wants much done to it, and if we continue here I hope it will be done. There is upon the back of the House a Garden of much greater extent than our Braintree Garden, but it is wholy for a walk & flowers. It has a Hawthorn hedge & Rows of Trees with a Broad Gravel walk.

How happy would it make me to see here my dear Brother, Sister, Nephew, Neices and to delight them with the prospect. Mr. Guile & Dr. Craigy dinned with us yesterday.[6] I find I have local attachments, and am more rejoiced to see a citizen of my own State than any other. Remember me affectionatly to my worthy Mother & Family, to Mrs. Palmer & family who I hope are comfortably situated, to Mrs. Brisler too. I hope she will be able to come this way before long.[7]

My Letter is written in haste, the weather very hot, and I too laizy to coppy.

Most affectionatly yours
A. Adams

Tell Lucy she must write to me.

Richmond Hill, August 9th, 1789

My dear Sister:

If I should ask why I have not heard from my sister or Friends, for several weeks past, would she not answer me by retorting the question? In replie I could only say that I had designd writing every day for a long time, but we have had such a lassitude of weather, and such a long continuence of it, that I have really felt unfit for every thing which I was not necessitated to perform, & for many of those which I have been obligated

---

[6] Andrew Craigie (1743–1819), of Boston, apothecary, financier, and speculator. During his service in the Revolution, Craigie was made Apothecary-General. In 1791 he purchased the Vassall house in Cambridge, now known as the Craigie-Longfellow house. Craigie married Elizabeth Nancy Shaw.

[7] Mrs. Palmer was Mary Cranch, widow of General Joseph Palmer (who died in 1788, leaving his wife and two daughters destitute) and sister of Richard Cranch (who married Mary Smith, the sister of Mrs. John Adams). One of the daughters, Elizabeth Palmer, married her first cousin, Joseph Cranch (who was the son of John, the brother of Mrs. Palmer and Richard Cranch). See the *New-England Historical and Genealogical Register*, vol. 27, pp. 40–1: "Richard Cranch and His Family."

to, from my situation, such as dressing, receiving & paying visits, giving dinners &c. I have never before been in a situation in which morning noon & afternoon I have been half as much exposed to company. I have laid down one rule which is, not to make any morning visits myself, and in an afternoon after six oclock I can return 15 or 20 & very seldom find any Lady to receive me. But at Richmond Hill it is expected that I am at Home both to Gentlemen & Ladies when ever they come out, which is almost every day since I have been here, besides it is a sweet morning ride to Breakfast. I propose to fix a Levey day soon. I have waited for Mrs. Washington to begin and she has fixd on every fryday 8 oclock. I attended upon the last, Mrs. Smith & Charles. I found it quite a crowded Room. The form of Reception is this, the servants announce & Col. Humphries or Mr. Lear, receives every Lady at the door, & Hands her up to Mrs. Washington to whom she makes a most Respectfull courtsey and then is seated without noticeing any of the rest of the company. The Pressident then comes up and speaks to the Lady, which he does with a grace dignity & ease, that leaves Royal George far behind him. The company are entertaind with Ice creems[1] & Lemonade, and retire at their pleasure performing the same ceremony when they quit the Room. I cannot help smiling when I read the Boston puffs, that the Pressident is unmoved amidst all the dissipations of the city of New York. Now I am wholy at a loss to determine the meaning of the writer. Not a single publick amusement is their in the whole city, no not even a publick walk, and as to dinners, I believe their are six made in Boston to one here, unless it is for some particular person to whom a Number of families wish to pay attention. There are six Senators who have their Ladies and families with them, but they are in Lodgings the chief of them, & not in a situation to give dinners—as to the mode of visiting, less time is expended in this way, than in sending word to each person & passing an afternoon with them, tho I own on the score of pleasure that would be to me the most agreeable. I have returnd more than sixty visits all of them in 3 or 4 afternoons & excepting at the Pressidents, have drank tea only at two other places and dined but once out, since I arrived.

Indeed I have been fully employd in entertaining company, in the first place all the Senators who had Ladies & families, then the remaining

---

[1] The earliest instance of the mention of "ice cream" in print seems to be that of 1744 in the *Pennsylvania Magazine of History and Biography*, vol. 1, p. 126: *Oxford English Dictionary, Supplement*, p. 490.

Senators, and this week we have begun with the House, and tho we have a room in which we dine 24 persons at a Time, I shall not get through them all, together with the publick Ministers for a month to come. The help I find here is so very indifferent to what I had in England, the weather so warm that we can give only one dinner a week. I cannot find a cook in the whole city but what will get drunk, and as to the Negroes, I am most sincerely sick of them, and I can no more do without Mr. Brisler, than a coach could go without wheels or Horse to draw it. I can get Hands, but what are hands without a Head, and their chief object is to be as expensive as possible. This week I shall not be able to see any company unless it is to Tea, for my Family are all sick, Mrs. Smiths two Children with the Hooping Cough, Charles with the dysentary, Louisa & Polly with a complaint similar. To Charles I gave a puke last night & his complaints have abated. Louisa & Polly are to take one to night. If we had not been so fortunate in our situation I do not know how we could have lived. It is very sickly in the City.

As to politicks, I presume many of the dissapointed candidates will complain. Some will quarrel with men & some with measures. I believe the President strove to get the best information he could, but there are some men who will get much said in their favour when they do not merit it. The News papers will give you the debates of the house. To the President, their system is as liberal as I could expect. I leave the world to judge how it is with respect to their vice President from whom they expect more entertainment. The House was New furnished for the President & cost ten thousand dollars as the Board of Treasury say. The use & improvement of this they have granted him, which is but just & right. He never rides out without six Horses to his Carriage, four servants, & two Gentlemen before him. This is no more state than is perfectly consistant with his Station, but then I do not Love to see the News writers fib so. He is Perfectly averse to all marks of distinction, say they, yet on the 4th of July when the Cincinnati committee waited upon him he received them in a Regimental uniform with the Eagal most richly set with diamonds at his Button. Yet the News writers will fib, to answer particular purposes. I think he ought to have still more state, & time will convince our Country of the necessity, of it. Here I say not any thing upon the subject. It would be ascribed to a cause I dispise if I should speak my mind. I hear that the vote which Mr. A[dams] gave in the Senate, respecting the Removal of officers by the President independant of the Senate, has been by some of his own state construed, as voting power into his own Hands, or having that in view, but his Rule through life has been to vote and act, independant of Party agreeable to the dictates of his conscience, and tho on that occasion he could have wisht on account of the delicacy of his situation not to have been obliged to have determind the Question, yet falling to him, he shrunk not.[2] Not a word did any of our state say when his vote reduced the duty upon molasses. All was silence then. They could not possibly asscribe it to any sinister motive but uneasy wrestless spirits are to be found in all quarters of the world.

And now my dear Sister I wish to know how you do. Mrs. Norton, Lucy not a line from either, nor a word from Sister Shaw.[3]

Mr. Bond will tell you that he saw us all. He was out two or three times. I wish you could come with our dear Brother Cranch & spend the Evening with us. We do not have company on Sundays. We go to meeting, but alass I do not find a Dr. Price.[4] I hope I shall visit Braintree next summer. I wonder Sister Smith has never written a word to Louisa. I am glad to find Tommy[5] has got a good Chum. I hope he will continue steady. Charles studies with Mr. Hamilton, goes to the office when his Father goes to Senate & returns with him at 4 oclock. He has not discoverd the least inclination for getting into company and has no acquaintance but George Storer.[6] Pray make my best regards to all my Friends. To my Mother present my duty. Remember me to

[2] On the question of whether the power of removal of federal officers belonged (according to the Constitution) to the President alone, or went hand in hand with the process of appointment, thus requiring confirmation, the Senate divided nine to nine, and "John Adams then performed one of the most important acts of his life" by giving his casting vote, as presiding officer, for free presidential power of removal. Adams cast the decisive vote twenty times—more frequently than any of his successors in office. Channing, *A History of the United States*, vol. 4 (1917), pp. 47–8.

[3] Elizabeth (Smith) Shaw (1750–1815), wife of the Reverend John Shaw of Haverhill, and subsequently the wife of the Reverend Stephen Peabody, who, suddenly becoming a widower, is said to have proposed to Elizabeth immediately after delivering the funeral sermon of her first husband.

[4] Richard Price (1723–1791), nonconformist minister and writer on morals, politics, and economics, was a famous preacher in London for many years. In 1771 he advocated the reduction of the British national debt, and in 1776 he attacked the justice and policy of the war against the American colonies. Price became the intimate friend of Benjamin Franklin, and in 1778 the Continental Congress invited him, without success, to remove to America. Apart from his *Review of the Principal Questions in Morals*, 1756, Price is chiefly famous for Edmund Burke's scathing denunciation of his approbation of the principles of the French Revolution. Mrs. Adams heard Price preach in London during the years 1785–1787.

[5] Thomas Boylston (1772–1832), son of John and Abigail Adams.

[6] One of the three children—Charles, George, and Mary—of Hannah (Quincy) Storer (1736–1826).

Mrs. Palmer and family. The Beautifull prospect here from every quarter makes me regret less than I otherways should do the spot I quitted. The rooms are lofty and was the House in good repair I should find it very convenient for my own Family. At present we are crowded for want of chamber room. My family consists of 18. How does the place look? I must get my Butter all put up & sent me from Braintree. I have Breakfasted constantly upon milk. I cannot eat the Butter here. I must write the Dr.[7] upon several subjects by twesdays post. I shall not get ready by this.

Pray let me hear from you. The season is plentifull. Let us rejoice & be glad. Cheer up my good Sister. A merry Heart does good like a medicine. We all send abundance of Love. I must go to look after my invalids.

       Ever yours
        A. ADAMS

        Richmond Hill, Sepbr. 1, 1789

MY DEAR SISTER:

I Received your kind Letters and meant sooner to have replied to them, but many avocations have prevented me. I am fully apprizd of all you mention in your Letter respecting your situation and wanted no apoligies for your conduct, but I still insist upon what I first wrote you, & it will pain me to hear you say any thing more upon the subject. I never could apply it more to my satisfaction. I shall never I trust feel the want of it. If I should and you are in a situation to render me service, I will then accept it. I regret that it is not in my power to assist my Friends more than I do, but bringing our minds to our circumstances is a duty encumbent upon us. We have lived through dangerous Times, and have reason to be thankfull that we are still in possession of our Liberty & so much of our Property; yet still there is no reason in our being cheated by our Friends as well as Robbed by our Enemies. I have reason to think that congress will take up the matter and Fund the debt.[1] I

---

[7] Dr. Cotton Tufts, who was acting as the steward of the Adams property in Braintree. See footnote 11 to the letter of June 28, 1789.

[1] Hamilton's proposal for funding the debt, or debts, of the United States, was not taken up till the second session of the First Congress. The fierce debate over his report concerned three different items:

  1. The foreign debt of the Union, $11,710,378, owed to France, Holland and Spain.
  2. The domestic debt of the Union, incurred by the Continental Congress, $42,414,085.
  3. The state debts, estimated at $25,000,000.

Everyone agreed that the foreign debt should be paid in full, but many persons bitterly

wish they would set about it before they adjournd or rather defered their adjournment, till they had compleated more buisness but they have had arduous work, and want a respit.

I fear they will Remove from this place. I am too happy in the situation of it, I fear, to have it lasting. I am every day more & more pleased with it. Should they go to Philadelphia I do not know how I could possibly live through the voilent Heats. But sufficient to the day; I am sorry to hear Mrs. Norton is unwell, but from your Letter suppose her situation will be mended by time and you will e'er long know that a Grandchild is almost as near to your Heart as your own children; my little Boys delight me and I should feel quite melancholy without them. William came from his Grandmamma Smiths an almost ruind child, but I have brought him to be a fine Boy now.

My dear Lucy I long to see her. I am glad she is gone from home to amuse herself a little. I wish she could come to Richmond Hill and she would say it was the most delightfull spot she ever saw. My Love to her and Cousin William.[2] Louisa is worried that her Mother does not write to her. I really am surprizd that she has not written a single line either to me or to her, because I wrote to her before I left home and I cannot suppose that she could take any umbrage at my taking her away; I wish you would write to her and let her know that Louisa is uneasy upon the subject, and has written to her I believe more than once.

I wish you would be so good as [to] see if you can procure me two dozen Bottles of Rose water and send by [Captain] Barnard who has saild for Boston.[3]

I propose to have Louisa inoculated for the small pox this Month. I have now nearly got through all the company, that we propose to dine this Session & I have not heard, that any of them were so near being drownd as to render it necessary to apply to the Humane Society. The Spirit of Rebellion is not yet quelld in Massachusets. The coals are blowing again and with a malice truly infernal. What will not dissapointed ambition stick at?

---

opposed the assumption of the state debts, and declared, moreover, that the domestic debt of the Union should be redeemed at its depreciated value. Hamilton's proposal prevailed, in the main: debts one and two were paid in full, and state debts were assumed to the extent of $21,500,000. Schouler, *History of the United States*, vol. 1, p. 145.

[2] "Cousin William" was one of the children of William Smith, the brother of Mrs. Adams. See footnote 4 to the letter of November 24, 1788.

[3] Probably that Captain Moses Barnard, then in command of the *Lydia*, which was captured by the French in 1799. See the *Columbian Centinel*, November 9, 1799.

> "O what a world is this, when what is comely
> Envenoms him that bears it."

> "Be thou as chaste as ice, as pure as snow, thou shalt not escape calumny."[4]

Pray present my duty to my worthy Mother & a kind remembrance to all inquiring Friends and be assured that I am, my dear Sister,

Most affectionately yours
A. ADAMS

P.S. I find the Author of the Libel (for such it is,) calld the Dangerous vice, is Ned Church,[5] a dissapointed [office] seeker. But why his malice should

---

[4] Lines 1 and 2: *As You Like It*, Act II, Scene 3, lines 14–5; the second quotation is from *Hamlet*, Act III, Scene 1, lines 140–2.

[5] Edward Church was the brother of the notorious Benjamin Church (1734–*circa* 1776), author, physician, poet, and traitor. There appeared in the *Massachusetts Centinel* for Saturday, August 22, 1789, a letter signed "A Republican," which contained parts of a "manuscript Poem, (said to have been written by a gentleman formerly of Boston) in which, among other popular topicks, the subjects of TITLES was introduced." The lines which annoyed John Adams follow:

> Be grateful then, YE CHOSEN! mod'rate wise,
> Nor stretch your claims to such preposterous size,
> Lest your too partial country—wiser grown—
> Shou'd on your native dunghills set you down.
> Ape not the fashions of the foreign great,
> Nor make your betters at your *levees* wait—
> Resign your awkward pomp, parade and pride,
> And lay that useless *etiquette* aside;
> Th' unthinking laugh, but all the thinking hate
> Such vile, abortive mimickry of State;
> Those idle lackeys, saunt'ring at your door,
> But ill become *poor servants* of the POOR;
> Retrench your board, for e'en the guests who dine,
> Have cause to murmur at your floods of wine:
> Think not to bribe the wise with their own gold,
> Though fools by flimsy lures shou'd be cajol'd;
> Places on places multiply to view,
> Creation on creation, ever new;
> Therefore in decent competence to live
> Is all that you can ask, or *justice* give.
>
> YE WOU'D BE TITLED! whom, in evil hour—
> The rash, unthinking people cloth'd with pow'r,
> Who, drunk, with pride, of foreign baubles dream,
> And rave of a COLUMBIAN DIADEM—
> Be prudent, modest, mod'rate, grateful, wise,
> Nor on your Country's ruin strive to rise,
> Lest great COLUMBIA's AWFUL GOD shou'd frown,
> And to your native dunghills hurl you down.

thus vent itself against Mr. A[dams] I know not, unless he thought himself neglected by him. I remember he wrote a letter to Mr. A. when we were abroad soliciting the place of consul to Lisbon which Mr. A. never answerd. I have past him I recollect two or three times in comeing from Town & I rember[*sic*] now that Mrs. Smith observed to me that he look'd so surly she hated to see him. It appears now that he offerd this peice to the Printers here who all refused to be concernd with it. He sent it [to] Boston & took himself off to Georgia. He never was the person that either visited or spoke a word to Mr. A. since he has been in N[ew] York. Mr. A. says, that one day at the Presidents Levee he was speaking to the President & Church bowed to him. He could not whilst addressing the President return his bow with Propriety. His intention was to have gone & spoken to him afterwards, but the Room being full he did not see him afterwards. This I suppose Church construed into Pride and contempt, & being dissapointed in obtaining a place from the Pressident, he vented all his malice upon the vice [President], & conceiving the Topick he took to be a popular one he has discoverd a temper as fit for Rebellion, Murder, Treason as his unfortunate Brother. I could wish that the Author might be fully known to the publick with regard to the subject of a proper title for the Pressident. Mr. A. never has or will disguise his opinion, because he thinks that the stability of the Government will in a great measure rest upon it. Yet the subject here is scarcly mentiond & the Boston News papers have rung more changes upon it, than all the News papers in the United States besides. I think in holding up Church to view, it would not be amiss to state his conduct with regard to the Spanish vessel.

       Ye faithful guardians of your Country's weal,
Whose honest breasts still glow with patriot zeal!
The lawless lust of POW'R in embryo quell,
The germ of mischief, the first spawn of hell;
Resist the VICE—and that contagious pride
To that o'erweening VICE—so near ally'd.
Within your sacred walls let Virtue reign,
And greedy MAMMON spread his snares in vain.
With unlick'd Lordlings sully not your fame,
Nor daub our PATRIOT with a LACKER'D name.
O WASHINGTON! thy Country's hope and trust!
Alas! perhaps her last, as thou wert first;
Successors we can find—but tell us where
Of ALL thy virtues we shall find THE HEIR?

A letter of protest against this effusion, signed "Togatus," appeared in the *Centinel* of August 26, 1789.

It was a relief to my mind to find the Author Church. I was really apprehensive that a Female pen had been dipt in full in consequence of dissapointed views. A Brute to attack me who never in thought word or deed offended him, or have ever been in this Country to Ball's, plays, or Routes.[6] But malice was his motive & Revenge his object. The Vice President ten times to one goes to Senate in a one Horse chaise, and Levee's we have had none. The Pressident only, has his powderd Lackies waiting at the door. So that under a Hipocritical mask he attacks one & hold [sic] the other impiously up & stiles him a Saviour & God. How inconsistant, railing at Titles & giving those which belong to the Deity.

How must a wretch feel who can harbour such a temper?

But adieu my dear Sister. Thus it is to be seated high. I pray Heaven to give me a conscience void of offence, and then the curse causeless shall not come.[7]

       Your[s] affectionatly
        A. A[DAMS]

      Richmond Hill, October 4th, 1789

MY DEAR SISTER:

I wrote you a Letter last week, but as it did not get to the Post office, I have detaind it with an intention of sending you one of a later date. I believe I have received all your Letters. Your last was dated Sepbr 8th. I have not written to any of my Friends so often as I ought to. You know very well that when a person is fixed to any particular spot, that very few subjects worth communicating can occur. As I have not been to any publick amusement, I cannot say any thing upon that score, but I can tell you something which may well excite your surprize. It is that I have cause every Sunday to regret the loss of Parson Wibird,[1] and that I should realy think it an entertainment to hear a discourse from him. Do not however tell him so, but except three sermons which three New England Clergymen have preachd to us, I have been most misirably off. Dr. Rogers where we usually attend, has been unable to preach ever

---

[6] "A fashionable gathering or assembly, a large evening party or reception, much in vogue in the eighteenth and early nineteenth centuries." *Oxford English Dictionary.* See, also, letter of Abigail Adams to Mrs. Cranch, written from London, April 6, 1786, in *Letters of Mrs. Adams,* C. F. Adams, Editor, Boston, 1840, p. 332.

[7] "As the bird by wandering, as the swallow by flying, so the curse causeless shall not come." *Proverbs,* XXVI, 2. See, also, the letter of June 6-8, 1797.

[1] Anthony Wibird (1728-1800), who was graduated from Harvard in 1747, was the minister at Quincy.

since I have been here and the pulpit has been supplied as they could procure *Labourers*—by Gentlemen who preach without Notes, all of whom are predestinarians and whose Noise & vehemince is to compensate for every other difficency.[2] To go to meeting & set an hour & half to hear a discourse the principals of which are so totally different from my own sentiments, that I cannot possibly believe them, is really doing penance. I have sometimes gone to St. Pauls. There I find much more liberal discourses, but bred a desenter and approveing that mode of worship, I feel a reluctance at changing tho I would always go to church, if I resided where there was no other mode of worship. The Clergymen here I am told are so Rigid that their company is very little sought after. They never mix with their people as they do with us, and there is in there Air and countanances that solemn Phiz and gate which looks so like mummery that instead of Reverence they create disgust, and they address their Audience with so much self importance and Priestly despotism that I am really surprizd at their having any men of sense and abilities for their hearers. I have seen but one exception to this character & that in a Dr. Lynd[3] who is really the best & most liberal of the whole sett. We have in Massachusetts a sett of clergy that are an honour to Religion, to Learning, & to our country, and for whom I feel an increased esteem & veneration since my Residence in New York. I do not however mean by my remarks that they are not Religious Moral Men here. I never heard a syllable to their injury, but they certainly are men of very mean capacities when compared to those of our State. There is no man of esteemed eminence amongst them even as a divine.

The adjournment of Congress leaves me a leisure which I most sincerly wish I could improve in visiting Braintree. If they had honestly

[2] John Rodgers (1727–1811), Presbyterian clergyman, was born in Boston. In 1728 his parents moved to Philadelphia, where, as a boy of twelve, Rodgers was dramatically converted by George Whitefield. In 1747 he was licensed as a preacher, and served in Virginia, Maryland, and Delaware. Having married Elizabeth Bayard, of Maryland, who died in 1763, Rodgers, in 1764, married Mary, the widow of William Grant, a rich Philadelphia merchant. In 1765 Rodgers began a pastorate of forty-five years in New York City, preaching to crowded congregations in the Presbyterian church which stood at the corner of Beekman and Nassau Streets. He was a distinguished patriot, and a friend of Washington. The New England Congregationalists regarded him as one of themselves, but they disliked the Calvinism of the Scotch Presbyterian pastors who served as his colleagues. For many years Rodgers was a punctilious and picturesque person as he walked the streets of New York.

[3] Probably the Reverend Dr. William Linn (1753–1808), who was attached to the Dutch Reformed Church in New York City. He married a daughter of Dr. John Blair. Dr. Linn delivered a funeral eulogy on George Washington, on February 22, 1800. *Eulogies and Orations on the Life and Death of General George Washington*, Boston, 1800, pp. 159–175.

adjournd to April, I say honestly for many of the southern members will not get here till then, I should not have hesitated in comeing on immediatly & spending the winter with my dear Friends in B[raintree]. But it has been my Lot to be fetterd one way or an other. The liberality of Congress obliged me to remove most of my furniture so as to make it quite inconvenient for us to pass a part of our Time at our own Home, without being at a considerable expence, and the prospect of a return in December very much discourages me in my progect. Mr. Adams's close & unremitting attention to Buisness during six months, has made a journey quite necessary for him, yet he will not go unless it is to his own Home. My son J. Q. A. proposes returning this week to Boston & Brisler leaves me tomorrow. How the Machine will get on without him I know not. I have offerd him what I esteem very liberal wages, & double what I can get others for, who would perform the mechanical part of Buisness as well perhaps as he but I know not where to find Honour, Honesty, integrity & attachment. He pleads the state of his family which I know it would be difficult to remove, but 200 dollars pr year are not so easily earned in Massachusetts, and are really more than we can afford. He has it at his option to return if he cannot succeed at home. I do not wish my offer to be known, and I think he will find it difficult to support his Family when he once comes to stand upon his own legs for them, which he has never yet done. From six years trial of him I can give him the best of characters, and I never expect to find an other so particularly calculated for me and my Family. His errors are those of Judgment or rather the want of judgment and upon that Rock I am fearfull he will split, when he comes to act for himself.—The Letter you mention for Mr. Bond was sent directly to his Lodgings upon our receiving it.[4]

I hope the appointments in the judicial Line will give satisfaction, notwithstanding some dissapointments. If I may judge by the News papers, there is no state in the union where there are so many grumblers as in our own. It has been my Lot in Life to spend a large portion of it in publick Life, but I can truly say the pleasentest part of it was spent at the foot of Pens Hill in that Humble Cottage when my good Gentleman was a Practitioner at the Bar, earnt his money, during the week, & at the end of it pourd it all into my Lap to use or what could be spaired to lay by. Nobody then grudgd us our living, & 25 years such practise would have given us a very different property from what we now possess. It

[4] Probably the father of William Cranch Bond (1789–1859), the astronomer. William C. Bond's mother was Hannah Cranch. See the letter of August 9, 1789.

might not have given us the 2nd Rank in the United States, nor the satisfaction of reflecting by what means & whose exertions these states have arrived at that degree of Liberty safety & independance which they now enjoy. If the United States had chosen to the Vice P's Chair a man wavering in his opinions, or one who sought the popular applause of the multitude, this very constitution would have had its death wound during this first six months of its existance. On several of the most trying occasions it has fallen to this dangerous *vice*, to give the casting vote for its Life.[5] There are several Members of the House & some of the S[enat]e who are, to say no worse, wild as—Bedlammites but hush—I am speaking treason. Do not you betray me.

Remember me kindly to all inquiring Friends, and believe me, my dear Sister,

Yours most affectionatly
A. ADAMS

Richmond Hill, October 11, 1789

MY DEAR SISTER:

Mr. Adams sets of tomorrow Morning on a visit to Braintree. I would gladly have accompanied him, but so many difficulties arose in the way, that I gave up the Idea. If I had come we must have gone to housekeeping, & by that Time I had got things any way convenient, I must have returnd, & that at a season of the year when it would have been cold & unpleasent travelling. I find myself attackd with my Rhumatick complaints upon the setting in of cold weather, and am obliged to be very circumspect.

The constant application to buisness for six months has made it necessary to Mr. Adams to take a journey and he promises me that he will go to Haverhill and visit his Friends, but you are like to have an other visiter. The Pressident sets out this week for a like excursion. He proposes to go as far as Portsmouth. He would have had Mr. Adams accept a seat in his in[*sic*] coach but he excused himself from motives of delicacy. We yesterday had a very pleasent party together. The whole family of us dinned with the President on Thursday, and he then proposed an excursion to long Island by water to visit Princes Gardens, but as Mrs. Washington does not Love the water we agreed that the Gentlemen should go by water and the Ladies should meet them at a half way House and dine together, and yesterday we had a most Beautifull day

[5] See footnote 5 to the letter of September 1, 1789.

for the purpose. The President, [the] V.P., Col. S[mith], Major Jackson,[1] Mr. Izard[2] &c went on Board the Barge at 8 oclock. At Eleven the Ladies, namely Mrs. Washington, Mrs. Adams, Mrs. Smith, Miss Custos [Custis][3] set out in Mrs. Washingtons coach & six & met the Gentlemen at Harlem where we all dinned together & returnd in the same manner. We live upon terms of much Friendship & visit each other often. Whilst the Gentlemen are absent we propose seeing one an other on terms of much sociability. Mrs. Washington is a most friendly, good Lady, always pleasent and easy, doatingly fond of her Grandchildren, to whom she is quite the Grandmamma.

Louisa & John A[dam]s [Smith] are both innoculated for the small pox on fryday last. I hope my son J. Q. A. arrived safe (as well as Brisler). I suppose he led you to think that I should visit you as he was very urgent for me to come. I think it not unlikely that there will be a summer recess next year & then I hope to see you all. I wish you would be so good as to get some Brown thread for me of Mrs. Field, three skains of different sizes. Mr. A[dams] will pay you for her, & for the Rose water, which you have procured. Ruthe Ludden, who lives with Mrs. Field, promised me that she would come and live with me whenever she was out of her Time.[4] If she holds of the same mind I will send for her in the spring either by Barnard or the stage. I wish you had Polly Tailor. To live alone she is a very excellent Girl, but she was never made for society, and Power was never worse used than in her Hands. I tell her sometimes that if I had taken Mrs. Brislers advice I never should have brought her. Of all things I hate to hear people for ever complaining of servants but I never had so much occasion as since I came here. One good servant attached to you is invaluable. The one who attends Mr. Adams is good for nothing that I know of but to look after his Horses. He has servd us as a coachman ever since I have been here. I hope Brisler will return, but I would not urge it too much, as the best people may take advantage of their own consequence and importance.

[1] Major William Jackson (1759–1828), who fought in the Revolution and was secretary to the convention which framed the Constitution in 1787. William Jackson served as one of the personal secretaries of George Washington from 1789 to 1791.

[2] Ralph Izard (1742–1804), Senator from South Carolina (1789–1795), and an ardent supporter of President Washington and the Federalists.

[3] Probably the eldest of the four children of Colonel John Parke Custis (1753–1781), stepson of George Washington: that is, Eliza Parke Custis (1776–1832), subsequently (1796) Mrs. Thomas Law.

[4] Ruth, daughter of Benjamin and Ruth Ludden, was born at Braintree in 1772. She did not become a servant of Mrs. Adams in New York.

How is Mrs. Norton? Does she begin to look stately? I shall want to see her. Lucy I hope is well. I pleasd myself for a week with the Idea of spending three months with you, but it cannot be.

I will thank you to look over Mr. Adams things for him & see that they agree with the list which I will send as soon as I know what he takes. Love to Mr. Cranch. Remember me kindly to my Mother & all other Friends.

Yours most affectionatly
A. ADAMS

Richmond Hill, Novbr. 1, 1789

MY DEAR SISTER:

A strange phenomanan has happend in our Family. I believe I wrote you that Louisa and John were both innoculated for the small pox but neither of their arms shew'd any proofs after the 2d day. Louisa was soon seizd with the cold & Fever which has so universally prevaild here. Upon the 10 day John was very sick, apparantly the symptoms of the small pox, but they lasted only one day. On the 17 day the child had an inflamation in his Eyes, a fever in his Head, was sick and oppressd at his stomach, but not the least redness upon the arm. We had no apprehension that it was the small pox. On the 19 day he began to have a small eruption upon his face, his symptoms went of & he has had the small pox finely, about a hundred which have filled. Louisa has been innoculated from him, and from the appearance of the arm we think it has taken. I hope she will have it as favourable as the child. He could not have taken it in any other way as he was not out of the House, but why he should take it, & Louisa not, cannot be accounted for in any other way, than that two disorders would not operate at the same time.

I yesterday received a Letter from Cousin Lucy of Ocbr 25, one from Tommy & one from Sister Shaw, and Last week yours October 12 came to hand. I put into Mr. Adams's trunk the cushion I promisd you. I should have sent it sooner, but hoped to have brought it. All the things on the Top belong to J. Q. A., as you will see. I wish you would send them to him, or let him know that you have them. When Brisler leaves the House I should be glad to have the things left inventoried, not that I fear loosing by the Family who are now there, but for my own satisfaction. There was one thing which I forgot to mention. I have papers in the Escritore which I lent Mrs. Bass.[1] The key is on the Bunch with

---

[1] Mrs. Bass, of Braintree, was an occasional servant of Mrs. Adams. See the letter of July 19, 1797.

Mrs. Brisler. I wish Cousin Lucy to go & take them away. Put them in a draw or Trunk at the other House. I hope to come to Braintree in the course of an other year, and see all my dear Friends. I wish the Dr. much happiness with his *Young wife*.[2] Is she not young for him? Mrs. Norton must have much satisfaction in the event, if she proves as I hope & doubt not she will a kind Aunt and an agreeable companion. I hope my dear sister has recoverd her sprits. None of us live without our anxieties, tho some are of a much more painfull kind than others.

How is our worthy uncle Quincy?[3] Mr. Adams I dare say will visit him as often as he can. I hope you will see our worthy President. He is much a favorite of mine, I do assure you. Tell Mr. Adams that Mrs. Washington says she has a present for him when he returns. It is true she says it is of no great value, but she will not tell me what it is, nor let me see it till he returns. I told her I would be jealous but it did not provoke her to shew it me. We are at present all very well, Louisa innoculated the 2 time on thursday last. I hope Mr. Adams will not put of his return so late as he talked of when he set out. The weather will be soon very cold and uncomfortable. Remember me kindly to all my Friends. I am very bad about writing; not half as good as when I was in England. The reason is I have few subjects, few new objects. The Men & Women here are like the Men & Women elsewhere, & if I was to meet a curious Character I should not venture to be free with it.

I wish to have our winter Apples, pears, Butter, some cheese, Bacon, Tongue &c all from our own state & what I cannot get from the Farm I would get put up in Boston, such as Hams & Tongues. I mentiond all these things to Mr. Adams, but do not know that he will be attentive about them. Any Letters which may be taken out of the post office addrest to the Vice Pressident of the United States, you may venture to open the covers of whether Mr. Adams is with you or not, for you may be sure that they come from Richmond Hill.

Adieu, my dear Sister, and believe me
Most affectionatly yours,
A. ADAMS

Mrs. Smith & Master William Magpye as I call him send duty.

[2] See footnote 11 to the letter of June 28, 1789.

[3] Norton Quincy (1716–1801), a brother of the mother of Abigail Adams, was graduated from Harvard in 1736.

RICHMOND HILL, NEW YORK CITY, 1790

BUSH HILL, PHILADELPHIA, 1787 　　　　　　　　　　　　　　　　　*J. P. Malcolm*

My dear Sister: Richmond Hill, Novbr. 3, 1789

I did not receive your Letter dated 25 untill Sunday Evening which made it too late to write by the last post in replie to it. I do not know any thing that I wisht more for than to have past the winter at my own House. For a summer situation this place is delightfull & the House convenient, and except its being Bleak and perhaps difficult of access in some parts of a severe winter, it is more to my mind than any place I ever lived in. In point of occonomy it would be very advantageous to be able to live at Home part of the year and the winter in particular, wood being the most expensive article here. Nut wood, what we call Walnut is 7 dollars pr cord and oak cost me five brought to our door between 40 & 50 cords of which we shall consume in a year, as we are obliged to keep six fires constantly, & occasionally more. The hire of servants is an other very heavy article part of which we might spair at Braintree. Our House we must keep & pay for, but I should wish if a recess of any length should take place again to spend it with my Friends at Braintree. My constant family is 18, ten of which make my own Family. Both Mrs. Smith & I am [*sic*] disposed to accommodate as much as possible, but difficulties will arise with the best servants sometimes, & we can neither of us boast that all ours are of the best kind.

I have a pretty good Housekeeper, a tolerable footman, a midling cook, an indifferent steward and a vixen of a House maid, but she has done much better laterly, since she finds that the housekeeper will be mistress below stairs. I wish Polly was in Braintree, and meant to have taken her with me if I had come, but I do not know what to say with regard to her suiting you. She is very far from being a Girl that will turn off work quick. Her constitution has been ruined by former hardships, and she is very often laid up. She has not method or regularity with her buisness. All her buisness here is to make 4 or 5 beds, & clean round Rooms which are almost coverd with carpets. All the Brass is cleaned by the footman. She helps wash & Iron, but I have been obliged to hire when I have wanted more cleaning than that done in a day, and every days work to pay 3 shilling a day for. I suppose I must keep her till spring, unless she should become more than usually quarelsome. With regard to drink I meet with no difficulty with her on that account, and she has an attention to my interest more than any servant I have besides, when Mr. Brisler is absent. She keeps no company, and is fond of the children, so that she has her good Qualities, for which I am ready to credit her.[1]

[1] For Polly Tailor, see footnote 7 to the letter of June 19, 1789.

I have written to Mr. Adams respecting the coachman, who certainly is not to be trusted with Keys of a cellar. He always slept in the stable & was never in the House but at meal times, or as a porter at the door when we had company to dine. He is a good coachman and that I believe is all. I hope Mr. Adams will return sooner than he talks of, for I am sure when Brisler goes he cannot be well accommodated in his own House, and the Roads will every day be proving worse. 200wt cheese, all the Butter from Mothers, my half from Pratts is what I should like sent. I should like a good Hog or two, but Pratts pork is not worth having, and I shall have some of my own here.

I think Brisler much in the right, both for me and himself. He will be better of than his master & may lay up more money, but what could he do at home to earn 200 Hard dollars. I think his Family may live very well upon one hundred. I have engaged 2 good Rooms for him for 32 dollars & a half. His wood I suppose will cost him 25 dollars, but suppose he only lays by 50 a year, tis more than he could do & mantain himself & family where he is.

I wrote to him by the last post. Let him know if his Family can come on without him & Mr. Adams wishes him to stay with him, that they shall come here till he & his Things arrive—but he must be here by the Time that Barnard is to look after his things.

I wish Mr. Adams would return with the President, as I know he will be invited to, & let Tommy[2] take his sulky & come on with that.

My Love to Mrs. Norton, to Cousin Lucy and all inquiring Friends. My most affectionate Regards to Mr. Cranch. Remember me to Mrs. Palmers Family.

Yours most affectionatly
A. ADAMS

[Richmond Hill], Janry. 5th, 1790

MY DEAR SISTER:

I begin my Letter with the congratulations of the season, to you and all my other Friends & for many happy returns in succeeding years. The New Years day in this state, & particularly in this city is celebrated with every mark of pleasure and satisfaction. The shops and publick offices are shut. There is not any market upon this day, but every person laying aside Buisness devote[s] the day to the social purpose of visiting & receiving visits. The churches are open & divine service performed begining

---

[2] Thomas Boylston Adams (1772–1832).

the year in a very proper manner by giving Thanks to the great Governour of the universe for past mercies, & imploring his future Benidictions. There is a kind of cake in fashion upon this day call'd New Years Cooky. This & Cherry Bounce as it is calld is the old Dutch custom of treating their Friends upon the return of every New Year. The common people, who are very ready to abuse Liberty, on this day are apt to take rather too freely of the good things of this Life, and finding two of my servants not all together qualified for Buisness, I remonstrated to them, but they excused it by saying it was New Year, & every body was joyous then. The V. P. visited the President & then returnd home to receive His Friends. In the Evening I attended the drawing Room, it being Mrs. W[ashington']s publick day. It was as much crowded as a Birth Night at St. James, and with company as Briliantly drest, diamonds & great hoops excepted. My station is always at the right hand of Mrs. W.; through want of knowing what is right I find it sometimes occupied, but on such an occasion the President never fails of seeing that it is relinquished for me, and having removed Ladies several times, they have now learnt to rise & give it me, but this between our selves, as *all distinction* you know is unpopular. Yet this same P[resident] has so happy a faculty of appearing to accommodate & yet carrying his point, that if he was not really one of the best intentiond men in the world he might be a very dangerous one. He is polite with dignity, affable without familiarity, distant without Haughtyness, Grave without Austerity, Modest, wise & Good. These are traits in his Character which peculiarly fit him for the exalted station he holds, and God Grant that he may Hold it with the same applause & universal satisfaction for many many years, as it is my firm opinion that no other man could rule over this great peopl & consolidate them into one mighty Empire but He who is set over us.

I thank you my dear Sister for several kind Letters. The reason why I have not written to you has been that the post office would not permit Franks even to the V. P. and I did not think my Letters worth paying for. I wrote you a long Letter a little before Mr. Adams's return, but being under cover to him, I had the mortification to receive it back again. I am perfectly satisfied with what you did for son Thomas, and thank you for all your kind care of him. It has saved me much trouble, but I do not think his Health good. He is very thin, pale & sallow. I have given him a puke, & think he is the better for it. Charls is quite fat. He is very steady and studious. There is no fault to be found with his conduct. He has no company or companions but known & approved ones, nor does he appear to wish for any other. I sometimes think his application too intence, but better so, than too remis.

I was really surprizd to learn that Sister Shaw was likely to increase her Family. I wish her comfortably through, but shall feel anxious for her feeble constitution. As to my Neice Mrs. Norton[1] I doubt not she will find her Health mended by becoming a Mother, and you will soon be as fond of your Grandchildren as ever you was of your own. I hope however she will not follow her cousins example, and be like always to have one, before the other is weaned. John does not go alone yet. William becomes every day more & more interesting. He is a very pleasant temperd Boy, but the other will require the whole house to manage him.[2] With Regard to the cellars I know if very cold weather should come we shall lose our red wine & porter, but as to the key, tis a point I do not chuse to meddle with tho all the Liquors should suffer by it. I did not leave it where it is, nor do I hold myself answerable for the concequences of neglect. The fruit which came here was like refuse, rotton & Bruised, a specimin of what I expected. But you know there are cases where silence is prudence, and I think without flattering myself I have attaind to some share of that virtue. We live in a world where having Eyes we must not see, and Ears we must not hear.

10 Janry.

I designd to have written much more to you and some other Friends, but publick days, dinning parties &c have occupied me so much for this fortnight, that I must close my Letter now or lose the conveyance.

Remember me affectionatly to all Friends. Living two miles from meeting obliges me to hasten or lose the afternoon service. Adieu.

Yours
A. Adams

Richmond Hill, Febry. 20, 1790

My dear Sister:

I yesterday received a Letter from Dr. Tufts and an other from Thomas informing me of the death of Mrs. Palmer. The good old Lady is gone to rest, happily for her, I doubt not, but what will become of her daughters Heaven only knows, Polly in particular.[1] I feel very unhappy

[1] Elizabeth (Cranch) Norton, wife of the Reverend Jacob Norton.
[2] William Steuben Smith (1787) and John Adams Smith (1788), sons of Abigail (Adams) Smith (1765–1813), previously referred to. See footnote 1 to the letter of November 24, 1788.

[1] Polly Palmer, daughter of the widow of General Joseph Palmer (died in 1788). See footnote 7 to the letter of July 12, 1789.

for them, and you I am sure must be still more so. I suppose you was too heavily loaded with care, and affliction to write me by the last post. They may continue in the House untill we want it, if it would any way serve them, but I presume there cannot be any thing for their support after their Mothers discease. I am sure you cannot help looking back for 20 years and exclaming, what a change! But such are the visisitudes of Life and the Transitory fleeting state of all sublinary things; of all pride that which persons discover from Riches is the weakest. If we look over our acquaintance, how many do we find who were a few years ago in affluence, now reduced to real want, but there is no Family amongst them all whose schemes have proved so visionary, and so abortive as the unhappy one we are now commisirating. Better is a little with contentment than great Treasure; and trouble therewith. It would be some consolation to the Sisters if they had a Brother in whom they could take comfort. If ever convents are usefull, it would be for persons thus circumstanced.

I did not write to you by Thomas as I thought he could give you every information you wish'd for respecting us. He writes that he got home well, but appears in some anxiety about the Measles. I would not wish him to avoid them, but only to be watchfull when he takes them and to be particularly attentive to himself during the period. This care I know you will have of him, if he should get them, and if he does not take them, he will always have an anxiety upon his mind increasing too as he advances in Life, every time he is liable to be exposed to them.

From all the Debates in Congress upon the subject of a discrimination, I presume the vote will be that there shall be none, but that some one or other of the plans proposed by the Secretary of the Treasury will be adopted.[2] It is thought that tomorrow will be the desisive day with respect to the question, as the vote will be calld for. On this occasion I am going for the first Time to the House with Mrs. Dalton,[3] Mrs. Jay & Mrs. Cushing to hear the debate. If you read the papers you will find some very judicious debates. Mr. Smith[4] of S[outh] C[arolina] who married a daughter of Mr. Izard, is one of the first from that state, & I

[2] Hamilton's proposal for funding the debt of the United States. See footnote 1 to the letter of September 1, 1789.

[3] Wife of Tristram Dalton (1738–1817), of Newburyport, who was graduated from Harvard in 1755. He was Senator from Massachusetts (1789–1791), and was defeated for reëlection in 1790. See, also, the letter of March 20, 1792.

[4] William Loughton Smith (1758–1812), of Charleston, South Carolina, who was elected as a Federalist to the first five Congresses; and appointed United States minister to Portugal and Spain on July 10, 1797.

might add, from the Southern States. Mr. Ames[5] from our state & Mr. Sedgwick[6] and Mr. Gerry are all right upon this Question & make a conspicuous figure in the debates. I hope some method will be adopted speedily for the relief of those who have so long been the sufferers by the instability of Government. The next question I presume that will occupy Congress will be the Assumption of the State debts, and here I apprehend warm work, and much opposition, but I firmly believe it will terminate for the General Good.

What a disgrace upon the Legislature of our state that they should permit such a Madman as Gardner[7] to occupy their time, to vilify Characters, to propogate grose falshoods to the world under their sanction. I should feel more trust for [sic] them if I did not foresee that good would come out of it in time, if the Bar possess that Honour which I presume they Have, they will combine to defeat Gardner and his Abetters and establish such Rules & Regulations as will tend to restore

[5] Fisher Ames (1758–1808), of Dedham, Massachusetts, one of the most gifted and persuasive, if anxious, of the New England Federalists. Ames's speech on Jay's Treaty (April 28, 1796) was "one of the greatest speeches ever made in Congress." Channing, *History of the United States*, vol. 4 (1917), p. 145.

[6] Theodore Sedgwick (1746–1813), of Stockbridge, Massachusetts, graduated from Yale in 1765, member of the House of Representatives in the first four Congresses, Senator (1796–1799), and Speaker of the House (1799–1801). Despite (or because of) his extremely humble origin, Sedgwick was overbearing to the common people, and habitually spoke of them as Jacobins and *sans culottes*.

[7] John Gardiner (1737–1793), lawyer and reformer, was the son of Silvester Gardiner (1708–1786), physician, land owner, and Loyalist, and the father of John Sylvester John Gardiner (1765–1830), Episcopal clergyman, who was rector of Trinity Church, Boston (1805–1830). John Gardiner was born in Boston and educated in Great Britain, where he was graduated from the University of Glasgow in 1755. As an ardent Whig, living in London, he became the friend of, and acted as counsel for, John Wilkes. In 1783, Gardiner returned to Boston, and in 1786 removed to Pownalboro, in the District of Maine, from which he was elected to the Massachusetts General Court in 1789. He was instrumental in abolishing entails and primogeniture in Massachusetts, and organized a mass meeting to agitate for the repeal of the law against theatres, but without success. As a vestryman of King's Chapel, Boston, Gardiner manipulated the shady deal by which that church, the property of the Episcopalians, eventually passed into the possession of the Unitarians. His tumultuous career was cut short when he was drowned off Cape Ann in the loss of the *Londoner*, October 17, 1793, while he was on his way to Boston to attend a meeting of the legislature. For a reproduction of his portrait by Copley, see H. W. Foote, *Annals of King's Chapel*, vol. 2, Boston, 1896, p. 357.

John Gardiner's father cut him off with one guinea; his son, in his discourse, "A Preservative against Unitarianism," June 8, 1811, observed: "The candor of an Unitarian resembles the humanity of a revolutionary Frenchman." Gardiner often attended services at Trinity Church, where he would disturb the congregation by refusing to read responses from the Book of Common Prayer, using, instead, a special prayer book which he himself had compiled.

their profession to the same Reputation which they held before the Revolution. You and I feel peculiarly interested in this matter as we have children rising into Life educated to the Law, without a competant knowledge of which no Man is fit for a Legislator or a Statesman. Let us look into our National Legislature. Scarcly a man there makes any figure in debate, who has not been Bred to the Law.

Pray give my Love to my worthy Brother Cranch & tell him that I sympathize with him in his affliction.[8] Remember me affectionatly to my Neices & Nephew and believe that your happiness is very near the Heart of your

Ever affectionat
A. ADAMS

New York, Feb'ry 28, 1790

MY DEAR SISTER:

On the 17 of this Month Cousin William[1] wrote his uncle, that he had carried his Cousin Tom[2] Home to Braintree with the symptoms of the Measles upon him; you will easily suppose that I waited for the next post with great anxiety but how was I dissapointed last Evening when Mr. Adams returnd from Town, and the Roads being very bad the post had not arrived. I could not content myself without sending into Town again before I went to Bed, but the servant returnd with two Newspapers only. Am the more anxious because I know that Thomas was not well during the whole time that he was with us. I gave him a puke, after which he appeard better. He appeard to me to have lost his appetite his flesh and his coulour, & I am fearfull he was in a poor state to take the measles. I know that he will have every care & attention under your Roof that he could have, if I was with him, and this is a great relief to my mind; but to hear that he was sick, and to be ten days in suspence, & how much longer I know not, has made me very unhappy. If you have occasion for wine as no doubt you will, pray send for the key and get it; and let Pratt bring you wood. The trouble you must necessarily be in upon the death of Mrs. Palmer, and the distrest situation of the Family, anxiety which I know you feel for Mrs. Norton, and now the Sickness of Thomas I fear will prove too much for your Health. I wrote to you by the last post and to Thomas, but tis a long time since I had a Letter from

[8] The death of his sister, Mrs. Palmer. See the letter of July 12, 1789.
[1] William Cranch (1769-1855).
[2] Thomas Boylston Adams (1772-1832).

you. I think the House had better be shut up than permitt any Body that I can think of, to go into it especially as I think it probable we shall spend a large part of the year there. I wish however that the Dr. [Cotton Tufts] might be consulted with regard to the safety of the House; pray write to me and relieve my mind as soon as possible.

I have never heard how Brother[3] got home with his charge.[4] Is Polly married?[5] I did not mention it to him while he was here, but Mr. A[dams] did. I knew it to be so much against his inclination that I thought it best to be silent. Our family is all well. Mrs. Cushing and Mrs. Rogers[6] spent the day with me yesterday. The judg and his Lady appear very happy, and well pleasd with their situation & reception at New York. I am very well pleasd to find that Gardner[7] is returning to his former insignificance. Strange that he should be attended to, or have any weight with sensible Men.

My Love to Cousin Lucy whom with the rest of my Friends I long to see. Believe me dear Sister most
                              Affectionatly yours
                                   A. ADAMS

                              N[ew] York, March 15, 1790
MY DEAR SISTER:
I last Evening received Your Letter of 28th of Febry which relieved my mind from a great weight of anxiety. I do not think that I have been so long a period, without Letters from some, or other of my Friends since I first came to New York, or else the anxiety I have been under for several weeks appeard to prolong the Time.

I have written to you 3 weeks successively but you do not mention having received my Letters. Last week I wrote to the Dr.[1] and not to you; in some of my Letters I proposed the Miss Palmers tarrying in the House as long as they could. I never expected any thing more from them, than a care of the House & furniture. I requested the Dr. to order them some wood which I presume he has done. I will mention to Gen'll

[3] William Smith (b. 1746). See footnote 4 to the letter of November 24, 1788.
[4] Betsy Crosby. See the letter of January 24, 1789.
[5] Probably Mary (Polly) Palmer, daughter of Mrs. Palmer, the recently deceased occupant of the old Adams house, and a niece of Mr. Cranch.
[6] See footnote 2 to the letter of October 4, 1789. Mary, widow of William Grant and second wife of John Rodgers, died in 1812.
[7] See the preceding letter.
[1] Dr. Cotton Tufts, who acted as steward for John Adams in Quincy. See footnote 11, to the letter of June 28, 1789.

Knox Mr. Cranchs request. Mr. Adams deliverd the Letter and talked with the Gen'll about him at the same time. The Genll mentiond him as a good workman & an honest Man. I will inquire of him when I see him if any thing can be done for Him. A Thought has just struck my mind. If we should not return to Braintree this summer, is Mr. Cranch Farmer enough to take that place to the Halves, provided he can do no better? I have not said any thing about it, for it this moment came into my mind. You may think upon it & give me your opinion without letting it go any further. Nothing would give me more pleasure than to be able to assist two worthy people. I shall wish to hear from Mrs. Norton as soon as she gets to Bed.[2] I think you told me that she expected this month and Sister Shaw too. It is really a foolish Buisness to begin after so many years, a second crop. I expect to hear next that our good friend the Dr. is like to increase his Family. Mine is like to be very prolifick if Mrs. Smith continues as she has set out. She has been gone a week on a visit to Long Island. Louisa grows tall, is the same diffident modest Girll she always was. I am sending her now to dancing. It is rather late for her to begin, but she learns the faster I believe. She has been only six weeks, & carried down a country dance in publick last week very well.

I hope my dear Sister you will make Thomas very carefull of himself & not let him go to Cambridge till he gets well of his Cough. The March winds are cold and piercing, and the Measles never mends the constitution, the Lungs being so much affected. Poor Mr. Otis I am grieved for him.[3] He told me to day on comeing out of meeting that he [never *cancelled*] did not expected [*sic*] to hear that his daughter was alive; for his last intelligence was that she was very near her end. This is a distress that neither you or I have yet experienced, at least not an age, when the loss is so very grevious, and Heavy. Yet can I most feelingly sympathize with those who have. It appears to me that more young ladies die of consumptions in Boston than in any other place. I cannot but think that there is some cause, arising from their manner of living, the two sudden change of air, from cold to Heat, & heat to cold, or a want of proper attention to their cloathing. I think it ought to be a subject of investigation by the Medical Society. My affectionate Regards to all Friends. Do not let it be so long again before I hear from you. I thank you for all your kind care of my son during his sickness. You have some times talkd of obligations, but sure I am you ought to be satisfied upon that Head, as

[2] Elizabeth (Cranch) Norton, wife of the Reverend Jacob Norton. See the letter of April 3, 1790.
[3] Samuel Allyne Otis. See the letter of June 28, 1789.

you so much oftner have the power of confering them, than I have of returning them to you, but you know that the will is good of
                    Your ever affectionate Sister
                              ABIGAIL ADAMS

                        N[ew] York, March 21, 1790
MY DEAR SISTER:
  I was in hopes of hearing from you by last Nights post, as I am solicitious to learn how Mrs. Norton does. I had Letters from Thomas and find that he is returnd to Cambridge very well he says, and he gives me the agreeable News of his Aunt Shaws[1] having got well to Bed with a daughter added to her Family.[2] I have been anxious for her; as her Health is so slender, and I know how to feel for you too the anxiety of a parent.
  Mr. Adams has spoken to Genll Knox upon the subject of your Letter; and has received a promise from him, that he will do something for Mr. Cranch within a forghtnight [sic]; I wish it may put him upon such a footing as to enable him to marry. Betsy will make him an excellent wife.[3] I wish their prospects were better. Present my Regards to her, and tell her that I shall always be happy to promote her interest, and wish it was more in my power.
  Pray what is the dismall story we hear of Mrs. Danfords jumping out of a 3 story window? Has she been long delirious? What was the matter with Mrs. Jones? She lookt as like to live last fall when she was here as any person of her age. How is Lucy Jones? I heard last fall a very allarming account of her Health. Our Good Aunt I hope makes the Dr. very happy. Is Mrs. Tufts like to increase her Family? I mean Young Mrs. Tufts. I hope nothing of the kind will take place with the other. I think it would be like to distroy the Harmony between the two Families.[4] I want to know all about the good folks in whose happiness I feel interested. I am sorry for what you write me respecting the one lately married, but I expected it. Do you remember the story of the Parissian Girl who insisted upon being hanged because her Father and her

[1] Elizabeth (Smith) Shaw (1750–1815), wife of the Reverend John Shaw, and subsequently Mrs. Stephen Peabody.
  [2] Abigail Adams Shaw, who subsequently married Joseph Barlow Felt (1789–1869), the famous antiquarian of Salem and Boston.
  [3] Joseph Cranch, son of the Reverend John Cranch, who died in Devonshire in 1746, married, May 2, 1790, Elizabeth Palmer, youngest daughter of General Joseph Palmer, and Mary Cranch, sister of Richard Cranch (1726–1811), husband of Mary, the sister of Abigail Adams.
  [4] See footnote 11 to the letter of June 28, 1789.

Grand Father were hanged? It is a sad misfortune when example can be plead to satisfy scruples—but there never was any delicacy of sentiment about her. I am sorry for her Grandmother, who I know it must Hurt.[5]

Mrs. Smith & children are gone on a visit to Jamaica [Long Island]. The House seems deserted. I expect their return soon, but not their continuence with me, as they are going to live in the city, and the Col[onel']s Mother and Family are comeing into Town to live soon. My Family has been so large for this year past, that we shall not make both ends meet, as they say. The expenses of Removing a Family, Furniture &c was a heavy burden, and the wages of servants is very high here, especially for such misirables as one is obliged to put up with— but I hate to complain. No one is without their difficulties, whether in High, or low Life, & every person knows best where their own shoe pinches. My Love to Mrs. Norton. Tell her to keep up a good Heart but be sure you do not let Lucy be with her. I know her make so well that she could not stand the trial.

I have had a Nervious Headache for this week past, which has quite unfitted me for any thing, and obliges me to make my Letter shorter than I designd.

Remember me kindly to all inquiring Friends and be assured of the affectionate Regards of

Your Sister
A. ADAMS

Mrs. Brisler Lucy & children are well.

MY DEAR SISTER: N[ew] York, April 3d, 1790

I congratulate you and my dear Neice upon the late happy event in your Family.[1] Can you really believe that you are a Grandmamma? Does not the little fellow feel as if he was really your own? If he does not now, by that time you have lived a year with him, or near you, I question if you will be able to feel a difference. Have you been so much occupied by these New cares as not to be able to write me a line upon the subject? It was from a Letter of Cousin William's[2] to Charles that I learnt the

---

[5] This letter from Mrs. Mary (Smith) Cranch is probably in the Adams Papers in the Massachusetts Historical Society. The story of the Parisian girl has not been found.
[1] The birth of a son to Elizabeth (Cranch) Norton, wife of the Reverend Jacob Norton, in March, 1790.
[2] William Smith, son of the brother of Abigail Adams. See footnote 2 to the letter of September 1, 1789.

agreeable news, at which I most sincerely rejoice. I doubt not as my amiable Neice has fullfild all the Relative duties in which she has been calld to act with honour to herself and satisfaction to her Friends, she will not fail to discharge the New one which has fallen to her share with equal ability. I wish my dear Sister I could go with you to visit her, as we used to do, and that I could personally tell her how much her safety and happiness is dear to me. I should receive more real satisfaction, in one hour, than in months of the uninteresting visits which my situation obliges me both to receive and pay. My old Friend Mrs. Rogers[3] has past the winter in N[ew] York and we have lived in our former intimacy. I shall regret her leaving it. Mrs. Smith and her Family the chief of them have been for three weeks at Jamica [sic] upon a visit. The House really felt so lonely after Master William went, that I sent for him back yesterday. John and he are both very fine children, but as yet my attachment to William is much the strongest. His temper is sweet and his disposition docile.

This place begins to reassume all its Beauty. I wish you could come and see it. For situation and prospect I know no equal. We have been gardning for more than a week. I always forgot to inquire of my Neices if the flower seeds succeeded last year. I fear my prospect of visiting Braintree will be cut of, by the short recess of Congress. The buisness before them is so important, and takes so much time to discus it, that they talk now of only adjourning through the Hot Months, and the breaking up a Family for a few months, the expense attending the journey with those domesticks which we must bring on, will out run the sum allotted by our generous Country, so that I see no prospect of visiting my Friends. I must therefore content my self with hearing from them as often as I can.

I wrote you a fortnight since that Genll Knox had given his word to Mr. A[dams] that he would do something for Mr. J[oseph] Cranch.[4] I presume he will not forget him. I shall dine there on Tuesday next, and as the Genll is always very civil polite and social with me, I will drop a word to him if opportunity offers. Mr. Jefferson is here, and adds much to the social circle.[5]

I wish to have some seed Beans of scarlet and of the white kind, the

---

[3] See the letter of November 24, 1788, and footnote 6 to the letter of February 28, 1790.
[4] For Joseph Cranch, see footnote 3 to the letter of March 21, 1790.
[5] Thomas Jefferson sailed from France in October, 1789, and arrived at "Monticello" on December 23. He proceeded to New York, where, on March 22, 1790, he became the first Secretary of State under the Constitution: 1790–1794.

pod of which is so tender. I forget the Name, but believe you will know. They grow in joints and are very fruitfull. Adieu. Tis time to go to meeting. O that it was to hear good Dr. Price,[6] or Mr. Clark[7] or Thacher,[8] or any body whose sentiments were more comformable to mine.

Ever yours
A. ADAMS

Richmond Hill, April 21, 1790

MY DEAR SISTER:

I received your two kind Letters of April 1 & 5. I am extreemly sorry to hear that Mrs. Norton is afflicted in the way that you write me she is, but tell her to keep up a good Heart. I can sympathize in her sufferings. A Bath of Hot Herbs was the most salutary means made use for me. A poultice of Camomile flowers is also very good, but I hope she is relieved before this time. Painfull experience would teach me upon the very first chill, to apply a white Bread poultice because those cold fits are always succeeded by a fever and complaints of the Breast always follow. I am glad to hear that my great Nephew [is] such a fine child.

When I wrote you last, you may remember that I told you I would speak to Genll. Knox in behalf of Mr. Cranch. I thought I had best do it before I said any thing to Mr. A[dams] about the place as the arrangments which the Genll. might make would prove more advantageous to him and require his attention upon the spot. I talkd with him and he engaged to send me a letter for him which is now inclosed to you. He told me that at West Point he would find a dwelling House work shop &c and two years employ if he would go there immediatly, that, he believed there was yet Buisness to be compleated at Springfield. There are many applicants so that Mr. Cranch should not be dilatory as there may be now a good opening for him. He will not fail of writing directly to Genll. Knox and giving him the information he requests. The Miss Palmers may continue in the House untill Mr. Cranch can accommodate them better. I wish my dear Sister that I could come to Braintree, but I do not see how it can be effected to any good purpose. Pray can you tell me where I could get a Boy of a dozen years. I would have him come round

---

[6] See footnote 4 to the letter of August 9, 1789.

[7] John Clarke (1755–1798), nephew of Timothy Pickering, and pastor of the First Church in Boston. For Clarke's sudden death, see the letter of June 27, 1798.

[8] Probably Peter Thacher (1752–1802), who was born in Milton, preached in Boston, and died in Savannah, Georgia.

in [Captain] Barnard if any one is to be had. Such a wretched crew as N[ew] York produces are scarcly to be found in any city in Europe. I am so much discouraged by every Body here that I dare not attempt to take one. I wish you would inquire of Ruthe Ludden whether she would be willing to come in Barnard & let me know.[1] Mr. Smiths Petter had a likely Boy that he askd me to take before I came here.[2] If he is not put out, and he will send him to me by captain Barnard I will take him. Let me hear from you soon. Mrs. Smith is going to House keeping in N[ew] York the 1 of May, the day when every Body removes as they tell me here. I shall feel lost. The children amuse & divert me much but they will be here half there time. William is down on his knees searching the pictures in Milton, whilst I write. Gammar, he says look here, the Man with a great sword going to cut them are Men all to peices. He is a lovely child with a temper as mild & sweet as one would wish. Adieu my dear Sister. I must quit to dress, as Mrs. Washington, Lady Temple, Mrs. Dalton, Mrs. King & several other Ladies drink Tea with me this afternoon.[3]

       Yours most affectionatly
         A. ADAMS

Wednesday Noon—Mr. Brisler desires me to ask if Mr. Cranch has got the Remainder of his money from Mr. Baxter[4] and prays he would see Mr. Baxter & let him know that he wants it.

       Richmond Hill, April 28, 1790
MY DEAR SISTER:

I designd to have written to you by the Monday post, but I was so very ill on Sunday that I could not set up. I have had the severest attack of the Rhumatism attended with a voilent fever which I have experienced for several years. I have not yet left my chamber, tho I am much relieved. The weather has been uncommonly wet and cold. Snow we have had in the course of this fortnight more than through the whole winter. Our House has been a mere Hospital ever since Saturday last. I have been confined in one chamber, Col. Smith in an other with a Billious attack, Charl[e]s in an other with a fever, my Housekeeper

[1] See the following letter.
[2] Mrs. Adams refers to the son of Peter, a servant of her brother, William Smith, merchant of Boston.
[3] For Lady Temple and Mrs. Dalton, see the letter of February 20, 1790. Mrs. King was the wife of Rufus King, Senator from New York (1789-1795).
[4] Father of Polly Baxter, a maid of Mrs. Adams.

confind to her chamber with Saint Antonys fire,[1] and a servant of Col. Smiths laid up with a voilent seazure of the Breast & Lungs, but thanks to a kind Providence we are all upon the Recovery. I was in hopes to have heard from you by last weeks post, & to have learnt how Mrs. Norton was, for whom I am much concernd. I am anxious for her from more disinterested motives than Swifts Friend, tho perhaps I can more feelingly sympathize with her for having "felt a pain just in the place where she complains."[2]

My last letter to you was accompanied by one for Mr. J[oseph] Cranch which I hope came safe to Hand. I wrote you something respecting Ruthe Ludden, but I wish now to be very particular, if her time is out with her Aunt as I think it was in March, and she is inclined to come. [Captain] Barnard will return here sometime in May. Her Passage by him will be six dollars which I shall pay. There is a Mrs. Laffen with whom Mr. Brisler is acquainted who went from here to Boston in Barnard and means to return again with him, so that she would not have to come alone. My terms to her will be three dollars a Month, and to give her the small pox. I wish to have an immediate answer because if she does not like to come, Mr. Brisler has a sister Betsy in Boston, who would be very glad to come and I shall write to her to come immediatly. I do not wish to send Polly home till I get somebody in her Room, but send her Home I must, or I shall never have a quiet family. This I must say of her, that I have never found her otherways than stricktly honest and I have not had the least difficulty with her on account of drink. In short it is next to imposible here to get a servant from the highest to the lowest grade that does not drink, male or Female. I have at last found a footman who appears sober, but he was Born in Boston, has lived a very short time in the city & has very few acquaintance there. You would be surprizd if I was to tell you that tho I have been long trying to get a Boy here I cannot find one that any Body will Recommend, and I should be very glad to get one from Boston, I mean Peters son. My Housekeeper who on many accounts has been the most Respectable Female I have had in the Family, is so sick and infirm that

---

[1] Any of certain inflammations or gangrenous conditions of the skin, especially erysipelas and ergotism, which in the Middle Ages were popularly supposed to be cured by the intercession of St. Anthony.

[2] See *The Poems of Jonathan Swift*, Harold Williams, Editor, Oxford, 1937, vol. 2, p. 557: "Verses on the Death of Dr. Swift" (1731), lines 135–6:

> Yet shou'd some Neighbour feel a Pain,
> Just in the Parts, where I complain;

she is obliged to leave me, partly I know because she will not live with Polly. If I could find any middle aged woman of a Reputable Character who understands Pastry &c in Boston I would send for her. I give 5 dollars a month to my Housekeeper. My kitchen and offices are all below stairs, and where there are a Number of servants there must be one respectable Head amongst them to oversee & take care that they do not run headlong as well as to overlook the cooking & to make Tea for me upon my publick Evenings, to make my pastry to assist in the Ironing &c. This is the Buisness which falls to her share. Ruthe I want for a house maid. She will have no concern with cooking at all, as I keep a woman solely for that purpose. I wish you would be upon the inquiry for me. If I had not Brisler with me I should be tempted to give up publick Life. The chief of the servants here who are good for any thing are Negroes who are slaves. The white ones are all Foreigners & chiefly vagabonds. I really know now more than ever how to Prize my English servants but I think when the cat is once gone I shall do much better. Do you remember the Fable of the Cat the Sow & the Eagle?[3] Scarcly a day passes that I do not think of it. Yet I have a real value for Polly. She has a great many good qualities, and alone in a small Family would answer very well, but Authority she can not bear to have the least. It is only by keeping her Humble that she is any way to be bourn with. In many things as Mr. Nothorp observed, she seems as necessary to me as my daily food, and but for that temper, I would not part with her. With that I could deal, but the eternal mischief between others, keeps the whole House in disorder, and gives a bad Name to the whole Family. Thus having detaild my whole Family grievences to you I bid you adieu. With Love to all Friends from your

Ever affectionate Sister
A. ADAMS

N[ew] York, May 30, 1790.

MY DEAR SISTER:

Your kind Letter of various dates came safe to Hand. I was allarmed at not hearing from you, & feard that you were all sick. The disorder

---

[3] See *Aesop's Fables*, "The Eagle, the Cat and the Sow." An eagle built her nest in the top of an old oak tree; a sow scooped out a home in its roots; and a wildcat lived in a hole half way between them. The wildcat persuaded the eagle to fear the sow, and the sow to fear the eagle, with the result that each starved to death, and the wildcat devoured the nest of eaglets and the litter of pigs—a warning against tale-bearing trouble-makers. La Fontaine, *Fables*, Book 3, Fable 6.

termd the Influenza[1] has prevaild with much voilence, & in many places been very mortal, particularly upon Long Island. Not a Creature has escaped in our Family except its Head, and I compounded to have a double share myself rather than he should have it at all. Heitherto he has escaped, not so the President. He has been in a most dangerous state, and for two or three days [I] assure you I was most unhappy. I dreaded his death from a cause that few persons, and only those who know me best, would believe. It appears to me that the union of the states, and concequently the permanancy of the Government depend under Providence upon his Life. At this early day when neither our Finances are arranged nor our Government sufficiently cemented to promise duration, His death would I fear have had most disasterous concequences. I feard a thousand things which I pray I never may be calld to experience. Most assuredly I do not wish for the highest Post. I never before realizd what I might be calld to, and the apprehension of it only for a few days greatly distresst me, but thanks to Providence he is again restored. Congress will set till July it is thought, and I fear adjourn to Philadelphia. I say I fear, for it would be a sad buisness to have to Remove. Besides I am sure there is not a spot in the United States so Beautifull as this upon which I live, for a summer residence. But personal inconveniency out of the question I do not see any publick utility to be derived from it, and I wish the Idea might subside untill time should make it proper to fix a permanant seat. I fear I must relinquish the Idea of visiting my Friends. I want to see you all and my Young Nephew whom you describe with all the fondness of a Grandmamma. Mrs. Norton will find her Health improved by Nursing I dare say. My Love to her and to Cousin Lucy. How I long to have you come and see me.

I am affraid my dear Sister I shall have to trouble you with the care of a commencement for Thomas,[2] like that which you so kindly made for his Brother, but I shall know more about his inclinations when I hear from him. I am unhappy at the account you give of Mrs. Turner. Poor Girl. She is going after her Mother at an early period of Life. You did not say if the child was living, but I presume it is.

I do not know what to do with our House if the Ladies remove.[3] I

[1] According to the *Oxford English Dictionary*, the word "influenza" first appeared in print in English in 1743, in the *London Magazine:* "News from Rome of a contagious Distemper raging there, call'd the *Influenza*."

[2] Thomas Boylston Adams was graduated from Harvard in June, 1790.

[3] The daughters of the late Mrs. Palmer, who were living in the old Adams house. See footnote 7 to the letter of July 12, 1789.

sometimes wish it was all in cash again. Do you know of any Body trusty enough to leave it with?

You will be so good as to have all Thomas things brought home and a glass which still remains at Mr. Sewalls. My best regards to Mr. Cranch & all other Friends.

Yours most affectionatly
A. ADAMS

MY DEAR SISTER: [Richmond Hill, June 9th, 1790]

I wrote to you ten days ago and informd you that my Family were very sick. I did not then conceive it to be, what I have since found it the Influenza. I have got better, but my cough & some other complaints still hang about me. Polly Tailor is so bad with it, that if she is not soon relieved the concequences threaten to be fatal to her. Louisa is very sick confind to her chamber. I keep a Bottle of Tarter Emetick and administer it as soon as they complain. Mr. Adams has kept clear of it yet, and he is the only one who has not been attack'd in a greater or less degree. Mrs. Smith has had a slight attack. The children appear to have it comeing and almost every Body throughout the whole city are [sic] labouring under it. This afternoon I heard that my Friend Mrs. Rogers lies dangerously sick. This distresses me greatly because it is not in my power to render her any assistance. I last Evening heard from Thomas, and that your Family were well, but he does not mention Mrs. Norton, by which I would fain hope that she is better. Mrs. Smith Removed last week, and this makes it necessary for me to request a few articles from my House in Braintree. I must request the favour of my good Brother Cranch to get me a case made for my large looking glass, and to be so good as to pack it for me & send it by [Captain] Barnard, with a note of the expence which I will pay to Barnard, my kitchen clock & press which stands in the kitchen, and two Glass Lanthern which are in the chamber closset & the stone Roller for the Garden. I should be glad to have all these things by Barnard. The Glass I do not know how to do without. The Top I have here. I cannot afford to Buy. Besides I have enough for the Braintree House, & should I purchase here, must sell them again at a loss. This House is much better calculated for the Glasses, having all the Rooms Eleven foot high. I have not heard from you since I wrote you respecting Ruthe Ludden. Mrs. Brisler has this disorder tho not Bad. I am impatient to hear from you. Pray let it be soon.

Yours most affectionatly
A. ADAMS

N[ew] York, June 13, 1790

My dear Sister:

I received your Letter of May 16, and was very happy to find that you were all upon the recovery. We have daily mercies to be thankfull for, tho no state is exempt from trouble and vexation. The one which at present Torments me is the apprehension of a Removal from a very delightfull situation, to I know not where, and I am too short sighted, or too much blinded, to see any real advantage from a Removal unless a Permanent seat was fixed. The fatigue and expence are objects not very pleasing in contemplation, and the Removal to a more southern state what I do not like, especially to Baltimore, where I am told we cannot in any respect be half so well accomodated. If I could see that the publick good required it, I should submit with more satisfaction, but to be every session disputing upon this subject, & sowerd as the members are, is a very unpleasent thing.[1] If we must move I must relinquish every Idea of visiting my Friends, and I had a latent hope that I should come for a few weeks merely on a visit, after Mrs. Smith gets to Bed, which I presume will be in July. I wish to hear from my Mother & Brothers Family. I know not what to do with the House. I must request you to have an Eye to it, and if any trusty Body could be thought of to go into the kitchen part I could wish they might, but I own I do not know of any Body. All the interest we have must go to destruction, and we can barely live here upon the publick allowence. Your Romancing Neighbours may amuse themselves, but their storys will never gain credit. There is a gentleman here, several indeed of whom I could inquire, but I am ashamed to ask, and indeed I do not recollect enough of the first part of the story to inquire properly about it, and I have every reason to think it all fabulous. They are all together the strangest Family I ever heard of. I last week accompanied Mrs. Washington to the Jersies to visit the falls of Pasaick. We were absent three days and had a very agreeable Tour.

I wish to have the articles I wrote for, sent by Captain Barnard. We have a fine growing season. Is it so with you? I wish to hear from you with respect to commencment. What will be necessary and how can it be

[1] For the intrigue and log-rolling which led to the choice of the site of Washington as the national capital in 1790, see Channing, *History of the United States*, vol. 4, pp. 74–9. In essence, the deal was a trade between Virginia and New England: Jefferson and Virginia supported Hamilton's plan for the federal assumption of state debts, and Hamilton rounded up enough New England votes in the Congress to put the capital on the Potomac. Until 1790, the seat of the government was New York, and, for the next ten years, Philadelphia. John Adams was the first President to live in the White House, which was ready for occupancy late in 1800. See footnote 4 to the letter of July 27, 1790.

managed? I fear it will give you a great deal of trouble especially as you are not very well accomodated with help, as it will be impossible for us to be at Home. I have thought that it might be dispenced with, yet as Thomas has conducted himself so well I could wish that he might be gratified if it is his desire.

Be so good as to let Mr. Smith know that Prince[2] is very well and quite contented. We are all well & Polly is better, than she was. Adieu. Write to me as soon as you can. Remember me affectionatly to all Friends.

Yours most tenderly
A. ADAMS

N[ew] York, June 27th, 1790

MY DEAR SISTER:

I have been expecting to hear from you every post, but I have not had a line from you since that dated May 10th. I wrote you once, I believe twice since I wish to know what has been determined upon respecting commencment as it is near at hand. I long more than ever to come Home especiall[y] since I am under some apprehensions of going further off. I am anxious to know what to do with our House. It is very hard that Mankind are so little trust worthy, that I cannot think of a single Family which might be placed there, who would not injure the House, furniture, & plunder me besides. Many through ignorance would not take proper care. I am sure that it will go to Ruin if it is not frequently lookd to. I have been thinking that when J. Q. A. has taken the Law Books to Town the remainder of the Books might be put into the small chamber next the garden or into the China closset above stairs. I fear they will receive injury from the weather in the office. I know not a word respecting the place any more than if it lay in the east Indies, and indeed it has proved of little more advantage to us than if it lay in the Moon. I look upon the Money expended there as lost. What has Woodard done with his place. Did he sell it? And to whom?

Mrs. Brisler wants much to hear from her sister. How are all our Friends? Mrs. Norton is getting Health & strength I hope fast. I pray she may not have children as fast as Mrs. Smith. It is enough to wear out an Iron constitution. I think she has lost much of her coulour and does not seem to be well at all; I feel very anxious for her, especially as she is like to have a very hot season to be confined in. She says not till

---

[2] A new servant of Mrs. Adams. See the letters of October 3, 1790, and March 12, 1791.

August, but I think she will not go so long as she looks very large. I have one or other of the children with me constantly. How is Uncle Quincy?[1] You say nothing about him. Dr. Tufts I find is married.[2] I dont hear half as often from him as formerly. Pray present my duty to him and tell him the Hams he procurd for me are fine and that I should be glad of a keg of Tongues.

Company call me of. Adieu.

Yours most affectionatly
A. Adams

N[ew] York, July 4th, 1790

My dear Sister:

A Memorable day in our calender. A Church beloning [*sic*] to the Dutch congregation is this day to be opened and an oration deliverd. This Church was the scene of Misiry & horrour, the Prison where our poor Countrymen were confined, crowded & starved during the war, & which the British afterwards destroyed. It has lately been rebuilt and this day is the first time that they have met in it.[1] They have done us the favour of setting apart a pew for us. The Clergyman is Dr. Lynn[2] one of the Chapling to congress and I think a better preacher than most that I have heard to day. An oration is [to] be deliverd by Dr. Livingstone[3] the other Minister belonging to this Church, but as to an orater, the oratory of a Clergyman here consists in foaming, loud speaking, working themselves up in such an enthusia[s]m as to cry, but which has no other effect upon me than to raise my pitty. O when when shall I hear the Candour & liberal good sense of a Price[4] again, animated with true piety without enthusiasm, devotion without grimace and Religion upon a Rational system.

[1] Norton Quincy (1716–1801). See footnote 3 to the letter of November 1, 1789.
[2] See the letter of June 28, 1789.
[1] The Reformed Dutch Church in Nassau Street, New York City, also called the Middle Collegiate, or the Rip Van Dam Church, which was rededicated and reopened on July 4, 1790, the British having used it as a prison and a riding-school during the Revolution. The church became the Post Office in 1845, and was demolished in 1882. Stokes, *Iconography of Manhattan Island*, vol. 1, plate 28, and description, p. 261; vol. 3, plate 105B, and description, pp. 725–6; and vol. 5, p. 1269.
[2] See footnote 3 to the letter of October 4, 1789.
[3] John Henry Livingston (1746–1825) was graduated from Yale in 1762 and began the study of law at Poughkeepsie. Livingston studied theology in Holland (1766–1770), where he took the degree of Doctor of Theology at the University of Utrecht. In 1783 he became a minister in New York City, where he preached chiefly in English, but occasionally in Dutch. He united all the Dutch churches in the country in 1772.
[4] See footnote 4 to the letter of August 9, 1789.

My worthy Friend Mrs. Rogers is returning to Boston. She has engaged to convey this to you with a Magizine which has for a Frontispeice a view of this House,[5] but the great Beauty could not be taken upon so small a scale, which is the Noble Hudson, as far distant from the House as the bottom of the Boston Mall is from the Governours House. If you see Mrs. Rogers, as it is probable you will at commencment, she will tell you how delightfull this spot is, and how I regret the thoughts of quitting it. I shall miss her more than half N[ew] York besides. We are very well, but impatient to hear from you and Family. I wish Congress would so far compleat their buisness as not to have an other session till the spring. I really think I would then come home and pass the winter with you. Mr. Adams wants some exercise. Ever since the 4th of Janry he has not mist one hour from attendance at Congress. He goes from Home at ten and seldom gets back till four, and 5 hours constant sitting in a day for six months together, (for He cannot leave his Chair) is pretty tight service. Reading long Bill [sic], hearing debates, and not always those the most consonant to his mind and opinions, putting questions, stating them, constant attention to them that in putting questions they may not be misled, is no easy task whatever Grumblers may think, but Grumblers there always was & always will be.

Adieu my dear Sister. Remember me affectionatly to all Friends.

Yours
A. ADAMS

Richmond Hill, July 27, 1790

MY DEAR SISTER:

I received your kind Letter of July 4th. The articles sent by Captain Barnard all arrived in good order, and I have to acknowledg Mr. Cranchs kind care in attending to them.

You have got through commencment and I hope have not been made sick with the trouble and fatigue. We had a pleasent day here, not over Hot and I pleasd myself with the hope that it was so with you. We got Thursdays paper, but had very little account of commencment. I know you must have been too much fatigued, and too buisily occupied to be able to write.

I do not know what to do with the House. I wish with all my Heart that Mears[1] would go in. I did not once think of her, but I do not know

[5] See the *New-York Magazine* (June, 1790), or Stokes, *Iconography of Manhattan Island*, vol. 1, plate 55A, and pp. 416-7; also footnote 1 to the letter of January 24, 1789.

[1] Mr. Mears was married to the sister of Mrs. Briesler, wife of the major-domo of John Adams.

any person I would so soon commit the care to. Mr. Brisler is anxious about the wine Casks. He says that there are only two Iron hoops on each and he fears the other will Rot off. If you have not the keys, pray get them and let me request you to have the things lookd to. The Rats he says may undermine the Bottled wine which is packd in sand. He is very anxious about it, and I am not less so. I beg you my dear Sister to accept of a dozen of the wine and present half a dozen bottles to my Mother.[2] If it is not drawn of let Thomas go, and do it, and send him for the keys. If the casks look like to give way, I must request that it may be New hoopd or otherways taken care of. I do not know when I shall see you. I think it would be a cordial to me, and Mr. Adams pines for relaxation, tho if one was to Credit the Clamours of the Boston papers we should imagine that there was nothing going forward but dissipation, instead of which, there is nothing which wears the least appearance of it, unless they term the Pressidents Levee of a tuesday and Mrs. Washingtons drawing of a fryday such. One last[s] two & the other perhaps three hours. She gives Tea, Coffe, Cake, Lemonade & Ice Creams[3] in summer. All other Ladies who have publick Evenings give Tea, Coffe & Lemonade, but one only who introduces cards, and she is frequently put to difficulty to make up one table at whist. Pray is not this better than resorting to Taverns, or even having supper partys? Some amusement from the Buisness of the day is necessary and can there be a more Innocent one than that of meeting at Gentlemens Houses and conversing together? But faction and Antifederilism may turn every Innocent action to evil.[4]

We are all well. You see my pens are bad beyond description, and dinner calls. Love to all Friends from

Your ever affectionate Sister
A. ADAMS

[2] Mother-in-law: Susanna (Boylston) [Adams] Hall. See footnote 4 to the letter of December 15–18, 1788.

[3] See footnote 1 to the letter of August 9, 1789.

[4] The session of the Congress during the summer of 1790 was made acrimonious by wrangling over two bills, the first of which fixed the national capital after 1800 on the Potomac; and the second of which provided for a limited assumption of state debts. The settlement was, in effect, a bargain between Jefferson and Hamilton. By the act of July 16, 1790, Philadelphia was to be the capital until 1800, by which time the Federal City was to be founded in a National District on the Potomac. By the act of August 4, 1790, $21,500,000 of state debts were to be taken over by the federal government. Massachusetts and South Carolina, each with four millions, and Virginia with three and one-half million, got more than half of the total sum. Schouler, *History of the United States*, vol. 1, pp. 154–6.

New York, 8 August, 1790

My dear Sister:

I have the pleasure to inform you that last Night Mrs. Smith got to Bed with an other fine Boy.[1] We could have all wisht it had been a Girl, but rest satisfied with the sex as it [is] a very fine large handsome Boy and both Mother and child are well. She spent the day with me on fryday, and I urged her as I had several times before, to accept a Room here, and lie in here, as the house in which she is is Small and Hot. She told me she would come out, and the next day intended to get her things ready for the purpose, but found herself so unwell on Saturday, yesterday that she could not effect it. I have been very unwell myself for a fortnight, so that she did not let me know she was ill, untill I had the agreeable intelligence of her being safe abed. I shall get her here as soon as possible. I have both the children with me. I have not heard a word from you since commencment, and I expect all my intelligence from you. Congress rise on twesday. I wish and long to come to Braintree, but fear I shall not effect it. How does Mrs. Norton stand the Hot weather? Your Grandson grows a fine Boy I dare say. I should be quite charmd to see him & my dear Cousin Lucy. When is she to be married to that said Gentleman? Pray give my Love to her and tell her she need not have been so sly about it. I had a few lines from Thomas [Boylston Adams] just before he set out for Haverhill. I expect him on here daily, and think he had best send his things Round by Barnard. I have nothing new to entertain you with unless it is my Neighbours the Creek savages who visit us daily. They are lodgd at an Inn at a little distance from us. They are very fond of visiting us as we entertain them kindly, and they behave with much civility. Yesterday they signd the Treaty, and last Night they had a great Bondfire dancing round it like so many spirits hooping, singing, yelling, and expressing their pleasure and satisfaction in the true savage stile. These are the first savages I ever saw. Mico Maco, one of their kings dinned here yesterday and after dinner he conferred a Name upon me, the meaning of which I do not know: Mammea. He took me by the Hand, bowd his Head and bent his knee, calling me Mammea, Mammea. They are very fine looking Men, placid countenances & fine shape. Mr. Trumble[2] says, they are many of them per-

[1] Thomas Hollis Smith (b. 1790), died in infancy. See footnote 1 to the letter of November 24, 1788.

[2] John Trumbull (1756-1843), famous American painter, whose best-known work is the "Signing of the Declaration of Independence," which occupied eight years. After six years in London and Paris, Trumbull turned up in New York City in December, 1789, in order to obtain portraits for his popular historical composition. Washington sat for him several times.

fect models. MacGillvery dresses in our own fashion speaks English like a Native, & I should never suspect him to be of that Nation, as he is not very dark.[3] He is grave and solid, intelligent and much of a Gentleman, but in very bad Health. They return in a few days.

Adieu my dear Sister. Remember me affectionatly to all Friends. I see Miss Nancy Quincy[4] is married. I wish her much happiness.

Yours
A. ADAMS

Sunday eve, N[ew] York, August 29, 1790

MY DEAR SISTER:

I last Night received your Letter which I have long expected, dated 9th of August, and thank you for your account of commencment, as well as your care. I have written to you a number of times and wonderd much at not hearing from you. By Dr. Jeffries[1] I wrote you an account of Mrs. Smiths getting well to Bed. She is very cleverly and has been once out to see me tho only three weeks last Night since she got to Bed, but the weather being so warm she has got the Air very soon or rather never shut it out. She was going to dine below stairs to day, and said if she was not asshamed she would go with me to take leave of Mrs. Washington, who sets out tomorrow for Mount Vernon. I am [going] into Town for that purpose, and shall part with her, tho I hope, only for a short time, with much Regret. No Lady can be more deservedly beloved & esteemed than she is, and we have lived in habits of intimacy and Friendship. In short the Removal of the principal connections I have

---

[3] Alexander McGillivray (c. 1759-1793), a Creek Chief belonging to the Wind Clan of the Upper Creek Indians, a Loyalist during the Revolution. From 1784 to his death in 1793, McGillivray, courted by merchants, speculators, filibusters, and by the governments of Georgia, the United States, and Spain, enjoyed a career of international significance. His chief interests were diplomacy, trade, planting, and drink. At one time he owned three plantations and about sixty slaves. For a lively account of the state visit of McGillivray to New York in July, 1790, see Schouler, *History of the United States*, vol. 1, pp. 171-2.

[4] Nancy Quincy (born 1763), daughter of Josiah and Ann Quincy, married on July 27, 1790, the Reverend Asa Packard, of Marlborough, Harvard, 1783, who died in 1843.

[1] John Jeffries (1745-1819), physician and scientist of Boston, Loyalist in the Revolution. Repairing to England, Jeffries made several famous balloon ascensions with the French aeronaut, François Blanchard (1753-1809)—one over London in 1784, and another crossing the English Channel on January 7, 1785, as the result of which Jeffries was complimented by Louis XVI and dined with Benjamin Franklin at Passy. Jeffries returned to Boston about 1790, where he established a large and profitable practice. For a description of this balloon flight, see Roof, *Colonel William Smith and Lady*, p. 72.

here serves to render the place, delightfull as it is, much less pleasent than it has been.

I have been almost upon the point of visiting Braintree. I even made several arrangments for that purpose in my own mind, but had it all overthrown by an arrangment for a Removal to Philadelphia this fall. Mr. Adams talks now of going there to look out a House, as he begins to think he shall be very miserable at Lodgings, but I will hope that I may come next summer, and be a Border with you for some Months if we should let our House. If the people you mention are responsible and worthy people I should have no objection to letting it to them with the furniture, the best carpet & china & glass tho not much, excepted—I know more injury may be done to furniture in one year than a House can easily sustain in several. A Hundred dollers goes but a little way in good furniture. Perhaps they may run away with a fancy that as the house is unoccupied we would readily let it for [a] trifle. The House I should rather let at a low Rent than it should stand empty, but not the furniture. 200 dollers a year or not much less I should expect to have for it including the Garden, Stables, &c. There are three Beds, two very good, and three carpets besides the best. At Philadelphia we must give four hundred for an empty house and that out of the City, but I shall [have] opportunity to write you more fully if they should have any fancy for taking it and I would consult the Dr.[2] about it.

We are anxious to get Thomas here and wonder that he does not come on. Pray hasten him as Mr. Adams is very desirious [sic] to have him here. My dear Sister I [will] never take the ten guineys so pray say no more about them. I am under obligations to you for the care and attention to my children which nothing pecuniary can repay. It hurts me that I have it not in my power to do as I wish—I hope our young folks will get into Buisness. I am glad Mr. Cranch will be like to get something for his hard Labour. I hope the remaining part of the debt will be provided for in less than ten years. Our publick affairs look very auspicious notwithstanding the grumbling. I have many more things to say to you but am obliged to close to go into Town, but will write to you soon again. We are all well. You may write by the post. They have not chargd us postage yet and I presume will not as the New act if it had past excepts the President and vice Pressident, and as it is known to be the intention

[2] Cotton Tufts. See footnote 11 to the letter of June 28, 1789.

of congress, I suppose they will not tax us with postage under the present act.[3]   Love to all Friends

Ever yours
A. ADAMS

MY DEAR SISTER: New York, October 3d, 1790.

Do you not pitty me my dear Sister to be so soon all in a Bustle, and weary of removing again, as much Boxing and casing as if we were removing to Europe? Our furniture may well be stiled *movables*. The expence attending the various removals would very handsomely furnish one House.[1] I feel low spirited and Heartless. I am going amongst an other new set of company, to form new acquaintances, to make and receive a hundred ceremonious visits, not one of ten from which I shall derive any pleasure or satisfaction, obliged to leave Mrs. Smith behind, and the Children to whom I am much attached, and many other things I have upon my mind and spirits which I cannot communicate by Letter. I live however upon the Hope that I shall come and see you next summer: I hope congress will not set [sit] out the Month of April.

I have wrote to the Dr. respecting the widow Owen and Rebecca Field I had rather they should be in the House than have it left empty through the winter. They must always remember that they must remove when ever we come to want the House, and that without giving us any trouble.

You wrote me about Rose water. If you have an opportunity to send me a dozen Bottles I should like to have it. I forgot to write to you sooner, but you may have it put up and addrest to Col. Smith New York when Barnard comes again. We expect to get our furniture on Board by the 20th of the Month. Charles is going to Board with his sister, and Thomas will go into an office in Philadelphia. I wish he could have gone into merchandize as I am sure he has more of a Turn for active Life.

[3] While Adams was presiding over the Senate in New York during the summer of 1790, his *Discourses on Davila*, a series of letters written as a running commentary upon an Italian's history of France, appeared in Fenno's *Gazette* at Philadelphia, and were copied by other Federalist papers. Adams seemed to be trying "to direct American sentiment against the new idea of complete equality and rights of man. . . . Adams himself, in later life, admitted that *Davila* largely helped to destroy his popularity, and wondered that he could ever have written that 'dull heavy volume.' " Schouler, *History of the United States*, vol. 1, pp. 192-3. For *Discourses on Davila*, see Adams, *Works*, vol. 6, pp. 223-339.

Enrico Caterino Davila (1576-1631) was born near Padua and murdered near Verona. Going to France to serve as a page of Catherine de Medici, Davila fought in the French civil wars until 1589. His chief work is *Storia della guerre civili di Francia* (1630).

[1] Congress convened in Philadelphia in December, 1790, and sat there for ten years, meeting in Washington for the first time on November 17, 1800.

How is Mrs. Norton & her Boy? We have got one with a Red Head. I do not know what part of the family he lays claim to. I forget whether I wrote you that they had Named him Thomas Hollis.[2]

Let Mrs. Field know that Lucy and Mr. Brislers children have the small pox. It has turnd and they have it very lightly. Lucy not more than 20 pock, Nabby not a dozen. Betsy is pretty full but has a good sort and is very cleverly. I had Prince inoculated at the same time. He has about a dozen, but has not been confined at all, nor sick, a little headache excepted. Be so good as to send his Father word if you have an opportunity.

Mrs. Smith is here to day and desires to be rememberd to all her Friends. When did you hear from Sister Shaw? I think I used to get Letters and write oftner when I was abroad than I do now.

Let me hear from you soon, and believe me

Most affectionately yours
A. Adams

Love to Mr. Cranch & Duty to Mother [mother-in-law]. I hope I shall see her again, good old Lady.

N[ew] York, October 10th, 1790

My dear Sister:

I wrote to you last Sunday, and on Wednesday received your kind Letter. We have begun to pack up our furniture, and expect to get it on Board by the 20th. Perhaps we may make it later, but I hope not as the weather will every day become more & more uncomfortable. The Idea of going so much further from you is painfull to me, and would be more so if I did not hope to spend the next summer with you. At present you have your Family with and near you, but it is my destiny to have mine scatered, and scarcly to keep one with us. My seperation from Mrs. Smith is painfull to me on many accounts. There is at present no prospect of their going with us, and if their prospects here were as fair as they ought to be, I should be less solicitious for them. With Regard to our House, I should have no objection to a carefull person living in the kitchin to take care of it, but as to letting it I cannot consent unless any person offers to take House and furniture all together. There is the other part of the House in which Bass lives that might be let, but then I should

---

[2] See the letter of August 8, 1790.

be loth that a shoe makers shop should be made of either of the Rooms. In short I do not know of any persons property so unproductive as ours is. I do not believe that it yealds us one pr cent pr Annum. I have the vanity however to think that if Dr. Tufts and my Ladyship had been left to the sole management of our affairs, they would have been upon a more profitable footing. In the first place I never desired so much Land unless we could have lived upon it. The money paid for useless land I would have purchase[d] publick securities with. The interest of which, poorly as it is funded, would have been less troublesome to take charge of then Land and much more productive. But in these Ideas I have always been so unfortunate as to differ from my partner, who thinks he never saved any thing but what he vested in Land. I am really however very uneasy with Pratt as a Farmer. He has got a great swarm of helpless children round him, labours hard but has no skill, and the place with the addition of Veseys[1] very little more than pays the taxes. I wish Mr. Beals could be induced to go upon it. The other place I know no more about than if it lay in the Moon. I have written to request that the Saint Germain pears and the best Russet Apples may be sent to me. The communication between Boston and Philadelphia is so frequent that I should suppose their could be no difficulty in it.

I had the pleasure of assembling yesterday Mr. & Mrs. Storer,[2] Mr. & Mrs. Atkinson, Mr. Charles, George & Mary Storer, Col. & Mrs. Smith and Miss Pegy Smith, who all dined with me and I felt more like Home than I have ever done since I left Braintree. Mr. Adams mourns that he could not make a visit Northward this fall. We are well. Brislers family all got through the small pox with only a day or two illness. Present me affectionatly to all Friends. I fear Mr. Cranch does not put on his flannel soon enough. I grow more and more in favour of the use of it and advise you to wear it next your skin. Make little waistcoats & put them on with the first comeing of cold weather, & I had as much spair Room in my stays as you have I would not be without them.

Poor Mr. Thaxter I am grieved for him, but who is without their troubles. I thank God that a larger portion has not fallen to the Lot of your ever

Affectionate Sister
A. ADAMS

[1] Mrs. Vesey was an aunt of John Adams. See *Letters of John Adams, Addressed to His Wife*, Edited by C. F. Adams, Boston, 1841, vol. 4, p. 249.

[2] See the letter of June 19, 1789.

N[ew] York, Sunday, October 17 [1790][1]

MY DEAR SISTER:

I arrived here last Night. My first inquiry was for a Letter from you, which I was happy enough to find, and great relief did it afford to my anxious mind. I sent to the post office to see if I could get any further intelligence last evening but was dissapointed. I am ready however to attribute it more to your not getting an opportunity of conveyance than to any unfavourable circumstance, and I was much incouraged yesterday by seeing Mrs. Judge Cushing, who told me of a cure performed upon Mrs. Hyslops leg after a mortification had really taken place. She made great use of Bark[2] and wine. I am sure my dear Sister neither Mr. Adams or I can ever think our wine used to a better purpose than in aiding the recovery of so dear & valuable a Friend, and we request you to get more from our cellar when that is expended. Can there be a greater pleasure in Life than rendering kindness to those we love and esteem and who we know are every way worthy of our regard. How many of my anxious & painfull hours did you in the summer past alleviate by your sisterly kindness. How much too am I indebted to my dear Lucy for her goodness. I am anxious for her Health, and full of the mind that a free use of the Bark would relieve her Nervious Headaches. Katy who is with me was relieved only in that way after a slow Nervious fever. I had a pleasant journey in point of weather. Mr. Adams found himself very weak and feeble when we came to travell. His Nerves were more affected than I was aware of before I left home. He has not had any return of his fever, but if I had not gone through all & more than he has sufferd I should be much more distrest. He gains strength by his journey, but what I fear is the buisness & company which he cannot avoid and which are very

---

[1] It is difficult to place this letter with certainty. Mrs. Adams plainly wrote, "N York, Sunday, October 17." The date "1790" was added in another hand, probably that of Mrs. Cranch, and the letter is endorsed: "Letter from Mrs. A. Adams (N[ew] York) Octr 17. 1790." Between the years 1787 and 1802, only in the year 1790 did October 17 fall on Sunday. Yet, in the following letter, of October 25, 1790, Mrs. Adams implies that she had not written to her sister since October 10, 1790, and the serious illness to which she refers makes it improbable that she did so. Beginning with the end of August, John Adams was absent from New York for about two weeks, looking for a residence in Philadelphia—the house at Bush Hill, to which he removed in November, 1790. He wrote to George Washington from New York on August 29, 1790, and to Samuel Adams from New York on September 12, 1790. Although her illness makes it seem unlikely, apparently Mrs. John Adams left "Richmond Hill" for New York City on October 16—if this letter is dated accurately.

[2] Jesuits' or Peruvian bark: the bark of various species of the cinchona tree, from which quinine is procured.

unfit for a person recovering from such a disorder. Thomas & Louisa are well. Mrs. Smith & Family I found well, but I cannot learn a word from Philadelphia.[3] Remember us all kindly to Mr. Cranch with our most sincere wishes for his perfect restoration to Health. I am my dear Sister,

Affectionatly yours
A. ADAMS

N[ew] York, October 25, 1790

MY DEAR SISTER:

After I had closed my Letter to you this day fortnight, I retired to my chamber, and was taken with a shaking fit which held me 2 Hours and was succeeded by a fever which lasted till near morning, attended with severe pain in my Head, Back, &c. The next morning I took an Emetick which operated very kindly and proved to me the necessity of it. On Tuesday I felt better and went below stairs, but was again seazd with an other shaking fit which was succeeded as the former by the most voilent fever I ever felt. It quite made me delirious. No rest for 5 Nights & days. It setled into a Regular intermitting Fever. The Dr. after having repeatedly puked me, gave me James's powders,[1] but with very little effect. I began upon the Bark the 10th day which I have taken in large Quantyties and it has appeard to have put an end to my fever, but I am very low and weak. I rode out yesterday and found no inconveniency from it. I shall repeat my ride to day. I have great cause to be thankfull for so speady a restoration, but I have a journey before me which appears like a mountain & three Ferries to cross. Very fortunate for me the winds have kept back the vessel from returning from Philadelphia which was to have been here the 20th to have taken our furniture. Mrs. Smith has been with me till yesterday. Her Baby is inoculated for the small pox, and she expects him to break out this week. But here endeth not all my troubles, for the day before yesterday Mrs. Brisler was taken sick of a Plurisy fever. She has been 3 times Bled & is Blisterd, and lies very

---

[3] This refers apparently to the news which Mrs. Adams was awaiting as to whether or not the house at Bush Hill was to be rented to her husband. John Adams was back in New York again by October 18, when he wrote to Samuel Adams.

[1] A febrifuge, very popular during the latter part of the eighteenth century and the beginning of the nineteenth; prepared by Dr. Robert James (1705-1776), who was graduated from Oxford in 1726, and in medicine from Cambridge in 1728. Dr. James compiled a *Medical Dictionary* (1743), to which his friend Samuel Johnson contributed. He patented his powder and pill in 1746. Oliver Goldsmith and George III were both addicted to the use of Dr. James's medicine, and each brought on serious illnesses from self-administered overdoses of it, Goldsmith dying as a consequence.

ill tho I hope not dangerous. I received your Letter by Mr. Cranch. He landed I believe only a few Hours. He went to Mr. Laurences[2] office, to Charles, and deliverd the two casks sent by Brother. The Ladies did not come on shore as the wind was then fair for them, and they had been out ten days, & much of the weather very stormy & Boisterous. He told Charl[e]s that they had been very sick. I am sure it would have given me great pleasure to have received & entertaind them or to have supplied them with any thing in my power.

I received a few days since by Mr. Durant[3] your kind Letter of October 11th, which I thank you for. Remember me affectionatly to Mrs. Eunice Paine.[4] Would a few Bottles of wine or Porter be acceptable to her? If they would will you take the trouble of getting it from our cellar for her. The Dr. has just left me and says he thinks Mrs. Brisler much relieved, and that she will be better in a few days. My Head I find as week as my body. You will therefore excuse my writing more at present than to assure you that I am as ever

Your affectionate Sister
A. ADAMS

Mr. Brisler would be glad the money may be sent by Mr. [Fisher] Ames when he comes to Philadelphia.

N[ew] York, Novbr. 7, 1790

MY DEAR SISTER:

I will not leave N[ew] York without writing you a few lines. I have not written a single letter since that which I addrest to you untill this day I attempted one to my son J. Q. A. I left my own House & I may say chamber, on twesday last, for I had not been able to stay below stairs, till I came to Town. I have been with Mrs. Smith ever since, and tho my fever still hangs about me I hope to set out tomorrow & make small stages. The Dr. think[s] the journy may be of service to me. The

[2] John Laurance (1750–1810), soldier of the Revolution, judge, United States Senator, who was born near Falmouth, England, and settled in New York City in 1767. He prepared and conducted the case against Major John André, in 1780. He was a leading Federalist in the first and second Congresses in 1789 to 1793, and served in the Senate from 1797 to 1800.

[3] Possibly John Waldo Durant of Philadelphia, father of Thomas Jefferson Durant (1817–1882), lawyer and politician.

[4] Probably Miss Eunice Paine (1733–1803) of Braintree, a sister of Robert Treat Paine. "Mrs." would be in this case a title of respect for an elderly lady; or possibly Eunice (Treat) Paine, wife of the Reverend Thomas Paine and the mother of Robert Treat Paine (1731–1814) and Miss Eunice Paine.

fatigue of removing has been doubly troublesome to me. I will write as soon as I can to you, and on the Road if I feel able.

Mrs. Smiths Baby has been very sick, and very near dying with the Small Pox. It would not come out. They were obliged to have it Bled & put into a warm Bath which relieved it. It is upon the Recovery. Mrs. Brisler is recoverd and I shall take her in the Carriage with me and her youngest child. Lucy & the eldest are gone with a maid of mine to Philadelphia. Our vessel saild on Thursday. I hope it will get there before me. All Friends here desire to be kindly rememberd to you. I wrote you to ask Mr. Cranch to send Mr. Brislers money by Mrs. Ames, but upon further consideration, Mr. Cranch will be so good as to pay it to J. Q. A. and I will repay it to Mr. Brisler. Adieu, my dear Sister.

Yours
A. A[DAMS]

[Bush Hill,] Philadelphia, Decbr. 12, 1790

MY DEAR SISTER:

I have received your two kind Letters one dated in October the 30 day I think & the 14 of Novbr. As the last came by a private Hand it did not reach me till last Evening. You will suppose that I might have written to you long e'er this, but as my letters would only have been a detail of grivences and troubles I was reluctant at taking my pen, and put it of from day to day. I reachd this city after 5 days journey. I was so weak as to be able to travel only 20 miles a day, but I gaind strength daily and was much better when I got here than when I set out. My Furniture arrived the day before me. I came up to the House expecting to have found every thing in readiness to put up the furniture agreable to promise but how was I dissapointed to find the painters with their Brushes and some of the most necessary matters untouch'd. The House had not been inhabited for four years & being Brick you may judge of the state of it. We had fires made in every part. The furniture must come in, and we must inhabit it unfit as it was, for to go with 14 or 16, for Brislers family were all with me, to Lod[g]ings was much beyond my Revenue: I expected to suffer. We got in on fryday. On the Monday following Louisa was taken sick. I gave her a puke & set her up again, but on the thursday following Polly Tailor was taken sick with a voilent Plurisy fever, confined to her Bed, bled 3 times, puked & Blisterd, and tho it is a month, she has got no further down stairs than to my chamber, for after the fever left her the old Ague took her in her Head and face. She is however upon the mending order. But this is not the worst of all my troubles. Thomas has been 18 days totally deprived of the use of his Limbs by the acute Rhumatism, attended with great inflamation and fever. The fever has abated. After having been 9 times Bled, puked and many other applications, he is yet unable to help himself. He is carried from his Bed to the Settee & fed like an infant. I have not left his Chamber excepting a nights and meal times for the whole time. The disorder seazd his Breast as well as his Limbs and produced all the complaints of Gravel by affecting his kidneys. I never knew him half so sick in my Life. I will not lay either of the disorders to this place tho I believe they were hastned & renderd worse by the dampness of the House. Polly has had 2 Fevers of the same kind since she has been with me, & Thomas Rhumatism has been comeing on for some time, yet they were peculiarly unfortunate to attack them at the time of Removal. Dr. Rush has attended them and I have found him a kind Friend as well as Physician.[1] I will not detail to you that in the midst of all this, the Gentlemen and Ladies solicitious to manifest their respect were visiting us every day from 12 to 3 oclock in the midst of Rooms heepd up with Boxes, trunks, cases &c. Thanks to a kind Providence I have got through the worst, I hope, of my difficulties and am in tolerable Health tho much fallen away in flesh. I have a source of anxiety added to my portion on my dear daughters account, Col. Smith having saild last week for England. His going was sudden and unexpected to us, but some private family debts which were due in England to his Fathers estate was one motive, and some prospects of assisting his Family by his voyage was a still further motive. I do not know what has really been the cause why he has been so poorly provided for in the distribution of offices. The P[resident] has always said that he was sensible to his Merrit & meant to Provide for him, but has not yet seen the way open to do it; She, poor Girl, is calld to quite a different trial from any she has before experienced, for tho the Col. was once before absent, she was in her Fathers House. Now she writes that she feels as if unprotected, as if alone in the wide world. One of his Brothers & Sisters remain with her during the Cols. absence. I have Johnny here with me, and would gladly send for her,

[1] Benjamin Rush (1745–1813), of Philadelphia, physician and patriot, signer of the Declaration of Independence. Dr. Rush completed his medical education at the University of Edinburgh, visited Paris, and returned to settle in Philadelphia in 1769. He was one of the early advocates of temperance, and was widely interested in politics and reform. John Adams appointed him Treasurer of the United States Mint, where he served from 1797 to 1813.

to pass the winter with me, but a young Baby and some other obstacles prevent. Pray my dear Sister, write to her and comfort her. No station in Life was ever designd by Providence to be free from trouble and anxiety. The portion I believe is much more equally distributed than we imagine. Guilt of conscience is the work of our own Hands and not to be classed with the inevitable evils of Humane Life.

Decbr. 14: I wrote thus far on Sunday. Thomas is very little better. Charles got here on Saturday and is a great assistance to me. I want my dear sisters & cousins. Notwithstanding I have been such a Mover, I feel in every New place more & more the want of my own near & dear connexions. I hope to see you all next spring. Pray let my son J. Q. A. know that his Brother is sick, that we should be glad to have him come here in Janry. or this Month if more convenient to him, but that I cannot write to him till the Next post. Adieu. I have only Time to say yours as the Post is going.

A. ADAMS

Philadelphia, Janry. 9th, 1791

MY DEAR SISTER:

I received your kind Letter of December 12th with one from my Nephew inclosing 4 Portraits. I instantly recognized my worthy Brother Cranch and my dear Sister together with our venerable Uncle Quincy. The other not one of us have skill enough to find out, by which I judge it is not a likeness. The three first are admirably executed and I have to request that the same hand would take my Mother[-in-law] and send it without letting Mr. Adams know for whom it is designd. You inquire how I like my situation.[1] I answer you the one I removed from, was in Burk[e]s stile, the sublime. This is the Beautifull. The House is better; that is the work within is superiour. The Architecture of the other House was Grand and the Avenue to it perfectly Romantick. The British Troops rob'd this place of its principal Glory by cutting down all the Trees in front of the House and leaving it wholly Naked. Behind the House is a fine Grove; through which is a gravell walk; which must in summer add greatly to the delight of the place. I am told for 8 months this place is delicious. In winter the Roads are bad and we are 2 miles & a half from the city. I have received every attention and politeness from the Gentlemen and Ladies which I could either expect or wish. Living

---

[1] Bush Hill was a suburb of Philadelphia, where Stephen Girard and Peter Helm assumed the direction of the new Lazaretto Hospital in September, 1793, during an epidemic of yellow fever. Schouler, *History of the United States*, vol. 1, p. 255.

here is more expensive than in N[ew] York, Horse keeping in particular, which we sensibly feel, as we are obliged to keep four, for during the sitting of Congress they frequently go six times to the city in the course of the day. We cannot purchase any marketting but by going into the city. We have had very severe cold weather from the beginning of December till the week past, when the snow has chiefly left us. I am thinking seriously of making arrangments to come to Braintree [as] early in the spring as the Roads will permit, for it is generally believed that Congress will not sit after March. If so I hope to be with you by the last of April or begining of May, and as I must leave Brisler and his Family here, I would look out early for some person in his stead. Can you inform me where Nathan Tirril is, and whether he was last summer engaged? He is a good Hand in a Garden and on many other accounts usefull. There are some articles which I shall want in the kitchin way, but it will be time enough to think of these things some months hence.

I feel the loss of Mrs. Smith and Family and it pains me daily that I could not have her with me this winter. It is in vain to say what we ought to have been able to do. I feel what I cannot do. The Cols. Family are all very kind to Mrs. Smith and treat her like a child, but a Fathers House is still the most desirable place. I hear every week from her. I have John with me. A fine Boy he is and the enlivener of the whole Family. We are a scattered family, and I see no prospect of our ever being otherways. Mr. Durant was here last week and said he was going to Boston in order to sail from thence for St. Croix, the River here being frozen up. I thought the Letter you sent to the care of Thomas would go best & soonest by him, so we gave it to him. Thomas is much better tho he does not yet go out except to ride. I have had a succession of sickness in my Family. When we have been well ourselves, our servants have been laid up. When I come to this place again I am determined to bring a *decent woman* who understands plain cooking with me. Such a vile low tribe you never was tormented with & I hope never will be. I brought all my servants from N[ew] York, cook excepted, and thought I could not be worse of than I had been. I have had in the course of 18 months seven, and I firmly believe in the whole Number, not a virtuous woman amongst them all: the most of them drunkards. I recruited with a new one last Monday, who brought written recommendations with her, and who to all appearence is very capable of her buisness, but on thursday got so drunk that she was carried to Bed, and so indecent, that footman, Coachman & all were driven out of the House. Concequently she has turnd herself out of doors. We know little of vileness in our state when compared to those cities who have such Numbers of Foreigners as N[ew] York and Philadelphia—I thank you my dear Sister for your kind care of your Nephew. He wanted it I believe. He mourns a want of employ, but all young men must have patience, especially in his profession. "There is a tide in the affairs of men."[2] Our young folks must watch for it.

I would ask Dr. Rush about a certain affair if I had a short detail of Names, circumstances, and time. If Cousin Lucy thinks it worth her time to give me some account of the affair, I am upon such an intimate footing with the Dr. since his practise in our Family that I could easily assertain all he knows about it, but the Story was so complicated that I am by no means mistress of the Subject.

My Love to Mrs. Norton & my young Nephew. I anticipate the pleasure of meeting you all. Pray heaven nothing may arise to prevent my realizing the satisfaction. Let me hear from you as often as you can and believe me at all times most

Affectionatly yours
A. ADAMS

Bush Hill [Pennsylvania], March 12th, 1791
MY DEAR SISTER:

I was just going to set down to write to you, when I received your Letter of [blank]. I am sensible I was much in Arrears to you, as well as to some other of my Friends. Since the Recovery of Thomas we have had Health in our dwelling, for which I have great reason to be thankfull. I have been happy with my three sons round me, but a sigh of anxiety always hung about my Heart, for Mrs. Smith, who ought to be with me during the absence of the Col. If I had remain in N[ew] York, we should not have lived seperate this winter, but my removal here, and the expence of the removal of a Family for 5 or six Months, was an obstical in the way. As the Col. is expected back in May, if he arrives as I hope he will, he will come immediatly into an office, which will afford to him and his Family a very handsome support. It will be a very Arduous office in the State of N[ew] York, but he is of a very active disposition, and very well calculated for the discharge of it. A prospect of a Provision for

---

[2] There is a tide in the affairs of men
Which, taken at the flood, leads on to fortune;
Omitted, all the voyage of their life
Is bound in shallows and in miseries.
Julius Caesar, Act IV, Scene III, lines 218–21.

himself and Family has releived my mind from a very heavy burden. I hope nothing will arise to detain him abroad longer than we expect, and this provision for him at Home, is much more agreeable to us all than any employment abroad, which would have carried from me my only daughter. Charles is returnd to his office in N[ew] York and Boards with Mrs. Smith. I suppose J. Q. A. will reach Boston by the time this Letter gets to you. He seems happy in the expectation of our passing the summer in Braintree, but he appears to have lost much of his sprightlyness and vivacity. He says that the want of Buisness in his profession and the dismal prospect for the practitioners of the Law in Massachusets, is the weight which depresses him, & that He should still be obliged at his age, to be dependant upon his parents for a support. Altho these feelings are proofs of a good mind, and a sensible Heart, I could wish that they did not oppress him so much. He wishes sometimes that he had been Bred a Farmer, a Merchant, or an, any thing by which he could earn his Bread, but we all preach Patience to him. Thomas follows his studies in the city with as much assiduity as his Health will permit, but he does not look well, and I think I cannot consent to leave him in this Hot climate during the summer. A journey may establish his Health, and prevent a return of that soar disorder the next fall, as his Blood retains yet much of the materials for making it. Every damp day warns him of the future, & reminds him of the past.

You wrote me in your Letter of Janry 25th of a Negro Man and woman whom you thought would answer for me this summer. If she is cleanly and only a tolerable cook I wish you would engage her for me. I had rather have black than white help, as they will be more like to agree with those I bring. I have a very clever black Boy of 15 who has lived with me a year and is bound to me till he is 21. My coachman will not allow that he is a Negro, but he will pass for one with us. Prince I believe I shall leave with Mr. Brisler. I shall bring Polly, and dismiss the rest of my servants. Tis probable we may hire the Black man part of the time as a Gardner, but I design to make those I bring with me work if I can. I will be obliged to you if you will go to the House, and look over the things and write me what you think I shall have absolutly need of towards keeping House. I have written to the Dr. to get Mr. Pratt to make me two kitchin tables and some other articles. There were some old Bed Steads in the House but none perfect. Will you ask Mr. Pratt if he can make me one that is movable like one which Polly says he made for Mrs. Apthorp with a sacking bottom and doubles up together. I do not know any Name for them to distinguish them by; I had one made in N[ew] York which I found exceedingly usefull when Thomas was sick. I have no coars ware neither milk pan, or bowl or dish, Broom or Brush. I shall want some tow cloth, ten or a dozen yds at my first arrival. I do not know if the Dr. [Cotton Tufts] has any Money in his Hands, to procure me these articles, but if he has not, I will send you some for the purpose, as I cannot think of comeing there with a Family, and then haveing every thing to look out for afterwards. Besides I shall not have Brisler to manage for me. I shall take some spoons & what little plate I may have occasion for with me. Mrs. Brisler left some chairs which I shall take of her. I think I have as much table & bed linnen as I shall want. I wish the Roads were such that we could set out immediatly, but that cannot be. I hope however to be with you by the first of May, and I look forward to it with great pleasure I assure you. I shall send by the first vessel a Trunk with some cloaths &c, as we wish to travell with as little Bagage as possible. I dinned yesterday at the Presidents. It was a take leave dinner. The President sets of this week on a Tour to those parts of his Dominions which he has not yet visited, Georgia & North Carolina. Our publick affairs never looked more prosperous. The people feel the benificial effects of the New Government by an increasing credit both at Home and abroad and a confidence in their Rulers. Some grumbling we must always expect, but we have as a people the greatest cause for Gratitude and thankfullness to the Supreme Ruler of the Universe for our present happy and prosperous circumstances as a Nation.[1]

Adieu, my dear Sister. Every blessing attend you and yours, is the sincere wish of your ever

Affectionate Sister
A. ADAMS

My kind regards to Mr. Cranch, to Mr. & Mrs. Norton, to Cousin William & Lucy and a kiss for my young Richard.[2]

[1] Hamilton's project for founding a national bank aroused intense opposition in and out of the Congress. Passing the Senate first, with the customary secrecy, the bill caused a long and bitter debate in the House. Washington asked both Jefferson and Hamilton for reports on the constitutionality of the bill as finally passed, and followed Hamilton's favorable report, of which the chief argument was the doctrine of "implied powers." The Bank of the United States got a charter for twenty years and was authorized to have a capital of ten million dollars, of which the United States was to subscribe two millions, and the public eight millions. For popular reaction to the setting up of the bank in the autumn of 1791, see Schouler, *History of the United States*, vol. 1, p. 198.

[2] Reverend Jacob and Elizabeth (Cranch) Norton, William Cranch (who married Anna Greenleaf), and Lucy Cranch (who married John Greenleaf). "Young Richard" is probably the son who was born to the Nortons in March, 1790.

Bush Hill, April 18, 1791

Dear Sister:

This day fortnight the 2 of May we propose to set out on our journey to Braintree. It will be the middle of May I presume before we arrive there if we meet with no accident, so that I will thank you to attend a little to my garden, have some sallid sown and what ever else you think proper. I wrote to you not long since requesting you to let me know what you thought I might want. You will not forget some Night Hawks.[1] Be so good as to get me a dozen yds of diaper for towels—I have not one there—and whatever else you think I stand in immediate want of. I cannot bear to go to a place unprovided, when a little forethought and care would save me much trouble, and I shall not have Brisler with me to provide for me. I have requested the Dr. to furnish you with the needfull. Vendues are so frequent in Boston that I may be provided with some things perhaps. I shall want a Tea kettle, dish kettle, chaffing dish, a set of Brushes, Brooms, pails, flat Irons, Tubs, Skillits, pots &c. I scarcly know what myself. I have not heard from you since I wrote to you respecting the Negro woman. I should like to have the House opend, cleand, and aird and to have her there when I get there, but I will write to you again and will let you know on what day tis probable I shall arrive. Remember me affectionatly to all Friends. I anticipate much satisfaction & pleasure with you this summer. I am with sincere regard & affection

Yours sincerely
A. Adams

New York, May 6th, 1791

My dear Sister:

I arrived here the night before last and found Mrs. Smith and Family well. We propose to tarry with her till Monday the 10th and in ten days more to be with you. Last night by the post I received your kind Letter of April 29th. A thousand thanks for your sisterly care and attention. A little Providence before hand saves a world of fretting and teazing. I have found inconvenience enough and additional expence too, from going

---

[1] No suitable meaning for "night hawk" has been found in the *Oxford English Dictionary*, which gives two definitions only, the first a kind of bird, and the second a nocturnal bandit. The late Albert Matthews kindly suggested the following solution. In the *Dictionary of American English*, "nighthawk" is defined as "a dish of some kind." This definition is based on the *Massachusetts Centinel*, July 10, 1784, which contains an advertisement of a sale of dishes in Boston. Among porringers, bowls, cups and saucers, pots and pans, and candlesticks, are listed "6 nighthawks."

to places quite inprovided. It is matter of comfort too to think I shall be like to find sober honest servants. I shall make much of all such. I think my dear Sister that as it is comeing Hot weather my oil cloth will do best for my parlour. I would wish to have it put down. What would be the expence of a New Tack. If ten or 12 dollors would put one up, tis so great a comfort that I should be glad to have one put up. Knives and forks I have put up, 1 dozen large spoons, 1 dozen & ½ Tea spoons. Suppose the Negro Man and woman have a bed and would not be against bringing it if I hire them both. A Matrass will do for the coach man & an other for the Boy. I hope Brother Adams[1] will not fail to procure us oats. We use 30 Bushels a month, and the coachman will have them, or other grain which is more costly & not so good for the Horses. Thomas is with us. Mr. Brislers Family moved in to our House the day I left it. I left to be put on Board Captain Cheeseman in the Brigg Ceares one Trunk of mine and one of Pollys, one Band Box & a small portmantua Trunk. If they should come before I get to Braintree I should be glad to have them brought up. I do not think of any other matter. I know you will be so provident for me that I am less anxious about any thing. I will write to you from some place on the Road so as to let you know with more certainty the day that I shall be with you. Let me find you at our House for I will be in before night. I shall avoid going through Boston. My Love to all my dear Friends. God send us a happy and joyfull meeting, prays your ever

Affectionate Sister
A. ADAMS.

Mrs. Smiths Love & Duty. Louisa would be glad if she knew how but she is one of the equal folks.

Philadelphia, October 30th, 1791.[1]

MY DEAR SISTER:

I wrote to you upon my journey whilst I was at Brookfield [Massachusetts] the Sunday after I left you and was sorry to find by your Letter, that you had not received it. I wrote to you from N[ew] York but have been so engaged in moveing, & so embarressd with company in the midst of it, tho only a complimentary call, that I have had scarcly a moment that I could call my own. It was kind in you [to l]et Mr. Cranch to superscribe your Letter. I thank you for [the] precaution, because I open

[1] Peter Boylston Adams (1738–1823), only living brother of John Adams.

[1] Readers will notice that Mrs. Adams is now back in Philadelphia, after having spent the summer in Braintree, later (1792) Quincy.

every Letter from you with trembling and fear. I rejoice most sincerely with you in your prospect of a recovering Limb. If the Life of our dear Friend is spaired, we cannot be sufficiently thankfull to a kind Providence, even tho the recovery should be long and Tedious. My Heart bled to leave you in such distress.

We have nearly got through the Bustle of Removal, but my House is no way to my mind. The Rooms so small and not able to lay two together, renders it very troublesome to see so much company as we must be obliged to. The weather is very pleasent and my Health better than for some months past. Thomas is less threatned with Rhumaticks than he was on our journey. Louisa as well as usual. Mr. Adams is much recovered to what he was, has been able to attend his duty in Senate, tho sometimes a good deal exhausted.

You mention in your Letter getting the House blockd up. I forgot to inform you that there was cider and potatoes to be put into the cellar and that Brother had engaged to see the cellar Bank'd up. But if it should not be done I would wish to have it secured before the Frost. For the Reasons above mentioned I directed Polly [Tailor] to leave the keys of the House with them, the keys of the cellar to bring to you. I wonder Mrs. Jeffry has not sent for Polly.[2] She appeard so solicitious to get her. I hope no one has done her an injury. Polly had qualifications peculiarly fitted for my Family, and might still have been in it, but for a little unruly Member. I like Katy very well and beleive I could not have been better suited. Mrs. Brisler is with me, feeble & sick, tho better than she was. I do not see but she must remain with me, unless Lucy returns to take care of her and her children. My things have not yet arrived from Boston. I fear I shall lose my Pears.

I am anxious for Billy Shaw[3] least he should be a criple all his day's.

Let me hear from you often for I am still anxious. Remember me kindly to all inquiring Friends.

Yours affectionatly
A. ADAMS

Philadelphia, December 18, 1791

MY DEAR SISTER:

I wrote to you on the 27 of Novbr. but company comeing in call'd me from my pen, and I have not since had leisure to reassume it. I have so

[2] Polly Tailor, formerly a servant of Mrs. Adams. See the letter of April 28, 1790.
[3] William Smith Shaw (1778–1826), nephew of Mrs. John Adams.

little Time that I can call my own whilst here that I think when I return to Braintree I ought without suffering from any reflections to be able to live retired. On Monday Evenings our House is open to all who please to visit me. On Twesdays my domestick affairs call for me to arrange them & to labour pretty well too, for the Wednesdays dinners which we give every week to the amount of sixteen & 18 persons which are as many as we can accommodate at once in our Thousand Dollors House. On Thursday the replacing & restoring to order occupies my attention. The occasional intercourse of dinning abroad, returning visits &c leaves me very few hours to myself. I feel that day a happy one that I can say I have no engagement but to my Family. I have a cleaver, sober, honest & Neat black woman as my daily cook. In this respect I am happier than formerly. I always hire for company. The greatest trouble I have, is that Mrs. Brisler is chiefly confind to her Bed wholy unable to do the least thing for herself or Family. She was better after I came here, but a return of the intermitting fever together with her old weakness & complaints not only deprives her of her usefulness but is a great incumberance to me, and takes up much of the Time of my help. In short I know not how I get through, for I have no other help than those I brought with me except the cook. I have been very well myself, till about a fortnight since, I have labourd under complaints. [*One line at the top of the page has been cut off.*] I am still afflicted. Mr. Adams is recoverd from his complaints but labours under a great cold. Thomas has escaped better than I feard from the Rhumatism. It threatned him for several weeks. Louisa is very well. Cealia requests me to inquire after her child & prays you would write to me & inform her if it is well. Mrs. Otis[1] & Cousin Betsy are well. We live socible & Friendly together. In many respects I am much better off than when I lived out of Town. Expence is not to be taken into consideration. That is almost beyond calculation. What a dreadfull blow this defeat of Sinclair & his Army?[2] My Heart bleads for the Relatives of as worthy officers as ever fought or fell but, the justice,

[1] Mary (Smith) [Gray], second wife of Samuel Allyne Otis (1740–1814). His first wife, Elizabeth Gray, daughter of Harrison Gray (1711–1794), died January 22, 1779.

[2] Arthur St. Clair (1736–1818) was born in Scotland and came to America in 1757 to serve with Amherst in Canada. He married Phoebe Bayard, of Boston, a niece of Governor James Bowdoin, from whom his wife inherited money. Having served in the Revolution, he was appointed Governor of the Northwest Territory in 1787. On November 4, 1791, he was surprised and overwhelmingly defeated by the Indians on a branch of the Wabash, not far from the present site of Fort Wayne. For a dramatic account of this defeat, and President Washington's reaction to the news of it, see Schouler, *History of the United States*, vol. 1, pp. 209–15.

the policy, the wisdom of this cruel enterprize lies with higher powers to investigate than mine.

Your kind Letters of Novbr 6th & 11th came safe to Hand and made me truly happy. So little hopes had I of the recovery of our dear and valuable Friend that I feard to hear from you; I could never have imagind that a Leg such as his was, & which appeard to be so far gone in a mortification, could possibly have been restored & that so soon, thanks to that all gracious Providence whose kindness has been so frequently displayd towards us. I heard last week from Mrs. Smith and her little ones. They were all well. You begin I suppose to feel anxious for Mrs. Norton. I hope to hear in due time that she has a daughter. I feel anxious about our House at Braintree. There was a place in the Roof that Leakd much. I sent for two Carpenters, but they could not find out the place. I wish it might be lookd too. I spoke with Brother about it, but fear he has not thought about it. I see by the paper that Mr. Jeffrie is gone to the Madaries for his Health. I want to know how Polly does & how she is likd. I often think of your Neighbours saying she was as necessary to him as his daily Bread. I miss her very much in things which it will be hard for any other person ever to make up to me, in that ready offerd service which prevented my wishes, and which is always so pleasing. Yet she balanced the account sometimes by the vexation which she occasiond me. I wish her well, and shall always value her good qualities, and freely credit her for them. Cealia is as good as I could expect, but would soon be led way if I did not strickly guard her. Katy has all the dispositions in the world [as] Sterne says, but wants experience, in a service which is quite New to her. She is faithfull in her duty, but poor Girl has her sister & two children to look after. In short I think sometimes it cost me as dearly for honesty & fidelity as it would for knavery and I seem to have got an entailment that follows me through the world, particularly a certain degree of sickness that I must take charge of. However it is I hope a part of the portion of good which I ought to do. If so I am in fault to complain. Remember me kindly to all Friends. Mrs. Payne I often think of. Give my Love to her & tell her I hope to see her early in the spring with my other Friends. Pray if I did not Mention the desk before give for it what you think it reasonably worth and ask the Dr. for the Money. Let me hear from you as often as you can and be assured of the sincere affection of

Your Sister
A. Adams

Philadelphia, Febry. 5th, 1792

My dear Sister:

I received your kind Letter of Decbr. and sincerely congratulate you and my Neice upon the Birth of a Son, tho I could have wishd it had been a daughter.[1] I have had the pleasure of having Mrs. Smith and William on a visit to me for 5 weeks. The Col. has been part of the Time here & Charles spent a fortnight with me. They expect to leave me in a week or ten days. This would be but a small matter to me as I should hope to see them again when I past through N[ew] York. But of that I have no prospect. The Col. has made a very advantagous contract with some Gentlemen which will carry him abroad and keep him [there] two years and accordingly he takes his Family with him and [they will] sail in the March Packet. This you may be sure is a heavy stroke to me, but I cannot wish them to decline it, as he goes upon a certain sure footing, and a probable great advantage. Mrs. Smith is in circumstances which will make me more anxious for her, but my Family are destined to be scatterd I think. I begin to long for the Time when I shall set out for Braintree. I fear it will not be earlier than the last year. My Health for six weeks has not been good. I still Labour under an Intermitting [fever] which I apprehend will increase with the warm weather. I am not confind, but am frequently obliged to decline going into company, of which this city is the General Resort during winter, and one continued scene of Parties upon Parties, Balls and entertainments equal to any European city. The Publick amusements tis True are few. No Theatre here this winter, an assembly once a fortnight, to which I have not been this season, but the more general Method for those who have Houses calculated for it, is to give Balls at their own Houses. The Indian War has been a distressing subject. Who & who have been in fault is not for me to say. Where a commander is to be found fit for the Buisness I believe will puzzel more wise Heads than one. The War is an [u]npopular one. If it is a necessary War as I presume it is, it is to be hoped that measures will be pressed to render it more successfull than it has yet been, but I believe those whose judgments are good have little expectation that it will be so.

What is become of Betty & her Husband? Cealia is very anxious about her child & very unhappy at the part her Mother has taken. I was glad to le[arn] that Polly was well & pleasd with her place. We have had

---

The second son born to the Reverend Jacob and Elizabeth (Cranch) Norton.

[*page torn*] weather here. The judge & Mrs. Lowell[2] have been a month here and by them I shall forward this to you. Mrs. Brisler is much better than she was. Her disorder proved to be an intermitting fever.

Let me hear from you and my Friends as often as you can. It will give great pleasure to your

Affectionate Sister
A. ADAMS

Philadelphia, March 20, 1792

MY DEAR SISTER:

I have obliged Louisa, much against her judgment, to give me a pen, Ink and paper, that I might make an effort however feeble to write a few lines to my dear sister. Tis now the sixth week since I have been out of the door of this Chamber, or moved in a larger circle than from my Bed to the chair. I was taken six weeks ago very ill with an Inflamitory Rhumatism and tho it did not totally deprive me of the use of my Limbs, it swelld and inflamed them to a high degree, and the distress I sufferd in my Head was almost intolerable. 3 Times was I let Blood, the state of which was like a person in a high Plurisy. I am now lame in my wrists from the 8th pr of Blisters which I have had. A week after the Rhumatism attackd me, the intermitting fever set in, and under that I am still Labouring. It was necessary to quell the inflamitory disease first, & Bark could not be administerd for that. I am now reduced low enough to drive away the Rhumatism, but the old Enemy yet keeps possession. The Dr. [Benjamin Rush] promises me the Bark in a few days, but my dear Sister, you would scarcly know me reduced as I am. I have scarcly any flesh left in comparison of what I was, but blessed be God my Life is spaired and I am really mending, tho it must be slowly whilst this fever which daily visits me remains. In the midst of my Illness my dear Mrs. Smith was obliged to leave me. Distress enough poor Girl. She then expected to have saild in 8 days but they have since determind to go in a Merchant Ship which is to sail this week. But tho absent from you my dear Sister & deprived of the Tender care of my only daughter, I have not been without my comforts. Louisa has been a watchfull and attentive Nurse. Mrs. Brisler has happily recoverd her Health and has been a comfort to me. But I have found in my old Friend Mrs. Dalton[1] a

---

[2] John Lowell (1743–1802), of Newburyport, and later Boston. In 1789 he became a United States judge for the District of Massachusetts.

[1] See the letter of February 20, 1790.

Friend indeed, and in my good Mrs. Otis[2] & kind Cousin Betsy,[3] all that I could wish or desire. One or other of them have been constantly with me, watching by Night & tending me by day as you my dear Sister would have done. I have experiencd from all my acquaintance the kindest solisitude for me, & tho so long a sickness, have always had more watchers to offer than I have had occasion to accept. I have had a most tedious cough through my disorder which has not yet left me. My weak state call[s] upon me to quit the pen & lay me down. If well enough tomorrow I will take it up again.

Wednesday, [March] 21, [1792]

I am much to day as yesterday. Had a tolerable Night, find rather more agitation upon my Nerves. Received a Letter from Mrs. Smith who was to have saild this day, but is prevented by the Cols. being taken sick with his old Billious complaint so as to be obliged to be Bled and Blisterd. I am not a little anxious for him. How soon may our fairest prospects be leveld with the dust and shew us that Man in his best estate is but vanity and dust?

I am almost too weak to think of any arrangments for a journey, but as soon as I am able to travel I shall set out for Braintree. If congress are not up, Mr. Adams will ask leave of absence. As I have not yet been out of my chamber, the middle of April is as soon as I can expect if I mend ever so fast, but that will soon be here. There is a little painting I wish I could get done to the House before I come. I mean the stairs and the Entry below & the china closset & the kitchen floor. I wish you would consult the the [*sic*] Dr. [Cotton Tufts] & have it done if you can. Mrs. Black has her small Room painted as I should like the Entry and closset. I hope my wood is ready which I engaged to have got in the winter. If I had been well I should have written to the Dr. respecting several things, but I am little capable of Buisness & Mr. Adams's whole time is taken up with the publick Buisness. I wish you to ask the Dr. if he does not think I had better have a Barrel of Brown Sugar bought provided it can be had. Good Sugars will rise. Oats I suppose it will be time enough to think of, yet if they are reasonable I wish the Dr. to secure us a hundred Bushel. I thank you my dear Sister for all the kind care you have taken

---

[2] Mrs. Samuel Allyne Otis, step-mother of Harrison Gray Otis (1765–1848).

[3] Elizabeth, daughter of William Smith, brother of Mrs. Adams. See the letter of April 20, 1792.

for me. I still continue to be troublesome to you. My Love to my Neices & all other Friends. I find myself too feeble to continue writing. Cealia is well, much concernd for her Child. Adieu. God grant us a happy meeting prays your ever

Affectionate Sister
A. ADAMS

Philadelphia, March 25th, 1792.

MY DEAR SISTER:

I received your kind Letter of March eleventh yesterday. I wrote to you last week which was the first time I had been permitted to use my pen, or indeed was able too, for six weeks. I have not yet been out of my chamber. The Weather has been very unfavourable this Month. I was to have tried the carriage to day but the weather is against me. I am so feeble & faint, if I move that I do not think I could get down stairs without being carried. Yet I grow impatient of confinement, and long to be well enough to set out on my journey. I fear I shall not have strength for it so soon as I wish. I would leave here the middle of April if I could.

You was so good as to make provision for me last year by procuring me those things which you thought necessary such as Loaf & Brown Sugar, Tea, Coffe, Meal &c. As to Brown Sugar I hope the Dr. [Cotton Tufts] will procure me a Barrel. I shall not have so many articles to provide as when I went last year in the furniture way, yet I did not arrive at a frying pan or Grid Iron I think. I dont know whether I wrote the Dr. to procure me candles. If I did not you will speak to him.

March 29th, [1792]

Bad weather yet. No riding out for which I am impatient. I yesterday received a Letter from Mrs. Smith [dated the] 24th. She writes me that the Col. was better & that they expected to sail the first fair wind. I have not learnt that they are yet gone. Indeed my dear Sister it is very hard to part with my only daughter. It has depressd my spirits very much through my sickness, but we must all have our trials, some of one kind & some of an other. As to Politicks, they begin to grow pretty warm. There are Honesters in Congress as well as in Boston. There are Grumblers and antifeadelist [sic], but very few from the North. The old dominion is in a Rage, because they could not carry the point of getting

THE ADAMS MANSION, QUINCY, 1787   E. Malcolm

more than there share of Representation in the Government.[1] All the attacks upon the Secretary of the Treasury and upon the Government come from that Quarter, but I think whilst the people prosper, and feel themselves happy they cannot be blown up. I most sincerely wish a stop could be put to the Rage of speculation, yet I think it is an Evil that will cure itself in Time. Tis very curious, just before the News arrived of Sinclairs defeat, Mr. Gerry made a motion for an Equesterian Statue to be Erected to the President, agreeable to a former vote of congress—now the Coin is not permitted to wear the stamp of the President because it would savor too much of Royalty.[2] So inconsistent are Men—and the same Men—But I feel that I must close. Presenting my affectionate Regards to you & yours I am most sincerely

Your affectionate Sister
A. Adams

Philadelphia, April 20th, 1792

My dear Sister:

I have just received your kind Letter as I was about to write to you to inform you that we proposed sitting out on our journey on Monday or tweseday next. The weather has been so rainy that I have not been able to ride so often as I wishd in order to prepare myself for my journey, and how I shall stand it, I know not. This everlasting fever still hangs about me & prevents my intire recovery. A critical period of Life Augments my complaints. I am far from Health, tho much better than when I wrote you last. I see not any company but those who visit me in my chamber. Nor have I once been out of my carriage, but to see my Friend

---

[1] As a result of the first census (1790), the House of Representatives was reapportioned among the states in the spring of 1792. Three bills were introduced into Congress, resulting in a three-sided quarrel between House and Senate, Federalists and Republicans, and New England and Virginia. The first bill was lost in the House; the second was vetoed by Washington—the first exercise of the veto power in our history. The third bill, allowing one representative for every thirty-three thousand people, took care of the fractional parts of the population in New England. After March 3, 1793, the House consisted of one hundred and five members. Schouler, *History of the United States*, vol. 1, pp. 206-7.

[2] "A Federal proposition in the House to put the President's head upon the new United States coins was assailed with more effect as an unrepublican imitation of Caesar's image and superscription, and the device of Liberty was finally substituted instead. Though in this instance and another, where plans were being pressed for erecting an equestrian statue to Washington . . . the real animus of the opposition was directed against the Hamilton clique. . . ." Schouler, *History of the United States*, vol. 1, p. 207.

Mrs. Dalton, who was sick before I got well, tho not till I was so much better as to do without her kind care. Cousin Betsy Smith[1] has been with me for the greatest part of the Time the last Month, and a good child she is, tender and affectionate as her good Mother was. I thank you for your care about my things. We have sent last week to Boston by the Brigg Isabella a number of Boxes & Barrels. They are addrest to the care of J. Q. A., but I wish you to ask the Dr. [Cotton Tufts] to be so kind as to see that a carefull Team brings them to Braintree, & that Hay or Straw is put into the cart, or the things will get Broken. The Bill of laiding was inclosed to Mr. Adams. I shall send by the Brig Maria my Trunk of cloaths &c. She is now here. I am glad to hear that spring is forward as I hope to find the Roads good in concequence of it, but I always fear for the fruit. If the things you mention could be accomplishd before we arrive, it would be a great relief to me. I am grieved for my dear Sister Shaw, tho I have not been able to write and tell her so, for I was seaz'd with an inflamation in one of my Eyes when I was first taken sick which has not yet left me. I could not bear a light in the Room, nor even the fire to Blaize. It is much better, but writing, reading or sewing are all painfull to me. Mr. Adams has not had any return of his Ague but lives in continual apprehension. Thomas is thin & pale but does not complain. We must leave him on account of his Studies. Yet it will be with apprehensions that I shall hear of his being sick—I do not particularly recollect any thing I want. You know as well as I & better for you provided for me before. If you go to Boston I should like to have a pr of Brass Andirons at about 8 dollars price, Tongues [*sic*] and Shovel proper for my best Room, but you need take no extra trouble for them. You will be so good as to have the Beds aird &c. If Betsy is in Braintree she may be engaged for to stay if you think best till Cealia gets Home. I shall send her by the vessel now here. I am not so perfectly easy on account of travelling Home as I should have been with Robert when he was sober, but he really got to such a pace that I have been obliged to part with him & have taken one who has not driven me more than once or twice, but I hope we shall reach Home safe. Terrible is the distress in N[ew] York, from the failure of many of the richest people there, and from the Spirit of Speculation which has prevaild & brought to Ruin many industerous Families who lent their Money in hopes of

---

[1] Daughter of William Smith, brother of Mrs. Adams and sister of Louisa Smith, who made her home with John and Abigail Adams. See footnote 4 to the letter of November 24, 1788.

Gain.[2] I was mortified to see our worthy Friend[3] stand so low on the list of Senators who I had been accustomed to see stand foremost, but such is the Instability of the people. Popular Leaders catch their ear and they are credulous to their own injury. In the House of Representatives of the U[nited] States matters are not going better. The Southern members are determined if possible to Ruin the Secretary of the Treasury, distroy all his well built systems, if possible and give a Fatal Stab to the funding system. In Senate they have harmonized well, no unbecomeing heats or animosity.[4] The Members are however weary & long for a recess one after an other are droping off, which gives weight to the opposite side. Many of the Southern Members have written long speaches & had them printed, which has had more influence than our Northern Friends are aware of who, depending upon the goodness of their cause, have been inattentive to such Methods to influence the populace. The V[ice] President, they have permitted to sleep in peace this winter, whilst the minister at War, & the Secretary of the Treasury have been their Game.[5] The Secretary of State & even the President has not escaped. I firmly believe if I live Ten Years longer, I shall see a devision of the Southern & Northern States, unless more candour & less intrigue, of which I have no hopes, should prevail. Should a war or any dire calamity assail us, then they would Hugg us. But politicks avaunt. My dear Mrs. Smith has been a Month gone. It pains me to the Heart. But who of us can say, that we have not our troubles? Our portion of happiness is no doubt equal to our deserts.

[2] The collapse of what the press called "scripophobia," a period of feverish speculation when the banks "soared like soap bubbles," starting in the summer of 1791. By the spring of 1792 there were many failures, and for large amounts.

[3] In 1792 the Senators from Massachusetts were Caleb Strong (1745–1819), of Northampton, and George Cabot (1752–1823), of Salem.

[4] "But in the Senate Chamber all was dignity, courtesy, and moderation; the Senators, never more than thirty-two in number in Philadelphia, appeared well powdered and in rich dress, and if a loud whisper disturbed the member who had the floor Vice-President Adams would restore order by gently tapping with his silver pencil-case upon the little mahogany table which stood in front of him." Schouler, *History of the United States*, vol. 1, p. 353.

[5] Because Henry Knox, Secretary of War, usually sided with Hamilton, who often carried Edmund Randolph, the Attorney-General, over to his way of thinking in disputes in the Cabinet, the Anti-Federalists, or Republicans, seized on the disaster of St. Clair's Defeat to strike at Hamilton by accusing Knox of inefficiency. When the Cabinet divided, Washington was left in the middle; but too often Randolph, as Jefferson liked to say, would give the "shells" to him and the "oyster" to Hamilton. Schouler, *History of the United States*, vol. 1, p. 275.

Adieu my dear Sister. I hope to see you in a few weeks. Remember me affectionatly to all our Friends. And believe me

As ever yours
A. ADAMS

MY DEAR SISTER: N[ew] York, Sunday, April 29, 1792

I left Philadelphia on Twesday Noon the 24 of April. My first stage was only twenty miles. I bore it better than I expected. The next day rode only 18. Rain came on & the Roads were miry indeed. We did not get to this place till fryday evening. Here I find a vacancy which cannot be supplied, tho all my Friends are good & kind. The first being who welcomed me to the House, and met me at the door, was Billys[1] little favorite dog who came skipping & hopping upon me. My feelings were awakened almost to Tears. Mrs. Smith I should have said moved into the Cols. House when he went away. N[ew] York is in great distress. Many of my particular acquaintance whose affluence was great & well founded when I lived here, and even when I passt through last winter, are now in Ruinous circumstances, thousands worse than nothing. Such is the wheel of fortune.

We propose setting out tomorrow but shall not reach Braintree (Quincy I beg your pardon)[2] till next week. I will endeavour to write you what day when we get into Massachussets, not perhaps till wednesday week. My Health is better than when I set out, but the Weather is very Rainy, & I dare not travell in bad Weather. My best Regards to you all. Adieu. Yours affectionatly
A. ADAMS

MY DEAR SISTER: N[ew] York, 25 June, 1795[1]

I yesterday received your Letter giving me an account of the distressd situation of Sister Smith.[2] I fear her disorder will terminate in a setled

[1] William, the eldest son of Abigail (Adams) Smith (1765–1813).

[2] Quincy, formerly part of Braintree, was established as Quincy on February 22, 1792. *Historical Data Relating to Counties, Cities, and Towns in Massachusetts:* Division of Public Records, the Commonwealth of Massachusetts, Boston, 1920, p. 52.

[1] Readers will notice that more than three years have elapsed since the preceding letter. Jefferson was no longer Secretary of State, Edmund Randolph having succeeded him on January 2, 1794. Hamilton, also, had retired, Oliver Wolcott, Jr., having become Secretary of the Treasury on February 2, 1795. Timothy Pickering became Secretary of War on January 2, 1795. William Bradford was Attorney-General after January 29, 1794; Joseph Habersham became Postmaster-General on February 5, 1795.

[2] Apparently the second wife of William Smith, the brother of Abigail (Smith) Adams. Smith first married Catherine Louisa Salmon.

distraction. Burrel shall have the Room & bed Room for Mrs. Smith at 12 dollors a year, but he shall have them only for her. That is he shall not consider himself at Liberty to let them to any one else if she should not continue with him. I mention this because when I let him the House there was a misunderstanding between us. But if she goes there, care should be had that she should have a sufficiency of good & wholesome food. They are poor people and live pretty near. Indeed they are obliged to. Mrs. Smiths place is let at much too small a Rent as produce is.

I was in hopes to have been on my way home by this time, but the Senate are not yet up, and Mr. Adams does not give me much hopes of its rising till Saturday. The Fate of the Treaty is not yet known. It is however the general opinion that it will be ratified. I say the out door opinion, for the Senate are secret and silent. It has been discussed with much calmness, coolness and deliberation, and considerd in all its various lights and opperations.[3] I hope the decision will be wise & judicious, satisfactory & benificial to the Country. The Grumblers will growl however. Party will shew itself, and be bitter. I have had letters from my sons [as] late as 24 April. They were well & desire to be particularly rememberd to all Friends at Quincy.

Mrs. Smith sends her duty & Love. She is well & so is Emelia,[4] a lovely Girl I assure you tho she has got red Hair which mortifies her mother not a little. John has the Ague poor fellow.

I hear frequently of your son,[5] & from every body the just praises which he merits. Mr. Greenleaf drank Tea here last week. He talks of

[3] For the acrimony and intrigue which accompanied the negotiation and ratification of this treaty, see the standard work, S. F. Bemis, *Jay's Treaty*, New York, 1923. Jay's Treaty, signed November 19, 1794, was the subject of such secrecy that John Trumbull, the painter, had to commit it to memory in order to give the text of it to James Monroe in Paris in December, 1794. Just as Washington was on the point of allowing a publication of the authentic document, Bache's *Aurora* of June 29 came out with an abstract of the substance of it. Bache got his copy from Stevens Thomson Mason (1760–1803), United States Senator from Virginia; he printed the text of the treaty in full in a pamphlet on July 1, 1795. For the popular reaction to the text of the treaty, see Schouler, *History of the United States*, vol. 1, pp. 310–2. The Senate ratified it on June 24, 1795. The House finally voted money to carry it into effect on April 30, 1796.

[4] Caroline Amelia Smith, who was born in 1795, married John Peter DeWindt.

[5] William Cranch (1769–1855) went to Washington in 1794 as lawyer for the North American Land Company, of which his brother-in-law, James Greenleaf, was one of the chief promoters. See James Edward Greenleaf, *Genealogy of the Greenleaf Family*, Boston, 1896, pp. 217–8, and the following note.

returning to Holland soon. The Girls here, I believe, wish his wife dead.[6] He is sufficiently a favorite where ever he goes, & seems too much of an American not to have all his affections, *all* centerd in this country. His manners are more like Nancys[7] than any of the rest of the Family. He looks like her. I asked how Polly [Tailor] was liked. He told me very much & Julia he said was well. I wishd him to go on to Boston that he [might] enjoy the happiness of his Brother[8] to which he had so much contributed. He said he must rejoice in it at a distance as his buisness would not allow him that pleasure.

Remember me affectionatly to all our Friends. Tell Brisler the week after next he may look for us.

Affectionatly yours
A. ADAMS

Springfield [Massachusetts], April 30, 1797[1]

MY DEAR SISTER:

I know you will rejoice to hear that we are so far on our journey without meeting any accident. My Quincy Friends and Neighbours who accompanied us as far as Westown could tell you that they parted with us in as good spirits, as the peculiar circumstances which preceeded our

---

[6] This remarkable man was James Greenleaf (1765-1843) of Boston, notorious speculator in land, the associate of Robert Morris (1734-1806) and John Nicholson (died in 1800) of Pennsylvania, in the North American Land Company. Greenleaf was American Consul-General in Amsterdam, and had a Dutch wife, through whose connections in Holland he planned to obtain investors in American land. The wars of the French Revolution diverted Dutch money to France, and emigrants who might have crossed the ocean died on the battlefields of Europe. The North American Land Company collapsed because of its ambitious scheme to promote and develop the new city of Washington. Greenleaf, Morris, and Nicholson went to jail. See the account of Greenleaf and his company in Channing, *History of the United States*, vol. 4, pp. 107-13; also, Schouler, *History of the United States*, vol. 1, p. 381.

[7] Nancy (Greenleaf) Cranch (1772-1843), sister of James Greenleaf (1765-1843), married William Cranch in 1795.

[8] John Greenleaf (1763-1848), who married his cousin, Lucy Cranch (1767-1846), daughter of Richard and Mary (Smith) Cranch.

[1] Readers will notice that almost two years have elapsed since the preceding letter. Mrs. John Adams, now the wife of the President, is on her way from Quincy to Philadelphia, where John Adams had been inaugurated on March 4, 1797. For his inaugural speech, see Adams, *Works*, vol. 9, pp. 105-11. President and Mrs. John Adams left their suburban home at Bush Hill and moved into the city of Philadelphia in 1791. In 1797 they occupied what was formerly the Robert Morris mansion, next door to the new Morris mansion at the southeast corner of Sixth and Market Streets. Washington resided there from 1790 to 1797. This dwelling was demolished in 1832. Pennsylvania built an Executive Mansion at Ninth and Market Streets, but neither Washington nor Adams lived in it.

leaving home would admit. We reachd Williams's and lodgd there.² It was fortunate that Mr. Brisler was with his wife, for in the Night she was taken with one of her sick turns, and was ill all night and part of the next day. Worry and fatigue had brought on what would have taken place without it as soon as the Hot weather commenced. Having effectually cleard her stomack, I hope she will proceed without any further inconvenience. The next day we reachd Worcester to dine, and Brookfield³ to lodge. How we got to Springfield to night, is not worth your while to inquire. The Attorney Generall[4] will not present us I presume, as we caught him on the Road, returning from Northhampton Court. But with a Family of thirteen persons it behoves us to get on as fast as we can, particularly when I consider my detention, and how necessary to the *Wheels* of the Presidents Family Brisler is. My Thoughts are continually like Noahs Dove, returning to the Ark I have left.

Whether like that I shall return no more, must be left with that Being, in whose hands my Breath is. I consider myself following where duty leads and trust the Event.

>Is Heav'n tremendous in its frowns? Most sure;
>And in its favours formidable too:
>Its favours here are trials, not rewards;
>A call to duty, not discharge from care;
>And should alarm us, full as much as woes;
>Awake us to their cause, and concequence;
>O'er our scann'd conduct give a jealous eye;
>And make us tremble.[5]

Such appears to me the situation in which I am placed, enviable no doubt in the Eyes of some, but never envy'd or coveted by me. That I

---

[2] Weston, the west precinct of Watertown, was established in 1713. In 1754 part of it was included in the new town of Lincoln. Boundaries between Weston and Waltham were established in 1766. *Counties, Cities, and Towns in Massachusetts,* p. 47. Williams's Inn was at Marlborough, Abraham Williams having erected a tavern there in 1665, which was still known by his name as late as 1907. Mary C. Crawford, *Little Pilgrimages Among Old New England Inns*, Boston, 1907, p. 160.

[3] Brookfield, now in Worcester County, was incorporated as a town in 1718. *Counties, Cities, and Towns in Massachusetts,* pp. 63–4.

[4] James Sullivan (1744–1808) was Attorney-General of Massachusetts from 1790 to 1807, and Governor, 1807–1808.

[5] Edward Young, *Night Thoughts:* "First Night: on Life, Death, and Immortality," lines 328–35. John Kieran of the New York *Sun* and "Information Please" deserves the credit for the placing of this quotation.

may discharge my part with honour, and give satisfaction is my most earnest wish.

My kindest regards await my Friends, particularly to Brother Cranch. Love to my dear Eliza. I hope she will not let her spirits faint or sink under her bereavement. How consolutary the reflection, that whom the Lord loveth, he chastneth.

You have the consolation of knowing that no part of your duty was omitted. All that the tenderest Love and kindest affection could do or perform was done by you, for the dear Girl whose loss we mourn. This with her dying Breath she bore witness too [sic]. [*At this point half a page is cut out.*][6]

Let Mrs. Howard know that Betsy stands her journey pretty well. The other Girls are very well. I forgot to mention to Mr. Porter to attend to the first catipillar webb and take them of as soon as they appear. Pray send him word. I see they are beginning upon the Road.

[A. ADAMS]

East Chester, [New York], May 5, 1797

MY DEAR SISTER:

We reachd here yesterday being thursday the 7th day from leaving home. We had very bad Roads, the Rains having washd all the stones bare, and the ruts were very deep. I was much fatigued. Brisler and Family went on to N[ew] York, Mrs. Brisler much mended in her Health by her journey. I hope when we get over our fatigue we shall all be able to say so. Betsy does not seem the worse for it, tho I think I have run a risk in taking so feeble a Being, but I hope it may be a means of restoreing a Good Girl to Health. I found Mrs. Smith and her Children in good Health. Mrs. Smith grows very fleshy, as much so I think as before she first went abroad, tho being older and more moulded into the form of woman, she does not look so burden'd. The Col[onel] has been gone a journey for a fortnight up to his New Lands. Tomorrow I go into New York and on Monday proceed for Philadelphia. I think it a very fortunate circumstance that Mr. Smith accompanied us. It has renderd the journey much pleasenter, and he has taken a good deal of care and

[6] The mother of John Adams, Susanna (Boylston) [Adams] Hall (1709–1797), died on April 21, 1797, at the age of eighty-eight. "Died at Quincy, 22 April, 1797, Mary Smith, daughter of the late Captain Smith, in the 22nd year of her age." *Columbian Centinel*, April 26, 1797. This Mary Smith was a niece of Mrs. John Adams. See *Letters of Mrs. Adams*, Boston, 1840, vol. 2, p. 237.

anxiety from my mind, which I should have felt if he had not been with me.

I want to hear how you all are; and how my Farming buisness goes on. I would wish you to go & look at them sometimes. My Love to all Friends and Neighbours. Mrs. Smith joins me in a kind remembrance.

Your affectionate Sister
A. A[DAMS]

Philadelphia, May 16, 1797

MY DEAR SISTER:

Most cordially welcome to me was your kind Letter of May the 4th, yet I have not found time since my arrival to thank you for it, or even to write a Line to any Friend. My Journey was as pleasent as my thoughts upon what was past, and my anticipations of what was to come would permit it to be. We reachd East Chester on thursday noon [May 4] and found Mrs. Smith and Children well. My reflections upon prospects there, took from me all appetite to food, and depresst my spirits, before too low. The Col[onel] gone a journey, I knew not where, I could not converse with her. I saw her Heart too full. Such is the folly and madness of speculation and extravagance. To her no blame is due. Educated in different Habits, she never enjoyd a life of dissipation. The Boys are fine Lads. I wish they were at Hingham under your care. I tarried one day & a half, and then went into N[ew] York. Charles lives prettily but frugally. He has a Lovely Babe and a discreet woman I think for his wife, quite different from many of the Family.[1] A Number of Ladies and Gentlemen visited me there. On Monday, the 8 of May, we left N[ew] York to persue our journey. On Wednesday morning about 25 miles from Town, I was met by my Friend who clameing his own, I quitted my own carriage, and took my seat by his side. We rode on to Bristol,[2] where I had previously engaged a dinner, and there upon the Banks of the Deleware, we spent the day, getting into the city at sun set. I found my Family of domesticks had arrived on Saturday without meeting any accident, which was very fortunate, for 40 miles through the Jersies was the worst Roads I ever travelld. The soil is all clay. The

---

[1] In 1798 Charles Adams (1770–1800) was living in Beaver Street, New York City. Stokes, *Iconography of Manhattan Island*, index, p. 288. His wife was Sarah Smith (1769–1828); his two daughters, Susanna Boylston (1796–1846), and Abigail Louisa (1798–1838). Mrs. Charles Adams was a sister of Colonel William Stephens Smith.

[2] Bristol, Bucks County, Pennsylvania.

heavey rains & the constant run of six stages daily, had so cut them up, that the whole was like a ploughd feild, in furroughs of 2 feet in deepth, and was very dangerous. To me you may well suppose such roads were more peculiarly distressing. They were so much so, as to confine me to my Room & Bed the greater part of Two days. By some applications I have in a great Measure recoverd, tho I am still a sufferer.

Yesterday being Monday, from 12 to half past two I received visits, 32 Ladies and near as many Gentlemen. I shall have the same ceremony to pass through to day, and the rest part of the week. As I am not prepaird with furniture for a Regular drawing Room, I shall not commence one I believe, as the Summer is to near at hand, and my Health very precarious. At the Winter Sessions I shall begin. Mrs. [Cotton] Tufts once stiled my situation, splendid misery. She was not far from Truth. To day the President meets both Houses at 12 to deliver His speech.[3] I will inclose it to you. I should like to learn the comments upon it, with a veiw to discover the Temper and Sentiments of the publick mind. We are indeed as Milton expresses it, "Thrown on perilious Times."

We have Letters from the Minister at the Hague[4] as late as 23 Feb'ry. I will send you in my next some extracts from them. They are in the same strain of information and intelligence with the former. The decission as it respected the Election here, was well assertaind in France & England & Holland, and it had its influence upon all those powers.

I pray you to Remember me affectionatly to all my Friends & Neighbours. I rejoice in your unanimity as it respect [sic] Mr. Whitney,[5] who you know is the Man of my choice, without any prejudice or dissafection to Mr. Flint.[6] The union was however unexpected but not the less agreable. The hour approaches to dress for the morning. My Love to Cousin Betsy. I wish she could run in as formerly. I do not however dispair of seeing her Here some future day.

I can say nothing to you of future prospects of returning to my own

---

[3] The first session of the Fifth Congress extended from May 15 to July 10, 1797. Adams read his message on relations with France on May 16, 1797.

[4] John Quincy Adams (1767–1848), who was commissioned by George Washington as minister to the Netherlands on May 30, 1794. For incomplete versions of seventeen letters which J. Q. Adams wrote to his mother, February 8, 1797, to April 14, 1801, from Holland and Prussia, see the second volume of *Writings of John Quincy Adams, 1779–1823*, W. C. Ford, Editor, New York, 1913–17.

[5] Peter Whitney (1770–1843), Harvard, 1791, became assistant to Anthony Wibird, minister in Quincy.

[6] Jacob Flint, of Reading, Harvard, 1794. He died in 1835. See the letter of November 15, 1797.

dear Home. That must be governd by circumstances. My pens are so bad I know not whether you can read. I am most affec'ly

Your Sister

A. ADAMS

Evening 8 oclock

The day is past, and a fatiguing one it has been. The Ladies of Foreign Ministers and the Ministers, with our own Secretaries & Ladies have visited me to day, and add to them, the whole Levee to day of senate & house. Strangers &c making near one Hundred asked permission to visit me, so that from half past 12 till near 4, I was rising up & sitting down. Mr. A[dams] will never be too big to have his Friends.

Philadelphia, May 24, 1797

MY DEAR SISTER:

I keep up my old Habit of rising at an early hour. If I did not I should have little command of my Time. At 5 I rise. From that time till 8 I have a few leisure hours. At 8 I breakfast, after which untill Eleven I attend to my Family arrangements. At that hour I dress for the day. From 12 until two I receive company, sometimes untill 3. We dine at that hour unless on company days which are tuesdays & thursdays. After dinner I usually ride out untill seven. I begin to feel a little more at Home, and less anxiety about the ceremonious part of my duty, tho by not having a drawing Room for the summer I am obliged every day, to devote two Hours for the purpose of seeing company. Tomorrow we are to dine the Secretaries of State &c with the whole Senate.[1] The Male [part of the *cancelled*] domesticks I leave wholy to Brisler to hire and to dismiss; the Female I have none but those I brought with me, except a Negro woman who is wholy with the Cook in the kitchin, and I am happy in not having any occasion for any others, for a very sad set of creatures they are. I believe this city is become as vile and debauched as the city of London, nay more so, for in the lower classes, much more respect is had to Character there. Speculation in Property, in politicks and in Religion have gone very far in depraving the morals of the higher classes of the people of our Country.

You will see by the Chronical, I presume, that the Tone of the Jacobins is turnd, and that the president has committed with them the unpardon-

[1] In 1797 the Cabinet consisted of five men, and there were thirty-two Senators. If we count Vice-President Jefferson, John and Abigail Adams must have invited at least thirty-eight guests to dinner.

able sin "by saying, that he was convinced that the conduct of the Government had been just and impartial to foreign Nations." Bache[2] opend his batterys of abuse and scurility the very next day, and has in every paper continued them, extracts of which I dout [sic] not the Faithfull Chronical will detail. The answer of the Senate[3] you will find equally firm and decided as the Speech. I call it a supporting answer. The House cannot yet get theres [sic] through. The Antis. want to qualify. They dare not openly countanance the conduct of France, but they want to court and coax her.[4] With Barra's [sic][5] insolent speech before their Eyes and Pincknys[6] dispatches, which fully prove the unbecomeing and indignant conduct of France toward the United States, these degraded Beings would still have their Countrymen "lick the Hand just raisd to shed their Blood." Amongst that number is Freeman[7] of our state, who yesterday appeard a full blood Jacobin in his speech in the House. Landgon [sic][8] in the Senate is more bitter than even Mason[9] or any Virginian. Mr. Otis[10] I am told appeard to great advantage, and was much admired in a speech of considerable Length.

I want to hear from you again. You must write to me once a week. How does Mr. & Mrs. Porter succeed? I will thank you to get from the

[2] Benjamin Franklin Bache (1769–1798), nicknamed "Lightning-Rod Junior," was a grandson of Benjamin Franklin. In 1790 he founded, in Philadelphia, the *General Advertiser*, better known later under the name *Aurora*, an Anti-Federalist, or Republican paper.

[3] To the address of John Adams, May 16, 1797, dealing with the strained relations with France. See Adams, *Works*, vol. 9, pp. 111–20.

[4] France and Great Britain had gone to war on February 1, 1793. The French government was offended with the negotiation and ratification of Jay's Treaty by the United States (1794–1795).

[5] Paul François Jean Nicolas Barras (1755–1829), member of the Directory (1795), appointed Bonaparte to the command in Italy, having, at the height of his power, arranged his marriage with Josephine de Beauharnais (1763–1814) in 1796.

[6] Charles Cotesworth Pinckney (1746–1825), of Charleston, South Carolina, appointed minister to France by Washington in 1796. When he arrived in Paris (December, 1796) the Directory declined to recognize his official status. For the four Pinckneys, see the genealogical note in Channing, *History of the United States*, vol. 4, p. 210.

[7] Nathaniel Freeman, Jr., (1766–1800), of Sandwich, member of the House of Representatives for Massachusetts (1795–1799).

[8] John Langdon (1741–1819), of Portsmouth, New Hampshire, was United States Senator (1789–1801).

[9] Stevens Thomson Mason (1760–1803), United States Senator from Virginia. See footnote 3 to the letter of June 25, 1795.

[10] Harrison Gray Otis (1765–1848), of Boston, son of Samuel Allyne Otis, Secretary of the United States Senate. Elected to succeed Fisher Ames, young Otis served in the House of Representatives (1797–1801). For his character and career, see S. E. Morison, *Harrison Gray Otis: Federalist*, Boston and New York, 1913.

table draw [*sic*] in the parlour some Annetts[11] and give it to Mrs. Burrel, and tell her to make her cheese a little salter this year. I sent some of her cheese to N[ew] York to Mrs. Smith and to Mr. Adams which was greatly admired and I design to have her Cheese brought here. When she has used up that other pray Dr. [Cotton] Tufts to supply her with some more, and I wish Mrs. French to do the same to part of her cheese, as I had some very good cheese of hers last year. In my best chamber closset I left a white Bonnet. Be so kind as to take it and give it for me to Mrs. Norton. In a small wooden Box is a new crape cap which I designd to have sent here, but omitted it untill my other things were gone. Will you get it & fasten it down to the Box by making a small hole or two and then putting a thread through the cap & Box. In my Bathing machine you will find a peice of canvass which will cover the Box. You will have it addrest & give it into Mr. Smiths care, who will send it to me. I have Bacon in Boston which I should be glad to have sent. Mr. Belcher knows about it. Dr. [Cotton] Tufts will pay the expence when requested.

My Respects to Brother Cranch & to Mrs. Welch. Love to Cousin Betsy from your

Ever affectionate Sister
A. Adams

Philadelphia, June the 3, 1797

My dear Sister:

The weather was so cold yesterday that we had fires in our Rooms. I suppose you have weather of a similar kind. We have had frequent showers and yesterday a fine rain. The House have at length got through the answer to the speech, 3 weeks debating whether, they should use the term indignation, or sensibility. The answer as reported and as finally agreed to, is a very handsome one, as well as a firm and decided one. It was carried 60 to 40. The Yeas & Nays were taken. Amongst the Nays will be found three of [the] Massachusetts delegation, Freeman,[1] who is a devoted ———, Varnum,[2] well known, and Skinner,[3] of whom better hopes were entertaind.

[11] Annet, an obsolete variant of anet—that is, anetseed—the seed of anet, or dill. *Oxford English Dictionary*.

[1] See footnote 7 to the letter of May 24, 1797.

[2] Joseph Bradley Varnum (1750–1821), of Dracut, Massachusetts, member of the House of Representatives (1795–1811), and Senator of the United States (1811–1817).

[3] Thomson Joseph Skinner (1752–1809), member of the House of Representatives (1797–1804).

The appointments of Envoys extraordinary, like every other measure of Government, will be censured by those who make a point of abusing every thing.[4] Mr. Marshall of Virginia is said to be a very fair and Honorable man, and truly American, a Lawyer by profession, against whom no objection is offerd, but that he is not Frenchman enough for those who would have sent Jefferson or Madison, Giles[5] or even Jarvis.[6] Judge Dana is known to be a decided Character, but not a party Man, nor any other than a true American. Yet Bache has undertaken to abuse the appointment, and the Chronical will not fail to retail it, that has more low Billingsgate than even Bache. But I can read them all with a true Phylosiphical contempt, and I could tell them what the President says, that their praise for a few weeks mortified him, much more, than all their impudent abuse does.

> There is no terror, *Cassius*, in your threats;
> For I am arm'd so strong in honesty
> That they pass by me as the Idle wind,
> Which I respect not.[7]

This day the House in a Body come at 12 to present their answer. The whole Hundred come.

I hope they will proceed to buisness with some dispatch. I see by the Chronical that you only have one side of the Question. I think Russel[8] ought to give the debates on the other side. We have Men from our state

---

[4] The famous "XYZ Mission." In the spring of 1797 John Adams chose C. C. Pinckney, of South Carolina, John Marshall (1755–1835), of Virginia, and Francis Dana (1743–1811), of Massachusetts, as envoys extraordinary to France. Dana declined to serve because of ill health; so Elbridge Gerry (1744–1814) was appointed in his place (June 20, 1797). Gerry was unalterably opposed to war with France because he feared an American alliance with England.

[5] William Branch Giles (1762–1830).

[6] Dr. Charles Jarvis (1748–1807), Harvard 1766, who, together with Benjamin Austin, was the leader of the Jeffersonians in Boston. In the Boston town meeting of April 25, 1796, Dr. Jarvis opened the debate in favor of a resolution which would have instructed members of the House of Representatives to veto Jay's Treaty, by refusing to vote for appropriations to carry the treaty into effect. H. G. Otis overwhelmed him and Austin by a vote of 2400 to 100. Jefferson appointed his son, William Jarvis (1770–1859), consul to Lisbon, where he served from 1802 to 1811.

[7] *Julius Caesar*, Act IV, Scene 3, lines 66–9. For some strange reason Mrs. Adams wrote "Jack cuss" instead of "Cassius."

[8] Benjamin Russell (1761–1845), journalist of Boston, founded the *Massachusetts Centinel and Republican Journal* in 1784, later the *Massachusetts Centinel*, and, in 1790, the *Columbian Centinel*. Russell was a thorough-going Federalist, but welcomed President Monroe to Boston in 1817, and coined the phrase "era of good feelings." He was among those who have been credited with the invention of the word "gerrymander."

who do great honour to it. Mr. Sewall[9] & Otis[10] are the principle Speakers. I must retract, however, what I have written as it respects Freeman & Skinner. They are on the question of agreeing to the address upon the *yea* side, but on most questions they vote with the *antis*. A Virginian who being *right* and *a new* member was misrepresented by Peter Porcupine[11] in his paper. Some Gentleman expresst his regret at it, upon which Mr. Evans[12] who was the Member, observed that Peter knew he was a Virginian, and so took it for granted that he must be wrong.

I inclose you a newspaper. It has in it a Letter of Thomas [Boylston Adams] to Mr. J. Quincy.[13] Tis said to be from Paris, merly as a cover, for you see the spirit of envy and Jealousy opperating and the misrepresentations respecting only the Change of Missions to *Berlin* instead of Lisbon.[14] At Portugal this present time, it was the opinion of the President & his ministers, that J. Q. A. could not be equally useful to his Country as at the Prussian court. A Treaty was to be renewd with that court, and various other reasons opperated which it would not be so proper to disclose. The appointment was made thus early to prevent his proceeding to Lisbon, where he would go on the arrival of his successor. But Malevelence is unbounded. The inclosed extract is from Bach's paper. Make the Chronical insert it.

Mr. Brisler has accomplishd the buisness for Mr. Cranch and I inclose the Bill. I have had but one Letter from you since I came here. We are all in pretty good Health. John Brisler has had the small pox & that very light. Remember me affectionatly to all Friends and Neighbours. I am, my dear Sister,   Affectionatly yours

A. ADAMS

[9] Samuel Sewall (1757–1814), of Marblehead, Massachusetts, member of the House of Representatives (1796–1800).

[10] See footnote 10 to the letter of May 24, 1797.

[11] "Peter Porcupine," the pen-name of the journalist William Cobbett (1763–1835), who was born in England, and died there. From 1792 to 1800 and 1817 to 1819 he lived as a political refugee in the United States, residing in Philadelphia during the last period. On March 4, 1797, he launched *Porcupine's Gazette & Daily Advertiser* to advocate alliance with England, war against France, and perdition for Republicans. The savage, sarcastic humor of the paper surpassed that of Philip Freneau and Benjamin Franklin Bache.

[12] Thomas Evans, member of the House of Representatives from Virginia (1797–1801).

[13] Probably Josiah Quincy (1772–1864), of Boston, member of the House of Representatives (1805–1813). On January 14, 1811, he first proposed the doctrine of secession in the Congress in a speech opposing the admission of Louisiana as a state.

[14] In 1797 President Adams first named his son, who was minister to the Netherlands, minister to Portugal, but his destination was suddenly changed to Berlin, where he negotiated a new treaty with Prussia.

Philadelphia, June 6, 1797

MY DEAR SISTER:

I received your Letter by this days post. I began to be anxious to hear from my Friends at Quincy. I cannot but say that I was astonishd at some of its contents. I could not believe that any Gentleman would have had so little delicacy or so small a sense of propriety as to have written a mere vague opinion, and that of a Lady too, to be read in a publick assembly as an authority. The Man must have lost his senses. I cannot say that I did not utter the expression, because it has always been my opinion that the people would not be willing to support two ministers, but little did I think of having my Name quoted on any occasion in Town meeting. If he had respected my publick Character only, he would have had some scruples upon that Head, I should have supposed. I shall always consider it as a want of delicacy in him, and a real breach of confidence to make use of my Name on the occasion. I am mortified to find a Gentleman of whom I had formed so favourable an opinion guilty of such a want of decorum. It will however serve as a lesson to me, to be upon my guard, & to be very close mouthed. I have not any remembrance of saying so, tho I think it very probable that I did. By your account of the whole transaction, he has not behaved like a Gentleman. I hope however we shall not be loosers in the end.[1]

I rejoice to hear our Farm looks well. The President is very desirious of seeing it. A journey some where will be absolutely necessary for him. Such close application for so long a period without any relaxation but a ride of a few miles, is too much for him & I see daily by a langour of his countanance that he wants rest. I fear he will not sustain himself unless congress rise so that we may quit this city during the Hot season.

I long for my rose Bush, my clover Field, and the retirement of Quincy, and the conversation of my dear Sister and Friends.

June 8th,[1797]

To day is post day to Quincy, and yesterday we had the Chronical. I think impudent as Bache is the Chronical has more of the true spirit of Satan, for he not only collects the Billingsgate of all the Jacobin papers but he add[s] to it the Lies, falshoods, calimny and bitterness of his own. For what other purpose could he design that paragraph,

[1] The use of the name of Mrs. Adams in the town meeting at Quincy had to do with the current discussion over finding an assistant to the Reverend Anthony Wibird. The letter from Mrs. Cranch, the contents of which "astonished" Mrs. John Adams, is probably in the Adams Papers in the Massachusetts Historical Society.

THE EXECUTIVE MANSION, PHILADELPHIA, 1790

THE MORRIS HOUSES, PHILADELPHIA, 1700

that the President was to receive one hundred & 14 thousand dollors for four years? The sallery every one knows is the same Nominal sum granted to President Washington without half its value. The 14 thousand dollors is no more the Presidents than the money voted to Rigg one of the Frigates building. Every dollar of it, is laid out for the use of the United States, and accurate Book accounts kept & vouchers taken, all of which will be regularly renderd in at our quitting the House. The son too, of 23 [sic] years old receiving this sallery of ten thousand dollors pr year.[2] These salleries are all setled by Law. A Minister Resident has 4 thousand 500 dollors pr year, a Minister plenipotentiary Nine thousand. He is not pickd out to receive more than any other, but his fault is being the son of the President. This wretched party are sinking very fast; but the mischief of these publications arises from their circulating amongst persons and in places where no inquiry is made into facts. Bache will publich [sic] on both sides. I wish Mr. Cranch[3] would make a true statement and see if the wretch would publish it. We give for this very House a thousand pounds a year. President Washington never gave more than 500. And every thing else in the same proportion, nay more than double—. But enough of this. I expected to be vilified and abused, with my whole Family when I came into this situation. Strickly to addhere to our duty, and keep ourselves unprejuced, is the path before us and the curse causeless shall not come.[4] I feel most sincerely for Mrs. Greenleaf and her situation. I know it will do no good to look back but you well know how anxious I was when it might have been of use to her. Mr. James Greenleaf it is said, is absconded.[5] Mr. Morris is confind to his House.[6] Each Party criminate the other, as you have no doubt seen by the Washington paper. I regret that there should exist any occasion for it, but know not the state of Facts, to judge between the parties. As soon as it is in my power I will endeavour to

[2] In June, 1797, John Quincy Adams was almost thirty, not twenty-three, as the Boston *Independent Chronicle & Universal Advertiser* alleged.

[3] Richard Cranch (1726–1811), and brother-in-law of Abigail Adams.

[4] See footnote 7 to the letter of September 1, 1789.

[5] With the failure of the North American Land Company in the panic of 1797, James Greenleaf of Boston sought refuge in the poor debtors' prison in Prune Street, Philadelphia. He obtained a discharge from prosecution by his creditors in 1798, under one of the earliest bankruptcy laws in the United States—that of Maryland. Channing, *History of the United States*, vol. 5, p. 193.

[6] Robert Morris retired to a country house and fortified himself there, holding out for months against creditors, collectors, and constables. He was subsequently lodged in jail. In 1800 Congress passed a federal bankruptcy act, by virtue of which he obtained his freedom in August, 1801. Channing, *History of the United States*, vol. 5, p. 193.

render Cousin William some assistance to enable him to purchase some Books. Say nothing about it. I will not forget him.

The time for the post to go out prevents my adding more. Tell Mrs. Howard that I think Betsy is getting better. She begins to look more like flesh and Blood. Nabby has been sick from some imprudence of her own, but is about again, Becky well, but I have a Lad who has been sick a week, and that from eating Ice creeme[7] when he was making it & hot. He brought on such a cramp in His stomack that his Life has been in danger ever since.

Remember me affectionatly to all Friends particuliarly to Dr. [Cotton] Tufts to whom I mean soon to write. My conscience accuses me that I have not.

Your affectionate sister,
ABIGAIL ADAMS

Philadelphia, June 23, 1797

MY DEAR SISTER:

I received your Letter of June 13th and thank you for it. The account you give me respecting my House and the Farm are very pleasing. I like your proposal of going to it and taking tea with my good Neighbours very much. I am very sorry to hear that Mrs. Beal is so unwell. I have feared that she would fall into a decline, for she has appeard to me, to look very unwell for many Months. She was a good Neighbour, and would be a very heavy loss to her Family.

I do flatter myself with the prospect of comeing to Quincy to pass the Months of August and Sepbr. I know it will be a tedious Journey, but I fear it will be more tedious here, and the President really suffers for want of a journey, or rather for want of some Relaxation. To day will be the 5th great dinner I have had, about 36 Gentlemen to day, as many more next week, and I shall have got through the whole of Congress, with their apendages. Then comes the 4 July which is a still more tedious day, as we must then have not only all Congress, but all the Gentlemen of the city, the Governour and officers and companies, all of whom the late President used to treat with cake, punch and wine. What the House would not hold used to be placed at long tables in the yard. As we are here we cannot avoid the trouble nor the expence. I have been informd the day used to cost the late President 500 dollors. More than 200 wt of cake used to be expended, and 2 quarter casks of wine besides

[7] See letter of August 9, 1789.

spirit. You will not wonder that I dread it, or think President Washington to blame for introducing the custom, if he could have avoided it. Congress never were present here before on the day, so that I shall have a Hundred & 50 of them in addition to the other company. Long tables are sit in the House with similar entertainment. I hope the day will not be Hot. I am like to be favoured with a cool one to day at which I rejoice, for it is no small task to be sit [sic] at table with 30 Gentlemen.

Judge Dana declines his appointment. I feard he would as the state of his Health has been infirm. The President has now nominated Mr. Gerry.[1] This I know will be cavilled at by some, and he will be blamed for it, but the responsibility rest [sic] with him, and he must bear it. He would not have nominated him if he had not thought him an honest Man and a Friend to his Country, who will neither be deceived nor warped. I hope he will not refuse.

The task of the President is very arduous, very perplexing and very hazardous. I do not wonder Washington wishd to retire from it, or rejoiced at seeing an old oak in his place. He has manifested his intire approbation of the measures persued by the Executive.

I thank you for your care of my things. Let Mrs. Hunt know that Nabby is well and I believe contented and that I shall want Betsy if I come as I expect, and I shall stand in need of some more female help, particuliarly a cook. I might here [sic] of some black woman in Boston perhaps who would undertake for two Months. I wish you would inquire.

I want to have the House white washed. I will thank you to see a little about it. It will be well to have the Garden attended to.

I inclose you a Ribbon I met with the other day, and I sent Cousin Betsy a short Gown to show her the fashion, by Mrs. Douse who was to send it to Boston to Mr. Smiths. I hope it will fit her. Adieu my dear Sister.

I am most affectionatly yours
A. ADAMS

I have not seen a speech more to the point than Genll Shepards,[2] but old men do not take so much pains to circulate their Fame as young ones. I enclose it for Mr. Cranch. Let me know if you get Fennos

[1] See footnote 4 to the letter of June 3, 1797.

[2] William Shepard (1737–1817), of Westfield, Massachusetts; Major-General of the Massachusetts militia in 1786 during Shays's Rebellion; member of the House of Representatives (1797–1803).

papers³ now. If you do not I will send them to you. Love to all Friends. Tell Polly Baxter, that I shall miss her very much when I come to Quincy, particuliarly in cooking. Betsy Howard I think is better, tho not [sic] able to go through but little.

Philadelphia, July 6th, 1797

MY DEAR SISTER:

I got through the 4 July with much more ease than I expected. It was a fine cool day, and my fatigue arose chiefly from being drest at an early hour, and receiving the very numerous sets of company who were so polite as to pay their compliments to me in succession in my drawing Room after visiting the President below, and partaking of cake, wine & punch with him. To my company were added the Ladies of foreign Ministers & Home Secretaries with a few others. The parade lasted from 12 till four oclock. Fenno has saved me further occasion of detailing the events of the day. He has given them with accuracy. I inclose his account of it.

You will see an intimation in his paper of some malpractices by a Senator. I inclose to you the Letter this day made publick. When shall we cease to have Judases? Here is a diabolical plot disclosed. When the Message was sent to the Senate with the original Letter Mr. Malcomb the Presidents Secretary met Mr. Blount[1] comeing out, who stopd and askd him what message he had got, upon which Mr. Malcomb replied it was a Secret and confidential one. Mr. Blount did not return untill after the Letter was read which threw the whole Senate into a consternation. Upon his comeing in, the Letter was again read. He turnd very pale, said he did write a Letter at that time to a Mr. Cary, but desired a coppy of it, and untill the next day to make his defence. It was granted, but Mr. Blount has not since been seen. Search was made after him yesterday and a vessel found which he had Charterd to go off in. Poor

---

[3] John Fenno (1751–1798), was born in Boston. Fenno's *Gazette of the United States* was founded in New York in 1789, but was published in Philadelphia beginning April 14, 1790. The *Gazette* had the aid of prominent Federalists, among them Alexander Hamilton.

[1] William Blount (1749–1800), of North Carolina and Tennessee, elected to the United States Senate and served from August 2, 1796, until he was found guilty "of a high misdemeanour, entirely inconsistent with his public trust and duty as a Senator," and was expelled on July 8, 1797. President John Adams was active in revealing Blount's plan to incite the Creeks and Cherokees to aid the British in conquering the Spanish territory of West Florida. Impeachment proceedings were instituted, but dismissed when it was decided that Blount, as a Senator from Tennessee, was not an officer of the federal government. Blount's letter to Cary, an interpreter in the Cherokee Nation, came into the hands of President Adams, who sent it to the Senate on July 3, 1797. The private secretary of John Adams during part of his presidential term was Samuel B. Malcom.

Pensilvanna [sic] keeps no Gallows, as Porcupine says. The Senate will expell him, & it belongs to the House of Reps. to impeach, but they have not yet reported. It does not appear that his offerd Service was accepted by the British, tho it is a glorious kettle for the Jacobines to swim in. How they rejoice. Corruption is corruption from whatever source it originates. This same Tenesse [sic] Senator was arrested for debt four different times on his return home last fall, and but for his Priviledge as Senator which screens him 20 days, he would have been lodged in Jail, which he no doubt richly deserves. He has a Brother in the House[2] who lately took fire at the *mention of French Faction* & challenged Mr. Thatcher [Thacher][3] in concequence of it. This Buisness tho communicated last tuesday to both Houses, is but just transpiring. The House have ordered all the papers to be published. I will send them as soon as they are publick.

I thank you for your kind Letter of 27 June. I derive much pleasure from your account of the Garden and rose Bush. I wish I could enhale the one & taste the other, but I fear not. I past an hour or two with Mrs. Wolcot last Evening, the Lady of the Secretary of the Treasury. Mr. Wolcot[4] seemd anxious at the Idea of the Presidents going so far from the Seat of Government at so critical a period. I know he will not leave here for any time if the Ministers think his presence necessary. We may truly say, we know not what a day will bring forth. From every side we are in Danger. We are in perils by Land, and we are in perils by sea, and in perils from false Breathern. Dr. Blair gave us an excelent discourse a Sunday or two ago. "Trust in the Lord, for in the Lord Jehovah is everlasting Strength."[5] If it was not for that trust and con-

[2] Thomas Blount (1759–1812), of North Carolina, member of the House of Representatives (1793–1799; 1805–1809; and 1811–1812).
[3] George Thacher (1754–1824), of Yarmouth, Massachusetts, Federalist member of the House of Representatives (1789–1801). Thacher removed to Maine, where he was judge of the Supreme Court (1820–1824), and died at Biddeford.
[4] Oliver Wolcott (1760–1833), of Litchfield, Connecticut, son of the signer (1726–1797), was a confederate of Alexander Hamilton, and his successor as Secretary of the Treasury (February 2, 1795). Throughout the years 1797 to 1800 he enjoyed the confidence of President John Adams, but secretly served Hamilton by conspiring with his fellow Cabinet members, Timothy Pickering and James McHenry. Adams foolishly failed to dismiss Wolcott in 1800, when he finally got rid of Pickering.
[5] Samuel Blair (1741–1818), the son of Samuel Blair (1712-1751), also a Presbyertian clergyman, one of whose pupils, the Reverend John Rodgers, was a colleague of the younger Blair, in New York City. This younger Samuel Blair, Princeton, 1760, Harvard, 1767, was minister at the Old South Church, Boston, 1766–1769; chaplain to the Continental Congress; and died at Germantown, Pennsylvania.

Dr. Blair's text will be found in *Isaiah*, XXVI, 4: "Trust ye in the Lord for ever: for in the Lord Jehovah is everlasting strength."

fidence our Hearts would often fail us. I inclose with this a part of a Letter written a day or two since, one part of which I thought proper to cut of, and am too laizy to coppy the remainder.

Congress expect to rise this week. I will write you again, as soon as I can determine what will be the result of our deliberations.

My Love to all inquiring Friends. Present me respectfully to Mrs. Welch and be assured I am, my dear Sister,

Most affectionatly your[s]

A. ADAMS

Let the Friends of my domesticks know that they are all well.

[Philadelphia, July 4, 1797?]

... Salute drank the Presidents Health gave 3 cheers and marchd off with perfect decorum & decency, next in order came the House of Rep's in a Body, and after them the Senate—Foreign ministers Secretaries and Ladies of those Gentlemen I should. . . .[1]

I have just this morning closed a long letter to your son. I congratulate you upon the Birth of an other Grandson. He wrote me a Letter last week upon a subject which it is like he will, or has communicated to you. I have I have [sic] given him the same advice I would a son of my own, so far as I was able to Judge, and have offerd to procure Law Books for him here to the amount of 200 dollors if he should judge it Eligible to persue the practise of the Law. I saw this week a Mr. Scott,[2] one of the commissioners from Washington, a very decent well informd Man. He dinned with us. I made particular inquiries respecting Mr. Cranch. He assured me he was very much respected and esteemed. Then I asked if he thought he would succeed in the practise of the Law there. He replied he did not doubt it. He must have patience & perseverence, but with the qualities Mr. Cranch possessd he had never known a person fail.[3]

[1] This letter was enclosed with the preceding. Most of the first page was cut off by Mrs. Adams.

[2] Gustavus Scott, a Scotsman, appointed a commissioner of the District of Columbia, August 23, 1794, died December 25, 1800. W. B. Bryan, *The History of the National Capital*, New York, 1914–16, vol. 1, p. 413n.

[3] After the failure of the North American Land Company and the collapse of real estate in Washington, William Cranch was appointed trustee in bankruptcy for James Greenleaf. The complicated affairs of Morris, Nicholson, and Greenleaf gave Cranch the legal experience which Mrs. Adams desired for her nephew, and must have taught him the patience which she felt he needed. In December, 1800, President Adams appointed this nephew by marriage to the Board of Commissioners of the District of Columbia, in succession to Gustavus Scott; two months later he put him on the federal bench, where he remained until 1855.

I cannot but think it will be better for him to remain there, than attempt a removal at an uncertainty and I have written him so.

I hope Mr. Gerry will not refuse to accept the mission to which he is appointed.[4] He has not given a decicive answer yet. I know he will not rashly decide, but he must know when a House is ready to burst into Flames. He deserves well of his country who will assist in putting it out. I cannot begin upon publick affairs. I am not certain but I lye exposed for having written some thing or other. A Letter to Mrs. Smith has not been received tho written 8th of June. It containd a post Note and I believe was taken from the office in N[ew] York.

[Philadelphia], July 11th, 1797

My dear Sister:

I have only time this morning by Mrs. H. G. Otis[1] to write you a Line and to tell you that we are as well as the Hot weather will permit. Congress having risen, I hope we shall go some where out of this city as the sickly season approaches.

I send you a handkerchief of the Mul mul kind which when well done up will look clear.[2] Pray accept it. The President says you must write, how the Barley has turnd out, how the corn grows, how it is in the meddow below the House—every thing you can find out about the Farm at all the places as he fears. That will be all he shall know about it this season. The key you mentiond is on the bunch, but the lock is bad and does not move easy. I send Mrs. Greenleaf a peice of muslin to make her some baby caps. I fear I should not have so good an opportunity if I kept it to make. I have not seen any lace to put on them, but I shall look out. My Love to her and Mrs. Norton. Tho so long a journey, I am dissapointed at not comeing to Quincy.

Adieu my dear Sister. Write me as often as you can. Give my Love and a kind remembrance to all Friends from

Your affectionate Sister
A. Adams

[4] See footnote 4 to the letter of June 3, 1797.

[1] Harrison Gray Otis, on May 31, 1790, married Sally Foster (1770–1836), the daughter of a Boston merchant.

[2] Mulmull, often shortened to "mull," a thin variety of plain muslin. The *Oxford English Dictionary* gives 1676 as the earliest date of the appearance of this word in print. "Mull" first appears in Jane Austen, *Northanger Abbey* (1798). See, also, the *Gazette of the United States*, January 16, 1798, in footnote 1 to the first letter of May 13, 1798.

P.S. I wrote to Sister Peabody[3] by Judge Livermore.[4] When you write let me know how Uncle Quincy does, Mr. Wibird,[5] and dont forget poor old Pheby. If she wants a Bushel corn, desire Mr. Porter to let her have it.

Philadelphia, July 19, 1797

My dear Sister:

If the Compass by which my course is directed does not vary again through unavoidable necessity I shall sit out for Quincy next week. We shall probably be 12 days in comeing. I shall want some preparation at Home. I will write to you from N[ew] York. Betsy wrote to her Mother to know if her Sister Nancy was at home & that I should want her during my stay at Quincy.

The Hot weather of July has weakend us all. Complaints of the Bowels are very frequent and troublesome. I received your Letter of 13 yesterday. I have suspected unfair dealings in the post office for some time, tho I cannot say where the fault is. As to the girls Letters I believe they were foolish enough to send them without any Frank. I received a Letter yesterday from your son who was well, and expected, to come to Philadelphia soon on buisness. I fear I shall be away, but I shall write him to come & put up at the House the same as if we were here.

Let Mrs. Porter[1] know that I should be glad she would have Mrs. Bass to clean up the House. I hope it will be white washd first. The post will be gone if I do not close.

Yours affectionatly
A. A[dams]

[Philadelphia, July 21, 1797]

My dear Sister:

The weather is Hot as we can bear. The whole city is like a Bake House. We have a House with large and airy Rooms, or I could not sustain it. I do bear it surprisingly well however, tho I long for a sea Breaze. I hope to leave here on Monday, and get on to Bristol [Pennsylvania] 18 miles the first night. I shall want several things put in order

[3] Elizabeth (Smith) [Shaw] Peabody (1750–1815).

[4] Samuel Livermore (1732–1803), of Portsmouth, New Hampshire, member of the House of Representatives (1789–1793), Senator of the United States (1793–1801).

[5] See footnote 1 to the letter of October 4, 1789.

[1] Wife of the gardener mentioned at the end of the letter of April 30, 1797.

at home for our reception. When I once get on my journey, I shall write to you so that you will learn our progress.

I heard from your son this week, and I wrote him yesterday. We are becomeing very intimate. I inclose to you the two last papers from thence. I have just read a peice, under the signature C.[1] I am at no loss for the writer, nor will you be when you read it. It does honour to the pen of the writer and proves him, no superficial observer. I expect to bring on with me William Smith to place him either at Hingham, or Atkinson.[2] I too, my dear Sister, have my troubles and anxieties.

When we get together, we may say to each other what would not be proper to write.

Louisa is better, but had an allarming turn of Numbness, so that she made no opposition to bleading, which with some powerfull medicine has restored her, but the side seazd was nearly useless for a day or two. Two years ago she had a number of these affections, but never one equal to this. She was, as well as I, pretty well allarmd. I hope she will be induced to be more active.

We are all so-so, none very sick. Mrs. Brisler has her turns. Little John[3] has had the Cholera Morbis. I thought him dead for ten minuts. Nabby & Becky are well. Betsy returns with me, and if she does not fail on the journey will do credit to Philadelphia, by looking like flesh instead of clay. Adieu, my dear Sister

Most affectionatly your[s]
A. A[DAMS]

East Chester, July 29th, 1797, Monday Evening[1]

MY DEAR SISTER:

We left Philadelphia on Wednesday last [July 19]. The day preceeding was very Hot. A partial Rain had waterd the Roads for 15 or 20 miles so as to render the first part of our journey pleasent. We were overtaken

---

[1] Apparently William Cranch (1769–1855).

[2] William Steuben Smith, eldest son of William Stephens and Abigail (Adams) Smith. See footnote 1 to the letter of November 24, 1788. William was ultimately placed as a boarder with Mrs. Adams's sister, Mrs. Stephen Peabody, at Atkinson, a town northwest of Haverhill, just across the border in New Hampshire.

[3] John Adams Smith (born in 1788), younger brother of William, mentioned above.

[1] This letter was written from East Chester, near the present site of New Rochelle, Westchester County, New York, where Colonel William Stephens Smith had a summer home. "Monday, July 29," however, is a date not possible for the year 1797. This letter was written on Monday, July 24, 1797. See the following letter.

by showers, and detaind by them, but on thursday we found clouds of dust for want of Rain. Troops and calvacades [sic] did not lessen it, and the Heat was intolerably oppressive, so much so as to nearly kill all our Horses, and oppress me to such a degree as to oblige me to stop twice in a few hours, and intirely undress myself & lie down on the Bed. At night we could not get rest. Small Rooms, bad Beds & *some company* obliged me to stretch my wearied Limbs upon the floor upon a Bed not larger than one of my Bolsters. From tuesday untill the afternoon of this day, we have not had any respite from panting beneath the dog star. I never sufferd so much in travelling before. The Rain I hope will cool the Air & enable us to proceed, but I fear we shall not reach Quincy this week. Mrs. Smith & little Caroline will be of our party.[2]

It is a long time since I had a Line from you—near a fortnight before I left home. I had a Letter from your son since I left Home. He writes me that he is well, and that his family are so. I wrote you inclosing to you a Hundred Dollars which I hope you duly received, as I found it necessary to give you some trouble to procure me several articles.

If I can get time on the Road I shall write you as I progress onward. Mrs. Smith desires to be kindly rememberd to you. So does your affectionate Sister

A. A[DAMS]

Saturday mor[nin]g
East Chester, 29 July, 1797

MY DEAR SISTER:

We leave this place this morning & hope to reach Home on fryday of the next week. I have written to Mr. Smith[1] to procure sundry articles for me in Boston which will require a Team to bring them to Quincy, & bags for oats. Will you be so good as to consult with Mr. Porter, and if Mr. Belcher can go to Town for them so as to get them up before we arrive, I should be very glad. Will you be so kind as to have some coffe burnt and ground, some Bread and cake made for me, and to be at our House on fryday when we hope to reach Quincy, and if you should hear of any intention of company meeting us on the road, to accompany us

[2] Mrs. Abigail (Adams) Smith and Caroline Amelia, her daughter, the granddaughter of Mrs. John Adams.

[1] "Mr. Smith's store in Boston." See postscript to the letter of November 24, 1788. William Smith, the brother of Mrs. Adams, kept a store in Boston. See the *Columbian Centinel*, April 28, 1798.

to Quincy, I must beg of you to make such arrangments of punch & wine as may be necessary. I have written to Mr. Smith on the subject and he will inform you. Wine you can draw from the casks in the cellar. Punch must be made by Gallons. You will procure spirit for the purpose, and in a Box in the North cellar which is naild up is some Jamaca spirit, that with some Brandy will answer.

I believe it would be best to get Mrs. Baxter to go to the House and assist in making Beds as she knows where my things are better than any one else. The Mattresses should be put on the Feather Beds, & two Beds put up in the new out Chamber for the Men servants. I have my two Grandson [sic] with me, but they can be provided for by some of my Friends if we cannot lodge them at first. We met at N[ew] York with so many unexpected things which we were not provided for, that I wish to have some arrangments made now previous to our getting home, particuliarly if we should meet company. You will find glasses &c enough. You will be so good as to have a table set in the dinning parlour, and every thing ready, to receive your truly affectionate

Sister & Friend
ABIGAIL ADAMS

Woster, [Massachusetts, Thursday,] October 5th, 1797

MY DEAR SISTER:

The day we left you, we proceeded to Flags to dinner. The weather very warm. We left there at half after 3 oclock and got to Williams's at half after six. Very much fatigued I was.[1] It is 35 miles from Quincy. Went to Bed at 8, slept but poorly. At 12 it began to rain & Thunder, continued showery all Night. In the morning cloudy & lowering. Sat out at 8, rode 8 mils to Sutbury. Stopd at Peases during a heavy Shower, then proceeded, but had not rode more than a mile before an other heavey shower overtook us.[2] We rode in the rain to this place,

[1] Mrs. Adams is writing from Worcester on her way back to Philadelphia from Quincy, where she spent the summer. John Flagg kept an inn at Weston at this time, and there, apparently, Mrs. Adams took her dinner on her first day out of Quincy. The Williams inn was at Marlborough, Abraham Williams having erected a tavern there in 1665, which was still known by his name as late as 1907. George Washington stopped at Flagg's and at Williams's in 1789. Mary C. Crawford, *Little Pilgrimages among Old New England Inns*, Boston, 1907, p. 160.

[2] Captain Levi Pease established a regular stage between Boston and Hartford as early as 1786. Worcester *Gazette*, January 5, 1786. Pease was born in Enfield, Connecticut, in 1740, but removed to Massachusetts, where Farrar's Tavern, at Shrewsbury, which he bought in 1794, is better known by his name. Crawford, *Old New England Inns*, pp. 36, 48, and 50.

where we were glad to stop the remainder of the day and night, during which time we had a deluge of Rain. This morning fair, windy & cold. In hopes of Letters from England by Col. Tudor.[3] When I orderd the things into the carriage, I saw a coat lined with Green Baize. Inquired to whom it belongd. No one knew. I presumed we had by mistake put Mr. Cranchs coat in with our own, as I heard you say he had a Lambskin one.

I would have returnd it by the stage but, they told us there was no security in sending it. I therefore wrote a Line & sent it to Mr. Packards [that *cancelled*] requesting them to send it on to Boston.[4] I have two cloase Lines both up. I wish when you see Mrs. Porter ask her to have one of them put up. We proceed as far as we can get to day. My best Love and regard attend you all. We are just sitting of.

Your affectionate Sister
A. Adams

East Chester, October 22, 1797

My dear Sister:

I have been from Quincy near 3 weeks. In all that time I have not heard a word from thence. I have written twice. I have not yet been into N[ew] York, and one might as well be out of America as in this village only 20 miles distant from N[ew] York, for unless we send in on purpose we cannot even get a Newspaper out. Yet are we in sight of the post road.[1] It is quite a village of Farmers who do not trouble their Heads about any thing, but the productiveness of their Farms. Mrs. Smith has lived here 18 months with making only one visit in the place. There is an Episcopal Church near here where there is divine service one [sic] a fortnight. Thiether we went last Sunday.

We have had some pleasent weather during the last week. I rejoiced in it, both on account of the Military parade & the Festival which was Brilliant indeed, and on Mrs. Norton's[2] account. I think it was the week she designd for her journey. Mrs. Smith is anxious to hear from

---

[3] Probably Colonel William Tudor, prominent merchant and scholar of Boston, who married Delia Jarvis and became the father of William Tudor (1779–1830), and Frederic (1783–1864), the Boston "Ice King."

[4] The Reverend Asa Packard (died 1843), Harvard, 1783, married Nancy Quincy, of Braintree, on July 27, 1799.

[1] The Boston Post Road, the highway between New York and Boston.

[2] Elizabeth (Cranch) Norton, wife of the Reverend Jacob Norton.

her Children. I fear in the multiplicity of Sister Peabodys cares, she will not think how desirious Mrs. Smith is of hearing from her Boys,[3] and she ought to receive all the comfort she can, for she has her full share of anxiety and trouble. I cannot leave her here this winter with not a single creature within 20 miles of her to speak a word to, or shorten the long solitary winter Evening.

I want her to take her little Girl & go with us to Philadelphia. Her feelings are such as you may suppose on such a proposal. What under different circumstances would have given her great pleasure, she now feels as a soar calimity [sic]. Yet I do not see what else she can do.

I make no reflections but in my own Breast. It is some comfort, to know that she has not been the cause, and that she could not prevent the misfortunes to which she is brought.

From the Col[onel] we have not heard, nor can I learn that his Brother has.

I hope you are well and the rest of our Friends. Tell Sister Smith[4] I will give her half a dollar pr pair for as many as she can knit for me, and I will send you the money to pay her and to get me some more cotton.

Tell Mrs. Brislers Friend, that I hear every day or two from him and that they are . . . .

[*The second page of this letter is missing.*]

East Chester, October 31, 1797

MY DEAR SISTER:

I have received but one Letter from you since I left Quincy now near a Month. I have been here three weeks, except 3 days which I past at my sons in N[ew] York.[1] Next Monday I leave here for Philadelphia, where it is thought we may now go with safety.

I was in hopes to have taken Mrs. Smith with me, but her situation is difficult, not having received any advise what to do, and she is loth to go for the present. I cannot say so much as is in my mind, the subject being a very delicate one, and wishing to have her do no one thing but what may prove beneficial to the whole. Sister Peabody has not yet

---

[3] William Steuben Smith, and John Adams Smith, grandsons of Mrs. John Adams, spent the winter of 1797-1798 with their great-aunt, Mrs. Elizabeth (Smith) [Shaw] Peabody, wife of the Reverend Stephen Peabody (A.B. Harvard, 1769), who was her second husband. The Peabodys lived in Atkinson, New Hampshire.

[4] Probably the second wife of William Smith, the brother of Mrs. Adams. The first wife of William Smith was Catherine Louisa Salmon.

[1] Probably in Beaver Street. See footnote 1 to the letter of May 16, 1797.

written to Mrs. Smith, which she regrets. I know how much she has been engaged, and fear the concequences upon her Health. She feels most keenly, and you know by experience what it is to pass through such a Heart rending trial. I wish these repeated summonses to the surviving Brothers might have a serious influence. The sisters are not unmindfull, but William has to me, the air of a too free thinker.[2]

Since I wrote you last I have Letters from my sons abroad, Thomas's late as 17 August. He has consented to go to Berlin with his Brother, who writes that he cannot by any means part with him, especially upon being sent into the center of Germany where I shall scarcly meet a Countryman twice a year," he says." and Thomas writes me, I intreet you to negotiate a successor to me, for I plainly see untill some such arrangement is made, I shall not be released. He says since I wrote you last, my Brother has been married and given me an amiable and accomplished sister.[3] He is very happy and I doubt not will remain so, for the Young Lady has much sweetness of Temper and seems to Love *as she ought*. Thomas speaks highly of the Family and of their kindness and attention to him, says they are about to embark for America & settle in the city of Washington, where Mr. Johnson has property. They will be an agreable acquisition to the city at which I rejoice for the sake of my Nephew and Neice.[4]

I have nothing of concequence to communicate. This place is as retired as you can imagine. We however keep up a communication with N[ew] York and Philadelphia. I had a Letter from Brisler, who was well with the rest of the Family yesterday.

I write merely to keep up our communication, and to tell you that we are all well. I will thank you to go to our House and see that particular attention is paid to the Carpets. I fear they will suffer. Adieu.

Yours affectionately
A. ADAMS

Philadelphia, Novbr. 15, 1797

MY DEAR SISTER:

I yesterday about 11 oclock went into the Presidents Room to see if John had returned from the post office. My good Gentleman was soberly

---

[2] "William" refers to Colonel William Stephens Smith, whose extravagance and long, silent absences from home were a source of great displeasure to Mrs. John Adams. Apparently the colonel's wife had appealed to his brothers and sisters for news of him.

[3] John Quincy Adams married Louisa Catherine Johnson, in London, on July 26, 1797.

[4] William and Anna (Greenleaf)Cranch. See footnote 8 to the letter of January 24, 1789.

standing at the fire with your Letter open and very gravely reading it. I scolded and very soon carried it of. I thank you for all your communications. The P[resident] says one of Sister Cranchs Letters is worth half a dozen others. She always tells us so much about home. And if he does not get them clandestinely he does not often see them. I wrote you a few lines the day before I left East Chester. On that day Mrs. Smith got Letters from her Brother Justice [Justus Smith] by a private hand, informing her that both he and the Col[onel] had written frequently by the post, and were astonished that she had not received any Letters, that by a private hand he had written and sent her some money in October. The Col[onel] was not then at Shenang [Shenango, Pennsylvania?], the Name of the place which Justice owns, but was expected in a few days. These Letters communicated some comfort. She came to N[ew] York with me in search of the Man by whom the money and Letter was sent. Since I have been here, I have had a Letter from her informing [me] that he had been sought where he formerly lived, but had removed from thence. I have contemplated the plan you mention. It may be put into effect if future circumstances require it. At present, it would be expensive and lonely, and not less subject to unpleasent feelings than being here on a visit, which is all that at present is expected, nor will she be obliged to appear on my publick Evenings, unless it is her choice.

I found Mr. and Mrs. Brisler and the Children very well and much the better for their country excursion. The Girls Becky and Nabby were very well, and both Mr. and Mrs. Brisler say, behaved with great prudence and discretion, quite to their satisfaction. I found every thing in the House in perfect good order, and all my old Hands escaped through the Pestilence.[1] One only of them had the fever. The others returnd as soon as Brisler got home, those whom he had dismisst when he went out, and those he retaind in pay, so that at present I could not wish to be better off than I am with respect to domesticks, which greatly enhances the comfort of Life.

I regret that there should be an opposition to Mr. Whitman,[2] and that

[1] Epidemics of yellow fever raged in Philadelphia in the summers of 1793, 1797, and 1798.

[2] On October 23, 1797, at a town meeting in Quincy, the Reverend Mr. Kilborn Whitman was offered the position as assistant to the Reverend Anthony Wibird, at a salary of five hundred dollars per annum and a house to live in. Mr. Whitman declined: see the letter of December 26, 1797.

it should principly arise from Mr. & Mrs. Black,[3] whom I very sincerely regard, tho I cannot say I respect their judgment in this case. I have not a doubt but Mr. and Mrs. Black will be reconciled in time. Reasoning and not railing will have the effect. Mr. Flint[4] was opposed by the latter. Present my compliment[s] to Mr. Whitman, & tell him if our State constitution had been equally liberal with that of New Jersey and admitted the females to a vote, I should certainly have exercised it in his behalf. As it is, he may be sure both of the Presidents and my good wishes for him, with a sincere desire for his settlement.

I have received one Letter from Sister Peabody written just after the death of Charles,[5] but Mrs. Smith has not had a line from her since her Children have been with her. Sister Peabody has so many cares that she has not much time to write, but I wish she would to Mrs. Smith. In her lonely hours she thinks much of her Children, and wishes to have from her Aunts hand some account of them. I have written her twice since I came from home, beside, one or two Letters just before I left home. I know not if she has received them. I am sorry to learn that Mrs. Cranch[6] is unwell. I have just been writing to him, and I have recommended to her to keep good spirits, and that it is a long lane which has no turn. Ask Cousin Betsy when I am to speak for the weding cap?[7] No Congress yet. A House but no Senate. Ben Bache is as usual abusing the President for *forceing* the respect from the people, degradeing this city by representing the military parade here as all forced. That it is a corrupt mass of Jacobinism, Quakerism and *abominationism*, I will most readily admit, but at the same time there are many worthy and respectable people here. Inclosd is a specimin of Bache Gall. But all will not do. I can see where the respect and attention is sincere. Many affecting proofs I have witnessed in this tour, one in particular of a private nature, at Brunswick [Maryland]. A white headed venerable Man desired to be admitted to the President. When he came in, he bowd respectfully and

---

[3] Probably Mr. and Mrs. Moses Black, who held the title to a mansion house in Quincy in February, 1788. Mr. Black's sister became that Mrs. Hall whose death, together with that of her husband, is mentioned in the letters of December 12 and 26, 1797.

[4] On July 31, 1797, at a town meeting in Quincy, the Reverend Jacob Flint, of Reading, was proposed as an assistant to Anthony Wibird, but refused the offer later because the salary was too small.

[5] Charles Smith, son of William Smith, brother of Mrs. John Adams, Mrs. Richard Cranch, and Mrs. Stephen Peabody.

[6] The wife of the brother of Richard Cranch (1726–1811).

[7] Elizabeth Quincy Shaw (1780–1798), daughter of Elizabeth (Smith) [Shaw] Peabody, by her first husband.

said he was happy to see him, inquired if that was his Lady? I came, said he, many miles this morning on purpose. I told my wife this morning that I would come, and she said why aint you affraid. No said I. Why do you think I should be affraid to go and see my Father? This was said with so much hearty sincerity, that to me it was of more value than the whole Military calvalcade [sic] of Pensilvannia.

Write me often, and remember me affectionatly to all Friends.

Yours as ever
ABIGAIL ADAMS

Philadelphia, Novbr. 28th, 1797

MY DEAR SISTER:

I received your kind Letter of Nov'br. 19th by this days post. I had previously received two others both of which I had replied to, but I do not know how to pass a week without hearing from you. At the same time I received your Letter, I also had one from Mrs. Smith informing me that she had received Letters from the Col[onel] of 2d of Nov'br and that he had written her word that he should be home soon. She accordingly gave up the thoughts of comeing to Philadelphia, which is a very great dissapointment to me. I fear she will be waiting & expecting, expecting & waiting, the rest of the winter, but I cannot advise her not to stay a reasonable time. She writes me in anxiety at not hearing a word from her Aunt. Sister Peabody did not use to be inattentive to her Friends. She knows the Boys are well and happy, but she should know that there Mother is not so, and for that reason is the more anxious for her Children, and wishes to have it to say that she hears often from them; for she may be blamed for placing them at such a distance from her, without considering the utility it is of to the Children. I have written repeatedly, so has Mrs. Smith, both to Sister and the Children. Before I left home I wrote & inclosed in one Letter a ten Dollor Bill. I never received any acknowledgment of it. Betsy[1] should write if her Mamma cannot. Pray do you represent the matter to her. I have requested that all Letters may be sent on under cover to the President at Philadelphia, and I will see them forwarded.

The city of Philadelphia is very Healthy at this time. I have had my Health much better than for several years past. I have not had a single days confinement since I left Quincy. The President took a bad cold by riding with the carriage windows down a very raw day in complasance

See footnote 7 to the preceding letter.

to the Military, and was confined ten days after we came here, but good Nursing got the better of it. The Senate and House have dispatchd their answers already to the speech.[2] I believe they were asshamd of their delay the last session. What, said the Duke de Liancourt[3] to the President, soon after the late constitution was adopted in France, do you think of our Constitution?[4] I think, replied the President, who was then Vice President, I think that the Directory are Daniel in the Lions Den. The Directory however, saw their Fate, and having an Army at their beck, banishd the Lions, before they devoured them. But still the Den ya[wns] for them and will sooner or later have them.

The measure of their iniquity is not yet full. They are instruments in the hands of Providence to scourge the nations of the Earth.

29th: Mr. Bartlet from Haverhill attended the Levee.[5] I requested the President to ask him to take a Family dinner with us, which he did, and I was happy to learn by him that he brought Letters to Mrs. Smith, so that I hope her mind is more at ease. I did now [sic] however get any, but that, as I hear they are well, I do not so much care for. I will thank you to make my Bacon for me, and when it is fit to smoak let Mr. Belcher carry it to the same place he got the other smoakd at. But I do not want it here. God Willing I will eat it at Home, & stay not an hour here longer than duty requires. I should like to have a Barrel of cheese sent if [it] can come immediatly. Otherways I fear we shall be frozen up. As to Butter I do not know as I am not there to make it myself I fear it will not be put up so as to keep. I hope Mrs. Pope will not forget me. Pork I should like to have a plenty of that.

[2] The second session of the Fifth Congress extended from November 13, 1797, to July 16, 1798.

[3] François Alexandre Frédéric, duc de La Rochefoucauld-Liancourt (1747-1827). This interesting nobleman founded on his estate, Liancourt, near Clermont, a model school for the education of the children of poor soldiers, called "École des Enfants de la Patrie," and was a member of the Estates-General in 1789, after which he was an emigré from France until the Consulate. As a result of his visit to North America, he wrote *Voyage dans les États-Unis, d'Amerique fait en 1795-1797* (1798), an English translation of which appeared as *Travels Through the United States of North America, the Country of the Iroquois, and Upper Canada*, London, 1799.

This duke is chiefly famous for the following colloquy with Louis XVI on the news of the fall of the Bastille, in 1789: "C'est une révolte?" "Non, Sire, c'est une révolution."

[4] The Third Constitution of the French Republic, that of 1795, which set up a Directory of five and a Legislature of two Chambers: the Council of Elders, and the Council of Five Hundred. This Constitution lasted till 1799, when it was replaced by the Consulate (1799-1804).

[5] Bailey Bartlett (1750-1830), of Haverhill, Massachusetts, member of the House of Representatives (1797-1801).

I inclose you a 5 dollor Bill. I forgot amongst my pensioners old Mrs. Hayden. Pray send her two, and get some salt peter & molasses with the other to do my Bacon. Will you be so good as to see that Pheby does not suffer for wood or any necessary.

I this moment have received a Letter from your son of 21 Nov'br, a very excellent Letter. He writes me that Mrs. Cranch was better, that Richard had been sick with the Quincy but was better. William had a bad cold.[6] He is doing well I hope. He writes in pretty good spirits. No News of Mr. Johnsons Family tho they saild the 10 of Sepbr.[7] I am under great fears for them.

I think Baxters resolution a good one. The next News I expect the parson will be courting. I am sorry to hear Mrs. Greenleaf has been so unwell. My Love to her and Mrs. Norton. A kind remembrance to all Friends.

Affectionatly your Sister
A. ADAMS

Philadelphia, December 12th, 1797

MY DEAR SISTER:

I received yesterday your kind favour of 29 Nov'br and 8th December. I had a few lines from you on Monday. I got my Letter to day to myself. I believe I shall not venture to communicate it. The President will be very angry with some of his Neighbours, if through their means we lose so good a Man, as is now in our power to settle.[1] The judgement of those in opposition is weak. I would sooner take the opinion of *Gains*, with regard to the merit of a preacher than either of them. I do not know what their objections are. Spear ought to know that the Scriptures combine the Gosple with the Law. I fancy Mr. B[lack]'s objection[s] are not much more forcible. I think Mr. Whitman ought not to decline merely on account of those persons, who all of them, I have not a doubt, will be conciliated by a prudent conduct. To Mr. Flint there was an obstinate intemperate opposition from a certain quarter which I always condemned, and tho I did not like Mr. Flint so well as Mr. Whitman as a preacher, yet both the President and I determined to sit down quietly

---

[6] Richard and William Cranch were sons of William Cranch (1769–1855), who married Anna Greenleaf (1772–1843) in 1795.

[7] Joshua Johnson, of a Maryland family, was the father-in-law of John Quincy Adams, and a brother of Thomas Johnson (1732–1819).

[1] For the choice of Kilborn Whitman as assistant to Anthony Wibird of Quincy, see footnote 2 to the letter of November 15, 1797.

with him if he had accepted the call of the people. I have a regard for, and Love my Neighbours but I cannot but condemn their conduct on this occasion and look upon it as mere obstinancy [sic] to make themselves of concequence. Poor Mrs. Hall & her Husband are both dead. They left a Child, but for some reason, I cannot devine what, her Brother will not let me, or any of the Family find it or see it, tho on Mr. Blacks account and from the regard I had for Mrs. Hall I have taken some pains to find it, and know how it was situated. I have written to Mrs. Black respecting it.[2]

Mrs. Smith is gone back to East Chester determined to wait there the arrival of the Col[onel]. We had a Letter from him this week. He was then at fort Stanwick[3] on his way to East Chester, he says. It was dated 29th November. It was directed to Thomas [Adams] supposing him, private Secretary to the President.

We have not any late Letters from London. I presume Mr. [J. Q.] Adams is gone to Berlin. I had a Letter from Thomas [Adams] dated the 10 of Sep'br. Thomas speaking of his new sister says, "She is indeed a most lovely woman, and in my opinion worthy in every respect of the Man for whom she has with so much apparent Cheerfulness renounced father and Mother kindred and Country to unite her destinies with his." This is a great deal for Thomas to say.

I inclose to you some remarks from Fennos paper upon some of Baches lies and abuse and a strip of paper containing Baches round assertion that the observations Printed in the Boston Centinel upon the Sermon of the Bishop of Norwich were *"Positively known"* to proceed from the pen of the Duke of Braintree, as he stiles the President.[4] If this has not been printed in any of our papers, let it be sent to the Mer-

[2] See footnote 3, to the letter of November 15, 1797.

[3] Fort Stanwix, on the Mohawk River, in Oneida County, New York. It was erected in 1758 by John Stanwix (1690–1765).

[4] See the *Columbian Centinel* for Wednesday, November 8, 1797. On February 17, 1797, Charles, Bishop of Norwich, preached in London at the Church of St. Mary le Bow, "before the society for propagating the gospel in foreign parts [sic]." After paying an elegant tribute to the character of George Washington, the bishop, probably with the thought of encouraging contributions, dwelt so feelingly on the need for spreading the gospel in North America as to make certain citizens of the United States think that he was describing their state of society as little better than that of savages. This letter of protest, signed "An American," occupies a column and a half on the first page.

Charles Manners-Sutton (1755–1828), grandson of John, third duke of Rutland, and a favorite with George III and his family, became Bishop of Norwich in 1792, Dean of Windsor in 1794, and, in 1805, against the wishes of William Pitt, who wanted the place for another, was made Archbishop of Canterbury. His son was Speaker of the House of Commons, and first Viscount Canterbury (1780–1845).

cury[5] to insert, that the world may see what bold and dareing lies these wretches are capable of. Yet when calld upon for proof, they have not a word to offer. The wretch who is supposed to have written this for the Aurora is a Hireling Scotchman Campbel[6] by name, who fled from England for publishing libels against the Government, and has been employd by the Jacobins here to excite a spirit of opposition to the Government. Who the writer of those remarks upon the Bishops Sermon was, is as well known to the Pope of Rome, as to the President. Scarcly a day passes but some such scurility appears in Baches paper, very often unnoticed, and of no concequence in the minds of many people, but it has, like vice of every kind, a tendency to corrupt the morrals of the common people. Lawless principles naturally produce lawless actions.— I have not heard from your son since I wrote you last. I am glad to learn that Mrs. Greenleaf is like to get rid of her complaint by a collection of the cause of it to one point. I dare say she will find herself better. Miss Alleyne is gone to Levingstone Manor to pass the winter with her sister. Mr. G[reenlea]f is yet confined, tho I believe he hopes soon to be liberated.[7] The vice President is come and dines here to day with 30 other Gentleman.

Remember me kindly to Mr. Cranch and respectfully to Mrs. Welch. Tell Cousin Betsy I will send her an old Maids cap, that will never be out of fashion.

Love to Mrs. Norton and family. How much charigned [sic] shall I feel if you write me that Mr. Whitman has given his answer in the Negative. I hate Negatives when I have sit my Heart upon any thing. Half the year I must sit under as strong Calvinism as I can possibly swallow and the other half, I do not know what is to come.

My paper reminds me to close, and my company that I must dress for dinner.

Yours most affectionately
A. ADAMS

[5] The *Massachusetts Mercury*, published in Boston.

[6] Possibly George Washington Campbell (1769–1848), who was born in Scotland, was christened George and added Washington to his name later. He was a member of the House of Representatives for Tennessee from 1803 to 1809, an ardent supporter of Jefferson, and an enemy of John Randolph of Roanoke.

[7] For the release of James Greenleaf (1765–1843), speculator in land, see footnote 5, to the letter of June 6, 1797. For James Greenleaf and his two wives, Antonia Cornelia Albertine Schotten (divorced 1800) and Ann Penn Allen, see Greenleaf, *Greenleaf Family*, pp. 217–8. For the Stuart portrait of Greenleaf, see Anne H. Wharton, *Social Life in the Early Republic*, Philadelphia, 1903, p. 30.

[*Enclosed with letter of December 12, 1797.*]

Mr. Bache and his correspondents appear to be in great distress least the respect shown to the President of the United States by the people of every City and Town through which he past on his journey to his own Home, and on his return to the Seat of Government, should be construed into a satisfaction with the Government, and an approbation of its administration. As Mr. Bache is but a youth of yesterday, when compared with the old Patriots who first stood forth in defence of the invaded Rights of their injured Country against the usurpation of Great Britain, I who am grown grey with years, and was witness to what I relate, can tell him, that the Testimonials of respect which have recently been offerd to the President of the United States, are no Novelties to him.

Previous to the meeting of the first Congress in the year 1774, the Members from Massachusetts, (our venerable President was one,) were met, escorted and Feasted, (if you please) in all the principal Towns and citys through which they past. The same publick marks of respect were again manifested with increased splendour, at the Meeting of Congress in the year 1775. In the year 1789 when the President was first Elected vice president, a Troop of Horse waited upon him at his Seat in Braintree, and escorted him from thence to the Governours in Boston accompanied by Numbers of citizens. From thence he was attended to Cambridge by a large, and respectable concourse of people, where he was again met by an other Troop of Horse.

Throughout the State of Conneticut he received the same marked attention. The citizen[s] of New York were not less Zealous on that occasion, than they have been, to do honour to him as President. Troops of Horse, and respectable citizens went as far as Kings Bridge,[8] and escorted him into the City of New York.

Every person who is acquainted with the Republican manners and habits of the President can witness for him, that every kind of show and parade are contrary to his tastes and inclination, and that they can be agreeable on no other ground, than as the Will of the People, Manifesting their determined resolution to support the Government, and the Administrators of it, so long as the administration is conformable to the Constitution. As to Mr. Baches polite allusion to Darby and

[8] Kings Bridge, or Phillipse' Bridge, or the Bridge at Spuyten Duyvil. This bridge connected the extreme northeastern tip of Manhattan Island with the mainland. John Adams was welcomed there at four o'clock in the afternoon of April 20, 1789, on his way to the home of John Jay. See Stokes, *Iconography of Manhattan Island*, index, pp. 328 and 458; vol. 1, plate 46; and vol. 5, p. 1238.

Joan,[9] I consider that as highly honorary to the domestic and conjugal Character of the President who has never given His Children or Grandchildren cause to Blush for any illegitimate ofspring.

Philadelphia, December 26, 1797

My dear Sister:

I received your Letter by this days mail of 17th. I am mortified at the loss of Mr. Whitman,[1] tho from what you wrote me I apprehended it would be so. Every one has a right to their own opinion, and my conscience suffers as much when I hear Mr. & Mr. & Mr. deliver sentiments which I cannot assent to & preach doctrines which I cannot believe, as my Neighbours because a Man does not wear Calvinism in his face, and substitute round Os for Ideas. But we must be doomed to a—a droomadery. I am out of patience, and yet I am brought down, for last week I was obliged to lose Blood, and confine myself for a week in concequence of one of my old attacks. I had some Rhumatism with it, but am getting better, and should have ventured to ride out to day if the weather would have permitted.

I could not see company on fryday Evening, nor the Gentlemen to day who attend the Levee. Mrs. Cushing[2] came last evening and took tea with me. I promise myself some society with her. Most of the rest is parade & ceremony. Next Monday is New Years Day and we shall have a tedious time of it. I thank you for the care of my Bacon & carpets. I had much rather they should be down on your floor than not. As to the Chair, I pray you take it. I had Letters from Mrs. Smith this week. She thought it best to part with Mr. & Mrs. King as her family were small, so that she now has only one Man to look after the Stock, and a Boy & Girl. In that manner she lives without a Human being to call upon her from one week to an other, buoyd up with an expectation of the Col[onel]'s return, which however I have very little faith in. The old Lady[3] is going out to stay with her now, which will render her situation more tolerable. I know she relucts at the thought of comeing here. If I was in private Life she would feel differently.

[9] Darby and Joan, a married pair who are said to have lived in the West Riding of Yorkshire in the eighteenth century. They are the subject of a ballad called "The Happy Old Couple," said to have been written by Henry Woodfall. The names first appeared in print in the *Gentleman's Magazine* (1735), vol. 5, p. 153.
[1] See footnote 2 to the letter of November 15, 1797.
[2] Wife of Justice William Cushing (1732–1810). See footnote 10 to the letter of January 24, 1789.
[3] Mother of Colonel William Stephens Smith, son-in-law of John Adams.

I was fully sensible that the Boys must be taken from all their connections to break them of habits which they had imbibed. There were a train of uncles and Aunts and servants to spoil them and very few examples such as I wisht to have them inrured to, and I dread their Fathers return least he should take it into his Head to take them away.[4]

I rejoice to hear that Mrs. Norton and Family are well. I hope Mrs. Greenleaf will recover her Health. Slip the inclosed into her Hand when you see her, and say nothing about it.

Where is Mr. Wibird[5] & is he this winter? multiplying and increasing as he was? 5 dollors are inclosed that you may apply them to the use of Pheby as her necessities may be. I have not heard from Washington[6] since I wrote you last.

I have been the communicator of very melancholy News to Mr. & Mrs. Black. I was much shocked when John returnd from Mr. Halls House and brought me word that they were both dead, and when the Baby at my request, was sent to me to see, I felt for the poor little orphan an inexpressible tenderness. It is a fine Baby and the Image of its poor Broken Hearted Mother, who the Physicians agree, dyed with fatigue and dejection of spirits without any symptoms of the fever. I hope Mr. & Mrs. Black will take the child, as soon as it is weaned.[7]

The President has agreed that he will not open any more Letters to me, and will be satisfied with such parts as I am willing to communicate. Accordingly he has not opend any since I scolded so hard about it. Pray if you have got the Song of Darby and Joan do send it me.[8] I do not recollect but one line in it, and that is, "when Darbys pipes out Joan wont smoke a whiff more." and I know they were represented as a fond loving conjugal pair. Baches object was to bring such a Character into Ridicule. True French manners in Religion and politicks is what he aims to introduce, but corrupt as our manners are, there is yet too much virtue to have such doctrines universally prevail.

Remember me to all our Friends whom I hope to see again in the Spring. And be assured I am, my dear Sister,

Your ever affectionate
ABIGAIL ADAMS

[4] William Steuben Smith, and John Adams Smith, who were spending the winter with their great-aunt, Mrs. Elizabeth (Smith) [Shaw] Peabody, in Atkinson, New Hampshire.
[5] See footnote 1 to the letter of October 4, 1789.
[6] That is, from her nephew, William Cranch, son of Mary (Smith) Cranch.
[7] See footnote 3 to the letter of November 15, 1797.
[8] See footnote 9 to the enclosure with the letter of December 12, 1797.

Philadelphia, Jan'ry 5th, 1798

My dear Sister:

I received your kind Letter of December and was surprized to find that my Letter should convey the first intelligence of the death of Mr. & Mrs. Hall to Mr. & Mrs. Black, as their Brother assured me he had written three weeks before.[1] I told him I would take charge of any Letter from him, and could nearly vouch for its going safely.

I was much dissatisfied when Mrs. Brisler sought the Child so earnestly and could not find it, and thought it my duty to inform Mrs. Black of it, as I did immediately upon his [Mr. Black's brother] sending the child to me.[2] My own conclusions were that it was at Nurse with some person, and in some place that he did not chuse my people should see. However this may be, the Nurse who brought the child and whom I saw Nurse it in my Chamber whilst she stay'd, is a very decent, respectable, healthy looking woman, above the common level of such persons here.

I have already written Mrs. Black my opinion of her and her replies to such questions as I put to her; I shall send some of my people to see the child as you say, when they are not expected, and I will have it brought me as often as once a Month, and I will let the Nurse know, that the Child has relatives who are much interested for it, and design to take it in the Spring, if the Child lives untill the Spring. The sooner Mr. Black comes for it, the better, for this city is a very unhealthy place for children.

As soon as Mrs. Brisler is well enough she will go with Betsy, and see the Baby. Mrs. Brisler has had one of her old ill turns, but is better.

I expect that your next Letter will bring me tydings of Abbe's death. I look upon it [as] a release to Pheby, but I am fully sensible her days of usefullness are nearly over and what is to be done with her I cannot

---

[1] See footnote 3 to the letter of November 15, 1797.

[2] Ann (or Anna) Hall, the orphan niece of Moses Black, of Quincy, and a distant relative of John Adams. "Moses Black's will left $1000 each to Anna Black Lamb and Mrs. Roxanna Blake and all his real estate in Quincy to his wife 'provided that if my said wife marry again, that I give and devise one-half of said Quincy real estate to Anna Hall.'" Daniel Munro Wilson, *Where American Independence Began*, Boston and New York, 1902, pp. 187-8. The interest of Mrs. John Adams in this infant Hall orphan probably sprang from the fact that some time after the death of the father of President John Adams, his widow married a "Mr. Hall." On the death of her second husband, Mrs. Susanna (Boylston) [Adams] Hall seems to have made her home with Mrs. Richard Cranch, probably because of the prolonged absence of John and Abigail Adams from Braintree, or Quincy. Both Abigail Adams and Mary Cranch were devoted to the aged mother of John Adams. She died on April 21, 1797. *Columbian Centinel*, May 3, 1797.

tell.³ For this winter she must remain where she is, but there is no reason that the whole of the House should be devoted to her as it is in a manner, for no other person will occupy it, who will give any thing for it, whilst she resides there, and she must have somebody to look after her. 12 or 13 years she has lived there, and never paid a sou. More than that she has lately received as much as her House rent from me, and as long as I am able I shall be willing to do for her, but I think some new plan must be struck out for her.

I received Letters from Sister Peabody yesterday for myself and Mrs. Smith. She thinks Mr. Atwood ought to have some acknowledgment made to him for his trouble. She says Charles left a New Watch worth 20 dollors.⁴ Suppose that should be given him, but I know not who has a right to do it. To Miss Sarah Atwood she also thinks some Handsome present ought to be made. Query who ought to make these presents? She ought to have what is reasonable and proper & handsome considering all circumstances, but the situation of Charles Family is well known. They are not in independant circumstances. I would not have them however receive from Strangers obligations which should be thought the Family ought to reward. Sister Peabody has twice written me upon this subject. She says Charles left in money about 40 dollors with which she has paid all extra Charges. His Cloaths which were given him by Mr. Atwood I think ought all to return to Mr. Atwood. He was his appretence [*sic*] and Mr. Atwood received from him all the service of his time &c. He treated him like a child in his sickness, and I shall ever esteem & respect the Family for it. I wish you would consult Dr. [Cotton] Tufts and Mr. [Richard] Cranch upon it. I will be at the expence of a Ring for Mrs. Atwood such as Cousin Betsy Smith has for Mrs. Rogers.⁵ Pray inquire of her and get her to have one made with Charles Name & present it to Mrs. Atwood for me, and I will pay for it. I do not want this known however beyond ourselves. Tis true he was my Nephew, but not the only relative I had or have who stands in need of pecuniary assistance. Marys sickness was much longer and more expensive. That, too, ought to be considerd.

³ Abbe is probably Mrs. Joseph Field, to whom a daughter was born in 1752, and Phebe is probably Phebe Trask, who married Henry Field in April, 1767. See the letter of June 4, 1798.
⁴ Charles Smith, son of that William Smith who was the brother of Mrs. John Adams, died in 1797. See footnote 5 to the letter of November 15, 1797. Charles Smith was apprenticed to Mr. Atwood.
⁵ Possibly a relation of John Rodgers. See the letter of October 4, 1789.

I wish you would write me fully upon the subject and whether you have had any Letters from William since the death of his Brother.

The News from abroad of the Peace made by the Emperor with the Directory of France (to call it a Republick would be a subversion of terms) is an Event big with concequences.[6] The treatment of our envoys, as rumourd, for the Executive has not received any communication from them since their arrival in France, excites however unpleasant sensations, for the insolent proposition & threat sent to Switserland a Nutral power shows us that tyrants stick at nothing.[7] The threatned invasion of England I do not much credit. They may be mad enough however to attempt it, for I believe they fear nothing so much as disbanding there [sic] Armies.

Our American Minister in England is making a Tour of it, so that at this most critical moment the Government is indebted to News Paper intelligence for all they have.[8] "I never left my post a moment but upon business for my Country during the whole war," crys—you know who.[9] But my paper is full, and the post will be gone. Adieu my dear Sister.

Affectionatly your[s]
[A.] Adams

[6] On April 18 and October 17, 1797, Francis II, Holy Roman Emperor—Francis I, Emperor of Austria, after 1806—first dealt with the government of revolutionary France by authorizing the signing of the treaties of Leoben and Campo Formio, the most important articles of which provided for the cession to France of the Belgian Provinces and the left bank of the Rhine. This left England standing alone as the only nation at war with the victorious French—a fact of great significance for the future.

[7] The "ancient inviolability" of the neutrality of the Swiss Confederation is a journalistic myth, dating approximately from 1914. As early as 1792 a French army entered the territory of Geneva, in order to "coöperate" with the "democratic" party of that city. On December 15, 1797, a French force seized Basle, and on March 6, 1798, the troops of Bonaparte captured Berne, the treasure of which, £800,000, was taken in order to provide pay for the conqueror's army. To "compensate" the plundered Swiss, the new "Helvetic Republic, one and indivisible," was proclaimed at Aarau. C. A. Fyffe, *A History of Modern Europe*, vol. 1, New York, 1881, pp. 151–3.

[8] Rufus King (1755–1827) was born in Maine, and settled in New York City in 1786, having married the only daughter of a wealthy merchant there. Serving as American minister to England from 1796 to 1803, King is said to have been "one of the most effective representatives the United States has ever had at London." Channing, *History of the United States*, vol. 4, p. 353.

[9] John Adams spent his summers on his farm at Quincy, Massachusetts. In 1798 Mrs. Adams was seriously ill, and the President of the United States stayed away from the seat of government at Philadelphia from midsummer to November, and at a most critical time, when relations with France were strained to the breaking-point.

Philadelphia, Janry 20, 1798

MY DEAR SISTER:

I do not know whether there is any getting over the Rivers. The Eastern Mail due yesterday is not arrived. The Ice has been broken up for two or three days past. Mr. B. Beals who has been here more than a week, talked of leaving the city yesterday.[1] I have given him a little matter addrest to Cousin Betsy. It is a small Box of the size of a little plate. In it you will find a shawl handkerchief which is for you and tho almost the only covering worn by our Ladies here, in the winter, you will think it more proper for April or May. My sattin fur Cloak is almost singular.

I wrote to Mrs. Black yesterday and shall certainly be very attentive to the Child. It grows finely.

We had some snow at the same time you had, but a much less quantity. We have had some very fine weather this Month, and it still continues. I wish our political Horizon look[ed] as bright as our Natural one does, but we have a dark prospect. I am at a loss to know how the people who were formerly so much alive to the usurpation of one Nation can crouch so tamely to a much more dangerous and dareing one, to one which aims not only at our independance and libety [sic] but a total annihilation of the Christian Religion, whose Laws, all which they have, are those of Draco, who are Robbers, Murderers, Scoffers, backbiters.[2] In short no crime however black or Horrid to which they have not become familiar. America must be punished, punished for having amongst her legislatures Men who sanction these crimes, who justify France in all her measures, and who would rejoice to see fire, sword and Massacre carried into the Island of Great Britain untill she became as misirable, as France is wretched.

O My Native State, wash ye, make yourselves clean from these abominations. You are Guilty of sending three such Men, V[arnu]m, F[reema]n, S[kinn]er.[3] Not a single state but what has some, Conneticut ex-

---

[1] Beals or Beal. Probably the captain of the frigate mentioned in the letter of May 29, 1798, plying between Philadelphia and Boston. See the letters of February 6, March 5, and June 13, 1798.

[2] Draco, or Dracon, an Athenian legislator who formulated the first code of laws for Athens, about 624 B.C. Because of the number of offences to which his code affixed the penalty of death, it was often said to have been "written in blood."

[3] See the letters of May 24 and June 3, 1797. Varnum favored national defence through the militia as against a standing army, opposed building the *Constitution* and other naval vessels, and denounced what he called the personal extravagance of President John Adams. Varnum was Speaker of the House of Representatives (1807–1811).

cepted, tho many of them would not go all lengths. Virginia has but two Federilists, North Carolina but one. Can we expect such measures to be adopted as the safety and security of the Country require? Every Man who sees the danger may toil & toil; like Syssaphass [Sisyphus], (I believe the Name is misspelt) the weight recoils. We have Letters from Mr. Murry.[4] A few lines from Mr. Marshall to him informs him: that the envoys were not received, and he did not believe they would be.[5] They dare not write, knowing that every word would be inspected. They have not been permitted to hold any society or converse with any citizen. In short they have been in a mere Bastile. We are in daily expectation of their return.

I expected from what you last wrote to hear of Abbes death. Pheby will be surrounded as long as there is any thing to eat or drink, and I suppose she will think [it] very hard to be obliged to alter her mode of living. But tho I am willing to assist towards her mantanance, I do not like to support all she may keep with her, and her whole income would not find her wood. Untill Spring it would be best she should remain where she is. I would have Mr. Porter let her have a Bushel of corn. The money I sent, you will lay out for wood or otherways as you think best. It would not do for me to order her any more wood but I would buy for her. That is an article she must have. Pray order her some when she wants and I will pay for it. The negro woman who lives with her should be obliged to find some, for she pays no rent. You will be so good as to let me know how she is.

Mrs. Smith is still at East Chester, waiting & expecting! I have just had a line from Sister Peabody of Jan'ry 5th. All well.

I could very easily forgive Mr. [Peter] Whitney, and should still like him for our minister. I am sorry he was not better advised. I suppose Mr. [Anthony] Wibird will not think of removeing now there is a female in the House. I do not know but Mr. Wibird himself may go and do likewise.[6] Remember me affectinatly [sic] to all our dear Friends.

Ever your affectionate Sister
Abigail Adams

[4] William Vans Murray (1760-1803), of Maryland, was a member of the House of Representatives (1791-1797), and a loyal Federalist and close adviser of Washington, who sent him as minister to the Netherlands in February, 1797. For some time Vans Murray was the sole official channel of communication between the French Directory and the government of the United States.

[5] C. C. Pinckney, John Marshall, and Elbridge Gerry were appointed envoys-extraordinary to France by John Adams in the spring of 1797—the "XYZ Mission."

[6] See footnote 5 to the letter of May 16, 1797.

Philadelphia, Febry [1–5], 1798

My dear Sister:

Your kind Letter of Jan'ry 14th I received last week. I shall not be dissatisfied with Mr. Whitney if the people are disposed to give him a call, but far otherways. I shall rejoice in the prospect of having so virtuous and sensible a Gentleman setled with us, to whom I doubt not, years will teach more knowledge of the word.

I can understand you well, tho you do not speak plain. I know you think that there may be allowd a greater latitude of thought and action at the Bar than in the pulpit. I allow it, and yet each Character be perfectly honourable & virtuous.

You ask me, What has Cox done that he is dismist.[1] I answer a Man of his Character ought not to have been employd where he was. At the Time the British were in [possession *cancelled*] this State, Mr. Cox then a young man, went from this city and joind them, and as a Guide led them into this city with a chaplet of ever Greens round his Head. When this Government was about to be establisht, he turnd about, and possessing some talents became a warm advocate for the Federal Government. He possess[es] specious talents. He got Col[onel] Hamilton to appoint him first Clerk in His office whilst he was Secretary of the treasury. In this office he continued till it is said Hamilton found him very troublesome to him, and not wanting to have him an Enemy, he contrived to get the office of Commissoner [*sic*] of the Revenue created, and Cox appointed to it. When Hamilton resignd, Cox expected to be appointed in his Room but finding Mr. Wolcot prefered befor him, he was much mortified.[2] And at the late Election for President, he became a writer in the papers and in pamphlets against the administration of Washington and a Partizen for Jefferson. But no sooner was the Election determined, than Sycophant like he was, worshiping the rising Sun outwardly, whilst secretly he was opposing and thwarting every measure recommended by the President for the defence of the Country. But

[1] Tench Coxe (1755–1824), of Pennsylvania, was the author of an able pamphlet, *An Examination of the Constitution of the United States* (1788), which marked him as an active Federalist. Coxe was made Assistant Secretary of the Treasury in 1789, and became Commissioner of the Revenue in 1792. Adams removed him in December, 1797; whereupon Coxe promptly went over to the "Republicans" and helped in the defeat of Adams in 1800, by publishing a letter which Adams indiscreetly wrote to him in 1792, blaming Hamilton for the appointment of Thomas Pinckney as minister to England. Hamilton struck back at Adams with his notorious election letter of 1800.

[2] Although John Adams gave no official reason for removing Coxe, it was commonly believed that his Secretary of the Treasury, Oliver Wolcott, Jr., persuaded him to take this step, even though Wolcott was a creature of Hamilton, and disloyal to Adams.

this was not all. He was constantly opposing and obstructing the Secretary of the Treasury in his department. A Man of no sincerity of views or conduct, a Changling as the Wind blow, & a Jacobin in Heart.

You will see by the papers I send you the debate continued by Congress for 15 days and yet undetermined, upon the foreign intercourse Bill.[3] These debates will be a clue to unfold to you the full system of the Minority, which is to usurp the Executive Authority into their own Hands. You will see much said about the Patronage of the President and his determination to appoint none to office, as they say, who do not think exactly with him. This is not true in its full extent. Lamb the Collector was not dismist from office for his Jacobin sentiments, but for his Peculation, Jarvis for Peculation, Cox for opposing the Government in its opperations.[4] The P[resident] has said, and he still says, he will appoint to office merit, virtue & Talents, and when Jacobins possess these, they will stand a chance, but it will ever be an additional recommendation that they are Friends to order and Government. President Washington had reason to Rue the day that he departed from this Rule, but at the commencement of the Government, when parties were not so high, and the Country not in danger from foreign factions, it was thought it would tend to cement the government. But the Ethiopen [sic] could not Change his Skin, and the Spots of the Leopard have been constantly visible, tho sometimes shaded.[5] I cannot think [the] Virgin[i]a

[3] Much of the time of the Second Session of the Fifth Congress (November 13, 1797–July 16, 1798) was consumed in the House of Representatives by the impeachment of Senator Blount, of Tennessee; consequences of the feud between Griswold, of Connecticut, and Lyon, of Vermont; and a long debate on what was called the Foreign Intercourse Bill—"A Bill Providing the Means of Intercourse between the United States and Foreign Nations." When Robert G. Harper, of South Carolina, brought this bill to the floor of the House, he caused an explosion of oratory which sputtered for weeks. The bill was designed to establish the diplomatic and consular service by means of amending the acts of July 1, 1790, and February 9, 1793. The opponents of the Federalists attacked it on principle, and also because the son of the President was minister to Berlin, and the unpopular William Loughton Smith, of South Carolina, had been appointed minister to Spain and Portugal on July 10, 1797. The opposition to the bill was led by John Nicholas (1756–1819), member of the House from Virginia. The Senate finally passed this bill as it came up from the House on March 13, 1798. *Annals of the Fifth Congress*, p. 521.

[4] John Lamb (1735–1800), a native of New York, became prosperous as a wine merchant and served with credit during the Revolution. In 1784 the New York Legislature, of which he was a member, appointed him Collector of the Customs of the port of New York. Washington renewed this appointment in 1789. In 1797 a shortage in the accounts of Lamb's deputy, a former criminal, forced Lamb to resign his office; he sold his lands to cover the lost funds, and died in poverty. For William Jarvis and Tench Coxe, see footnote 6 to the letter of June 3, 1797, and footnotes 1 and 2 above.

[5] "Can the Ethiopian change his skin, or the leopard his spots? then may ye also do good, that are accustomed to do evil." *Jeremiah*, XIII, 23.

declamation will make many converts, for how stupid would that man be thought in private Life who should put the care and oversight of his affairs into the Hands of such persons as he knew would counteract all his instruction, and destroy all his property?[6]

Vague and contradictory accounts are in circulation respecting our Envoys. One thing is certain. No official communication has been received from them, from whence I judge they do not think it safe to make any. Bache is in tribulation. He publishd last Saturday an attack upon the Secretary of State for receiving as he said 5 dollors for a pasport which should have been deliverd Gratis. One Dr. Reynolds appears to have been at the bottom of the buisness, an Irish scape Gallows who fled here from the justice of his country charged as he was with treason against it, and a reward of a hundred Guineys was offerd for him by the British Government. A person wholy unknown to the Secretary but one of Baches slanderers and employd by him as it is said to write libels. I hope the Rascals will be persued, to the extent of the Law.[7]

It is time to leave politicks for my paper is already full. We had a very heavy storm last week and it looks more like winter now than since I have been here.

Mr. Greenleaf has been sick, but I believe he is quite recoverd. I hear

---

[6] What Mrs. Adams called the "Virginia declamation" were the long and formidable speeches in which John Nicholas, of Virginia, attacked the Foreign Intercourse Bill. Nicholas used three chief arguments in opposing this bill:

1. He hoped "to bring back" the consular and diplomatic service to the "simple" days of 1789.
2. He accused John Adams of filling up appointments to the foreign service with his partisan supporters, that is, with Federalists.
3. He thought that the United States would be better off if it were to have no ministers at all!

Nicholas was a crank, and consequently one of the very first American "isolationists"— "Mr. Nicholas considered the subject of this bill as one of the most important that could come before the Legislature, for he attributed all our misfortunes to this source. He thought we ought to have no political connexion with Europe, but be considered, in relation to that continent, as mere buyers and venders [sic] of their manufactures." *Annals of the Fifth Congress*, p. 922.

In 1803 Nicholas removed to Ontario County, New York, and died destitute in 1819.

[7] On November 12, 1796, Thomas Wotherspoon, a Scottish merchant, got a passport in Philadelphia, for which he gave one of the clerks of Timothy Pickering a gratuity of five dollars, in silver. Over a year later, Bache published the story of this transaction in the *Aurora* of January 24, 1798. Pickering dismissed both his first and second clerk, and wrote to the *Aurora*. Bache gave Dr. James Reynolds as the source of his information, possibly the same James W. Reynolds whose so-called wife, Maria Lewis, blackmailed Alexander Hamilton in 1791 and 1792. Maria Lewis sometimes called herself the wife of Jacob Clingman, a confederate of Reynolds. Charles W. Upham, *The Life of Timothy Pickering*, Boston, 1873, vol. 3, pp. 308–12.

WILLIAM STEPHENS SMITH, 1786 *Mather Brown*

of him frequently and I am told that no comfort or convenience is wanting but that of Liberty, that unfortunately there is but too much company, for I have been Credibly informd that as many as two Hundred Heads of Families and persons formerly in good circumstances are now in confinement. Mr. Greenleaf expects soon to be liberated by a Law of this State which is now before the Legislature.[8]

I had Letters from Mrs. Smith last week, the col[onel] was not returnd, nor do I much believe that he will. I believe I mentiond to you to get Sister Smith to knit me some Stockings, but I wholy forget whether I sent any money either to buy cotton or pay her.[9]

I wish you would mention to Mrs. Black to make a cap for the Baby and inclose it to me. It will have a good Effect I know in fixing in the mind of the Nurse a Certainty that it has Relations who attend to it. I inquired of the Nurse if it was well provided fir [sic]. She said it had sufficient for the present, and she always brings it clean and well enough drest. I know it will give you pleasure to learn that Mr. & Mrs. [J. Q.] Adams had arrived safe at Hamburgh in October & left it for Berlin on the 2d of Nov'br. We learn this from Mr. Murry by a Letter of Novbr 7th.[10] We have not received any letters of a later date than Sep'br. We are all at present in the enjoyment of Health. Mrs. Cushing came in last Evening in the sisterly manner & past the Evening with me. With Mrs. Otis and her I could fancy myself at Quincy.[11]

I bear my drawing Rooms, sometimes crowded, better than I expected, tho I always feel the Effects of the lights the next day.

My affectionate Regards to all Friends young or old from your
Sister
A. ADAMS

P.S.
Pray let me hear from Polly. I am very uneasy about her.

Just as I had written the last sentance yours of 20th was brought me. Alass poor Polly. My Heart aches for her. I shall dread to hear again. If she wants wine pray send from my cellar as much as she may have

---

[8] James Greenleaf was discharged from bankruptcy in 1798, under "one of the earliest American bankruptcy laws . . . that of Maryland." Channing, *History of the United States*, vol. 5, p. 193.

[9] "Mrs. Smith" is Abigail (Adams) Smith, wife of Colonel William Stephens Smith. "Sister Smith" is Martha (White) Smith, wife of William Smith, the Boston merchant, brother of Mrs. John Adams.

[10] For William Vans Murray, see footnote 4 to the letter of January 20, 1798.

[11] For Mrs. Justice William Cushing, see footnote 10 to the letter of January 24, 1789. Mrs. Samuel Allyne Otis was the wife of the Secretary of the Senate, 1789–1814.

need of. They cannot buy such. If she lives do go & see her again. I wish I could do her any good. I really Loved her.[12] The post will be gone.

Yours
A. A.

Philadelphia, Feb'ry 6th, 1798

My dear Sister:

I was very anxious to receive a Letter from you this morning, and Betsy was wishing yet dreading to hear from her sister. That she yet lives, is some hope for to build upon. Mr. Brisler has just brought your Letter from the office dated 29th Jan'ry. I believe I have written you every week, but fancy the Ice may have prevented the post from arriving. I wish Polly was where you could often see her. I have a great opinion of cabbage leaves. I would apply them to her feet, to her neck & to her Head. You know how opprest she always was at her Lungs if any thing ailed her. I want to be doing something for her. Tell her I am very anxious for her and hope she may yet recover. But great care and tenderness is necessary or she will be lost. Pray take care. But why should I ask what I am sure is always done. Pray tell Mr. Cranch to take great care of himself, and, my dear Sister, my cellar is always open to you. Do not let so good a man want wine to make his Heart glad, when you know where it can be had with a hearty welcome. I have written to Dr. Tufts to get my Room & chamber new painted and that as soon as it can be done in March the closset floor & the entrys and stairs. They will have time then to dry sufficiently. I had a letter on Saturday from Mrs. Smith. The Col[onel] returnd last week and has notified his Credittors to meet him in order to adjust with them his affairs.[1] I cannot suppose that he has it in his power to satisfy the demands they have, but if he can settle so as to be able to do any buisness in future it will be a great relief to my mind as well as to hers. But I am affraid of vissions, of Ideal Schemes &c. At any rate I am glad he has returnd. It really seemd to me at times, as if Mrs. Smith would lose

[12] Probably Mary Carter Smith, niece of Mrs. Adams, who died on April 28, 1798. See footnote 1 to the letter of May 7, 1798.

[1] Colonel William Stephens Smith, the son-in-law of John Adams, had plunged heavily into speculation in western lands on his return from London to the United States in 1788. As late as 1812, however, he was living on a farm, "Smith Valley," which he owned in Lebanon, Madison County, New York. From there he was elected as a Federalist to the Thirteenth Congress (1813–1815).

herself. She has sometimes written me that existance was a burden to her; and that she was little short of distraction. I have been more distresst for her than I have been ready to own. You know she always kept every thing to herself that she could, but she writes in better spirits, and is at least relieved from that worst of States, I think, a constant anxious expectation, and anticipation.

I have had Letters from my sons abroad to October. They were then well, but none since they left London. I hope they are safe at Berlin long before this time. You saw a Letter or rather an extract of a Letter in the Centinal from [J.Q.A. *cancelled*] dated as if written at Paris about a fortnight since in order the better to disguise the source.[2] It is probable you may see publishd from Fennos paper some observations upon the operation of the French constitution as exemplified in the transactions of the 4 Sep'br by the same hand.[3]

You complain of always having a share of Rhumatism. That is just my case. I have it floting about, sometimes in my head, Breast, Stomack &c, but if I can keep of fever I can Parry it so as not to be confined. Dr. [Benjamin] Rush is for calling it Gout, but I will not believe a word of all that, for Rhumatism I have had ever since I was a Child. When I feel any thing like fever, nitre in powder of about 6 Grains with a 6 part of a Grain of tarter Emetic & a 6 part of a Grain of Calomil in each taking 3 powders in a day, generally relieves me.

Inclosed is a ten dollor Bill out of which be so good as to give two to the widow Green, Mr. Pratts Mother, and to pay Sister Smith for the stockings knit, and supply her with Cotton. Buy Pheby a load of wood if necessary. I know you Love to be my almoner. I wish it was in my power to do more abundantly. If there is any thing in the way of oranges, Milk, Bisquit &c, which will be for Pollys comfort do be so kind as to procure it for her and send to her for me.

I hope captain & Mrs. Beal are recoverd and that Mr. & Mrs. Black are well. I pray you to remember me to Brother Adams & Family when

---

[2] See the *Columbian Centinel*, January 27, 1798, for the "Copy of a Letter" dated "Paris, September 21, 1797," in which J. Q. Adams stated that he saw no prospect of success for the "X.Y.Z. Mission" because the new revolution in Paris, by expelling two Directors and one-half of the legislative body, had driven the moderate men from power.

[3] John Fenno's *Gazette of the United States*, an organ of the Federalists. Mrs. Adams refers to the *coup d'etat* of September 4, 1798, the 18th Fructidor, when the three Republican directors, Barras, Rewbel, and La Révellière, defeated their colleagues, Barthélemy and Carnot. See footnote 4 to the letter of April 13, 1798.

you see them. My Love to Mrs. Norton, to Mrs. Greenleaf, & respects to Mrs. Welch.[4] From your ever
Affectionate Sister
ABIGAIL ADAMS

When you see Mrs. Pope, ask her about the Butter, the quantity & price. I should wish to pay for it, as well as two or three of her Cheses.

Philadelphia, Feb'ry 15, 1798

MY DEAR SISTER:

I have not received a Line from you since the last of Jan'ry. Betsy is much distresst to hear from her sister and I am not a little anxious. I hoped the twesday post as usual would have given me some information. I must attribute it to the weather. For, my dear Sister, write me a line every post if only to tell me how you all are. You will see much to your mortification, that Congress have been fitting [fighting], not the French, but the Lyon, not the Noble British Lyon, but but [sic] the beastly transported Lyon.[1] I am of the Quakers mind whom Peter Porcupine quotes. Speaking of the Irish, he says, "There is no mediocrity, or medium of Character in these people: they are either the most noble, brave, generous and best Bred: or the most ruffian like dirty and blackgaurd of all the creation." What a picture will these 14teen days make upon our Journals?! Yet are the supporters of Lyon alone to blame: *the Gentlemen* the real federilist would have expeld him instantly, and if it were possible a federilist could be found thus to have degraded himself, he would not have cost the Country 14 days debate, besides the infamy and disgrace of sitting again there.[2] I inclose you a paper containing a speach or two upon the subject. The Brute has not been in the house

---

[4] For Captain Beal, see footnote 1 to the letter of January 20, 1798; for Mr. and Mrs. Black, footnote 3 to the letter of December 22, 1799. "Brother Adams" is Peter Boylston Adams, younger brother of the President. Peter Boylston Adams (1738-1823) had four children by Mary Crosby: Mary (March 4, 1769), Boylston (April 24, 1771), Ann (April 19, 1773), and Susanna (August 11, 1777). The others are Mrs. Elizabeth (Cranch) Norton, wife of the Reverend Jacob Norton; Mrs. Lucy (Cranch) Greenleaf, wife of John Greenleaf; and the wife of Dr. Thomas Welsh, of Quincy.

[1] Matthew Lyon (1750-1822) was born in County Wicklow, Ireland, and came to America in 1765, settling in Vermont. He was elected to the House of Representatives in 1797, and was mercilessly lampooned as an ignoramus by the Federalist press. On January 30, 1798, in the House of Representatives, he spat in the face of Roger Griswold, of Connecticut, who had derided his military record.

[2] On February 12, 1798, a resolution for Lyon's expulsion was lost in the House, having received a majority, but not the requisite two-thirds vote.

for several days, but he is unfealing enough to go again, and if he does, I have my apprehensions of something still more unpleasent.[3]

These Philadelphians are a strange set of people, making pretentions to give Laws of politeness and propriety to the union. They have the least feeling of real genuine politeness of any people with whom I am acquainted. As an instance of it, they are about to celebrate, not the Birth day of the first Majestrate of the union as such, but of General Washingtons Birth day, and have had the politeness to send invitations to the President, Lady and family to attend it. The President of the United States to attend the celebration of the birth day in his publick Character of a private Citizen! For in no other light can General Washington be now considerd, how ever Good, how ever great his Character, which no person more respects than his Successor. But how could the President appear at their Ball and assembly, but in a secondary Character, when invited there, to be held up in that light by all foreign Nations. But these people look not beyond their own important selves. I do not know when my feelings of contempt have been more calld forth, in answer to the invitation. The President returnd for answer, "that he had received the card of invitation, and took the earliest opportunity to inform them, that he declined accepting it."—That the Virginians should celebrate the day is natural & proper if they please, and so may any others who chuse. But the propriety of doing it in the Capital in the *Metropolis* of America as these Proud Phylidelphians have publickly named it, and inviting the Head of the Nation to come and do it too, in my view is ludicrious [*sic*] beyond compare. I however bite my Lips, and say nothing, but I wanted to vent my indignation upon paper. You must not however expose it, nor me. It will be call'd pride, it will be calld mortification. I despise them both, as it respects myself, but as it respects the Character I hold—I will not knowingly degrade it—

Let me know whether a Letter coverd to Mr. Cranch for Dr. Tufts has reachd you safely. We are all as well as usual. The Baby was here on Sunday and is very well.[4] Remember me kindly to all Friends.

Your ever affectionate Sister
A. Adams

---

[3] On the very day Mrs. Adams wrote this letter, Roger Griswold beat Lyon with his cane, while the latter defended himself with the fire-tongs. Both encounters took place before the House had actually been called to order.

[4] The infant orphan daughter of Mr. and Mrs. Hall. See the letters of December 12 and 26, 1797.

Philadelphia, Feb'ry 21, 1798

My dear Sister:

I received your kind Letter of Feb'ry 9th and was quite rejoiced to hear that Mrs. Baxter was like to do well, when I feard to open the Letter least it should inform me of her death.[1] I have been Confined with a cold like the influenza for several days past. I have dreaded least it should prove one of my Feb'ry attacks. It came on with a very soar Throat and hoarsness and terminated in sneezing. It has made me quite sick. I have not been out of my Room since Saturday. I hope however it is going of. I have a company of 33 to dine with me tomorrow, Eleven of whom are Ladies, and Louisa is in much trouble on account of being obliged to act as Principle tomorrow.[2] She would have had me sent [sic] cards of apology to defer it, but I could not consent, as most of the Ladies are well known to her, and it is good sometimes to oblige young people to come forward and exert themselves. Amongst the Ladies is Mrs. Law, the Grandaughter of Mrs. Washington, who lives in the city of Washington. She is a very pleasing, agreable Lady, and I loved her for the kind and affectionate manner in which she spoke of Mr. & Mrs. Cranch and Betsy Elliot, whose absence she says they all regret.[3]

I have some expectation of seeing your son here in a few days. I hear he is comeing upon Mr. Greenleaf['s] affairs. Mr. Morris deliverd himself to his bail and went to Jail last week.[4] If ever said Mrs. Law, I had felt a disposition to extravagance, I should have been cured by a visit to Mrs. Morris. Two years ago, Mrs. Morris was a remarkable well looking

[1] Probably the wife of that Thompson Baxter mentioned in the letter of January 7, 1800.

[2] Louisa, the daughter of William Smith, the brother of Mrs. John Adams. This Louisa was the favorite niece and lived with Mr. and Mrs. Adams for many years.

[3] Thomas Law (1756-1834) was born in Cambridge, England, and died in Washington, D. C. On March 20, 1796, Law married Eliza Parke Custis, step-granddaughter (and adopted child) of George Washington. This marriage ended in a Vermont divorce, Law distributing gifts of imported English china among his friends by way of celebrating his release. Law was the son of the Bishop of Carlisle and the brother of Lord Ellenborough. He made a fortune in India, most of which he invested in real estate in the District of Columbia, and lost. He was eccentric and dictatorial, and given to writing poetry. For his strange character and checkered career, see Charles Moore, *The Family Life of George Washington*, Boston and New York, 1926, chapter 10; and, also, Allen C. Clark, *Greenleaf and Law in the Federal City*, Washington, 1901, pp. 219-44. Betsy, or Elizabeth Eliot, is probably one of the five daughters of Samuel Eliot, a prosperous merchant of Boston, grandfather of Charles William Eliot, President of Harvard.

[4] Robert Morris (1734-1806), the financier, was finally arrested for debt in February, 1798, when he was taken to Prune Street, the debtors' prison in Philadelphia, where he remained for three years, six months, and ten days.

woman, Maria, my companion, gay and blith as a bird, blooming as a rose in June.[5] I went to visit Mrs. Morris, & met her without knowing her, so alterd that I was shockd. Maria pale, wan, dejected & spiritless. Such is the change. Here I cannot refrain quoting a passage which struck me in reading it, as applicable not only to that Family, but to one with which I am more closely connected.[6]

"The man who loses his whole fortune, yet possesses firmness, Philosophy, a disdain of ambition and an accommodation to circumstances, is less an object of contemplative pity, than the person who without one real deprivation, one actual Evil is [first?], or is suddenly forced to recognise the fallacy of a Cherished and darling hope. All speculative wealth has a shallow foundation, but that its foundation has always been shallow is no mitigation of dissapointment, to him who had only viewed it in its superstructure, nor is its downfall less terrible to its visionary elevator because others had seen it from the beginning as a folly or Chimera: Its dissolution should be estimated, not by its romance in the unimpassioned examination of a rational looker on but by its believed promise of felicity to its credulous projector."

I am sometimes ready to exclaim when I see one bubble bursting after an other, all is vanity and vexation of spirit.

You write me that I have amused and entertaind you by my communications. I am sure I must mortify you by a detail of some late proceedings in congress. You must have heard of the spitting animal.[7] This act so low, vulgar and base, which having been committed, could only have [been] dignifiedly resented, by the expulsion of the Beast, has been spun out, made the object of party, and renderd thus the disgrace of the National legislature, by an unfortunate clause in the Constitution which gives the power into the hands of the minority, requiring two thirds to concur in an expulsion of a member. The circumstances were so fully proved of Lyons being the base agressor, that as Gentleman I could not have belived they could have got one third of the members to have consented to his continuence with them. But you will learn the state of the buisness from the documents I send you. I know not where it will end. In the mean time the buisness of the Nation is neglected, to the great mortification of the federalists.

[5] Robert Morris married Mary White, of Maryland, called "Maria," daughter of Colonel Thomas White and sister of William White (1748–1836), first Protestant Episcopal Bishop of Pennsylvania.

[6] Mrs. Adams was apparently thinking of her sense of disappointment with her son-in-law, Colonel William Stephens Smith, and her son, Charles Adams.

[7] Matthew Lyon of Vermont. See footnote 1 to the letter of February 15, 1798.

You will have received before this my Letters, which contain a reply to some of your queries.

I want to say a word to you by way of advise. The Farm which has been disposed of, I hope may prove a relief to Mr. Cranch as well as an advantage to him and that the income from the money if vested in publick Securities will yeald you more real profit than the Land, yet that was solid money fleeting. My request is that the sum during Brothers Life may not be broken in upon with an Idea of assisting Children. They are young and can better bear hardships and care, than those who are advanced in Life. I hope therefore nothing will lead to a dispertion of the capital, tho you have as deserving children as any person need desire. I repeat pray do not let the bank be touchd. I have seen too many instances of parents dependant upon Children. Tho there are instances which do honour to humane nature, there are more which disgrace it.

As to the Carpet you speak of, you may use it, and when I return I will let you know whether I will part with it. Adieu my dear Sister.

Most affectionatly your[s]
A. ADAMS

Philadelphia, Feb'ry 28th, 1798

MY DEAR SISTER:

I have this moment received your kind Letter of Feb'ry 18th, prevented by the bad Roads from reaching [me] sooner, and I have got now to be as anxious and as solisitious for the arrival of the Eastern post, as I used to be at Quincy for the arrival of the Southern. I thank you for all your communications. I saw the centinal last Saturday and thought I knew my own Letter, but did not know whether it was an extract from one to you, or to Mr. Smith, to whom I sometimes freely scrible.[1] In my last I believe I gave you some account of the intended

---

[1] *Columbian Centinel*, February 17, 1798. The letter to which Mrs. Adams refers was apparently prepared for the *Centinel* by Richard Cranch from information he obtained from the letters Mrs. Adams wrote to his wife. The letter is as follows:

"A writer in the *Chronicle* of yesterday, under the signature of Plain Truth asserts 'that the President of the United States received dispatches from France *a month ago*, notwithstanding which the most profound secrecy has been maintained on this all-important subject.' Under this assertion, the writer proceeds to abuse the President and deceive the public. To prevent this incendiary from deceiving the public, you may from good authority declare the assertion of Plain Truth, to be without the least foundation. By letters from Philadelphia to the 6th February, not a word at that time had been received by the Executive from our envoys at Paris. Letters had been received from Mr. King as late as October, and from Mr. Murray, at the Hague, to the 10th November. Those gentlemen at that time were as much in the dark with respect to our Envoys, as we are here. The character of the President for patriotism and integrity is too firmly fixed with every true American, to be injured in the least by the abuse of such a vile incendiary as Plain Truth.
February 16. A CORRESPONDENT."

Birth Night Ball, & the Presidents reply, which on the morning of the day, appeared in Baches paper, to my no small surprize, tho I cannot say I was sorry to see it. It was however accompanied by insolence and abuse, and fully shews the temper of even those who were the Managers of the Birth Night Ball, not of *the President* of the United States, but of a private citizen. The publication had however a direct contrary effect to what was intended. It threw a Gloom & damp upon the whole proceeding. Every one was inquiring the why? & the Wherefore? Many who had subscribed upon the Faith that the President was going, refused afterwards to attend, amongst whom in justice to him I must say was the Vice President, who declared himself shockd with the impropriety of the thing when he first heard of the Proposal, but was led to lend his Name because he would not give offence. This is certain he did not go, and I have my my [sic] information so direct that I know what his opinion was. Yet these very persons who sit the matter on foot are now endeavouring to make it believed that he was the first mover in order to give offence to the President—give the d[evi]l his due, but lay no more than he deserves to his Charge.[2] I have been informd that of 150 who subscribed 15 only were present of Ladies, and they have been so mortified that not a word has been publishd in their News papers respecting it. I hope in time they will learn how to appreciate themselves as a Nation. They have had, & now have a Head, who will not knowingly Prostrate their dignity & character, neither to foreign Nations, nor the American People.

My dear Sister your son has been with us ever since he came, which is a week tomorrow.[3] Next to my own children I love those of my sister. He is very well and says Mrs. Cranch and the Children are so. But he will write you himself.

Tell Mrs. Black I shall see the Baby tomorrow.[4] I had a Bonnet made for it which I gave it a fortnight ago. I think it wants a dimity Cloak which I will get for it. I will write her the result of my conference with the Nurse.

I shall take Cousin Betsy in hand shortly.[5] At present I fear the post

[2] If Adams was not quite tactful about the "Birth-night Ball" for Washington on February 22, 1798, Jefferson was not quite frank. He wrote privately of this tempest in a teapot: "The late birth-night certainly has sewn tares among the exclusive federalists." Morison, *H. G. Otis*, vol. 1, p. 133.
[3] William Cranch (1769–1855), son of Richard Cranch (1726–1811), husband of Mary (Smith) Cranch (1741–1811).
[4] See the letters of December 12 and 26, 1797.
[5] See footnote 4 to the letter of December 15, 1788.

will go out without my Letter if I do not immediatly close after presenting my kind regards to all Friends from

> Your ever affectionate Sister
> A. ADAMS

Philadelphia, March 3d, 1798

MY DEAR SISTER:

To communicate pleasure, is reflecting happiness. The Secretary of State came smiling in my Room yesterday [upon which *cancelled*] I said to him, I know you have got dispatches, upon which he took from his pocket two Letters from my dear son at Berlin.[1] Tho they were publick Letters and upon publick buisness, they informd us of his safe arrival at Berlin on the 7th of Nov'br, 4 days from Hamburgh. On the 10th he had an audience of the Prussian Minister. The King was informd of his arrival, and directed his Ministure [*sic*] to assure Mr. Adams, that he received with great satisfaction this mark of attention from the United States and that he regreetedly [*sic*] exceedingly that his extreem illness renderd it impossible for him to give him the first Audience.

"On the 17th Mr. Adams writes, The King of Prussia died yesterday morning at 9 o'clock at Potsdam. He was immediately succeeded by his son Frederic William the 3d. My Credentials cannot now be presented. I must request New ones to the Present King may be forwarded as soon as possible."[2]

I hope the mission begun so contrary to his wishes and so injurious to his Private interest, will become more auspicious. He had made his arrangement for going to Lisbon, hired a house there, taken and paid his passage, when he received news that he must go to Berlin—and this without any additional allowence, and only half the sum allowd for the outfit of a minister going from this Country, tho his expences must amount to the same.

I received, he observes, an office, tho no promotion, at once invidious in appearance and oppressive in reality, but I have done. My Country has every claim upon me. If her Service were [really *cancelled*] merely a Bed of Roses, it would not be a worthy incitement to ambition.

[1] Timothy Pickering (1745–1829), bringing letters from John Quincy Adams, minister to the Court of Prussia. For portions of the texts of these letters from Prussia, see *The Writings of John Quincy Adams, 1779–1823*, W. C. Ford, Editor, New York, 1913–1917, vol. 2, February 8, 1797—April 14, 1801.

[2] Frederick William II (1786–1797), nephew of Frederick the Great, and Frederick William III (1797–1840).

I inclose you an other paper upon the Foreign intercourse Bill.[3] A stranger would be ready to suppose that The President, instead of having appointed only one single Minister since he came into office (the Envoys excepted, who were only for a particular object,) that [sic] he had Nominated an incredible Number and increased or wanted to increase their Salleries. The House of Rep's have not by the constitution any right to judge of the propriety of of [sic] sending foreign Ministers, nor the courts to which they shall be sent, nor the Grades. The Constitution has given that power solely to the President as it has to the House of Reps the granting of Money. As well might the President assume to himself the disposal of Money, unappropriated. Yet have they according to calculation expended as much Money by the length of the debate as would pay the salleries of all our Ministers for two years to come.

Mr. Otis & Mr. Harper have very abley replied to Mr. Gallitin whose speaches I will send you as soon as they are printed.[4]

Your Son is well and talks of returning the beginning of the week.

I would have my stockings kept till I return.

I had Letters from Mrs. Smith. She was well. My Love to Mrs. Norton, Greenleaf & their Families. Poor Suky Warner.[5] I am grieved for her. I am, my dear Sister, with unalterable affection,

Your Sister
A. ADAMS

Philadelphia, March 5th, 1798

MY DEAR SISTER:

I received on Saturday Evening the 3d March your kind Letter of 25 Feb'ry. You estimate much too highly the little services I am able to render to my Friends, and you depreciate the value of your own, the benifit of which I have too often experienced to sit [a *cancelled*] lightly [value upon *cancelled*] by them, for whilst you visit the widow,

---

[3] See footnote 3 to the letter of February 1–5, 1798, and the postscript to the letter of March 5, 1798.

[4] Abraham Alfonse Albert Gallatin (1761–1849), of Pennsylvania, Secretary of the Treasury (1801–1814), was one of the leaders of the opponents of the Federalists in the House of Representatives in 1798. Harrison Gray Otis, son of the Secretary of the Senate, was a member of the House from Massachusetts, and Robert Goodloe Harper (1765–1825) was a member of the House from South Carolina.

[5] Susannah Warner, daughter of that Mrs. Warner, of Gloucester, who became the second wife of Dr. Cotton Tufts, died at Weymouth on April 7, 1798, aged twenty-two. *Columbian Centinel*, April 28, 1798.

the orphan, the sick, and console them by your presense, enliven them by your conversation & prescribe for their necessities, you prove that it is possible to be very benevolent and Charitable tho with small pecuniary means. When you do all the good in your power, you enjoy all the happiness the practise of virtue can bestow, and long may you receive the Reward.

Your son has been with us near a fortnight. I feel very loth to part with him. He must leave us, he says, tomorrow. I believe he has just received Letters from Mrs. Cranch. I will stop and ask him how she is.

I have read Nancys Letter. She and the Children are both well. It is dated the 27 Feb'ry. She is very anxious for her Brother, which is very natural.[1] I know not how she could be otherways, for tho unfortunate belevolence [sic] has been a striking trait in his Character—Mr. and Mrs. Law have been three weeks in this city.[2] You know he married Miss Custos, who seems to inherit all the benevolence of her Grandmother. She is a charming woman. The more I see of her the more amiable she appears. She is to spend the day with me tomorrow, in the family way, for which she seems to be found [sic]. I loved her the more for the friendly manner in which she expresses her Regard for your son and for Mrs. Cranch and Betsy Eliot who she says, she misses very much. Mrs. Law is so easy, so tranquil, so unaffected, that her first appearance preposses[es] you in her favour, so different from most of the formal Ladies of this city. Yet there is sociality enough here amongst some of them. I always however sit it down when I meet with it, that N. England comes in for some share of it. I have visited sometimes & sit half an hour in company in some families with whose reception and manners I have been particularly gratified [with *cancelled*]. Upon making inquiries of my intellingenser, Dr. [Benjamin] Rush, who knows everybody and their connections, I discover that Grandfather or Mother or some relative originated from N. England. Two Nations are not more different than the N. Englanders and many Natives of this city. I must not however be too local. Which has the preference I have not said—

You will learn that at length dispatches have arrived from our commissoners, but with them, no prospect of success. We have letters to the 9 Janry. I inclose you the paper which contains the message from the President with the Letter to both Houses of Congress. We shall now see how the American pulse beat. I fear we shall be driven to War,

[1] Anna (Nancy) Greenleaf, wife of William Cranch, mentioned above, and sister of James Greenleaf, the speculator in land and the partner of Robert Morris.
[2] See footnote 3 to the letter of February 21, 1798.

[to *cancelled*] but to *defend* ourselves is our duty. War the French have made upon us a long time.[3]

I cannot learn what is become of Mr. Beal. Is he not yet got to Quincy?

Let Mrs. Black know that the Nurse and Baby were with me yesterday. It had had a bad cold but was better. We put on the cap and it lookd very pretty. I gave the Nurse the 5 dollors sent by Mrs. Black for which she was very thankfull, and says Mrs. Black may assure herself that she shall take the best care of the child. She told our people Mrs. Brisler and Betsy, that Mr. Black complain a good deal of the expence, but she could not keep it for less. She had to give at the rate of 15 dollors pr cord for wood, which I know to be true, and that she could not do any other buisness than look after the two Children. She seems to think that carrying the Children by water when the weather becomes pleasent will be less fatigue to them than by land, but this for a future days consideration. Louisa desires the letter to her sister may be sent to her if she is gone to Atkinson [New Hampshire].[4] Thank Mr. Cranch for his kind Letter. I would have the floor painted in the kitchin & the stairs a plain yellow unless the floor is too thin. I believe it is much worn, the closset too. The best time for painting is when there can be time enough for it to dry without any persons treading upon it, and that makes me earnest to have it done quite early, and with boild oil. I should be glad [if] Mr. Billings would new lay the wall against the Garden as soon as the frost is out the Ground. Be so good as to desire Mr. Porter to lay in a load of Charcoal. Dr. Tufts will give him money to pay for it. We cannot do without it when we are there. I hope too he will get wood enough home. I must get you to have an Eye to the painting or I fear it will not be done to my mind. As soon as the season will permit I would have persons enough employd to compleat what is to be done. And my strawberry bed Stutson [Stetson] must attend to very soon in the Spring. I should not like any other person should [*sic*] touch it. As to the rest of the Garden, I must look to Tirril to do it, I suppose. But more of this an other time. I had rather prepare to come Home than to go from it. Adieu, my dear Sister,

Most affectionately your[s]
A. ADAMS

[3] The American commissioners to France in the "XYZ Affair": John Marshall, Charles C. Pinckney, and Elbridge Gerry. See Schouler, *History of the United States*, vol. 1, pp. 386-97.

[4] Atkinson, New Hampshire, a village about three miles northwest of Haverhill, Massachusetts, where Mrs. Adams's sister, the former Mrs. John Shaw, resided with her second husband, the Reverend Stephen Peabody. See footnote 3 to the letter of August 9, 1789.

Foreign intercourse the Question upon Nicolas motion was taken to day & regected by the 52 Gentlemen. 44 in favour of it. 3 federilist absent.[5]

Philadelphia, March 13th, 1798

My dear Sister:

I received on Saturday your favour of March 3d. The reason why Letters are longer from hence to Quincy than to Boston, is oweing to their making up the Mail but once a week for Quincy, whereas they make them up twice for Boston; Mr. [William] Cranch did not leave us untill Wednesday Morning the Roads were so bad: I do not perceive any alteration in him, except that he has caught some of the Southern Complexion; none of their Manners: his principles were too well fixd to be easily altered. He went twice with us to meeting to hear Dr. [Samuel] Blair and said it was quite a Feast to him to go again to publick worship.[1] Mr. [James] Greenleafs situation worried him, and I am fearfull that his 3 or 4 years labour, has been toil and trouble, without any gain; or that he will finally lose what is due to him. This for a young Man just sitting out in Life is a very hard lesson but he has too feeling a Heart to deal with people embarressd in their circumstances. He found [Robert] Morris in Jail, and if he sufferd he could not say: you must pay me. What distress, what Ruin, have these immense speculators involved themselves, their families, their connections, and thousands of others in? What is past cannot be remedied. We seldom learn experience untill we get too old to use it, or we grow callous to the misfortunes of the world by Reiterated abuse.

> And Nature, as it grows again towards Earth
> Is fashioned for the journey, dull and Heavy.[2]

What an alteration of honour has desperate want made!
> What viler thing upon the Earth than Friends
> Who can bring noblest minds to basest ends![3]

[5] Actually, the House of Representatives, on Monday, March 5, 1798, rejected the Nicholas Amendment by a vote of 52 to 48. *Annals of the Fifth Congress*, p. 1234, and *Columbian Centinel*, March 17, 1798. This Nicholas Amendment would have limited the salaries of ministers to London, Paris, and Madrid to $9000 a year, and the salaries of all other ministers to $4500 a year. The second proposal, of course, was an oblique blow at John Quincy Adams, who had been transferred from the Netherlands, or the Batavian Republic, to Berlin for the purpose of negotiating a new treaty with Prussia to replace the one of 1784.

[1] See the letter of July 6, 1797.
[2] *Timon of Athens*, Act II, Scene 2, lines 227-8.
[3] *Timon of Athens*, Act IV, Scene 3, lines 470-1.

I have been led into these reflections in contemplating the unhappy situation of Mr. Morris, Nicolson & others. You can scarcly form an Idea of the great Change which has taken place in this city in the course of 5 years, and a greater still awaits it.[4]

I am sorry to learn that Cousin Betsy has a Cough. Let her not neglect it. She should get some of Churchs Cough drops.[5] This climate tho subject to great Changes, is very little subject to Coughs. The Air is not half so keen in the coldest weather.

I expect your next Letter will bear me the melancholy tidings of Suky Warners death. She has been vibrating upon a thread for several years. Tell Cousin Betsy if her cough does not soon mend, to lose a few ounces of Blood. She can spair it well, and it may prevent dangerous concequences.

I cannot say what Congress mean to do. The dispatches are but just decypherd. Whether the President will think proper to make any further communications is more than he himself can yet determine, but it must strike every Body, that every thing which might endanger our Envoys, who are still in Paris, for any thing to the contrary which we know, must and will be kept Private, clamour who will. Enough is already known to excite wrath and indignation agains[t] a Goverment who refuses even to receive Messengers specially appointed. "Peter [Porcupine] says, All men now agree that Congress ought to do something, and that immediatly, and if they do not, they may expect to bring on themselves all the odium attachd to such indecisive measures, I had almost said Criminal—every one knows that the Snail like mode of proceeding which we have long beheld is not the fault of the President. He has taken care that his Character, either as an American, or as the Chief Majestrate of America, shall not suffer, let the result be what it may. The Senate are ready to support him:—"

Peter says many good things, and he is the only thorn in Baches side. He [Bache] is really affraid to encounter him [Peter], but he [Peter] frequently injures the cause he means to advocate for want of prudence

[4] For the North American Land Company of Robert Morris, John Nicholson, and James Greenleaf, see footnote 6 to the letter of June 25, 1795. See, also, Clark, *Greenleaf and Law in the Federal City*.

[5] "Church's Cough Drops are prepared and sold (only) by the inventor and sole proprietor, Dr. James Church, at his Medicine Store, No. 1 South Third-street, next the Market, Philadelphia; and by appointment, at New-York, by Messrs. Staples & Co., 169 Pearl-street, and Miss Wedman, 112 William-street.

"Dr. Church may be consulted every day, at his office, 158 South Front-street, Philadelphia." *Gazette of the United States*, January 9, 1798.

and discretion. I have a great curiosity to see the Creature. There is a strange mixture in him. He can write very handsomely, and he can descend & be as low, and vulgar as a fish woman.

I had Letters last Evening from Mrs. Smith. She is well, and writes in rather better spirits, at least with more calmness and composure. Inclosed is a Letter which she sent me for Mrs. Guile.

My Love to Mrs. Norton, Greenleaf, and to the Dr. and Mrs. Tufts. Tell them I sincerely sympathize with them under their affliction. Mrs. Otis desires to be rememberd to you. They always dine with us on Sundays. The Judge and Mrs. Cushing have promised to call and see you on their return. Mrs. Cushing can tell you all about us. Inclosed is a ten dollor Bill. Will you be so good as to tell Mr. Porter to lay in a load of Charcoal and call upon you for the pay. Half a load will answer, but sometimes we could not get a part. I would rather he should take a whole load. And I would wish you to get me garden seeds. I speak in time, but a Letter does not reach you in a week. Will you ask Mr. Porter whether the young man who worked with him last year Soal is to be had this. If so he had better engage him for Nine Months. I do not conjecture when we shall get away, but you know I love to have every thing done in season. I am affraid the President will be overwhelmd. Buisness thickens upon him. Officering all the frigates, contemplating what can be done at this critical period, *knowing what he thinks ought to be done*, yet not certain whether the people are sufficiently determined to second the Government, is a situation very painfull as well as responsible—All Good people ought to pray Heartily for him and for our Country—Good Dr. Blair prays "that he may hear a voice saying unto him this is the path, go thou in it."

I thought I was just going to finish upon the opposite side, but here I am half way down the other. I must however bid you adieu to write to my sons by a vessel which is this week to sail for Hamburgh.[6] I am, my dear Sister,

Affectionatly your[s]
A. ADAMS

Philadelphia, March 14th, 1798

MY DEAR SISTER:
Yesterday dispatches were received from Mr. King up to the 9th Jan'ry.[1] In a post scrip he says, I have just learnt that Mr. Adams has

[6] John Quincy Adams and Thomas Boylston Adams (1772–1832).
[1] See footnote 8 to the letter of January 5, 1798.

JOHN ADAMS, 1789 *John Trumbull*

been received by the new King notwithstanding his commission was to his Father. This is civil and will enable him to proceed with buisness.[2] I received a Letter from Dr. Tufts yesterday that allarmd me. I thought I inclosed him some Bills. I might, as I wrote you the same time [have] put them into yours, for the Dr. in a post scrip says that you had written him that you had them. When the Dr. writes to me inclose his Letters in yours, for as those are *held sacred* now by a promise not to open them, I shall receive them, in a way I wish. The Dr. and I have some buisness transaction [*sic*] which are between ourselves.[3]

Nothing new transpires but what your Boston papers have; warm words in congress must be apprehended, whilst some are for going shares with France submitting intirely to her will and quietly disposed to receive every lash she pleases to inflict. Northern Blood boils, and I do not know what will take place. I hope they will be cooler to day, but Giles has just opend his batteries.[4]

Pray, is Betsy going to steal a wedding upon us? She inquires the fashions. They are as various as the Changes of the moon. The young Ladies generally have their Hair all in Curls over their heads, and then put a Ribbon, Beads, Bugles or a Band of some kind through the fore part of the Hair to which they attach feathers. The Band is put upon Ribbon, sometimes on wire. Frequently two are worn which cross each other. They tye behind [under *cancelled*] over the hind Hair & then a small Bunch of Hair turns up behind in which a small comb is fixd and the ends of the hind Hair fall Back again in curls. The Gounds [*sic*] are made to have only one side come forward and that is confind with a belt round the waist. The waist made plain. Some sleaves are drawn in diamonds, some [Robbins *cancelled*] Robins drawn up & down with bobbin in 5 or 6 rows.[5] In short a drawing room frequently exhibits a specimin of Grecian, Turkish, French and English fashion at the same time, with ease, Beauty and Elegance equal to any court—What a medley are my Letters. I had yesterday to visit me after the Presidents Levee, the Kings of 3 Indian Nations. One of them after sitting a little while rose and addrest me. He said he had been to visit his Father, and

[2] See the letter of March 3, 1798.

[3] Mrs. Adams refers to her having angrily forbidden her husband to open any more letters addressed to her. See the letters of November 15 and December 26, 1797.

[4] William Branch Giles (1762–1830), member of the House of Representatives from Virginia from 1790 to October 2, 1798, when he resigned.

[5] "Robin," a variant of "robing," a trimming on clothing: 1748, Richardson, *Clarissa Harlowe; Oxford English Dictionary*.

he thought his duty but in part fulfilld, untill he had visited allso his Mother, and he prayd the great spirit to keep and preserve them. They all came and shook me by the Hand, and then took some cake and wine with me. There were nine of them. One of them spoke English well. They then made their bow and withdrew, much more civil than the Beast of Vermont.[6] Adieu, my dear Sister.

I am most affectionatly your[s]
A. ADAMS

[Philadelphia], March 20th, 1798

MY DEAR SISTER:

I write you a few Lines this mor'g just to inclose to you the Newspaper of yesterday which contains an important Message from the President. It is a very painfull thing to him that he cannot communicate to the publick dispatches in which they are so much interested, but we have not any assurance that the Envoys have left Paris and who can say that in this critical state of things their dispatches ought to be publick? Our foreign Ministers can never be safe, or they will cease to be usefull to us abroad, if their communications are all to be communicated. This was not the case during our revolution. Under the old Congress, dispatches were never made publick. I expect the President will be represented as declaring War, by taking off the restriction which prevented Merchantmen from Arming.[1] It was always doubtfull in his mind, whether he had a Right to prevent them, but the former President had issued such a prohibition, and he thought it best at that time to continue it. You see by the papers that Bache has begun his old bilingsgate again, because Mr. J. Q. Adams is directed to renew the treaty with Sweeden which is now just expiring, and for which not a single sixpence will be allowd him as the King of Sweeden will empower his Minister at Berlin to renew it there. Dr. Franklin made the treaty in Paris with the Sweedish minister, and the President made the Treaty with Prussia in Holland, yet this lying wretch of a Bache reports that no treaties were ever made without going to the courts to negotiate them, unless

---

[6] Matthew Lyon. See footnote 1 to the letter of February 15, 1798.

[1] See Schouler, *History of the United States*, vol. 1, p. 395. On March 27, 1798, however, as the result of a conference attended by the "Republican" members of the Congress, Richard Sprigg, Jr., member of the House of Representatives from Maryland, offered three insidious resolutions: the first against war with the French Repbulic, the second against the arming of merchant vessels, and a third in favor of protection for the seacoast of the United States.

the power where they were made, were concernd in them, and says it is all a job in order to give Mr. [John Quincy] Adams a new outfit & additional sallery at every Court. But there is no end to their audaciousness, and you will see that French emissaries are in every corner of the union sowing and spreading their Sedition. We have *renewed information* that their System is, to calumniate the President, his family, his administration, untill they oblige him to resign, and then they will Reign triumphant, *headed by the Man of the People*. It behoves every pen and press to counteract them, but our Countrymen in general are not awake to their danger. We are come now to a crissis too important to be languid, too dangerous to slumber—unless we are determind to submit to the fraternal embrace, which is sure and certain destruction as the poisoned shirt of Danarius.[2] Adieu my dear Sister. I intended only a line but I have run to a great length. We have had snow and rain for three days. What has been your Weather? Love and a kind remembrance to all Friends from

> Your ever affectionate Sister
> ABIGAIL ADAMS

> Philadelphia, March 27, 1798

MY DEAR SISTER:

I received yesterday your kind Letter of March 19th, I expect a Letter every week if you have nothing else to say, but as Sterne observes, "how the Shadows Lengthen, as the Sun declines." And this may be applied to the Moral as well as the Natural [world *cancelled*] System. As we descend the Hill of Life, our gay and vissionary prospect vanish, and what gilded our Meridian days, our Zenith of Life, as the Shadows lengthen, we see through a different medium and may justly estimate many of our persuits, as vanity and vexation of spirit.

"But theres a Brighter world on high" which opens to us prospects more permanant, and pleasures more durable. To that let us aspire in the sure and certain hope, that by a patient Continuence in the path of Religion and Virtue, we shall assuredly reap, if we faint not, the happy fruits of a glorious immortality.

When I took my pen this morning, with the rising Sun, I did not think of moralizing thus, but the visions of the Night had left an impression upon my mind, and those visions were occasiond by reflections

[2] Dejanira, the wife of Hercules, whom Nessus, the Centaur, tried to kidnap. Dejanira prepared the shirt which caused the death of her husband, after which she hanged herself.

upon the dangerous and Hazardous situation into which our Country is brought, by that demoralizing, wicked and abandoned Nation, or Government of France. When no sacrifice on their part was required, when justice and Equity is all we wanted, when two repeated offers of accommodation have been generously offerd to them, they turn a Deaf Ear and refuse to listen eitheir [sic] to the voice of Reason, or the call of Honor; but answer only by renewed insults and more audacious plunder. In this situation our Country is calld upon to put themselves in a *state of defence*, and to take measures to protect themselves by Sea. This is calld a declaration of war on the part of the President, by those who would gladly see their Government prostrate, Religion banishd and I do not know if I should judge too hardly if I said our Country Shared by France. That war will not be the concequence of the conduct of France towards us is more than I can say; it certainly leads to it, as the most probable Event. But the President did not make our difficulties, nor has the Government. No Nation has more strictly adhered to nutrality, none sufferd so much, none [bore *cancelled*] bourn with more patience the spoiling of their Property.

Union is what we want, but that will not be easily [be *cancelled*] obtaind. It is difficult to make the people see their danger, untill it is at their doors, or rouse untill their country is invaded. The Senate are strong. They are much more united in their measures than the House. There is an attempt in this city to get a petition signed to congress declaring their determination not to go to war with France, and they hope to sit this measure in opperation through the different States. Is it possible that any person can suppose this Country wish for war by which nothing is to be obtaind, much to be expended and hazarded, in preference to Peace? *But in self defence* we may be involved in war; and for that we ought to be prepared, and that is what the President means. What benifit can war be to him? He has no ambition for military Glory. He cannot add by war, to his peace, comfort or happiness. It must accumulate upon him an additional load of care, toil, trouble, malice, hatred, and I dare say Revenge. But for all this he will not sacrifice the honor and independance of his Country to any Nation, and if in support of that, we are involved in war, we must & we ought to meet it, with firmness, with Resolution & with union of Sentiment.

I shall sigh for my retirement at Peace Feild, before I shall reach it.[1] If I can leave here in May, I shall be content, but I cannot say posi-

---

[1] "Peace Field," an old name for the Adams Mansion in Quincy.

tively. The Roads will not be tolerable untill then; I should like to have what I proposed done as soon in the season as it can be with advantage.

The President says you may keep a Cow at the Farm through the season.

I had a Letter from your son two days after he got home. He found little William had been dangerously sick with a fever, but he was on the recovery. And he mournd the loss of a very valuable Friend a Mr. Deakins who dyed in his absence, a Man possessd of a most estimable Character in whom he says he had found an other Father.[2] Mr. and Mrs. [Thomas] Law returnd last week.[3] I really think she is a truly worthy woman.

I inclose to you a News paper because it contains a speech of Mr. Reads [Reed] upon the foreign intercourse Bill.[4] It contains as much good sense and is more to the point than the three & four hours Harangues of some others. Mr. Read very seldom speaks.

What, have I got so near the End of my paper before I was aware. I have more to say yet, but Louisa warns me to Breakfast, and I bid you adieu for the Present.

Affectionatly your[s]
A. ADAMS

[Philadelphia], March 31, 1798

MY DEAR SISTER:

I write you a few lines this morning merely to inclose a Letter which I will thank you to cover and forward to Atkinson [New Hampshire]. I have not time to write this morning to Atkinson. Inclosed I sent you a specimin of the Manners, Religion & politeness of one of the 44 Gentlemen, who can come and Eat of my Bread, & drink of my wine, one whom the Virginians consider as a Paragon of politeness, whom they have plumed themselves upon as a promising [young *cancelled*] Man, and a man of Property, one of their best speakers.[1]

[2] William Deakins, Jr., was the eldest of the three sons of William Deakins, Sr., of Prince George County, Maryland, himself a son of John Deakins, who came to the United States in the seventeenth century. William Deakins, Jr., and his brothers, Francis and Leonard, all became residents of Georgetown some time before the Revolution. See Clark, *Greenleaf and Law in the Federal City*.

[3] Thomas and Eliza Parke (Custis) Law. See footnote 3 to the letter of February 21, 1798.

[4] John Reed (1751–1831), of West Bridgewater, Yale, 1772, Federalist member of the House of Representatives (1795–1801).

[1] Possibly William Branch Giles (1762–1830), of Virginia, an active opponent of the Federalists; or probably John Nicholas (1756–1819), of Virginia, who harangued the House of Representatives for several weeks against the pending Foreign Intercourse Bill. See the following letter.

I know not what can excite their wrath to such a degree, but that they think there is yet some Religion left in the Country, and that the people will have some respect to it, & to those Rulers who acknowledge an over over[sic] Ruling Providence. Bache you see is striving to render the Proclamation Ridiculous and with his Atheistical doctrines spreading French principles far and wide.² But I trust and hope we may as a people be of that happy Number, whose God is the Lord, and never [get *cancelled*] forget that it is Righteousness which exalteth a Nation, whilst Sin is their Reproach. Adieu, my dear Sister,

Affectionatly yours
A. A[DAMS]

[Philadelphia], April 4, 1798

DEAR SISTER:

The eastern post will go out this morning and I take my pen to thank you for your Letters of the 20 & 26th of March. We had received intelligence of the wisdom of Roxbury & Milton, their petitions having reachd their Representitives in Congress.¹ The reply to them may be found in the dispatches of our Envoys yesterday communicated to congress.² The publick exegiency of our Country, and the real in some,

² Proclamation for a national fast, March 23, 1798. See Adams, *Works*, vol. 9, pp. 169–70. The fast was set for May 9, 1798.

¹ On March 20, 1798, at a town meeting in Roxbury, Massachusetts, a petition to Congress was prepared, and voted, against the arming of merchant vessels, as likely to bring on war with France. On March 22, Milton followed suit, in a town meeting at which Seth Sumner was chosen moderator. If merchant vessels were to be armed, it was argued, this measure should be taken by an act of Congress, not by executive order. See the Milton Records (1775–1808), pp. 301–303, and the Roxbury Records. See, also, the reports of these town meetings and letters in regard to them in the *Columbian Centinel*, March 24, 1798; the *Independent Chronicle and Universal Advertiser*, March 19–22 and March 22–26, 1798, and the *Massachusetts Mercury*, March 23, 1798. J. B. Varnum presented the Milton petition in the House of Representatives on April 2, 1798, *Annals of the Fifth Congress*, Washington, 1851, vol. 2, p. 1367. On April 13, Varnum presented a similar petition from Cambridge, and on April 23, two others, from the towns of Harvard and Lexington. *Annals of the Fifth Congress*, vol. 2, pp. 1414 and 1522. When Mr. Dana objected to the petition of Cambridge being referred to the Committee of the Whole, the question was put, and he was defeated by a vote of 38 to 35.

The Roxbury Records are locked up in the vaults of the Liberty Mutual Insurance Company, Boston. The editor wishes to thank Mr. George G. Wolkins, of the Massachusetts Historical Society, for having called his attention to microfilms of these records in the Boston Public Library.

² As a result of a resolution of the House of Representatives, April 2, 1798, John Adams, on April 3, transmitted to Congress the dispatches from "the envoys extraordinary of the United States to the French Republic" with the request that they might "be considered in confidence." On April 5, the House voted to print twelve hundred copies of these dispatches. *Annals of the Fifth Congress*, vol. 2, pp. 1374–8. Adams withheld only the names and descriptions of Talleyrand's unofficial agents, Hottinguer, Bellamy, and Hauteval, who, in the deciphered dispatches, were designated as "X," "Y," and "Z."

and the Pretended unbelief of others, produced a torpor, and an indicision which call'd for Conviction & proof as strong as holy writ, that all, and more than was exprest, in the Presidents last message, was necessary to be done to put our Country on its gaurd and to inspire them with a determined resolution to preserve their Rights, their freedom and independance, all of which are attack'd by the most base, profligate and abandoned Culprits which were ever permitted to scourge the Nations of the Earth; The Algerines lose all their venality & tyranny when Compared to them.[3]

The Proofs of this will now be laid before the publick as soon as they can be printed. Out of fears for the safety of our Envoy's they would not have yet been published, if the House of Reps. had not calld for them. Gallitan, the sly, the artfull, the insidious Gallitan knew better than to join in the call.[4] Giles was heard to say to his Friends in the House, You are doing wrong to call for those dispatches.[5] They will injure us. These Men knew that the President would not have exprest himself in such strong terms in his Message, if he had not possesst convincing Evidence, and tho they lie to the publick, they believed all that was asserted in his Message, "that all hopes of accommodation was at an End." I have never seen the dispatches, but I have learnt from the Members who yesterday visited me, what I had before suspected, that Tallyrand & the Directory would have been bought. The wretches even stipulated a certain sum to be paid them for the Presidents saying in his speech at the opening of the summer session, "that we ought to show France that we were not a degraded People." They wanted to prove him deficient in knowledge, a false man, by making us tributary to them and that by the consent of the of the [sic] very ministers he had sent to negotiate with them. But I will not mutilate further what I have only learnt by incorrect details. As soon as the dispatches are publishd I

---

[3] From one point of view, the American outcry against the French proposal that the "XYZ" commissioners should grease the palms of the Directory in 1798 was odd. As early as 1784 Adams, from London, had thought that the only way to deal with the Corsairs of the Barbary Coast (Algiers, Tunis, Tripoli, and Morocco) was to buy them off. In 1786, a treaty was concluded with the ruler of Morocco providing for the annual payment of American tribute. On April 10, 1792, Washington submitted to the Senate a treaty, according to which the sum of $40,000 was to be given to the pirates of Algiers to keep them quiet. Adams continued the policy of paying blackmail to the pirates of the Mediterranean. Jefferson put an end to the practice in 1805. See Channing, *History of the United States*, vol. 4, pp. 44 and 264–9.

[4] See footnote 4 to the letter of March 3, 1798.

[5] See footnote 4 to the letter of March 14, 1798.

will send them to you. The Jacobins in Senate & House were struck dumb, and opend not their mouths, not having their cue, not having received their lessons from those emissaries [which they make; which Tallirand *cancelled*] which Tallyrand made no secret of telling our Envoys are spread all over our Country; and from whence they drew their information. I believe T[alleyra]n[d] is not too scrupelous to take a *fee*. We are ensnared. We shall be destroyd unless the snare is broken, and that speedily. Thus you see Town meetings can judge!

I was much shockd yesterday at reading in the Paper [of yesterday *cancelled*] the death of Mrs. Quincy.[6] I had only heard by way of Mrs. [Samuel Allyne] Otis the day before, that she was unwell. What was her complaint? It must have been sudden I think, or you would have mentiond it. The Glory of the family is departed. Mrs. Quincy was in all respects the first Character in it. I mourn with all her Friends most sincerely, for by them her loss must be deplored. Mrs. Gill is an other of my Friends & connections whose loss I lament.[7] She was however at an age when we could not expect her much longer continuence. Yet I feel these ligaments giving way one after an other. I feel their loss to society and the warning voice to myself, "This Lifes a dream, an empty Show."

How is your weather? Last week we had three or four days when we were obliged to sit with our windows open, and for these three days past we have had a voilent east storm of wind and Rain. We had sallid, and the Trees in our Yard are budding & would have Blossomd in a few days. The Roads had got tolerably good so that I just began to ride out of Town but this great rain will spoil them again.

If we have many troubles we have also many blessings, amongst which & not the least I consider Health. Both the President & I have enjoyd our Health better this winter & spring than usual, but the constant care, application and anxiety will wear out the firmest constitution.

I received Cousin Betsys Letter and shall write to her soon.

Your truly affectionate Sister
ABIGAIL ADAMS

[6] Mrs. Abigail Quincy, widow of Josiah Quincy, Jr. (1744–1775). See the *Columbian Centinel*, March 28, 1798. Mrs. Quincy was the daughter of William Phillips (1722–1804), and sister of Lieutenant-Governor William Phillips (1750–1827), benefactor of Phillips Academy, Andover, Massachusetts.

[7] Mrs. Rebecca Gill, wife of Lieutenant-Governor Moses Gill, of Massachusetts, died at Princeton, Worcester County, at the age of sixty-nine, on March 19, 1798. *Columbian Centinel*, March 24, 1798.

I send you a pamphlet just publishd, said to be written by a Mr. Hopkinson, a young Lawyer, whose father was a judge & Author of the battle of the Kegs.[8]

[Philadelphia], April 7th, 1798

MY DEAR SISTER:

The Senate on thursday voted to have the dispatches from our Envoys made publick, and orderd them Printed, but not the instructions. I hope however that those too, will be published: The People will then be convinced that every word Contain in the Presidents Message of the 19 of March can be justified both by the instructions given, and by the dispatches received, and that what Jugurtha said of Rome is literally applcable [sic] to France.[1] When the Instructions were read in the House, the words of Milton might have been applied to the Jaco[bin]s

> Abash'd the devil stood
> And saw virtue in her own shape
> How Lovely.[2]

Not one of the clan have dared to say, that they themselves would have been willing to have conceded more; or that more could have been granted "consistant with the Maxims, for which our Country has contended at every hazard: and which constitutes the basis of our National Sovereignty."[3] Some of those who have been voters, more than speakers

---

[8] Francis Hopkinson (1737-1791), of Philadelphia, a signer of the Declaration of Independence, published in 1778 "The Battle of the Kegs," which celebrated the first attempt to employ mines in warfare, and is the best known of all his works. His son was Joseph Hopkinson (1770-1842), congressman and jurist, and author of "Hail Columbia." See the letter of April 26, 1798.

[1] Having successfully bribed a majority of the Roman Senate to approve of his process of disposing of his cousins (and rivals) by murder, Jugurtha, King of Numidia, the bastard grandson of Masinissa, observed that "Everything was for sale at Rome." "As he was leaving Rome, he is said to have exclaimed at last, after frequently looking back on it in silence: 'that it was a venal city, and would quickly perish if it could only find a purchaser.'" Sallust, *The Jugurthine War*, Chapters 20, 28, and 35.

[2] . . . abasht the Devil stood,
And felt how awful goodness is, and saw
Vertue in her shape how lovly, saw, and pin'd
His loss; but chiefly to find here observd
His lustre visibly impar'd; yet seemd
Undaunted.   *Paradise Lost*, Book 4, lines 846-851.

[3] "Message to Both Houses of Congress; Transmitting Despatches from France," March 19, 1798: ". . . consistently with maxims for which our country has contended at every hazard, and which constitute the basis of our national sovereignty." Adams, *Works*, vol. 9, p. 157.

came forward and declared their intire satisfaction in the conduct of the President and their conviction of his sincere desire to preserve Peace, their astonishment at the profligate demands of France, and an abhorence of her conduct. These are some of those who have been decived [*sic*] and declare so, but their is yet a Number of a different sort, those whom the French boast of as their Partizens who will not leave them, very wicked Men, who tho now convicted will only shift their ground, retreat for a little while seeing the current without doors sits so strongly against them, but return to the Charge again, as soon as their plans are concerted and matured. It is however come to such a crissis, that they will be adjudged Traitors to their Country. I shall not be able to send you the dispatches untill tuesday next. In the mean time I inclose you Fennos paper, which will give you a few of the out lines. If the communications should have the happy effect which present appearences lead me to hope, that of uniting the people of our Country, I shall not regret that they were calld for. Out of apprehension what might prove the result of such communications to our Envoys, if they still remain in Paris, the President forbore to communicate them and in his Message was as explicit as was necessary for those who reposed confidence in him. But such lies and falshoods were continually circulated, and base and incendary Letters sent to the house addrest to him, that I really have been allarmd for his Personal safety tho I have never before exprest it. With this temper in a city like this, materials for a Mob might be brought together in 10 minuts. When the Language in Baches paper has been of the most insolent and abusive kind, when Language in the House of Rep's has corresponded with it, and anathamas have been thunderd out by Members without doors, and a call upon the people to Humble themselves before their Maker, treated with open contempt and Ridicule, had I not cause for allarm? But that which was meant for evil, I hope may terminate in Good.

    I am not [without *cancelled*] without many fears for our Envoys. The wretches may imprison them and since they avow Algiers for their pattern, oblige us to Ransome them at an enormus price; They are like the three Children in the Furnace.[4] I wish they may have as safe a deliverence. But none of these fears should transpire. Poor Mrs. [Elbridge] Gerry with such a family as she has, may be very misirable with the apprehension if she should know that it is feard they will not be permitted to leave France.

[4] Children of Israel: Shadrach, Meshach, and Abednego. *Daniel*, III, 12–30.

Let Mrs. Black know that my Little Ward has quite recoverd from the small pox. I expect it here tomorrow.

I have received cousins Letter and have answerd it by a little Box which is to be put on Board a vessel going to Boston committed to the care of Mr. Smith & addrest to him. I shall say more to her when I write to her upon the Subject.

I know not when I shall see you, but I exhort the Members to dispatch buisness so as to rise in May. I hope their will subsist more harmony & union, peace and good will in the House than has appeard this Session. May the people be united now they have before them such proof of the base veiws and designs of France to Plunder us of all we hold dear & valuable, our Religion, our Liberty, our Government and our Property.

My kind Regards to Mr. Cranch, to Mrs. Welch, to Sister [Mrs. William] Smith, and all others who interest themselves in the happiness of your

Ever affectionate Sister
Abigail Adams

Philadelphia, April 13, 1798

My dear Sister:

I inclose a Letter to Cousin Betsy, who has been very frank with me upon the subject of her approaching connection. I hope they will live to enjoy mutual happiness.

I believe I have been deficient in not mentioning to you that Mr. [James] Greenleaf was liberated from Prison on Saturday week. I have not seen him. Mr. [Samuel B.] Malcomb was present at Court and heard the examination. He returnd quite charmed with Mr. Greenleafs manners and deportment, tho not so with the counsel against him, who he said used Mr. Greenleaf in a very ungenteel manner but still Mr. G[reenlea]f did not forget what belongd to himself, by which means he obtaind many advocates.[1]

I know my dear Sister you will rejoice that I can hear from my Children publickly, that is officially, tho I have not received any Private Letters. Mr. King writes that he has put on board a vessel bound to Liverpool Letters from Mr. Adams to his Family.[2] That vessel I presume waits to

---

[1] See footnote 6 to the letter of June 25, 1795, and footnote 7 to the letter of February 1–5, 1798.

[2] See footnote 8 to the letter of January 5, 1798.

sail under the convoy granted. The Secretary of State has received by the British packet duplicates of Letters from Mr. Adams at Berlin dated 6 December in which he writes that he was received by the New King of Prussia on the 5th of December, that the King had waved [sic] the common ussage with respect to him, considering the distance of the United States, and received him. Upon presenting his Credentials, he assured the King that he had no doubt that new ones would be sent him, and that he doubted not he should be warranted by his Government in assureing him of the interest the United Stat[e]s take in his welfare and prosperity, and that he should but fulfill their wishes by reiterating to him the sentiments of Friendship and good will which he had in Charge to express to his Royal Father and Predecessor. To which his Majesty answerd, that he was much gratified by the mark of attention which the United States had shown to the Government, and wished to assure him of his repriocal [sic] good will, and good wishes for their happiness and prosperity, that the similarity of the commercial interests of the two Countries renderd the connection between them important, and might be productive of mutual benifit. On the same Evening Mr. Adams had an Audience of the Queen Mother.[3]

This is rather different from the treatment which our Envoys meet with from the 5 Kings in France.[4] The publick opinion is changeing here very fast, and the people begin to see who have been their firm unshaken Friends, steady to their interests and defenders of their Rights and Liberties. The Merchants of this city have had a meeting to prepare an address of thanks to the President for his firm and steady conduct as it respects their interests. I am told that the French Cockade so frequent in the streets here, is not now to be seen, and the Common People say if J[efferso]n had been our President, and Madison & Burr our Negotiators, we should all have been sold to the French—It is evident that the whole dependance of the French is the devision amongst ourselves. Their making such a Noise & pretending to be very wroth at the Presidents speech, is designd only to effect a Change in the chief Majestracy. They dare not openly avow it, but the declaration that all vessels should be subject to capture which had passports on board signd with the Presidents signature is one amongst the many personal insults offerd, but they have sprung a mine now which will blow them up. They have discoverd

[3] Louisa of Hesse-Darmstadt, second wife and widow of Frederick William II, King of Prussia (1786–1797).

[4] Barras, Rewbel, La Révellière, Merlin, and François made up the French Directory as of October, 1797. See footnote 3 to the letter of February 6, 1798.

a greedy appetite to swallow us all up, to make us like the Hollanders, to cut us up like a capon, and deal us out like true Gamesters.

I sent and bought Kings Pantheon as soon as I found myself foild in my recollection.[5]

I shall write to your son tomorrow. I have not heard lately from him.

I don't care whether Mrs. Pope puts me down any butter, if she will only let me have fresh when I come home. I could never find any body who would take the pains which she does, and make so good Butter in the heat of summer.

My Love to Mrs. Norton & Greenleaf. To each I have sent a cimplicity [sic] cap.[6] Respects to Mr. Cranch & Mrs. Welch, from

Your truly affectionate Sister
ABIGAIL ADAMS

Philadelphia, April 21, 1798

MY DEAR SISTER:

I believe I have not written to you before this week. I have been much engaged in writing to my Children, from whom I have had the pleasure of receiving Letters last Saturday, and again this day. My Letters, of the last week were Decbr. 28th, giving me an account of the various disasters which befell them. J. Q. A. writes thus. "I saild with my little Family from London to Hamburgh, which place we reached after a stormy, but not a long passage. From Hamburgh we proceeded heither by—Land I was going to say; but it is rather an ocean of a different description, or what Milton would call, 'a windy Sea of Land,' that is about 200 miles of continual sand banks, converted by the wetness of the season into bogs of mud.[1] We reachd Berlin on the 7 of last Month, and three days after began my severest affliction. My Wife and Brother one after the other were seized with violent and dangerous illnesses. At a Tavern—in a strange Country—unacquainted with any humane Being in it, and Ignorant of the Language in a great measure, you can judge what we all sufferd. Mrs. Adams was so ill for ten days that I could

---

[5] *An Alphabetical List of the Subscribers to the King's Theatre, Pantheon: with references to their different boxes* . . . , London, 1791; or *Description of the Allegory, printed for the curtain of the King's Theatre, Pantheon*, London, 1791.

[6] A small, plain cap, worn either in the house or out of doors, under large hats. These caps were ironed flat, and were used indoors on informal occasions.

[1] So on this windie Sea of Land, the Fiend
Walk'd up and down alone bent on his prey.
Paradise Lost: Book 3, lines 440-1.

scarcly leave her Bedside for a moment, and Thomas seazd with an allarming inflamitory soar Throat & high fever, threatned with an attack of the Rheumatism at the same time. In the midst of our mischances we had the good fortune to find a good Physician, an Englishman who has for many years been settled in this Country. My Wife & Brother, thanks be to God, are now quite recoverd." Thomas delicately explains the sickness of Mrs. Adams, in the following manner. "The extraordinary exertion and fatigue of our voyage and journey proved too much for the delicate constitution of Mrs. Adams, and since our arrival she has undergone severe illness, illness of such a nature as an experienced Matron would easily divine upon calculation and comparison of dates, but which a young Batchelor knows not how to describe, but by the use of terms which practise very properly renders familiar only to professionals.—I conceive that you take my meaning, notwithstanding the veil of Mystery which is thrown over it."—Thomas then goes on to say, that they were "obliged to pass a Month at a publick Hotel before appartments could be found for their accommodation. We are at length settled in a snug family way, tho in point of lodgings we are misirably provided. It is the fashion here for two or three Families to dwell under the same Roof, and tho the houses are large, they are not sufficiently so to accommodate completely the numbers that usually inhabit them." He then proceeds to give an account of the city, and of the King & Queen &c. The King has a very amiable Character. The Perusal of the Letters would give you pleasure, but I do not yet know how to spair them. To day I received an other Letter of 31 of Jan'ry in which he acknowledges receiving Letters from me written in November & December, which is some satisfaction. These Letters are full of information, but it would be spoiling them to curtail them. One Anecdote I will however copy.—"The Great and important object which now raises the most voilent discussions at Paris, relates to the seizure of *certain cloaks* at Lyons, which were Embroidering for the Costume dress of the Legislatures. It appears they were Casimiers of English manufacture, purchased at Sedan and sent to Lyons, to have the appearance of proceeding from the National Looms—But under the late decree of the Directory, commanding the seizure as contraband of all goods of English manufacture; the *Costume cloaks* themselves were laid hold of and subjected to the common destiny—as soon as the counsel of 500 heard the fate of their *Embroidered* Cloaks they took fire, and sent a Message to the Directory complaining of the outrage offerd to the Legislative Body by the minister of police, intimating that they expected him to be punished, and insisting upon having their *precious Cloaks* deliverd up to their committee of Inspectors. The Directory answer that the committee shall have the Cloaks, but that the Embroidering is not finished, and that without an explanatory Law, the Cloaks must be deliverd in their incompleat state. The counsel then with no little Indignation pass an explanatory Law, declaring that they will have their Cloaks with all *the Embroidery* or not at all. And thus ends the momentous affair, which at least serves to shew the condition of their National Manufactures, and at the same time the means used to give them a coulour of Prosperity. At the same time the great expedition to conquer and ruin England and give a directory to the Republic of Albion is going on with great ardour."

The state of our own internal affairs ware a better prospect, as it respects union and dispatch in Buisness. The people who can see and judge for themselves are disposed to do right, but the Ethiopean cannot Change his skin, and the Emissaries were never busier or more active than the vile junto are at present.[2] Bache has the malice & falshood of Satin, and his vile partner the Chronical is equally as bad.[3] But the wretched will provoke to measures which will silence them e'er long. An abused and insulted publick cannot tollerate them much longer. In short they are so criminal that they ought to be Presented by the grand jurors.—I have not a doubt that a late writer in the Chronical under the signature of a Republican has been in concert with the vile liar (Findley who during this session has written a Letter full of falshoods as may be proved from the journals of the Senate, from the treasury Books). This writer has been replied to by one under the signature of Marcus in the Centinal. Republican says the President & his son have received 80,000 dollars in two years. Every one knows from every Almanack and Registure that the sallery for President & Vice President has been the same from the commencment of the Government to this day; and the Man who dare say that a sou more has been received is a Liar, and is calld upon for his proof. Mr. J. Q. Adams has received exactly the same with other Ministers of the same Rank from this Country, a sallery of 4500 as minister Resident, an outfit of that sum when he left the Country. But when his destination was changed, he received only half the sum he would have done if he had gone from this Country. As minister Plenipoteniary, he has 9000 dollors pr year, but was only

[2] See footnote 5 to the letter of February [1–5], 1798.
[3] The *Independent Chronicle and Universal Advertiser*, of Boston, published by Thomas Adams.

allowd half that sum as his outfit. He never received a copper in concequence of his having been appointed to Lisbon, because he did not go tho he had been at the expence of hireing a House there, & actually sent his Books there & paid his own passage, when he received orders to go to Berlin, so that he was actually a looser. Yet these wretches thus deceive the people. These are facts. Let them bring proof to the contrary. Let them go to the treasury Books & they will see how they are abused. I inclose that wicked old Findleys Letter.[4] Their system is evident in every part of the union. Perdition catch them. We had as good have no devil if he does not claim his own. Forgive me if I have been Rash. My indignation is excited at these Hypocrits.

Yours
A. A[dams]

Philadelphia, 22 April, 1798

MY DEAR SISTER:

By the post of yesterday I received yours of April 15. As the post will now go more frequently I hope you will get Letters more regularly.

It was very unfortunate for Mrs. Porter, to have Mr. Sole taken sick the very day after he came, and the more so because she is now encumberd with more buisness. I have written the Dr. [Cotton Tufts] that I think it would be best to through [throw] two Chambers into one and to have access to it from without by stairs, which Chamber may hold all the Books in regular order, and be a pleasent Room for the President to do buisness in, as we are so confind in the House. There are in the granery some Book Shelves which may be made to answer in addition to those we have, and may be new painted. I mean to have the whole executed without Mr. Adams knowing any thing of the accommodation untill he sees it. And when the building is finishd for the Book Room, I must request Brother Cranch to see the putting [them cancelled] the Books up in order. The Room now used for the Books will serve Mrs. Porter for a Lodging Room.

[4] In the spring of 1798, there occurred a most unbecoming controversy as to just how much money in salaries and allowances John Adams and John Quincy Adams were drawing from the federal government. William Findley (1741–1821), a "Republican" member of the House of Representatives from Pennsylvania, seems to have begun it with the letter which Abigail Adams enclosed in her letter to her sister. The controversy was continued in Boston in the pages of the *Independent Chronicle and Universal Advertiser*, published by one Thomas Adams, and the *Columbian Centinel*, published by Benjamin Russell. A "Republican" repeated the charges of Findley in the *Chronicle;* and "Marcus," "Philo-Marcus," and "Detector et Flagellator" defended John Adams and his son in the pages of the *Centinel*. See the *Columbian Centinel* for March 21 and 31, April 4, 11, and 14, 1798.

The Gentlemen say they will let me go home early in June, but it is difficult to keep the good men together. There are now absent nine Federal Senators from some excuse or other, some for a fortnight, some for three weeks, and some for the remainder of the session [which *cancelled*]. I think it difficult to excuse [them *cancelled*] absence at so Critical a period. The Antis all stick by. Tho the Senate are strong, yet they appear to be weak from the absence of so many federal men. In the House they are become so strong, as to do Buisness by a considerable Majority. The Jesuit Gallatin[1] is as subtle and as artfull and designing as ever, but meets with a more decided opposition, and the Party, tho many of them as wicked as ever, are much weakened by some whose consciences will not let them go all lengths with them. As the French have boasted of having more influence in the United States, than our own Government, the Men who now espouse their cause against their own Country, and justify their measures, ought to be carefully markd. They ought to be brought into open light. Addresses from the Merchants, Traders & Underwriters [have *cancelled*] have been presented and signd by more than 500 of Men, of the greatest Property here in this city, highly approveing the measures of the Executive. A similar one from the Grand Jurors, one from York Town, and yesterday, one from the Mayor, Aldermen & common counsel of the city, a very firm and manly address. Others are comeing from N[ew] York, from Baltimore, and I presume Boston will be no longer behind than time to consult upon the measure. They must in this way shew the haughty Tyrrants, that we are not that divided people we have appeard to be; their vile Emissaries make all our trouble, and all our difficulty. A Report is in circulation that our Envoys left Paris for London on the 16 Feb'ry but nothing has been received from them here later than Jan'ry 8th tho many Rumourd accounts of dispatches, has been circulated.

I would recommend to my countrymen the judicious observation of Mr. Burk, who says, "A Great State is too much envied, too much dreaded, to find safety in humiliation. To be secure, it must be respected. Power and Eminence, and consideration are things not to be begged. They must be commanded and they who suplicate mercy from others, can never hope from [for] justice through themselves.... Often has a Man lost his all because he would not submit to hazard all in defending it."[2]

[1] See footnote 4 to the letter of March 3, 1798.

[2] *Burke: Selected Works*, E. J. Payne, Editor, Oxford, 1892, "Letters on the Regicide Peace," pp. 11–12: Letter I (1796).

See the opinion of the French minister at Berlin upon our Naval defence. Mr. Adams writes, "I have had some conversation with the French Minister here concerning the New law against Neutral navigation which he admitted as contrary to the Law of Nations.[3] But he says it is only a necessary Retaliation against the English, and if the Neutral Nations will suffer the English to [seize] all their vessels, the French must do the same. I told him without being disposed to justify or apologize for the Predatory practise of England, which I utterly detested, I must say they never had been carried to an extent any thing resembling this regulation—that besides England was now making indemnification for many of the depredations committed under coulour of her Authority, that if the Principle of Retaliation alledged as a warrant for this new measure on the part of France were founded there could never be any such thing as Neutrality in any maritime [sic] war, for that it would require every Neutral power to make war upon the first instance of improper capture of a vessel under her flag.—No said he, that is not necessary, but the Neutral powers should shew a firm countanance, and determined resolution to maintain its [sic] Rights and send all its commerce under convoy.—I askd him what a power was to do that had no ships of war to give as convoys?—He said *they must raise* sufficient for the purpose." This you see is the opinion of even a French Minister. Yet no longer ago than fryday, our House of Rep's sit till near 8 oclock combatting Gallatins motion, that the President should be restricted from useing the ships built & to be built as convoys in time of Peace, thinking, I presume, as he could not prevent their being built, he would Defeat the use of them at this present time, as France had not declared war, and it was not probable we should. The Federilists cast out the motion by 50 to 34.[4]

I believe I have wearied you with politicks. I wrote Mrs. Black last week, and in hopes that she might get the Letter sooner inclosed it to Mr. Smith, who when it arrives may be absent, which I regreet. Please to tell her that I received her Letter of the 16 yesterday, that since I

[3] See the *Memoirs of John Quincy Adams*, Philadelphia, 1874, vol. 1, pp. 214–5. The diary of John Quincy Adams, *as published*, contains no entry covering this conversation. In 1798, the French minister to Berlin was Antoine-Bernard Caillard (1737–1807), who served under both Louis XVI and the Republic! Adams first met Caillard in St. Petersburg, when he (Adams) was serving as the secretary (1781–1783) to Francis Dana, American minister to Russia. Caillard persuaded Prussia to acknowledge the Rhine as the eastern boundary of the French Republic.

[4] For the warlike measures adopted by the Congress against France in the spring of 1798, see Schouler, *History of the United States*, vol. 1, pp. 397–401.

took the child from Mr. Black, he nor his Housekeeper have not been near it, that they retaind all the Cloaths which the child had except what it had on, and those which Mrs. Black sent it. I knew it must have more clouts or it could not go the journey, never having had more than 8. I have therefore got some diaper and made 13 for it, a couple of yellow flannel coats & two calico slips, all of which we have made and if Mr. Black does not think proper to give up the other things, I will see that the Baby shall have every necessary article. I shall be answerable to the Nurse for its Board, but they made the poor thing sick by taking it out in the Evening and giving it Rum, the Nurse says to make it sleep. It was more uneasy and gave her more trouble than when it was sick with the small Pox. I was quite unhappy about it. It is better now, and I expect to see it to day. I believe I should have lost it, if they had kept it a week, and gone on in the way they began.—I shall rejoice when I hear it is safe with its *Patron* and *Benefactress*—Let me know when the Box for Cousin Betsy arrives. Has Mrs. Norton been unwell? I hope it is not *her old sickness*—My Love to her. When she is Blessd with a daughter I shall think she deserves well of her Country, and need no further aid it with Recruits. I quite long to see you all. I do hope the buildings will be all finished so that Mrs. Porter may be able to remove into them when we come. I should like to have the kitchin floor & stairs painted, and the Chamber floor where the Girls used to sleep. I hope particular attention will be paid to the chimny peice in the parlour to get the smoak of[f], that it may dry.

I inclose 5 dollors. Will you be so good as to get something of the value of a couple of dollors & present to Mrs. Porter. Perhaps a new Bonnet might be acceptable. I will not confine you to two dollars. Please to pay Sister Smith as she knits & keep her supplied with cotton. I will put ten dollors instead of 5 in, that you may draw upon it for a load of wood to Pheby if she wants or Bread corn.

I sent to get an other of Mr. Harpers Books to send to the Library, but tho two thousand were Printed they are all gone. A new Edition is comeing out.[5] I am, my dear Sister, most affectionatly

Your Sister
A. Adams

Mrs. Otis, who with her Family always dine with us on Sundays, desires to be rememberd to you. We live like Sisters.

[5] Robert Goodloe Harper (1765–1825), of Virginia, published in 1797 his *Observations on the Dispute Between the United States and France*, which attracted great attention at home and in Europe, and ran through many editions. Harper was an able and ardent Federalist.

My dear Sister the Aniversary of this day awakens all my feelings—Is poor Suky yet living?[6]

[Get some thing of two dollors value for Mrs. Norton *cancelled*.]

The Baby has been to see me to day. It grows very fast since it had the small pox. I dont think it half so pretty since, as it was before. Yesterday the nurse went to Mr. Blacks, and they sent it what things it had. They had got over their anger, but said they would take it away at the end of a fortnight, but I do not believe them. My pens are very bad but I cannot copy my scrawls.

[Philadelphia], April 26, 1798

My dear Sister:

I inclose to you a National Song composed by this same Mr. Hopkinson.[1] French Tunes have for a long time usurped an uncontrould sway. Since the Change in the publick opinion respecting France, the people began to lose the relish for them, and what had been harmony, now becomes discord. Accordingly their had been for several Evenings at the Theatre something like disorder, one party crying out for the Presidents March and Yankee Doodle, whilst Ciera was vociferated from the other.[2] It was hisst off repeatedly. The Managers were blamed. Their excuse was that they had not any words to the Presidents March—Mr. Hopkinson accordingly composed these to the tune. Last Eve'ng they were sung for the first time. I had a Great curiosity to see for myself the Effect. I got Mr. Otis to take a Box, and silently went off with Mr. and Mrs. Otis, Mr. & Mrs. Buck to the play, where I had only once been this winter.[3] I meant now to be perfectly in cogg, so did not sit in what is

---

[6] The mother of John Adams, Susanna (Boylston) [Adams] Hall (1709-1797), had died just one year before. "Suky" is Susannah Warner, daughter of the second wife of Dr. Cotton Tufts. See footnote 5 to the letter of March 3, 1798.

[1] "Hail Columbia," composed by Joseph Hopkinson (1770-1842), at the request of a young actor and singer of his acquaintance, Gilbert Fox (1776-1807), who was born in England and settled in Philadelphia. Fox was not only a singer, but an actor and an engraver of some note. Years afterward, Hopkinson wrote that Fox had asked him for the song on Saturday, that he had composed it on Sunday, and that it was first sung on Monday evening. April 25, 1798, however, fell on Wednesday, not on Monday.

[2] "Ça ira," the first popular song of the French Revolution, was sung in 1789 by the insurgents as they marched to Versailles. The music was extremely popular under the name ,"Carillon National," which was a great favorite with Marie Antoinette. The words were suggested to Ladré, a street-singer, by Lafayette, who remembered hearing Franklin say, when asked for news at various stages of the American Revolution: "Ça ira, Ça ira."

[3] The scene was the New Theatre in Chestnut Street, Philadelphia, and the companions of Mrs. Adams were Samuel Allyne Otis, Secretary of the Senate from 1789 to 1814, and

calld the Presidents Box. After the Principle Peice was perfor[m]d, Mr. Fox came upon the stage, to sing the song. He was welcomed by applause. The House was very full, and at every Choruss, the most unbounded applause ensued. In short it was enough to stund [*sic*] one. They had the song repeated—After this Rossina was acted.[4] When Fox came upon the state [*sic*] after the Curtain dropt, to announce the Peice for fryday, they calld again for the song, and made him repeat it to the fourth time. And the last time, the whole [Gallery *cancelled*] Audience broke forth in the Chorus whilst the thunder from their Hands was incessant, and at the close they rose, gave 3 Huzzas, that you might have heard a mile—My Head aches in concequence of it. The Managers have requested the President to attend the Theater, and twesday next he goes. A number of the inhabitants have made the same request, and now is the proper time to gratify them. Their have been six differents [*sic*] addresses presented from this city alone; all expressive of the Approbation of the measures of the Executive. Yet dairingly do the vile incendaries keep up in Baches paper the most wicked and base, voilent & caluminiating abuse—It was formerly considerd as leveld against the Government, but now it is contrary to their declared sentiments daily manifested, so that it insults the Majesty of the Sovereign People. But nothing will have an Effect untill congress pass a Sedition Bill, which I presume they will do before they rise[5]—Not a paper from Bache press issues nor from Adams Chronical, but what might have been [prevented *cancelled*] prossecuted as libels upon the President and Congress. [They *cancelled*] For a long time they seem as if they were now desperate —The wrath of the public ought to fall upon their devoted Heads.

I shall send a paper or two because your Boston papers cannot take

---

Daniel Buck (1753–1816), Federalist member of the House of Representatives from Virginia (1795–1797), and their wives.

[4] What Mrs. Adams calls "the principal piece" was "The Italian Monk," a play in three acts, interspersed with songs, and presented for the second time in America. This was followed by "More Sack," an epilogue in the character of Sir John Falstaff, to be spoken by Mr. Warren. Then Gilbert Fox sang "Hail Columbia" to the tune of the "President's March," "accompanied by the full band and a grand chorus." This was encored four times. The evening concluded with a favorite comic opera, in two acts, "not acted these two years," called "Rosina." See the *Gazette of the United States and Philadelphia Daily Advertiser*, April 25 and 26, 1798.

[5] For the texts, and the unpopular results of the Naturalization Act (June 18, 1798), the Alien Act (June 25, 1798), the Alien Enemies Act (July 6, 1798), and the Sedition Act (July 14, 1798), see Henry S. Commager, *Documents of American History*, New York, 1934, pp. 175–8. Pickering pressed for the full enforcement of these ill-advised laws, and to the detriment of Adams.

in one half of what these contain. Mr. Otis's Letter is a very judicious, sensible, patriotic composition, and does him great honour.[6]

You may rely upon it from me, that not a single line from our Envoys have been received but what has been communicated, and nothing has been received from them since the last communication.

I received your Letter of the 20 this day. I am very sorry the closet should be omitted because it wanted painting very much and does not easily dry. I wrote to the Dr. [Cotton Tufts] and proposed having the outside of the house new painted, and the Garden fence also which never was more than primed, but I would not put too many Irons at once in the fire.

If you have got Cousin Betsys Box or she has, as I see the vessel is arrived, you will then find what a drapery dress is, and the Young Lady will teach how it is to be put on. A Cap for you should be made as you usually wear yours, and as I wear mine, of handsome muslin with a pleated border or a lace—I wear no other but upon publick Evenings when I wear a Crape dress cap.

I do not wear the drapery dress myself as I consider it too youthfull for me. I have both sides alike, but they both come forward upon the top & then fall away and are worn with a coat or the Apron lose.

Will you desire Mr. Porter to get some slips of the Quince Tree and sit out in the lower garden.

Adieu my dear Sister. My pen, I think, is scarcly ever dry.

Yours in Love, affection

ABIGAIL ADAMS

P.S. Since writing the above the song is printed. Bache says this morning among other impudence that the excellent Lady of the Excellent President, was present, and shed Tears of sensibility upon the occasion. That was a lie. However I should not have been asshamed if it had been so. I laughed at one scene which was playd, [to] be sure, untill the tears ran down, I believe. But the song by the manner in which it is received, is death to their Party. The House was really crowded, and by the most respectable people in the city.

[6] *Letter to General Heath* (1798). The Roxbury town meeting was "warned" on Monday, March 19, for Tuesday, March 20, 1798. General William Heath (1737-1814), a farmer of Roxbury and a veteran of the Revolution, acted as chairman of the meeting. According to the town records, 113 voted in the affirmative on the motion to petition Congress against permitting merchant vessels to arm in their defence. According to General Heath, only four voted in the negative. On Wednesday, March 21, General Heath wrote to Harrison Gray Otis, whose district included the town of Roxbury. Otis answered him on Friday, March 30, and his letter was published and circulated widely. See Morison, *H. G. Otis*, vol. 1; pp. 68–71 and 88–9. See, also, the *Columbian Centinel*, March 24, 1798, for a letter, signed "Norfolk," attacking this town meeting and General Heath.

Philadelphia, 28 April, 1798

My dear Sister:

I have just received yours of the 23 April and I sit down to answer your inquiries respecting the building. I wrote to Dr. Tufts my Ideas upon it. I should think the East Chambers the best for a Library and I do not see any inconvenience from having the Stairs to it without doors like going into a store, as Mr. Tufts Store is built. I pray neither the Dr. or Mr. Black when he comes will say any thing about the Building. I mean to have it all done snug, and the Library removed if I can before I come, and I pray the Dr. to inform me of the cost, which I design to secure monthly from my expences here. I know the President will be glad when it is done, but he can never bear to trouble himself about any thing of the kind, and he has no taste for it, and he has too many publick cares to think of his own affairs.

You mention Betsys [sic] Shaws illness. I did not know she had been sick, except the beginning of the winter. I am allarmd for her.[1]

The caps are at the bottom of the Box sent to Cousin Betsy. I see by the papers that the vessel is arrived. If she is not at home you may open the Box. I never received the Letter in which the Dr. mentions having inclosed the plan. Tell the Dr. if four or 5 Hunderd dollors will meet the object, I will remit the remainder to him as he shall have occasion.

The Child is very well. Let Mrs. Black know. The weather yesterday was very Hot and is like to be so to day. I had a very full Drawing Room last evening. I must close them in May. I cannot have them in Hot weather. I went yesterday to return some visits, and where ever I past, I received a marked notice of Bows & *the Friends* in the Street *in their way* noticed me. I thought nothing of it, untill my attention was caught by a Bunch of Tradesmen they lookt like, who at the corners of the Street saluted me as I past with their Hats—In short we are now wonderfully popular except with Bache & Co who in his paper calls the President old, querilous, Bald, blind, cripled, Toothless Adams. Thus in Scripture was the Prophet mocked, and tho no Bears may devour the wretch, the wrath of an insulted people will by & by break upon him.[2]

---

[1] Probably Elizabeth Quincy Shaw (1780–1798), daughter of Elizabeth (Smith) [Shaw] Peabody.

[2] "And he [Elisha] went up from thence unto Bethel: and as he was going up by the way, there came forth little children out of the city, and mocked him, and said unto him, Go up, thou bald head; go up, thou bald head.

And he turned back, and looked on them, and cursed them in the name of the Lord. And there came forth two she bears out of the wood, and tare forty and two children of them." 2 *Kings*, II, 23–4.

I have not time to add more than my Love and Regards to all Friends from your
Affectionate Sister
A. ADAMS

Philadelphia, May 7th, 1798

MY DEAR SISTER:

Mr. [Moses] Black got here on thursday night. I was rejoiced to see him. It seemd next to being at home. I yesterday received your Letter of April 29th. I had heard before both of Sukys death and my dear little Mary's.[1] I felt hers the more sensibly, because she was more endeared to me from having been more with me than either of the other Children. My Heart is grieved for Mr. and Mrs. [William] Smith who for this Month Past have seen one continued scene of affliction from the [frequent *cancelled*] repeated Bereavements of Friends, and Relatives. If any thing can effectually wean & detach us from this world, it is the loss of those who render Life pleasent and agreable to us. Yet we are apt to cling closer to those which remain, and Even what are call'd Mrs. Thrails [Thrale] three warnings in her Dialogue between Death and Man, are insufficent too frequently to find us ready to depart, loss of Limbs, loss of Sight & loss of Hearing.[2] I recollect my Mother[-in-law] once said to me after she was Eighty four years old, I *really believe* if I was now sick, I should want to get well again. So strong a principle is the Love of Life. If it was not for the sure and certain hope of a superiour state of existance beyond this transitory scene of Noise, Bustle, pain & anxiety—we should be of all Beings the most misirable. The Present state of the world exhibits in the Revolution of France one of the most astonishing spectacles ever [exhibited *cancelled*] acted upon the stage to scourge the Nations of the Earth. Voltair[e] Predicted that Popery should be overturnd by Atheism.—What is to be our future Lot, and Destiny, remains to be unfolded. I hope we may still Continue to be "that happy people saved of the Lord." That we were sinking into a state of Langour, of Supineness, of Effimanancy & Luxury is but too evident from our stand-

[1] Mary Carter Smith, daughter of "William Smith, Esq., Merchant," niece of Mrs. Adams, died at the age of seven. See the *Columbian Centinel*, April 28, 1798. The *Boston Directory* (1798) lists "William Smith, merchant, No. 53 State Street, house Court Street."

[2] "The Three Warnings. A Tale" is a sprightly poem, in the style of Swift, by Hester Lynch (Salusbury) [Thrale] Piozzi (1741–1821), in which Death, having been persuaded by a young bridegroom to call for him later on in life, pays his second visit only to find the lover of years past lame, deaf, and blind, and no longer unwilling to die. *Autobiography: Letters and Literary Remains*, Boston, 1861, pp. 247–9.

ing in need of such severe & repeated scourging to arouse us to a sense of Danger, and to compell us to rise in defence of our Religion, our Liberties & independance. We are to day at 12 oclock to have a moveing and stricking spectacle, no less than between 7 & 8 Hundred young Men from 18 to 23 in a Body to present an address. Upon this occasion the President puts on his uniform, and the whole House will be thrown open to receive them. A number of Ladies will be present upon the occasion with me. The address and replie will appear in the paper and I will send it to you.[3]

I was pleasd with Mr. Nortons choice of a Text for the subject of his Fast sermon. Peter [Porcupine] I see in his paper of Saturday has been thinking upon the same subject, *that Man is* a very extraordinary [Man *cancelled*] creature. When he pleases he writes admirably, and is the greatest scourge of the french Faction which they have in the Country. His shafts are always tipt with wit, and his humour is such as frequently to excite more of good than ill.

I inclose to you a number of Letters from my sons; Some I have sent for Mrs. Johnson to read, who has not yet received any Letters.[4] Mrs. Johnson in her last Letter writes me, that Mr. Johnson had invited Mr. Cranch to come to George Town and take an office vacant by the death of a Mr. Cook, a Nephew of Mr. Johnsons. She says Mr. Johnson had put all his Papers into Mr. Cranchs Hands. I hope Mr. Cranch will find in Mr. Johnson an alleviation for the loss of Mr. Deakings.[5] Has he written you any thing upon the subject? Mr. Greenleaf has liberty to go out daily, which he does. He may be attended by an officer, and I believe he is, but his confinement is not close as it was. I have ever been an advocate for his intentions, but it is very hard for those who are smarting under the presure of a loss of all they possesst, and that without the least beneifit [*sic*] derived from him, to be reduced with their Families from affluence, to poverty and indigence, to refrain from bitter reflections, and imputations inconsistant with candour and a confidence in the integrity of his heart. I never knew untill this week, that our Friend Mr. Smith of Boston was a looser by him to the amount [of] Eighteen thousand dollors. Do not however mention it to Mr. Smith, as he never hinted the thing himself to me—What a Besom of destruction is this Spirit of Speculation.[6]

[3] Of Adams's answers to addresses from different parts of the United States (1797–1801), fifty-six are printed in *Works*, vol. 9, pp. 180–236; for this reply, see pp. 187–9.

[4] Mrs. Joshua Johnson, of Maryland, mother of Louisa Catherine, wife of John Quincy Adams.

[5] See footnote 2 to the letter of March 27, 1798.

[6] See Clark, *Greenleaf and Law in the Federal City*, p. 195; and the letter of June 1, 1798.

I hope our people will proceed with the buildings as tho I was to be at Quincy the beginning of June. I regret as the Roof is raised that the building was not continued the whole length of it, but the Dr. [Cotton Tufts] did not think of so extensive a plan, any more than I did at first, and the plan which he writes that he inclosed to me never came to Hand—Let me know how it progresses. Have you got the Box I sent to Betsy? The weather has been as Hot for this fortnight past as it was last year in June. The Country looks delightfull. I ride almost every day and enjoy it. I fear we shall be detain here much longer than I wish. I would have the building painted a Stone coulour, and I hope the Dr. poor man if he is able will have the out side of the House painted over white as it now is, but it wants a new coat—I wish the Dr. would try calomil upon himself. I have a great opinion of its efficacey. Return me the Letters as soon as you have read them. Love & respects to all inquiring Friends from your

       Affectionate Sister
        A. ADAMS

       Philadelphia, May 10th, 1798
MY DEAR SISTER:

Rumour at a distance magnifies and seldom reports truth. I have not written you a word upon a subject which I know would have made you at least very uneasy. About three weeks ago, a Letter was sent, or rather brought here of a Sunday Evening by two young women of the City, one of whom said passing the House a few days before She took up a paper in a small alley which runs between our house & our Neighbours. It was wet by lying at the Edge of a gutter which passes through the passage. The Girl, finding it in this way opend the Letter, and read it, but being allarmd at the contents, knew not what to do. Her mother, who was absent at the Time, returning & finding what she had done, directed the Girl to bring it herself, & relate the circumstances. The purport of the Letters [sic] was to inform the President that the French people who were in this city had formed a conspiracy with some unsuspected Americans, on the Evening of the day appointed for the fast to sit fire to the City in various parts, and to Massacre the inhabitants, intreating the President not to neglect the information & the warning given, tho by an annonimous Hand, signd a Real tho heretofore a misguided American. The President conceived it to be an incendary Letter written to allarm & distress the inhabitants. An other Letter of the same purport was sent ten days after, thrust under the door of Mr. Otis's office. These with some Rumours of combinations got abroad, and the Mayor,[1] Aldermen &c kept some persons upon the watch through all parts of the city, & the Governour gave orders privately to have a troop of Horse in case of need.[2] The Young Men of the city as I wrote you on Monday to the amount of near Eleven Hundred came at 12 oclock in procession two and two. There were assembled upon the occasion it is said ten thousand Persons. This street as wide or wider than State Street in Boston, was full as far as we could see up & down. One might have walkd upon their Heads, besides the houses window & even tops of Houses. In great order & decorum the Young Men with each a black cockade marchd through the Multitude and all of them enterd the House preceeded by their committe. When a Young Gentleman by the Name of Hare, a Nephew of Mrs. Binghams, read the address, the President received them in his Levee Room drest in his uniform, and as usual upon such occasions, read his answer to them, after which they all retired.[3] The Multitude gave three Cheers, & followd them to the State House Yard, where the answer to the address was again read by the Chairman of the committe, with acclamations. They then closed the scene by singing the new song, which at 12 oclock at night was sung by them under our windows, they having dinned together or rather a part of them.[4] This scene burnt in the Hearts of some Jacobins and they determined eitheir, to terrify, or Bully the young men out of their Patriotism. Baches publishd some saussy peices, the young men resented and he would have felt the effects of their resentment if some cooler Heads had not interposed. Yesterday was observed with much solemnity.[5] The meeting Houses & churches were fill'd. About four oclock as

[1] Hilary Baker, mayor of Philadelphia at this time, died in office of yellow fever on September 25, 1798. For a description of the circumstances in which this mysterious letter of warning as to arson and murder was found, see Morison, *H. G. Otis*, vol. 1, pp. 110–111, where the source of information is given as "General Correspondence of John Adams, 1797–1798," pp. 173 and 175, in the Adams Manuscripts, which are locked up in the Massachusetts Historical Society.

[2] Thomas Mifflin (1744–1800), merchant, member of the Continental Congress, and soldier of the Revolution, served three terms as governor of Pennsylvania (1790–1799). His wife, Sarah Morris, was described by John Adams as "a charming Quaker girl."

[3] The famous Mrs. William Bingham, one of the daughters of Thomas Willing (1731–1821), Philadelphia banker, who was at one time a partner of Robert Morris. Willing's thirteen children made up a numerous and influential clan in Philadelphia. This nephew of Mrs. Bingham was Robert Hare (1781–1858), distinguished chemist, the son of Robert and Margaret (Willing) Hare. See Morison, *H. G. Otis*, pp. 133–6.

[4] "Hail Columbia." See the letter of April 26, 1798.

[5] Wednesday, May 9, 1798, was observed as "A Day of Public Humiliation, Fasting and Prayer, throughout the United States." *Columbian Centinel*, May 9, 1798; Adams, *Works*, vol. 9, pp. 169–70; and footnote 2 to the letter of March 31, 1798.

is usual the State House Yard, which is used for a walk, was very full of the inhabitants, when about 30 fellows, some with snow Balls in their Hats, & some with tri-coulourd cockades enterd and attempted to seize upon the Hats of the Young Men to tear out their cockades. A scuffel ensued when the Young Men became conquerors, and some of these tri coulourd cockades were trampled in the dust. One fellow was taken, and committed to Jail, but this was sufficient to allarm the inhabitants, and there were every where large collections of people. The light Horse were calld out & patrold the streets all Night. A gaurd was placed before this House, tho through the whole of the Proceedings, and amidst all the collection, the Presidents name was not once mentiond, nor any one grievence complaind of, but a foreign attempt to try their strength & to Awe the inhabitants if possible was no doubt at the bottom. Congress are upon an Allien Bill.[6] This Bache is cursing & abusing daily. If that fellow & his Agents Chronical, and all is not surpressd, we shall come to a civil war. I hope the Gen'll Court of our State, will take the Subject up & if they have not a strong Sedition Bill, make one—Before I close this I shall send to the post office.

Quincy address and a Letter from Brother Cranch, News papers but not a line from my sister. Well, I trust the next post will bring me some.

I must now close my Letter or the post will be gone. The Nurse & childern and Nabby Hunt are all going on Board this morning. Nabby holds me to my word that I would let her go home this spring, no difficulty or uneasiness on either part. She is wrong for herself. I have given her a dollor pr week ever since she has been with me, paid her doctor, and she is now going to ——. She will find the difference. I suppose she thinks she may get a Husband at home. Here there is no chance.

Your ever affectionate
A. Adams

Mr. Black was here & well to day.

Philadelphia, May 13, 1798

My dear Sister:

I write you a few lines by Mr. Black altho I know the post will go quicker. I hope to get Letters to day from Quincy. Now a week since I heard. We are thank God all well. The President is most worn down. I

[6] The Alien Act, and the Alien Enemies Act, passed June 25 and July 6, 1798. Commager, *Documents of American History*, pp. 176–7.

tell the Gentlemen if they do not give him a respit soon, it will be too much for him. The Numerous addresses which pour in daily in abundance give him much additional writing. They are however a gratefull and pleasing testimony of the satisfaction of the publick mind, assurances to support the Government, notwithstanding the pains which has been taken to poison it.

I send you my dear Sister a peice of Muslin for two Crowns of caps. It must be done up with great care. It is calld Deca Muslin.[1] It does not look well to tell the price of any thing which is for a present, but that you may know its real value, I will tell you that it was six dollors pr yd. It is accompanied by a peice for a Border which to get the blew out you must put in vinigar & water. I have also sent you a narrow lace for to put on them. If you put a double Border there will be enough for only one. Let me know, because when I find a pretty Edging I will send you enough for the other. You will want to run the lace upon a narrow peice of Muslin. Ladies of your age wear such fine Muslin, with white Ribbons made like the dress close caps, with a little Hair seen at the Ears. I have not time to add more, than

Yours,
A. A[dams]

Philadelphia, May 13, 1798

My dear Neice:[1]

If I have not written to you my dear Neice it is not because I have not frequently thought of you. Through the winter, your good Mother has often informd me of your welfare and that your little Girl was well. I have sent by Mr. Black a little token of my Remembrance to her, not because I thought you had not pretty things in Boston, but merely that she might have a slip of my giving her. If she is in short coats, and what I

---

[1] "Imported (via New York) on the ship Hero, from Madras and Calcutta, and for sale by the subscriber, at No. 61 Chestnut Street . . . the following articles . . . Dacca worked muslins . . . Mull Mull handkerchiefs . . . Samuel Wilson." *Gazette of the United States*, January 16, 1798. "Dacca muslin is an exceedingly filmy and fragile textile, manufactured at Dacca, in Bengal, and much used by women for dresses and by men for neckerchiefs in England about 100 years ago. The Dacca Muslin now employed resembles the modern Madras Muslin, and is used for curtains." S.F.A. Caulfield, *Dictionary of Needlework*, London, 1885.

[1] This letter was addressed to Mrs. Lucy (Cranch) Greenleaf (1767–1846), wife of her cousin, John Greenleaf, who was the brother of James Greenleaf of the North American Land Company.

send would make two, with the addition of half a yd more, pray inform me and I will procure it. Mr. Black goes from hence this morning. It has been a Great pleasure for me to see him, both as a Friend and Neighbour. I hope he will get the little orphan safe Home. It will not then suffer for those it has lost.[2]

I mourn with you & with all who knew, your Faithfull, Learned, good and Benevolent Pastor, your loss.[3] Many of my Friends and acquaintance are gone, since I left Home, tho only six months since. My Love to Mrs. [William] Smith when you see her. I most sincerely sympathize with her, under the repeated shocks she has sustain'd. My dear little Mary is amongst the number of those I shall miss, when I return, which I hope I may be able to, in the month of June.[4] My kind regards to Mr. [John] Greenleaf.

From your affectionate Aunt
ABIGAIL ADAMS

Your uncle & Louisa desire to be rememberd.

Philadelphia, May 18, 1798

MY DEAR SISTER:

What, no Letters from Quincy, has been repeated every day for a week upon the return of every messenger from the post office. I was hunting up my pen this morning & going to sit down and inquire whether my dear sister was sick when yours of May 10th was brought me. You can hardly judge how impatient I feel if I do not hear once a week. But have you not received a Letter from me inclosing a Bill of Laiding of the Box which was addrest to Mr. Smith & which Bill I desired you to forward to him? I sent such a one to you before the vessel sail'd. Pray have it inquired for. Two of Mrs. Goulds daughters who was formerly of Boston went in this vessel. Mrs. Gould must be known to Mr. [William] Smith. The address arrived last week and Mr. Black carries the answer to it & placed his name to it here. He intended reaching Quincy this day. He can tell you all about us, and about Philadelphia & the spirit of the times. I am rejoiced to see that the pople [sic] are roused to a sense of their danger, and to a determination to support their Rights. The Good

---

[2] See the letters of December 12 and 26, 1797.

[3] Probably the Reverend John Clarke (1755–1798), who died suddenly on April 2, 1798. See footnote 2 to the letter of June 27, 1798.

[4] See footnote 1 to the letter of May 7, 1798.

sense & property of the Country must be in its support. They cannot suppose that their President can have any object in view for himself or Family, from the whole course & tennor of his Life, incompatable with the honour, dignity and independance of his Country. He has his all at Stake, & more than any other individual, because of his high responsibility. The numerous addresses do honour to our Country, tho they load the President with constant application to his pen, as he answers all of them and by this means has an opportunity of diffusing his own sentiments, more extensively & probably where they will be more read and attended to than they would have been through any other channel. His manner of Receiving the youth of this city and his replie to them, I am told has attachd them so much to him, that a word to them from him upon any subject will not fail of [his *cancelled*] its influence. Of this he had a trial this week, upon a trivial subject, it is true, but it was one which might have had concequences. But his opinion signified to one of the Committe instantly was complied with—A Bill has been before the House empowering the President to receive voluntary Choirs [Corps, *see below*] in case of need. Varnum and Gallitin have opposed it vehemently. It was yesterday carried by a Great Majority in the House.[1]

I am equally anxious with Col. Daws for the fate of our Envoys.[2] With the best intentions I fear they have been too believing, and submitted to more humiliation than their country required of them, by remaining after the last decree of the Directory. I send you the last dispatches—and I sometimes add a news paper, supposing it contains more than you can get otherways. I long for the time to come when I may sit my face Northward. I have not received any account of the Dr. [Cotton Tufts] receiving a Bill of a hundred dollors sent I believe in my last Letter to him. He mentions having received the Letter to you, so I presume he got it. I hope he will be able to write me soon. The President received a Letter from him this week. I pray Heaven to prolong his usefull Life.

Return the Letters from my Children, as soon as you can. I inclose you one from your son, and one from my Friend Mrs. Johnson, which you will be so good as to return me.[3] I have but little time to write now as the post will go out at 12 oclock, but I congratulate you upon a brighter

[1] See the Act of May 28, 1798. Schouler, *History of the United States*, vol. 1, p. 397, note 3.
[2] Probably Thomas Dawes, father of Harrison Dawes (1794–1835), who married Lucy Greenleaf, the daughter of Lucy Cranch and John Greenleaf.
[3] See footnote 4 to the letter of May 7, 1798.

prospect for him. I have bespoken for Mrs. Cranch the kind and Material regard of Mrs. Johnson, and told her, that like her own daughter she had been seperated from all her natural connections. I have written to Mr. Cranch & his uncle has written the Letter he requested for Mr. Carrol.[4] I am anxious for Betsy Shaw. A change of Air might serve her. She is [in] too high & keen a situation, I fear, for the State of her Lungs.[5] My Love to Mrs. Black. I long to hear she has got her little Girl.

Most affectionatly your Sister
ABIGAIL ADAMS

Philadelphia, May 20th, 1798

MY DEAR SISTER:

I was sorry to read to day in the Centinal of the 16th an account said to be written by a member of congress to his Friend in Conneticut [an account *cancelled*] so contrary to truth. If the writer had said the State House Yard or Gardens, instead of the Presidents House, he would have written the Truth, but most assuredly there was no appearence of any persons round this House, or near it, untill the Gaurd of light Horse came. You will hear many a Goblin story I doubt not, but you may rest assured we are not ourselves apprehensive.[1] The ardour and attentions of the Citizens is so great, that if a House takes fire a gaurd [*sic*] is placed round us. On the Evening the allarm was, you will recollect that I wrote you a great concourse of persons were assembled in the street before our doors, but it was not untill the affray took place in the State House Yard that the light Horse were calld out, or that any persons assemblied here, & then they were citizens I believe from the orderly behaviour & silence which was preserved.

---

[4] Daniel Carroll, of Duddington, a large holder of land in the District of Columbia, and a nephew of Daniel Carroll (1730–1796), one of the commissioners of the Federal City, that is, Washigton, D.C., until his resignation in 1795. Clark, *Greenleaf and Law in the Federal City*.

[5] Probably Elizabeth Quincy Shaw (1780–1798), daughter of Elizabeth (Smith) [Shaw] Peabody. See footnote 1 to the letter of April 28, 1798.

[1] As an instance of the touchiness of Adams and his wife in regard to trifling errors in the newspapers, see the *Columbian Centinel* for May 16, 1798: "May 7, 1798. This day at 12 o'clock, the Young Men of this city assembled at the *Merchant's Coffee House*, from whence they marched in a body, attended by an immense concourse of their fellow-citizens, forming a body of upwards of 1200, bearing the American Standard, and wearing the American cockade, to the house of the President of the *United States*, where they presented to him their address." The correction offered by Mrs. Adams is of no importance.

I also see a Letter from Mr. Bourn in the paper respecting our Envoys.[2] Government have not received any such account, altho there are letters from Mr. Murrey [sic] & Mr. King[3]—I cannot however take it upon me to deny the fact, tho I think it the worst News we could hear, because suppose it true, I believe it only calculated to deceive and amuse us, the more effectually to devour us. When I hear of an order to stop all depredations upon our commerce and to restore what has been unjustly robd from us, then shall I believe that they consider our Friendship of some use and value to them, not that they are acting from Principles of equity or justice, whilst they are dealing such vengence to other Nations. If they approach a step towards us, it is because there is some formidable combination taking place with some other powers against them,—I hope it will not damp the ardour of Patriotism which is just rousing from its stupour. The best negotiaters we can possibly have, are our addressers pledging their Lives and fortunes. Our Preliminaries are fortifications, Armed vessels and voluntary [Choirs *cancelled*] Corps.

21 May, [1798]

Upon a further attention to the Letter of Mr. Bourn I find not the least inducement to believe that it refers to any thing of a later date than the dispatches received by [the] Government dated in Febry. There are letters from Mr. Murrey [sic] ten days later and no mention is made of any such event or expectation; that Spain & other powers

---

[2] In the *Columbian Centinel*, May 16, 1798, the following letter and editorial note appeared:

Amsterdam, March 20, 1798.

Mr. Benjamin Russell,
Boston.
Sir,
  I avail myself of the first opportunity to acquaint you that the ship *America*, Capt. Henshaw, from New-York, lately brought in here by a French cruiser, has been immediately released by the Consul of that nation; and I am happy to add, that every thing will be done here to support and protect the intercourse with the United States.
  My letters by the last mail from Paris mention, that our Envoys had lately have [sic] several conferences with the Minister of Foreign Affairs—result not known.—
I am, your obedt. servt.
Sylvanus Bourne.
Another letter from the above gentleman says, that Mr. Gerry had informed him, that the Envoys had had three conferrences [sic] with the Minister for Foreign Affairs, and that the negotiation appeared to be in good train.

[3] For Rufus King, see footnote 8 to the letter of January 5, 1798. For William Vans Murray, American minister to the Netherlands and envoy to France (1799–1800), see footnote 4 to the letter of January 20, 1798.

appear to be assumeing more spirit is true. Hear before you blame, is a good maxim, but it seems as if our Envoys were of the bird or cat kind to be fasinated [with the *cancelled*] by the serpents of France. They know not to what a pitch the pulse of their countrymen Beat.

I am very sorry Mr. Cabbot [*sic*] declined accepting the Secretaryship of the Navey.[4] No body but himself doubts his ability to have executed the trust well. On such occasions as the present, every hand should be put to the plough. I fear congress will continue to sit far into the Month of June. I think sometimes if they do not rise & give [their *cancelled*] the President a respit, they will have Jefferson sooner than they wish.

I never saw Mr. Adams look so pale, and he falls away, but I dare not tell him so. His spirits are however [are *cancelled*] good, but he wants a ramble in the clear air of the Country, and a new Scene. I stand it, better and have my Health better this Spring, tho an ill turn of a day or two at a time, is scarcly worth mentioning when compared to the weeks of confinement I have experienced.

You mentiond in your Letter that Dr. Tufts wanted only 200 hundred dollors. I did not know whether you meant in addition to what I had sent. I however inclose one which you will deliver to him; if another is wanted I can send it the begining of June. I dont know how I shall send a trunk to Boston. There are so many French Privateers cruizing that I dare not venture.

You must write to me once a week certainly, no matter whether you have a subject of more concequence than our mere domestick affairs. How does the building go on? Have you seen it lately? I hope the Book Room will be large enough and that it will be pleasent. My best regards to Dr. Tufts, who I hope is better. I think [it *cancelled*] his disorder Rhumatick. I am very anxious for Betsy Shaw. When do you expect Cousin Betsy back? Have you not got the Box yet? Captain Bradford of the schooner *Sally* was the vessel by which it went. I sent you the Bill of laiding with a request that you would forward it to Mr. Smith. Love to all Friends from

Your ever affectionate Sister
A. ADAMS

Write as soon as you receive this & send your Letter to Boston if not post day. We get news papers in 5 days now.

[4] George Cabot (1752–1823), who, weary of politics, resigned his seat in the Senate in May, 1796, retired to private life, and refused an appointment as the first Secretary of the Navy in 1798.

Philadelphia, May 26, 1798

MY DEAR SISTER:

Yours of the 18 I received on thursday 23, and I rejoice to hear Mr. Black got home so soon, as I think he could dissipate your anxiety on our account. I may be too confident, but I do not feel as if any body wanted to hurt or injure us. Bearing neither malice or ill will towards any one, not even the most deluded, I cannot be particuliarly apprehensive. I wish the Laws of our Country were competant to punish the stirer up of sedition, the writer and Printer of base and unfounded calumny. This would contribute as much to the Peace and harmony of our Country as any measure, and in times like the present, a more carefull and attentive watch ought to be kept over foreigners. This will be done in future if the Alien Bill passes, without being curtaild & clipt untill it is made nearly useless.[1] The Volunteer Corps which are forming not only of young Men, but others will keep in check these people, I trust. Amongst the many addresses have you particuliarly noticed one from the state of N[ew] Jersey with the Govr. at their head, as commander in chief?[2] It is from all the officers, and they are not vain and empty tenders, for a deputation from their Body is comeing to Present the address on Monday next, and to tender their services as a volunteer Corps. I wish with you that I could see as great a Change for the better in Morals as in politicks, but it is a part of Religion as well as morality, to do justly and to love mercy and a man can not be an honest & Zealous promoter of the Principles of a True Government, without possessing that Good will towards man which leads to the Love of God, and respect for the Deity; so that a proper appreciation of our Rights & Duties as Citizens, it is a prelude to [of *cancelled*] a respect for Religion, and its institutions. To destroy and undermine Religion has been the cheif engine in the accomplishment of this mighty Revolution throughout Europe. We have felt no small share of the balefull influence of the Age of Reason, but to have a thorough Idea of the deep laid system, you must read a work lately publishd calld proofs of a conspiracy against all the Religions and Governments of Europe, by John Robison, Professor of

---

[1] See footnote 6 to the letter of May 10, 1798.

[2] Richard Howell (1754–1802), soldier of the Revolution, Governor of New Jersey (1793–1801). Howell helped suppress the "Whiskey Insurrection," wrote the popular song, "Dash to the Mountains, Jersey Bell," and was described as "The soul of honor, friend of human kind."

Natural Philosophy in the university of Edinburgh.³ This Book I have sent to Dr. Belknap with a request that if he possesst a Copy, that he would send it to Mr. Cranch.⁴ If he has not, he will lend it to him. You will read the Book with astonishment. What led me to send the Book at this Time, was from a Letter from my son at Berlin, who I know from his manner of writing had not seen the Book. It was first publishd last Sep'br in Edinburgh. In his Letter he mentions a society calld a *Theo Philanthropick*,⁵ and describes it as a [mixture of *cancelled*] a [*sic*] Theological & political mixture of deism, morality and Anti-Christianity—that to propagate these doctrines, persons had been sent lately to Hamburgh; and that *Dupont de Nemours* was talkd of as comeing out to America to establish such societies here.⁶

I have made the extract from his Letter at length, and sent it to Dr. Belknap together with Robisons work, which fully unfolds the whole scheme, and displays the effects of the Principles in the Revolutions in Europe to their full extent. I thought I could not do a better service than to put our Countrymen upon their Gaurd. The son of this Dupont [Victor Du Pont] has just arrived in this city from Charlstown, S[outh] C[arolina], where he was Consul. He is now sent here in order to super-

³ John Robison (1739–1805), "one of the greatest mathematical philosophers of his age," was graduated from the University of Glasgow, where he later lectured on chemistry. He served in Canada with Wolfe, and became professor of Natural Philosophy in the University of Edinburgh in 1773, and-first general secretary of the Royal Society of Edinburgh in 1783. He was a copious contributor to the *Encyclopædia Britannica*. Although James Watt, the engineer, said of him: "He was a man of the clearest head and the most science of anybody I have ever known," Robison, who was himself a Freemason, published what has been called "a lasting monument of fatuous credulity"—*Proofs of a Conspiracy against all the Religions and Governments of Europe, carried on in the secret meetings of Freemasons, Illuminati, and Reading Societies*, Edinburgh, 1797. A fourth edition of this book appeared in London and New York in 1798. This was the absurd book which Mrs. Adams was reading. It was Robison who passed on to posterity the famous story of General Wolfe's having quoted Gray's *Elegy* from memory the night before his death at the capture of Quebec.

⁴ Jeremy Belknap (1744–1798), Congregational clergyman, author of the *History of New Hampshire*, 1784–1792, and the *American Biography*, 1794–1798, and founder of the Massachusetts Historical Society.

⁵ Theophilanthropy, a system of Deism based on a belief in the existence of God and in the immortality of the soul, which appeared in France in 1796 and died out about 1801. *Oxford English Dictionary*. "Larévellière de Lépeaux enjoys the distinction of having invented a new religion of his own; but 'Theophilanthropy' ('a kind of hotch-potch of Rousseau, Voltaire, Socrates, Seneca, and Fénélon') soon outlived an ephemeral popularity." J. R. Moreton Macdonald, *A History of France*, New York, 1915, vol. 3, p. 75.

⁶ Pierre Samuel Dupont de Nemours, who was born at Paris in 1739, and died near Wilmington, Delaware, in 1817, was a French political economist and politician, a friend of Thomas Jefferson, and the founder of the Dupont Family in the United States.

ceed Le Tomb [Joseph Philippe Létombe], as consul-general.[7] He told a Gentleman who mentiond it at the drawing Room last Evening that his Father was gone to Hamburgh in order to embark for America, which corresponds with the account given by Mr. [J. Q.] A.—and he added that he found the spirit of the times such, that he should be very sorry to have his Father come out. The intention was that he should have come out to accompany the Marquiss La Fayett & Family. By this means you see, he would naturally have been cordially & kindly received, and have crept unsuspected into the Bosoms of Americans, untill he had bit like a Serpent and stung like an Adder.[8] Was there ever a more basely designing and insidious people? Burk was right, when he described the French republick to be [founded *cancelled*] founded upon Regicide, Jacobinism and Atheism, and that it had joind to those Principles: a body of systamatick manners, which secured their opperation.[9]

Robisons Book will shew you how much the corruption of manners has aided in the destruction of all Religious and moral Principles. All the new institutions strike at the root of our social nature. Mr. Burk goes on to observe in his Letters upon the Regicide Directory, "that other Legislators knowing that marriage is the origin of all Relations, and concequently the first Element of all duties, have endeavourd by every Art to make it sacred." The following observation ought to be [indelliably *cancelled*] indelbly [*sic*] written upon every mind. "The Christian Religion by confining it to pairs and by rendering that Relation indissoluable, has by these two things, done more towards the peace, happiness, settlement and civilization of the world, than by any other part in this whole scheme of divine wisdom."[10]

I objected to the answer to the Boston address upon the same Principle you mention.[11] I did get an alteration in it, but between ourselves, I think the address itself as indiffcrent as most any one which has been sent. But this is confidential.

Inclosed is a Letter [from *cancelled*] for Mr. Black, which I return as he requested. I hear nothing yet of the Box sent for Cousin Betsy. I hope it is not lost.

[7] In 1798, Talleyrand replaced Joseph Philippe Létombe as consul-general at Philadelphia with Victor Marie du Pont (1767-1827). See footnote 1 to the letter of July 17, 1798.

[8] "At the last it [wine] biteth like a serpent, and stingeth like an adder." *Proverbs*, XXIII, 32.

[9] *Burke: Selected Works*, "Letters on the Regicide Peace," pp. 70-2, Letter I.

[10] *Ibid.*, p. 74, Letter I.

[11] Adams, *Works*, vol. 9, p. 189.

We have had some delightfull rains these two days past. I want to escape the cage & fly to Quincy but know not when to say it will be. I am, my dear Sister,

Affectionatly yours

A. ADAMS

P.S. Louisa desires me to inquire when you expect her sister back. My Letters to you are first thoughts, without correction.

[Philadelphia], 29th May, 1798

MY DEAR SISTER:

I just write you a line to day, to tell you we are well, and to inclose Letters from my Family. We have not any thing new since I wrote you last, except a fine rain, which is truly a blessing, for the Grass and Grain were in a suffering condition, and the dust so intollerable as to render riding very dissagreable. I am to drink tea on Board the Frigate *United States* this afternoon if the weather permits—On Saturday the Captain hopes to go out—I was glad to see by the papers of yesterday that Captain Beals was arrived. I should have been sorry if he had lost his place on Board the Frigate.[1]

I inclose to you a paper containing a number of addresses and answers. I think [Benjamin] Russel might enlarge his paper and take some of them in, that the knowledge of the prevailing spirit & sentiments might be diffused, especially as not a Jacobin paper publishes one of them, but an Insolent impudent thing of 14 or 15 Grenadeers with a St. Domingo captain at their head, has found its way into all there papers.[2] But

[1] This frigate of 44 guns was one of those designed by Joshua Humphreys expressly to outclass the existing type of frigate in the British and French navies. It was built in 1798, and became famous. In 1799, Chief Justice Ellsworth and Governor Davie boarded her at Newport, Rhode Island, at the command of John Adams, and, after a prosperous voyage across the Atlantic, entered the Taguo on one of the last days of November. The two commissioners landed finally near La Coruña, from which place they pushed on to Paris to join Vans Murray. On October 25, 1812, the *United States* engaged and captured the 44-gun British frigate *Macedonian*, and brought ship and crew into Boston Harbor. See Channing, *History of the United States*, vol. 4, pp. 205–6 and 476–7.

[2] After the completion of the ratification of Jay's Treaty in 1796, the United States extended *de facto* recognition to the quasi-independent government of Toussaint L'Ouverture, the Negro chieftain who had dispossessed French authority in Santo Domingo. The ports of that island were excepted from the non-intercourse law against France until June 26, 1799. The British used the ports of Santo Domingo for their naval patrol of the West Indies, where their search and seizure of American ships added fuel to the flames of sympathy for France in the United States. See [*John*] *Russell's Commercial Gazette*, May 28, 1798; the *Massachusetts Spy and Worcester Gazette*, May 30, 1798; Charles R. King, *The Life and Correspondence of Rufus King*, New York, 1894–1900, vol. 2, p. 285, and Appendix 2, pp. 616–634; and S. F. Bemis, *A Diplomatic History of the United States*, New York, 1942.

Russels paper is pretty much like what Peter [Porcupine] says the N[ew] York papers have been of late, "not worth a curse." The Mercury might like to publish some of them.[3] How does the Farm look, says the President? Oh that I could see it, and ramble over it. Does not Sister Cranch say a word about it? Have you heard lately from Atkinson [New Hampshire]? Poor little Caroline has got the Ague & fever.[4]

Yours affecly
A. ADAMS

Philadelphia, June 1, 1798

MY DEAR SISTER:

I was indeed greatly afflicted by the contents of your last Letter. I received it yesterday, and having a large party of Ladies and Gentlemen to dine, I felt but Little spirit to receive or entertain them. I did not communicate it to the President untill the Evening, when he insisted upon it, that I had some dissagreable News which had affected my spirits. Least [sic] he should suppose it greater, or of a different kind, I told him. He most sincerely participates with the distresst family. It hurts him, as you know all, & every thing which afflicts his Friends, does. I have all anxiety for our worthy Friend Mr. Smith, least he should be materially affected by it. His loss by Mr. Greenleaf was very heavey.[1] Like his Father, he is the Friend in secreet, as well as openly, and his own troubles he surpresses. I fear Mr. J. Q. A. must be a sufferer. I know he left his little all in the Drs. [Thomas Welsh's] Hands. He has since his absence directed his Brother Charles to draw upon him for a sum, I do not exactly know how much, & vest it in real estate; This he did, but afterwards was prevaild upon to let it go, & what security he now has I know not. Knowing the Family difficulties, and that it is a [difficult *cancelled*] hard thing to keep clear of them, I got some knowledge from a Quarter which I dared not disclose, that the Property was in Jeopardy. I then wrote to Mr. J. Q. A., advising him to employ Dr. Tufts in future as his Agent. He then wrote me that he had written Dr. Welch to lay out his

---

[3] *The Massachusetts Mercury*, published in Boston. Benjamin Russell, Federalist publisher of the *Columbian Centinel*. See footnote 8 to the letter of June 3, 1797.

[4] Caroline Amelia Smith, daughter of Abigail Adams and Colonel William Stephens Smith.

[1] Mrs. Adams refers to financial losses resulting from the speculations of James Greenleaf. "Mr. Smith" is not her brother, William Smith, but probably that "William Smith, Esq." who was elected one of the selectmen of Boston, standing third in the poll of seven victors, on Monday, May 14, 1798. See [*John*] *Russell's Commercial Gazette*, May 17, 1798.

Property in a freehold in Boston; I know not what to do.[2] I believe I had better write to Charles, and if I find he has the property secure, to hold it untill he can hear from his Brother.

The longer we live in the world, the more do troubles thicken upon us, yet we hug the fleeting shadow. Have you heard from Haverhill, or rather Atkinson? I am anxious for Betsy Q[uincy] Shaw. I think a change of air might be good for her.

I am glad to learn that the buisness goes on so rapidly at Quincy. I do expect to see it, the beginning of July, I fear not sooner. Pray desire Mrs. Porter not to use the Bacon, but to have Beef procured. I found so much difficulty to get any good when I was at home [that was good *cancelled*] that I should be loth not to have enough. In about 6 days I will remit what the Dr. wants. I should like to know that what I sent to you for the Dr. had arrived safe. I have not learnt how Mrs. Blacks little Girl got to Quincy. I think Nabby Hunt was a foolish Girl to go home and relinquish a dollor pr week which I have given her ever since I first hired her, for a very easy kind of Buisness, and go home to Poverty. I did not send her away, for Nabby was a solid honest Girl. But for the buisness, I have got a much better one. Let me know how far the building is compleated. I hope it will all be finishd before I get home and all the workmen gone. If you think the walls will not be sufficiently dry for papering, that can be omitted untill an other season. With the kindest Regard for all our dear Friends and a sympathy in their troubles I am, my dear Sister,

Your ever affectionate
A. ADAMS

Mrs. Brisler is much afflicted at the death of her Mother. The answer to the Quincy address tho short was from the Heart.[3]

Philadelphia, Monday, June 4, 1798

MY DEAR SISTER:

I received on Saturday yours of May 28th. I wrote you on Saturday previous to my receiving yours. I am very sorry if the Box I sent should be lost. It was a square Box covered with canvass, the same you sent my cap in last summer, addrest to Mr. Smith—The dress in it together with the handkerchief, Ruffels &c was of 30 dollors value. I intended it for Betsys wedding dress. The vessels Name the *Sally & Polly*, Cap. Brad-

[2] For Dr. Thomas Welsh, see Adams, *Works*, vol. 9, pp. 571-2.
[3] Adams, *Works*, vol. 9, p. 197.

ford. I was rejoiced to learn that Mrs. Blacks little Girl was safely arrived. She is not very fair, nor do I think her so pretty as she was when younger, but she was tand with the water no doubt. I did not have any conversation with Mr. Black respecting Mr. Whitman.[1] I thought as he had been so constant and determined in his opposition, that it would be to no purpose, and if the thing cannot work its own cure I do not believe persuasion will. A prudent, discreet conduct on the part of Mr. Whitman will have the greatest effect. Yet we must suppose that Mr. Whitman has his feelings, & that he cannot go to Mr. Blacks without a new invitation after having been so much opposed by him. I think the first step should be taken by those in opposition towards Mr. Whitman, unless affliction assails any of them. Then the man should forget his feelings, and the true spirit of Christianity induce him to do good even to those who have despightfully used him. When Mr. Black lost his Brother & Sister Mr. Whitman should have visited them—then was the time for him to have won them. Mr. Black has a tender feeling Heart, all alive to distress, and actively benevolent.—I will however when I return use my good offices to unite them.

I have not heard from your son nor from Mrs. [Joshua] Johnson since I wrote you last. Mr. Johnson, I understand, has sufferd very much since the war, between France & England, and he is obliged to attend very closely to his affairs here, where he had large sums oweing to him.

Dr. [Thomas] Welch and Family are never out of my mind. I know not what to say to them by way of comfort or consolation. I have written to Mr. [William] Smith asking his opinion of sending Thomas to Berlin to Mr. [John Quincy] Adams in lieu of T[homas] B[oylston] Adams, who is determined to return home this fall, and who begs me to send some body in his Room.[2] Thomas is a solid Lad, Loves Mr. Adams, was brought up with him, and it will be a living for him for a year or two, and prepare him for future buisness, and I should suppose that the proposal would be agreable to him at this time, when he must be dejected with his Fathers situation. I would have him go to Hamburgh, and from thence he may soon proceed to Berlin. I would have him go directly after taking his degree.

We are distrest at the stay of our Envoys, who seem to be in a delirium. They will assuredly suffer in some way or other, if the knowledge of the

---

[1] Kilborn Whitman declined the position as assistant to the Reverend Anthony Wibird See the letter of December 26, 1797.
[2] Thomas Welsh, Harvard, 1798, son of Dr. Thomas Welsh.

dispatches arrives there, and the concequent temper of the Pople [*sic*] reaches, before their orders arrive for comeing away. My only hope is that the winds of Heaven were propitious in carrying their orders to them. But my astonishment is, that after the decree past the Directory for seazing all Nutrals who should have any kind of British Manufactor on Board, 24 hours should not have past before pasports had been demanded. They ought not to have hesitated a moment what part to have acted. Do not however repeat these censures from me. They may be asscribed to a *higher* source. But I greatly fear the delay occasiond by the *obstinacy of one Man*.[3] You will hear reports, I suppose, but they shall not come from me, nor will I give Ear to them, untill more solid proof, more demonstration, obliges me too—The News Papers say that dispatches have arrived from our Envoys to the 4 April. It is not so. Those are dispatches from Mr. King, & from Mr. Adams but not a line to [the] Government since those which have been made publick from our Envoys in France. There is a private Letter from Mr. Pinckney to Mr. King, which Mr. King has sent a copy of, but it is not publick, but a private Letter from one Gentleman to an other. By some means or other this has leakd out—and given rise to the report of publick dispatches.

I think our next accounts from England must be highly important. God Grant the fate of Pharoah [*sic*] & his Hoast, to those who attempt to cross the channel. England is the only Barrier between France & universal domination. There I trust is some true Religion, & piety, some respect to Law & Government, some Rational Liberty, Benevolence & Philanthropy, for whose sake I hope & trust the Nation will be saved.

Braintree address is received, and answerd. So is Cambridge & Medford, which last is an admirable one. Who drew it? It is out of the common stile. It is designd by some Gentlemen to collect them all together & publish them in a vol'm. I pray you present my kind and affectionate Regards to all my Friends. How many of my acquaintance I shall miss when I return! Mrs. Field is relieved from the infirmites under which she sufferd, and having acted well, very well, her part in Life, will, I doubt not, have her reward. As a Neighbour I loved, valued & esteemed her, & all who belonged to her, as I have fully proved by my

[3] Elbridge Gerry, who, as a member of the famous "XYZ Mission," remained in France when Charles Cotesworth Pinckney left Paris and Marshall decided to return to the United States. Talleyrand had persuaded Gerry that France would declare war if he left, but Gerry refused to negotiate alone without further power. See "Message of John Adams to Congress": *Columbian Centinel, Extraordinary*, April 16, 1798.

connection with so many Branches of her Family. Considering her Education few women have exhibited more Prudence, industry, patience under trying afflictions, equanimity of temper, and indeed every christian virtue. I [have *cancelled*] experienced her kindness from my first becomeing her Neighbour, when I was young and unexperienced. Her [kindness *cancelled*] Benevolence was always manifested without any boast or expectation of reward. I never wanted help, eitheir in sickness or Health, when some of her Family was not ready to afford it, and that long before [she *cancelled*] I was in a station to do more for them than others. I shall ever revere her memory.[4]

How is Brother Adams, Suky & Boylstone?[5] Not a word of them, or from them have I heard but by Mr. Black. Mr. Adams wrote to his Brother & told him he must write him word about his Farm and Town affairs, but he has not. You say we must not sit our Faces towards you this Month. I fear it. I do not expect to get from here untill the last of June. I hope all will be accomplishd then.

My Love to Mrs. Black, & kind Regards to Dr. Welch & Family. I would write if I knew what to say.

I do not hear from Haverhill, Atkinson [New Hampshire] I mean. The Children write to their Parents which Letters I forward; but not a line to me. Louissa is quite out of Patience with Betsy.[6] She has had but one Letter from her since she left Quincy. My Paper says, leave off.

Yours as ever
A. ADAMS

Philadelphia, June 8th, 1798

MY DEAR SISTER:

I received yours of June the first. I am quite delighted at the account you give of the season, and the appearance of vegetation. I was out yesterday at a Farm of Judge Peters calld, Belmont.[1] It is in all its Glory. I have been twice there, when I lived at Bush Hill, but he has

---

[4] This Mrs. Field was probably one of the forebears of that John Quincy Adams Field who flourished in Quincy during the nineteenth century, and possibly, therefore, connected by marriage with the tribe of Adams. See footnote 3 to the letter of January 5, 1798.

[5] Peter Boylston Adams, only surviving brother of the President, and two of his four children, Susanna and Boylston.

[6] Louisa Smith, the devoted niece who made her home with John and Abigail Adams, and her sister Elizabeth.

[1] Richard Peters (1744–1828), lawyer, soldier of the Revolution, judge, and farmer, lived at "Belmont," near Philadelphia. Washington appointed Peters to the federal bench in 1792. Judge Peters, an authority on maritime jurisprudence, married Sarah Robinson, by whom he had six children.

improved both the House and Gardens since. After being six Months in a city, you can hardly conceive the delight one feels at entering a wilderness of sweets. The Grass, the Grain, the profusion of Beautifull flowers, Jasmine, Hyacinths & Roses, all in full Bloom, climing arond the windows & Piazzas and Porticos of the neat building, formd such a pleasing contrast to the bare brick Buildings and the throng of conechigo Waggons which are ranged in rows through our street, that it appeard a mere Paridice to me.[2] The House is an ancient building with a Hall through it, like Jeffries at Milton which opens into the Garden.[3] In front is a lawn and from the House there is a view of the Noble Hudson [sic: Delaware], and at the foot of the Hill much nearer flows the Schuylkil. After walking in the Garden we returnd and found the table spread with 6 or 8 quarts of the large Hudson Strawberry, gatherd fresh from the vines with a proportionable quantity of cream, wine & sugar. Our taste and smell were both regaled, whilst ease, sociability and good humour enhanced the pleasure of the repast. The Judge is an old Friend and acquaintance of the President from the first Congress & served with him as one of the Board of war. Mrs. Peters has all that ease and affibility, united to good sense and fine spirits which render her manner truly pleasing. They have a number of children, 2 Grown son[s] & a daughter with 3 younger. They reside in the city during the winter.

You will learn with pleasure that the Bill for calling of all intercourse with France past the Senate by 18 to 4. There are 10 Members absent most of whom, I believe all, would have joind the Majority. Mr. Fosters Resolutions will be taken up this day, the amount of which will be to declare our Treaty with France no longer binding. You will see them in your papers.[4]

Addresses increase untill the President can find scarcly any thing new to say. He has however [one] in answer to the old Colony.

His old Friend W[arre]n did not sign it. His son has. I received a kind of an apology in a Letter from her, "He addresses none but the Supreem Being." But he wishes well to the Government and the Administrator of it. Her Letter was that of an old Friend.[5]

[2] "Conechigo waggons" may possibly mean garbage wagons. See *Webster's New International Dictionary:* "Connach, v.t. to spoil, to waste. *Scot.*"

[3] John Jeffries (1745–1819). See footnote 1 to the letter of August 29, 1790.

[4] Dwight Foster (1757–1823), Federalist representative and Senator from Massachusetts. At this time Mr. Foster was a member of the House of Representatives.

[5] James Warren (1726–1808), Massachusetts political leader, was born at Plymouth, graduated from Harvard in 1744, and settled as a merchant and gentleman-farmer in his native town. He was the husband of Mercy (Otis) Warren (1728–1814), the historian, by whom he had five sons.

We have just got a Pamphlet from France, abusive as Thom. Paines against Washington, part Prose & part Poetry, the very language of their Party here, the very wrods of Bache & Volney in some parts of it.[6] But the time is past for their currency here. When I read it I said to Louissa, this is the production of that unhangd Rascal Church.[7] You must know that there were such complaints made from Portugal of him & his conduct had been so base & enimical to his Country, that one of the first acts of the Presidents, was to displace him. This you may be sure, excites all his vengance, tho he disguises it. Genll. W[ashingto]n used sometimes to give a man an office of whom he was *affraid*. This was the case with Goveneer Morris & Church, but it has ended as all the appointments have, which were made with a *concilatory view*.[8] Neither Love or fear will prompt the Present Commander in chief to give an office to an undeserving Character knowingly. [Many *cancelled*] Some no doubt, will prove unworthy of their trust.

People are not sufficiently on their gaurd with respect to recommendations, and by them alone can the President judge of a very great proportion of those whom he appoints to office. It was Gen'll W[ashingto]n's wish to make Friends of foes, and he aimd at converting over those who were luke warm. You did not hear at that day so much Noise of *Executive Patronage*. The reason the Reason [*sic*] is evident. Lambs Services, Munroes, Randolph, Church & Morris, with many others of similar sentiments, shared the loaves and fishes. A different conduct is now observed and wisdom taught by experience.[9]

[I do not *cancelled*] Mr. Johnson went from Cambridge in the vacancy to visit his parents, and they have concluded that he should finish his Education at Annopolis college. It is not well judged I think, and I

---

[6] Thomas Paine (1737-1809), in his *Letter to George Washington*, 1796, accused the President of bad faith and indifference to him. Paine helped organize the Theophilanthropists. See footnote 5 to the letter of May 26, 1798. Comte Constantin François de Chasseboeuf de Volney (1757-1820), was a French scholar and author. He travelled in Syria and Egypt (1783-1787) and in the United States—was a member of the Constituent Assembly, and was ennobled by Bonaparte and by Louis XVIII.

[7] Edward Church, the brother of the notorious Benjamin Church, who was born in 1734 and died some time after 1776. See footnote 5 to the letter of September 1, 1789.

[8] Gouverneur Morris (1752-1816), of New York, was named as minister to France by President Washington early in 1792. The nomination was fought bitterly in the Senate because of the aristocratic views of Morris, and his very bad manners. He was confirmed by 16 to 11, and was very successful in Paris—the only minister who refused to leave the capital during the Reign of Terror.

[9] For John Lamb (1735-1800), see footnote 4 to the letter of February 1-5, 1798.

have ventured to express such a sentiment. I have not heard since I wrote you from Mrs. Johnson or your son.[10]

Mrs. Otis desires to be kindly rememberd to you. She is distresst for Mrs. Welch & Family. She knows how to sympathize, and really does.

You must let me know how things go on. Take particular care of the Letter inclosed for Dr. Tufts. I have just sent a trunk on Board [with *cancelled*] a vessel for Boston and hope it will not be long before I shall follow; The Rumour of yesterday ends in vapour but tho not true, I hope I hope [*sic*] it will be soon. Church as I conjectured, is said to be the writer of this base libel. It is an abuse upon the President for his speeches to Congress, of which you see Tallyrand says the Directory complain. Poor wretchs. I suppose they want him to cringe, but he is made of the oak instead of the willow. He may be torn up by the Roots, or break, but he will never bend.[11]

Yours
A. Adams

Quincy—I mean Philadelphia—June 13th, 1798

My dear Sister:

But I was thinking so much of Quincy, that I mechanically dated from thence; When I sent Letters for Louissa, Mrs. Brisler &c by yesterdays Mail, I could not get time to add a line of my own, being engaged in writing to Berlin by the British packet. Since my last to you, I have received a Letter from Mrs. Johnson inclosing Letters to her, both from Mr. & Mrs. A[dams], at which I rejoiced. She has thought [it] hard that, I should hear so much oftner from our Children than she should, but Mr. Adams writes duplicates, & by different ways. I dared not venture to send you the Letters as I should have liked to, but I thought it would be a breach of confidence, and I have returnd them to Mrs. Johnson—I copied a part of Louissa's Letter. Her first date is 17th of Jan'ry, when she says Mr. Adams returnd from Court, and found her writing to her Friends, but threw her into great agitation, by telling her that she must be presented to Court on the next day, and that her Cloaths were not any of them ready. To use her own words, "You know Mamma *my Partiality for Great Companies* and will therefore

---

[10] "Mr. Johnson" was a son of Joshua Johnson, of Maryland, and a brother of Mrs. John Quincy Adams.

[11] See La Fontaine, *Fables*, Book 1, Fable 22: "Le Chêne et le Roseau." The fable refers not to a willow, but to a reed, which obliged the wind by bending, when the unpliable oak was torn up by the roots!

readily conceive what I felt at the thought of going into a society so intirely strange to me, that I had never even seen the Lady who was to present me. However I got ready and went & considering all things, got through this dissagreable buisness pretty well. But from that day to this the first of Feb'ry we have not been permitted to spend an evening at home, which is so extreemly unpleasent to me, that I am obliged to pretend sickness, to avoid it. The King and Queen are both young, and I think the Queen one of the most beautifull women I ever saw. She is now pregnant with her fourth child, and is but just 21 years old. She goes into company, and dances from 6 in the Evening untill 6 in the morning, notwithstanding her situation. The Courts are twice a week, one of which is a Ball & the other a card party. The Etiquet and usage of the Court, require all Ministers & their Ladies to attend, so that I am obliged to make one in this *Elegant Mob*. On every Monday Evening I am obliged to pay my respects to the Princess Henry, a Great Aunt of the Kings, where I am necessitated to sit 2 or 3 hours at whist. Once a fortnight we are obligated to visit Prince Ferdinand, who is Great Uncle to the King.[1] The Princess is an old Lady who has been very Handsome. She is remarkable kind to me, and has interested [me very *cancelled*] herself very much about my Health. Her sister, some years Younger than herself, is the most Elegant woman I ever beheld. She has been pleasd to take such a fancy to me, as to make me sit down with her, at her work table, and talks whole evenings with me. I was invited to a Ball the other Evening, and she undertook to find me partners.

Yet after all this, my dear Mamma, I do not think I am calculated for a Court. To a Child Educated like yours, for domestick society, such a round of constant dissipation, makes me wish I was once more among my beloved Friends."

Mr. J. Q. Adams in his Letter to Mrs. [Joshua] Johnson expresses himself thus: "Since the recovery of Mrs. Adams, she has been presented at Court, and to the Several Princesses, belonging to it. Her Personal appearance, as well as her manners & deportment, which are such unequivocal indications of her Character and disposition, have been every where pleasing."

Thus you see, my dear Sister, I have been amused, and entertaind like a partial fond mother and knowing how much you interest yourself in my pleasures I have communicated them to you. I now inclose

[1] Princess Henry was the wife of Henry of Hohenzollern, the second of the three younger brothers of Frederick the Great (1740–1786). Henry died in 1802. Ferdinand of Hohenzollern, who died in 1813, was the youngest brother of Frederick the Great.

to you what will be more interesting to you, a Letter received from your son. If he does not get time to write so often to you, as you wish you will learn how he has been employd.

I yesterday received Letters both from Mr. and Mrs. [Stephen] Peabody. The account she gives me of Betsy are [sic] painfull and allarming. I hope she too, will not be added to the Number who fall victims to the slow underminer, a consumption, yet the constant fever is very like it. Few instances occur here, and a cough is rare, oweing, I believe, to the less keen air. Disorders here are more sudden, and inflamitory.

Letters from Mr. Murrey to the 12 of April, in which he says, "Switzerland is broken down after a most bloody conflict with the army of Bernes in which seven thousand, including women, who fought bravely, have fallen on the side of the Swiss Army. That Bern was aristocratic was the Pretence."[2]

In this Letter he says, "I learn that France will treat with Mr. Gerry *alone*. The other two will *be orderd* away." Can it be possible, can it be believed that Talleyrand has thus deluded and facinated Mr. Gerry, that he should dare to take upon him such a responsibility? I cannot credit it, yet I know the sin which most easily besets him is obstinacy, and, a mistaken policy. You may easily suppose how distrest the President is at this conduct, and the more so, because he thought Gerry would certainly not go wrong, and he *acted* his own judgment, *against his counsellors*, "who have been truer prophets than they wish themselves." Gerry means the Good of his Country, he means the Peace of it, but he should consider, it must not be purchased by national disgrace & dishonour. If he stays behind, he is a ruind Man, in the estimation of his Countrymen. This is all between ourselves. You will be particularly reserved upon this subject. I would not be the mean's of hurting Mrs. Gerrys feelings, or even of judging [sic] hardly an old and steady Friend, for whom I am really distrest.

Adieu my dear Sister. Tomorrow I promise myself a Letter from you. We have abundance of wet weather. How is the season with you? Has Mrs. Porter got help? I wish if she has, that she would whiten me a cotton sheet or two & some towels which are in a trunk in the Garret. Let me know when you think all things will be in readiness? I shall not leave here till after the 4 July. We shall be overwhelmd with Military

---

[2] William Vans Murray was stationed at The Hague as United States minister to the Batavian Republic from June 7, 1797, until he went into France in February, 1800. For Bonaparte's conquest of Switzerland, see letters of January 5 and May 20, 1798.

Parade on that day. Love, affection &c &c where ever due. The President will put young Beals name on the list.[3] If he applies to Capt. Sever & gets an approbation from him, the President will appoint him.

Yours as ever
A. ADAMS

Quincy [Philadelphia], 19 June, 1798[1]

MY DEAR SISTER:

I expected to have heard from you on Saturday, but no Letter came and on Wedensday but still no Letter. I was dissapointed, but knowing your many avocations I concluded it must arise from thence, I hope not from sickness, tho you wrote me you was not well. I who have more leisure, and no care of Family affairs but my orders can, and do devote almost every morning in writing to some Friend or other. You will hear before this reaches you of the arrival of Mr. Marshall at N[ew] York. Mr. Pinckney is gone to the South of France with a persuit for the Health of a daughter suposed in a consumption. Mr. Gerry stays untill he hears from our Government, which as appears to me, is a very wrong step.[2] The Government you will be informd received last week an other dispatch of a Letter from Talleyrand, and a very lengthy reply by our Envoys, which being in a press copy & part cypher, two copies being to be prepared of it, could not be got ready in one or two days. In the meantime Talleyrand [by the *cancelled*] had sent out to Bache his Letter for to be publishd here, & without the replie of our Envoys. This he exultingly gave to the publick on Saturday. It really appears a very fortunate circumstance that, our government, should have received tho by an other conveyance the dispatches about the same time, and so soon be able to counteract the villany intended by Talleyrand. It has an other good effect, that of convinceing the most unbelieving of the close connection between the Infernals of France & those in our own Bosoms. And in any other Country Bache & all his papers would have been seazd and ought to be here, but congress are dilly dallying about passing a Bill enabling the President to seize suspisious persons, and their papers. We shall be favourd soon I suppose with the pamphlet written by the Clerk in Talleyrands office—All this however works for good, and will tend to work out our salvation I hope.

[3] Probably Richard Beal, who was third lieutenant of the *Constitution*. *Columbian Centinel*, May 26, 1798.
[1] See the letter of June 13, 1798.
[2] See Channing, *History of the United States*, vol. 4, pp. 187-8.

I will send the papers as soon as publishd. In the mean time I send you some pamphlets to be distributed for the publick Benifit, and send one in my Name to Mrs. Webb with my compliments.

We are all well but a servant who has been voilently attackd with an inflamitory Soar Throat, & very dangerously sick for several days. We hope he has past the worst. The season has not yet been uncommonly Hot, [The *cancelled*] I am weary of conjectures, so shall say nothing of when it is probable Congress will rise. I believe they will decarle [*sic*] war against the French first.

Mr. Marshalls arrival will hasten the buisness—O Mr. Gerry! Mr. Gerry, that you had but been wise enough & resolute enough to have come too.

Mrs. Malony got home yesterday morning, in six days. I have not seen her. I have only heard that she is come.

With a kind remembrance to all Friend[s]

Yours
A. A[DAMS]

Philadelphia, June 23d, 1798

My dear Sister:

The weather has been so oppressively Hot for this week, and the streets of the City so nausious that I expect the concequences which must follow. They already begin. Complaints of the Bowels are frequent & an inflamitory soar throat. Frederick has got below after 5 bleedings, Blistering &c. Becky is now sick with it. Hers is less upon her throat, more in her Bowels, not much fever. I hope hers will not prove very Bad. Several of the rest of us have had a touch. It comes with a stifness & pain in the neck & back part of the Head. In some parts of the city the old fever is making its appearence.[1] Congress are anxious to rise, but will not sooner than they did last year, I fear. O how much precious time did they waste this winter in that dirty affair of Lyons, and disputing whether Mr. Smith & J. Q. A. should be ministers Resident, or Plenipos, with which they had no buisness, any more than who should be of the Directory in France.[2]

[1] Yellow fever, or *maladie de Siam*. See College of Physicians of Philadelphia, *Facts and Observations Relative to the Nature and Origin of the Pestilential Fever which Prevailed in the City of Philadelphia in 1793, 1797, and 1798*, Philadelphia, 1799.

[2] For the feud between Matthew Lyon and Roger Griswold, see the letter of February 15, 1798. John Quincy Adams was American minister to Prussia. "Mr. Smith" is William Loughton Smith (1758–1812), of South Carolina, son of a rich merchant, educated in Eng-

I have put under cover to Mr. Cranch a Letter for William Shaw, supposing he might be at Quincy & the papers and handkerchiefs are for him. You will send them if he is gone home.[3] You will find in them what Mr. Marshal brings and the state in which things are in France.

I received your Letters of the 10 & 15th. The President is delighted with your account of the clover and Barley Fields. He most sincerely pines after them, but he is tied to his table 9 Hours of the day. Some of the addressers complain that his answers are too short. They do not consider nor know how numerous they are, or what other buisness there is to attend to. Some fore noons he is calld from his Room 20 times in the course of it, to different persons, besides the hours devoted to the Ministers of the different departments, the investigation necessary to be made of those persons who apply for offices or are recommended, the weighting the merits, and pretentions of different Canditates [sic] for the same office &c &c &c. His Eyes, which you know used to be very troublesome to him, are quite well, and he is enabled to read and write with ease to himself, which is a great favour.

I am glad you have got the Box. Betsy did not say to me that she was going to be married directly, but she wrote what I took to be her determination soon. Poor dear Betsy Shaw, must she too follow our dear Mary, Charles and Suky Warner?[4] My heart aches for our sister. I know not how she will sustain the shock. I think our physicians are too fearfull of Bleeding in early complaints of the Lungs.

I shall be satisfied with the kitchen floor as it is. I hope all will be done by the beginning of July, for I shall want all the Room I can find and, more than all. I do expect Mrs. Smith will come with me to make her Children a visit. As I have sent the papers I need say nothing about politicks. Our Legislature have done nobly in Massa[chusetts]. What Life & vigor does a good Patriot give to a whole state when placed at the

---

land and Geneva. Smith was the author, in 1792, of a pamphlet (*The Politicks and Views of a Certain Party, Displayed*) attacking Jefferson, which is usually attributed to Alexander Hamilton. In 1794 he was burned in effigy in Charleston, in company with images of Benedict Arnold and the Devil! Although Hamilton and Washington felt that Smith's personal unpopularity debarred him from conspicuous appointment, John Adams made him minister to Portugal, July 10, 1797. Jefferson relieved him on September 9, 1801.

[3] William Smith Shaw (1778–1826), Harvard, 1798, became secretary to his uncle by marriage, John Adams, after his graduation. Adams, *Works*, vol. 9, p. 45.

[4] Charles Smith, who died in 1797, and Mary Carter Smith, who died in April, 1798, aged seven, were children of William Smith, the brother of Abigail Adams. Susannah Warner, who died in April, 1798, was the daughter of Mrs. Susannah Warner, of Gloucester, the second wife of Dr. Cotton Tufts.

Head of it.[5] I wish our Legislature would set the example & make a sedition act, to hold in order the base Newspaper calumniators. In this State, you could not get a verdict, if a prosecution was to be commenced.

My pen is bad. I know not whether you can read it. And the damp air spoils the paper.

I am in haste. The post will leave me before I assure you of what my Sister knows and believes, that I am allways her

Affectionate Sister
A. ADAMS

Philadelphia, June 25, 1798

MY DEAR SISTER:

I write you a few lines to day, but the weather is so Hot and close, and the flies so tormenting that I can not have any comfort. The mornings instead of being pleasent as with you, are stagnant. Not a leaf stirs till nine or ten oclock. I get up & drop into my chair; without spirits or vigor, breath a sigh for Quincy, and regreet that necessity obliges us to remain here. It grows sickly, the city noisome. My Family are thanks to God, recoverd from their illness, and no New one taken down. We have began the use of the cold Bath, and hope it will in some measure compensate for want of a braceing Air. The largness and hight of our Rooms are a great comfort and the Nights are yet tolerable, and I have freed myself for the season of any more drawing Rooms. Dinners I cannot.

I send you the last dispatch which has yet got printed. I expect Congress will decare [sic] war before they Rise. They are impatient now to rise, but will not be permitted to untill several more important Bills are matured and past. You will see by the paper inclosed the reception give to Genll. Marshall.[1] He is deserving of it all. I cannot but feel hurt for Mrs. Gerry. O that [he cancelled] Mr. Gerry had, but have thought with his Employer and with his Colleagues. They would all have been here long before this time. We must wait the Event. You will find that in the toast Given at the dinner to Mr. Marshal no notice or mention [was made] of Mr. Gerry.

[5] Increase Sumner (1746–1799) was elected Governor of Massachusetts in 1797, 1798, and 1799. He died in office at the beginning of his third term. See the letter of December 4, 1799.

[1] On June 18, 1798, John Marshall arrived at New York on the *Alexander Hamilton*, after a voyage of fifty-three days from Bordeaux. "General" Marshall entered Philadelphia in triumph on June 25, 1798. A. J. Beveridge, *John Marshall*, Boston, 1916, vol. 2, pp. 343–5.

I had a Letter from Mrs. [William Stephens] Smith on Saturday. She desires to be rememberd to you and all her Friends. She was in N[ew] York on a visit to Col. Smiths Mother, who had been sick. Caroline was better. I want to hear of Betsy Shaw every week, but alass I fear she is too far gone to receive any comfort from hearing of her. I send a handkerchief to old Mrs. Welch with my respects, and a little bit of Muslin for Sister Smith a couple of caps. How does she do?

Inclosed is a Book for Mrs. Porter. Do you get Peters paper Regularly?[2] I am, my dear Sister,

Affectionatly yours
A. ADAMS

The President received last week a polite and Friendly Letter from Genll. Washington inviting us to make a visit to Mount Vernon when Congress rises.

One of the handkerchiefs for my dear Sister Cranch. [*Written on the outside of the letter.*]

Philadelphia, June 27th, 1798

MY DEAR SISTER:

The reflections which this morning have occupied my mind previous to taking my pen, have been of a solemn & melancholy Nature. Wherefore O Lord art thou thus contending with thy people, that one prop after an other is taken from them? The Sudden death of Dr. Belknap has filld my Heart with Sorrow.[1] Following so soon after Dr. Clark, and I presume from the account in the paper, in as sudden a manner, calls upon us to make the inquiry, and that with suitable Humiliation, why at this season of uncommon danger to the Religion of the Gospel of Christ, we are deprived of its ablest supporters and defenders?[2] Why when our Country is in danger from within & from without, its steadiest

---

[2] William Cobbett's *Porcupine's Gazette and Daily Advertiser*, which advocated alliance with England, war against France, and perdition for "Republicans."

[1] Jeremy Belknap, pastor of the church in Federal Street, died suddenly in Boston on June 20, 1798. See 1 *Coll. Mass. Hist. Soc.*, vol. 6, 1799, pp. x–xviii (from the *Columbian Centinel* of June 25, 1798), and *Proc. Mass. Hist. Soc.*, vol. 66, pp. 96–106: Samuel A. Eliot, "Jeremy Belknap: A Paper in Recognition of the One Hundred and Fiftieth Anniversary of the Massachusetts Historical Society."

[2] John Clarke (1755–1798), pastor of the First Church in Boston, suffered a stroke of apoplexy in the pulpit on the afternoon of Sunday, April 1, and died the following day. See the letter of April 3, 1790. Oddly enough, Clarke was the fourth pastor of the First Church to suffer this fate: John Norton (1663), John Oxenbridge (1674), and Thomas Foxcroft (1769), having experienced a similar misfortune. See 1 *Coll. Mass. Hist. Soc.*, vol. 6, pp. iii–ix.

friends in the midst of their days, and in the height of their usefullness should so awefully be snatchd from us?—Two of our ablest divines, men of distinguished learning, industery, integrity, virtue & Patriotism, are releasd from their Labours, [and *cancelled*] but their works will survive them. Dr. Belknap was engaged in a very usefull & Labourious work, that of his American Biography, the 2d volm of which is now at the press, and as he wrote me on the 14 of this Month will be out in July. In the course of the last month I had exchanged several Letters with him, and I had undertaken to get a subscription paper filld for him. On Monday I closed a packet to him, little thinking that he had fled to the world of spirits. His stile of writing was plain, simple and clear. I recollect with pleasure the only time I ever heard him preach. It was at the Accademy meeting at Hingham, a sermon well worthy publication. His late Fast sermon he sent me, and as I had been, I hardly know how, drawn into a correspondence with him, I had contemplated with pleasure, a more intimate acquaintance with him upon my return to Massachussets, but of this, and many other, Scources [*sic*], I have been deprived in the short space of seven Months absence. But his examples & his Precepts will not I hope be lost. To use his own words, "It is impossible to conceive how much good may be done by our example. It may do good after we are Dead. The Remembrance of what we have been, and what we have done, may long outlive us,—and unborn Posterity may be the better for it."

He must have left a very distresst family I think. Tell Mr. & Mrs. Black, that I am a sincere mourner [with them *cancelled*], and sympathizer with them. The President mourns his loss, not less than I do. He was one of his best Friends. He mourns not only for himself, but for his Countrys loss, and for Society in General. My path to Massachusets is spread with sorrow, and coverd with mourning. The death of so many of my friends, the distress of Dr. Welch and Family, the prospect of an other melancholy Scene at Atkinson [New Hampshire] together with the dark & thick cloud which hangs ready to Burst upon our Country, all combine to wound and distress me. The dark side of the picture is a deep shade.

I would not however forget the Blessing which remain, nor be ungratefull for what of Good is yet continued to me—nor [forget *cancelled*] be unmindfull that I hold all by a frail tenure.

I cannot commence any other subject, but Subscribe your ever
Affectionate Sister
A. ADAMS

[Philadelphia], July 3d, 1798

MY DEAR SISTER:

The extreem heat of yesterday & the no less prospect of it this day, is beyond any thing I ever experienced in my Life. The Glasses were at 90 in the Shade Yesterday. Tomorrow will be the 4 July, when if possible I must see thousands. I know not how it will be possible to get through. Live here I cannot an other week unless a Change takes place in the weather. You had as good be in an oven the bricks are so Hot. I can only say to you that yesterday the President Nominated Gen'll. Washington to be commander in chief of the Army to be raised, and as soon as the Senate pass upon it, the Secretary of War will be sent express to announce it to him.[1] His Country calls. No Man can do so much for it in that Line. "The knowledge that he lives" is a Bulwark. It will unite all Parties in the Country. It will give weight, force and energy to the People, & it will dismay our Enemies.—I cannot think that he will decline the station.[2]

Mr. Soper from Braintree was here yesterday, & he disclosed my whole secret about my building. The President had a hearty laugh & says he is sorry it was not carried clear along. He is affraid it is upon too small a Scale, so tell the Dr. [Cotton Tufts] we shall not incur any blame.

I inclose you the paper of this day. You will see how Politicks are. Tis so Hot I cannot think or write more than

Yours as ever
A. ADAMS

Philadelphia, Monday, July 9th, 1798

MY DEAR SISTER:

I have not a Letter from you to day. I hope however to hear from you by the next post, but if you have had weather like what we experienced

---

[1] James McHenry (1753–1816), the fourth choice for the post, succeeded Timothy Pickering as Secretary of War in January, 1796. Adams forced his resignation from the Cabinet in May, 1800. See the letter of July 17, 1798.

[2] Mrs. Adams is quoting from one of sixteen toasts drunk at the "sumptuous dinner" at the "Concert Hall" in Boston, in celebration of George Washington's birthday, in 1798. Most of the officers of the state were present, and General Benjamin Lincoln presided. The second toast, that to George Washington, reads as follows:
"May his name be still a rampart, and the knowledge that he lives, a bulwark against all open and secret enemies of our country." The third toast was drunk to President Adams, with a proper verbal tribute. The fourth toast was drunk to Vice-President Jefferson—but without comment. "Nineteen Volunteer" toasts followed. Apparently the number of formal toasts at the time—usually sixteen—was determined by the number of states then in the Union. *Columbian Centinel*, February 24, 1798.

here for three days, I do not wonder that you could not write. We have had ever since the 4 July very comfortable days and nights, frequent showers, no hard or severe thunder, a prospect of a fine season. This morning I have to congratulate you upon the first Gallic trophy to the Arms of the United States. Captain Decateur in the Deleware has captured a 12 Gun Privateer & 70 Men, which he has brought in.[1] She had taken a ship two days before bound [for *cancelled*] from this port for Liverpool. The Men she put on board a vessel bound for Boston. So stupid will the merchants here be, as still to send their vessels out unarmd. The French Man thought himself attackd by an English ship of war, but upon finding that it was an American, he askd the Captain if America was at war with their Nation? No, replied the captain, but you are with mine. O, says the frenchman, I have a commission for what I do. And so, replied captain Decateur, have I. When he saw the American flag hoisted over his, he stormed and swore at a terrible rate. Mon Dieu, I had rather see my ship sunk, blown up in the Air. The captain told him, he would soon put him below with the Men if he did not conduct himself properly. I rejoice to see the spirit & Bravery of my Native State. Let the vipers cease to hiss. They will be destroyd with their own poison. Bache is in duress here, & Burk in N[ew] York.[2] I inclose to you the dareing outrage which calld for the Arm of Government.

This mornings Centinal announces the death of Sheriff Thayer.[3] What was his disease? Quite a middle aged Man. Was it an Apploplexy

[1] Stephen Decatur, Sr., (1752–1808), naval officer, and son of a French seaman of the same name, was commissioned captain in the United States Navy on May 11, 1798, at the outbreak of hostilities with France. He put to sea in the *Delaware*, and in July captured the French privateer, *Le Croyable*, renamed *Retaliation*, the first prize of the war, and of the new American Navy. He was the father of the more famous Stephen Decatur (1779–1820).

[2] *Gazette of the United States*, July 7, 1798: "We are credibly informed that John D. Burk and Dr. James Smith have been arrested in New-York, for a most infamous libel against the President of the United States, published in the *Time-Piece*. Their bail are Colonel [Henry] Rutgers, Aaron Burr and Peter R. Livingston."

John Daly Burk (1775–1808), dramatist, was born in Ireland and came to America in 1796, evidently as a political refugee. He was among the earliest to put an American battle scene on the stage, in *Bunker Hill, or the Death of General Warren*, produced first at the Haymarket Theatre, Boston, February 17, 1797. One character refers to nightingales singing in Boston! President Adams saw the play in New York, and said to the manager: "My friend, General Warren, was a scholar and a gentleman, but your author has made him a bully and a blackguard." For a short time Burk was the publisher of the *Time-Piece*, in New York City. He was killed in a duel with a Frenchman at Petersburg, Virginia.

[3] Atherton Thayer, Sheriff of Norfolk County, died at Braintree at the age of thirty-three. *Columbian Centinel*, July 4, 1798.

[*sic*] or fever? I have been affraid to hear from you, least you should be the bearer of the death of Mrs. Lincoln, who I heard was dangerously sick with a Billious fever. Not seeing her death in the paper of to day I am led to believe & hope that she is upon the recovery. I had a Letter from Sister [Stephen] Peabody stating according to my request Betsys [Elizabeth Quincy Shaw (1780–1798)] case from its commencment, which I consulted Dr. [Benjamin] Rush upon. He is of opinion that she has an abscess forming in her side, that a fatal mistake was made at the commencment of her disorder in neglecting to Blead and Blister, which might in a few days at that time have relieved her. The Man, whom I had, seizd voilently with an inflamitory Soar throat, was Bled 5 times & 60 oz of Blood taken from him. He was below stairs in a fortnight and tho pale, is very well and able now to perform his duty, picking up fast. The Dr. does not like to advise without being able to see the particuliar state in which Betsy is, but as her circumstances are described, he thinks he should take 4 oz of Blood from her, & keep Blisters upon her side, as soon as one heald put on an other. Give her gentle exercise and vegatable food. But she may be too far gone for all this. I fear from the Numbness, the cough, the waisting & the Night Sweats, that her doom is fixed [and *cancelled*]. I hope, my dear Sister, that my friends will conquer the aversion to the Lancet, which I believe is not used sufficiently early in inflamitory diseases. But this climate calls for it more than ours. Consumptions are not common here.

Congress are going on very well at the Eleventh hour. Tho timid they will do all but one thing before they rise. That however would save them much trouble. Why, when we have the thing, should we boggle at the Name—The Secretary of War went express this morning to Mount Vernon—I hope and trust that the Gen'll will not refuse an appointment made, it is true, without his knowledge or consent. It was one of those strokes which the Prospect and Exigency of the times required, and which the President determined upon without consultation. It however meets with universal approbation and will concenter more Hearts than any other possible appointment. "His Name a Host, & the Knowledge that he lives a Bulwark."[4]

I wish you would tell Dr. Tufts that I would have a table made for Mrs. Porter, and half a dozen chair[s] if she wants them.

Yours, ever yours
A. ADAMS

[4] See footnote 2 to the letter of July 3, 1798.

Philadelphia, July 12, 1798

My dear Sister:

By Mrs. Otis, who leaves here this week, I send a waistcoat Pattern for William Shaw, which I designd should have reachd him before commencment. I send it to you because I presume he will be at Quincy. If you will get it made for him you may charge it to me. The stripes should go round the body. I have put some lining in. The waistcoat should be linned throughout. I hope he will be attentive to arrange all the Books up in the Book Room & to replace all he pulls down. Order strick order, & method will be required of him in the place designd for him. Every Letter & paper are placed in Alphabitical order in desks & places designd for them, and every different department relative to War office, Marine office, Secretary & Treasury office distinct, so that no trouble occurs in searching for papers.[1]

I do not expect to leave here in ten days, as the Senate must set after the House rise.

Yours affectionately
A. A[dams]

Philadelphia, July 13, 1798

My dear Sister:

I begin my Letter by saying that Mr. Cranch was so much better on the 7th, the date of Mrs. Johnsons last Letter, as to conclude to go to the Court the next day. I would not make a long preparation to allarm or distress you, or write you a word upon the subject untill Mrs. Johnsons 2d Letter came, for I would not have you feel as I did, upon reading the first part of hers of the 4 of July, upon any account. I veryly thought I should drop it before I found out the cause. To save a long detail I inclose you her Letters tho there are several confidential communications in them which you will not permit to go out of your Hands. Perhaps you may have received a Letter from Nancy with more particulars. I know when Mr. [William] Cranch was here, he gave me some account of the Party quarrels and animosities, but said he had been happy enough to keep clear of them.

You will learn by Mrs. [Joshua] Johnsons Letter that in taking Mr. Cooks buisness, he [William Cranch] was engaged for Mr. Cooks clients, and Mr. [James] Ray being one of them, he was also engaged in his buisness. This it seems was the cause of [Captain William Mayne]

[1] William Smith Shaw (1778–1826), nephew of Abigail Adams. See footnote 3 to the letter of June 23, 1798.

Duncansons animosity against him. Duncanson is a Scotchman who had held a command in the East Indies and came over to this country when Mr. [Thomas] Law did.[1] I saw them both frequently at Col. [William Stephens] Smiths in N[ew] York the summer I made a visit there. Ray is an Englishman. The dispute between them is concerning a vessel which they fitted out for the East Indies coverd as American Property, but which was taken by the English upon suspicion that she belongd to British subjects, and Ray pleads that tho a partner, he became so after the vessel was purchasd. Duncanson thinks himself cheated by Law & Ray, and has been hardly used as dispassionate people say. But the quarrel has arrived at such a pitch as to throw all George Town into two strong Parties. Property in the federal city, in different parts of it, is an other Source of contention. I really pitty Mrs. Johnson, who is come into the very heart of contention, and will judge of All America, I fear, from what she sees & hears round her. The warm interest she has taken in behalf of Mr. Cranch, who is indeed the much injured Man, makes her too deeply interested as a Partisan with the Ray, & Law, people.

I was surprizd to find Mr. Dalton becomeing Bail for Duncanson, but suspect he had a family reason for it.[2] Indeed, intemperate and

[1] For the complicated and unfortunate business and legal relations of these men, see W. B. Bryan, *A History of the National Capital*, 1914–16, vol. 1, *passim*. Most of the trouble sprang from James Greenleaf's operations in real estate in the District of Columbia. George Washington expressed his disapproval of Greenleaf's methods in a personal letter to Daniel Carroll, one of the commissioners of the District. Washington observed that the price Greenleaf offered the commissioners for land was too low, and that Greenleaf was obviously planning to obtain a monopoly of the land and make an "immense" profit. When James Greenleaf went bankrupt, William Cranch, his lawyer and brother-in-law, was appointed his trustee. Captain William Mayne Duncanson, James Ray, his partner in the commission business, and Thomas Law were all Englishmen who had come to the United States in 1794 and invested heavily in Greenleaf's scheme to "promote" the District of Columbia. Thomas Law was the only investor who was shrewd enough to obtain mortgages from the North American Land Company for the purchases which he made. When Greenleaf failed, all the other investors were in the hopeless position of "general unsecured creditors." Bryan, *National Capital*, vol. 1, p. 245. Lawsuits over Greenleaf's operations went on for fifteen years, including an appeal to the United States Supreme Court. For Thomas Law, see footnote 3 to the letter of February 21, 1798. See also, Clark, *Greenleaf and Law in the Federal City*.

[2] Tristram Dalton (1738–1817), of Newbury, former Federalist Senator from Massachusetts (1789–1791), inherited large means, most of which he lost speculating in real estate in the District of Columbia. As early as 1793 he helped to found a mercantile establishment in Washington: Lear & Company, the partners of which were Tobias Lear, former secretary to George Washington, James Greenleaf, and himself. After this company failed, Adams appointed Dalton to succeed William Cranch as one of the commissioners of the District of Columbia. President Jefferson made Tobias Lear the United States commercial agent at Santo Domingo. Bryan, *National Capital*, vol. 1, pp. 221 and 415.

unjustifiable as Duncanson was towards Mr. Cranch he is said to be much injured, and kept out of money due to him, by his opponents, but he should have waited untill the Law decided. A responsible Bondsman is no disgrace to the injured Party, and I cannot see it in the light which it appeard to Mrs. Johnson when in her warmth & agitation she wrote first. You will see there were heavey Bonds required.

I could not know the state of things to my satisfaction, untill I sent for Mr. Stodard the Secretary of the Navey, who is a man of great modesty, worth and integrity.[3] He came from George Town and he conversed freely upon the subject with me, giving me the true state of the Parties. He spoke in high terms of the fair & honorable Character which Mr. Cranch sustaind, and particularly of his Prudence in keeping himself clear of party animosities.—I found that he himself and two others were the only persons who had not taken their sides. I have just been writing to Mr. Cranch. Mr. Greenleaf came in great distress to me yesterday, having got by Rumour a report of the Matter. He talkd like a friend, and felt like a Brother.—He looks very well and so does his dear Nancy.[4]

I received a Letter from you this day. Congress will rise on Monday next. The House I mean, the Senate will yet remain in session. The appointment of officers cannot be made without them. I mean Gen'll officers and the Secretary of War cannot get back untill next week from Mount Vernon. The President would not nominate any other officer untill he received an answer from Gen'll Washington. Return my Letters as soon [as] you have read them. The weather is now delightfull. I find that it was as hot at N[ew] York & Baltimore & Boston as here. I thought it would have killd me, for I was not well and the heat added to the pressure of my complaints. We were happily relieved on Tuesday afternoon by Rain and Wind, since which the weather has been agreable. I long however to see my friends. *Those which remain to me, should be doubly dear and precious.* O that I could slide along to them, unnoticed and without parade.

I presume William [Smith] Shaw will be with you. I have sent him a white waistcoat pattern by Mrs. Otis. You will take charge & have it

[3] Benjamin Stoddert (1751–1813), of Maryland, was the first Secretary of the Navy, George Cabot (1752–1823), of Salem, Massachusetts, having refused Adams's appointment of him to the post in 1798. See footnote 4 to the letter of May 20, 1798.

[4] Anna (Nancy) Greenleaf, wife of William Cranch, who was the nephew of Mrs. Adams, was the favorite sister of James Greenleaf, promoter of the North American Land Company.

made. I set my Heart upon going to commencment this year; but the publick would not let me.

I have heard from Atkinson [New Hampshire], but I get no comfort or consolation. That poor Girl has in my mind been sacrificd by a wrong management by her Physicians in the first instance. If she had been early Bled, she might have been saved. At least that is my sentiment, tho I would distress her mother by saying so. I think there is no doubt that an abscess is forming in her Side.

I shall want you to procure me some stores. I will give you notice and send you money for the purpose.

I am, my dear Sister,
Affectionatly your[s]
ABIGAIL ADAMS

P.S. Thank you for Nancys Letter. Tis a very good one. In the first instance Mrs. [Joshua] Johnson attended from my recommendation, but both Mr. & Mrs. [William] C[ranch] require only to be known to be loved.

Philadelphia, July 17th, 1798
MY DEAR SISTER:

I had a Letter yesterday from Mrs. [Joshua] Johnson of the 12 July, in which she says Mr. Cranch had just returnd from the Court to which he went, the Judge being indisposed; that his wounds were getting well fast, and that he did not suffer any inconvenience except a headache, by his ride, that he had written to you a full account of the whole buisness. Congress rose yesterday. The House. The Senate are obliged to sit a few days longer. Mr. McHenry is not yet returnd from Mount Vernon—He is expected to day. I hope we shall be able to leave here next week, but I cannot possitively say. We do not design that it shall be known here the day we are to sit out. We wish to avoid military Parade. We get no News from abroad, and Mr. Gerrys stay [puts *cancelled*] is a plausible pretence for the Jacobins to circulate Lies and falshoods in abundance. Le Tomb [Joseph Philippe Létombe] has circulated the report, that Mr. G[erry] was received and was negotiating & that a French minister might daily be expected here—If one should come, he will not find America a resting place, 24 hours, but I have not any Idea of such an Event.[1]

I wrote you in my last that I should want some stores, a couple pound Hyson Tea, ditto souchong, Hundred Brown Sugar, several dozens Hard Bread, half Hundred coffe, Gallon of Brandy, Quarter pd Nutmegs, pd cinnamon, Mustard, Pepper, 2 oz Maize [mace], half pd Cloves—I want also for one Bed a Bed tick. It is for a common one. Mrs. Porter can tell you. I think I must have a couple of Bedsteads. I shall have 4 Men Servants. I would have them saking bottoms. Would it not be best to get them of Bedlow? I have Bedsteads enough out in the Grainary chamber, but they are such lumber that I do not know if any thing could be done with them. If they could I should not regret their being cut for the purpose. They put up with screws which screws are in the store closset some of them & some of them over the Top of the Granary chamber window. If any of them should be put up, I shall want some straw Beds to be made to put upon them before the others are laid on. I also wish you to purchase me a peice of Russia sheeting and sit Nabby to make it. I have not half sheeting enough for these People which is stout. I also want you to get me a peice of the plain Russia towelling. The sheeting & toweling take a receipt for as thus, "for the use of the Household of the President of the U S."—I also

[1] S. E. Morison, "Du Pont, Talleyrand, and the French Spoliations," *Proc. Mass. Hist. Soc.*, vol. 49, pp. 63–79, has proved, with documents found in the French Archives, that peace between the United States and France in 1798 was maintained chiefly by the decisive influence of Talleyrand, who learned from Victor Marie du Pont (1767–1827), French consul at Charleston, and elder son of Pierre Samuel Dupont de Nemours (1739–1817), that the Directory had over-estimated the strength of sympathy for France in the United States. Having been refused his exequatur at Philadelphia by John Adams when he was appointed consul-general to succeed Joseph Philippe Létombe, Victor du Pont had a long talk with Thomas Jefferson on May 31, 1798, and then sailed for France on June 7, on the *Benjamin Franklin*. He reached Bordeaux on July 3, and forwarded a long report to Talleyrand on July 21. Talleyrand sent a copy of this report to the Directory on July 27. The decree ending depredations on American commerce was published July 31, 1798. Although Pickering denied the sincerity of France in reporting to the Senate on January 31, 1799, Adams based his spectacular change of policy a few weeks later on this very decree, taking his hint from Richard Codman, a Boston speculator who was living in Paris at the time. After talking with young Victor du Pont, Talleyrand warned the Directory that for France to go to war with the United States would be merely to fall into the Anglo-Federalist trap.

By the time Davie, Ellsworth, and Vans Murray, minister to the Netherlands, presented their credentials at the Tuileries on March 8, 1800, Bonaparte, by the revolution of the 18th Brumaire (November 9, 1799), had overthrown the Directory, and had made himself First Consul, assisted by Cambacérès and Lebrun, and Talleyrand was entrenched as foreign minister of the Consulate. After long bickering, peace between the United States and France was signed at Mortefontaine, September 30–October 1, 1800.

want some Tea pots & a coffe pot or two, some tea spoons for the kitchin. Any thing which you may think I want beside you will be so good as to provide. I inclose you a Bill of an Hundred dollors. It runs in my mind that I want some yellow dishes & plates, some kitchin knives & forks, half dozen pd spermiciti candles, flask sweet oil. I have a small field Bedstead in the Garret which might be put either in the little Chamber or the one Mrs. Porter used to occupy. It wants a little mending if I remember right.

I have put things down just as I have thought of them and without much order.

Mr. McHenry is just returnd and brought with him Genll Washingtons acceptance of his appointment, but the Printers without any Authority have published that he was expected to come on to Philadelphia, whereas no such thing is at present intended. The present opperations necessary can be carried on by communicating with him and by other and younger officers, who will this day be nominated.[2] As Congress would not proceed to a declaration of war, they must be answerable for the concequences. With a kind remembrance to all Friends, and in the hope of seeing you e'er long I am sincerely and affectionatly

Your Sister
ABIGAIL ADAMS[3]

[2] In organizing an army for the proposed war with France in 1798, President Adams induced George Washington to accept the command of it, and was persuaded, much against his will, to make Hamilton Inspector-General. Henry Lee was placed at the head of the brigadiers. For Adjutant-General, Adams picked his son-in-law, Colonel William Stephens Smith, a brave and able veteran of the Revolution, but Pickering, the Secretary of State, "lobbied so effectively against Smith that he received only five votes." At Washington's suggestion, Smith was made the colonel of a regiment. Channing, *History of the United States*, vol. 4, pp. 191-4, and *Annals of the Fifth Congress*, vol. 1, p. 623. For a defense of the innocence of Hamilton in this intrigue and for an explanation of the motives of Pickering, see S. F. Bemis, *The American Secretaries of State and Their Diplomacy*, vol. 2, New York, 1927: Henry J. Ford, "Timothy Pickering," p. 236. When, in December, 1800, Adams nominated his son-in-law, Smith, to be Surveyor of the Port of New York, "Hamilton successfully exerted his influence in favour of confirmation by the Senate."

[3] The gap of almost fifteen months which follows, except for one letter, is explained by the fact that in the summer of 1798 Mrs. Adams was taken seriously ill at Quincy and did not return to Philadelphia until the autumn of 1799. The letter of January 17, 1799, which follows, probably was written during a visit with her daughter, Mrs. William Stephens Smith, in New York. Most unfortunately for himself and the duties of his office, President Adams was absent from the seat of government from mid-summer until November, 1798. Channing, *History of the United States*, vol. 4, p. 194.

[New York?], Janry. 17, 1799

My dear Sister:

I received your kind Letter of Janry and intended writing you yesterday, but I know not how it is, I have less time for writing than formerly. I believe it is partly oweing to my not being able to improve the morning as I used to. When I can sleep I indulge myself more—as it is not light enough to see to write till after seven oclock. Our Weather is too warm. We shall have a sickly spring. Colds are very common. Poor little Caroline has been threatned with the Quincy or Hives. She is very sick now but I hope not dangerous. It is a very allarming complaint.[1]

I am rejoiced to learn that we shall once more be a setled people. Any thing I have is at your service. I inclose you ten dollors towards purchasing a Gown for Mr. Whitney as my part.[2]

I know you will rejoice that I have heard from Mr. [J. Q.] Adams, tho the Letter is four Months old. It is dated at Dresden 7th Sep'br when he was about returning to Berlin. He says he was quite recoverd & Mrs. Adams's health much mended.

Do you want to see a specimin of Virgin[i]a Democracy, politeness, *independance*, Respect for Authority couchd in language decent, polite and Manly? Read the inclosed from litterally a Beardless Boy, a child in voice and face, the most purile figure you ever saw for his age, which is said to be 26. Let the public judge.[3]

I can only add my Love to all Friends from your
      Truly affectionate
       A. A[dams]

Sunday eveng, Brookfield, October 13, 1799

My dear Sister:

I got to Westown [Weston] on Wednesday by four oclock and was met two miles from Town by Mrs. Otis, accompanied by Mrs. Marshall, who insisted upon my putting up with them.[1] I accordingly went,

---

[1] Caroline Amelia Smith, daughter of Abigail Adams and Colonel William Stephens Smith.

[2] Peter Whitney (1770–1843), who became the assistant to Anthony Wibird, minister at Quincy.

[3] Early in 1799 John Randolph of Roanoke (1773–1833), a noisy disciple of the philosophers of the French Revolution, became a candidate for the House of Representatives.

[1] Colonel Thomas Marshall (1718–1800) commanded the Tenth Massachusetts Regiment at Saratoga in 1777. Son of Captain Christopher Marshall, an officer in the British service, he was a merchant-tailor in State Street, Boston, before the Revolution. He purchased the confiscated estate of a Tory at Weston, where he died on November 18, 1800. The Marshall house was moved in 1882 from Highland Street to Church Street, where it

and was very kindly and hospitably received by the Col. and his Family. The old Gentleman who is now more than 80 years, still retains much of the fire and sprightlyness of youth. He is very infirm in health, but delights in the company and society of his Friends and acquaintance. Mrs. Marshall you know. She is a charming woman; and strives to render the Col. comfortable and happy. Thursday was so rainy, that we could not go out of the House. On fryday morning we set out, and got on 27 miles to Peases, which being a neat good house, and good Beds, we put up for the night, and yesterday proceeded to this place, where it has been my lot oftner to keep Sabbath, than in any other Town upon the Road.[2] We have renderd it more agreable to day, by attending public worship, and hearing two good sermons, and some delightfull singing. Tomorrow we hope to reach Springfield, and get along by degrees, but the young Farmer whom James has founderd by giveing him grain, is very lame, and unpleasent travelling with. I heard of the President, who got to East Chester on Monday last, almost sick with a voilent cold.[3] I am very anxious about him. I pray you to write me how Brother Cranchs [cold] is. Direct your letters to me at East Chester. Write by Brisler, who will call upon me. Remember me kindly to all Friends.

Your affectionate Sister
A. ADAMS

East Chester, [New York], October 20th, 1799

MY DEAR SISTER:

I reachd this place yesterday morning and found Mrs. Smith and Caroline very well. Mrs. [Charles] Adams and her two little Girls have been here three weeks. N[ew] York still distresst with the fever. Tho many of the inhabitants have returnd to the city, yet several of them

---

now stands. Appletons' *Cyclopaedia of American History;* Francis S. Drake, *Dictionary of American Biography*, Boston, 1872, p. 600; *Massachusetts Soldiers and Sailors of the Revolutionary War*, Boston, 1902, vol. 10, p. 265; and Daniel S. Lamson, *History of the Town of Weston, Massachusetts: 1630–1890*, Boston, 1913, p. 63.

[2] For Captain Levi Pease and his inn, see footnote 2 to the letter of October 5, 1797.

[3] Colonel William Stephens Smith had two homes in New York. On March 25, 1795, he bought the eastern section of the Van Zandt farm, a tract of twenty-three acres lying between the East River and the Boston Post Road, on Manhattan Island, extending north and south between what are now East 58th and 62nd Streets, New York City. This was his winter home. He spent the summers in East Chester, Westchester County, where he bought the property known as the Vincent Halsey house, three miles from what is now New Rochelle. Roof, *Colonel Smith and Lady*, pp. 226–7.

have fallen since, and from the return of so many persons, new cases have been increased.

I found a Letter from the President, who writes, that he was oppresst with one of his old heavey colds—that he could get but a small Room & Bed Room at Trentown [New Jersey] for his accomodation, that the fever still was so bad in Philadelphia that it would not be thought prudent to attempt going in untill the Black frosts of Novbr came—I found here old Mrs. Smith & Nancy just returned from Baltimore. They past through the city of Philadelphia. They said that tho it was Evening when they got there, yet they would not have remaind a Night, for the smell of the city was so offensive that they could not endure it—They therefore procured a carriage & got 5 miles out. I left Mr. Otis and Family at a neat Inn about 7 miles from hence. Mrs. Smith is gone out this morning to see if she can procure lodgings for them in this place—We had a very agreable journey save that young Farmer proved so lame as to oblige me to hire an other horse, and have him led on.

I am desirious to hear from you. A Letter directed to East Chester to the care of the post master New Rochell will reach me. I mentiond to Mr. Beal that I would have the garret entry painted & the back stairs. I would have them done before he leaves the House. The kitchin floor stands in need of painting. I think it will be best to do it, even tho I should make the alteration in the kitchin which I contemplate. You must write a word about the cellar unless the Letters come immediatly to me.

Remember me to all our Friends. Mrs. [William Stephens] Smith & Caroline & Mrs. [Charles] Adams desire to be rememberd to you. Louissa will write for herself.

Your affectionate Sister
A. Adams

East Chester, October 31, 1799

My dear Sister:

I received your Letter on Saturday the 26th by Brisler, who with his family arrived here in safety. John was taken with the Mumps the day before. He was not so sick, as to prevent their proceeding to cross the Ferry—I have not heard of him since, but expect to, this day. Louissa has had the Mumps, so as to be swelld up to her Eyes. They have been a week upon her, and are not yet gone. Caroline was seizd last week with the worst inflamation in her Eyes that I have ever seen a child have. It threw her into a fever. She has been blisterd for it, and kept without light, which she could not bear a Ray of. It seems to be going of, but is still bad. Mrs. Smith had designd to go on to Philadelphia with me, and remain untill the Col. got into his winter quarters in the Jersies, and then go to him and pass the winter with him. It was my intention to have gone from hence on Monday the 4th of November, but I fear Caroline will detain me longer. The President is still at Trenton. We keep up a communication by the post at [New] Rochell, which is three miles from hence; and there I requested you to direct a Letter for me, but after this week I think you may address them to Philadelphia. Mr. & Mrs. Atkinson calld with Nancy Storer to see us this morning on their way to N[ew] York, all well, and yesterday I met Col. & Mrs. Morton, Mrs. Quincys Brother, returning.[1] Mrs. [Charles] Adams and Nancy Smith went in on Tuesday. I expect they will return on Saturday to take in the children. Tell Mrs. Norton I should like to present my Granddaughters to her sons; They are sprightly lively children. Susan is very forward and intelligent for three years, and would stand all day to hear you read stories, which she will catch at a few times repeating, and has got all goody Goose stories by Heart as her uncle J. Q. Adams did Giles Ginger Bread.[2] She tells me all her Letters and would read in a month if she had a good school. Abbe went alone at nine months, and is very pretty, more so than Susan, having the advantage of sprightly Eyes. Both have fine complexions.[3] But I cannot look upon them my dear Sister with that Joy which you do upon yours. They make my Heart ache, and what is worse, I have not any prospect of their being better off. But shall we receive Good, and not Evil? Yet it is a trial of the worst kind. Any calamity inflicted by the hand of Providence, it would become me in silence to submit to, but when I behold misiry and distress, disgrace and poverty, brought upon a Family by intemperence, my heart bleads at every pore.

When I get to Philadelphia I will write to Mr. [William] Cranch, and enjoin it upon Thomas [B. Adams] to do so. He will rise superiour to

[1] Eliza Susan Morton, daughter of John Morton, merchant, of New York, was the wife of Josiah Quincy (1772–1864). Nancy Storer was the daughter of Charles Storer, private secretary, at one time, to John Adams. Adams, *Works*, vol. 8, p. 310.

[2] *The Renowned History of Giles Gingerbread: A Little Boy who Lived upon Learning.* This book for children, attributed both to John Newbury and Giles Jones, appeared about 1765. *Cambridge Bibliography of English Literature*, 1940, vol. 2, p. 561.

[3] Susanna Boylston (1796–1846) and Abigail Louisa (1798–1838), daughters of Charles (1770–1800) and Sarah (Smith) Adams (1769–1828). Charles Adams died of drink on November 30, 1800.

his troubles. He has no vices to disgrace himself and Family. His misfortunes have arisen from trusting to the honesty of others.[4]

I am exceedingly anxious for my dear son abroad. The last accounts from him lead us to fear, that the next will bring us an account of the death of his wife. He too, had been sick of an intermitting fever. Where is the situation in Life which exempts us from trouble? Who of us pass through the world with our path strewed with flowers, without encountering the thorns? In what ever state we are, we shall find a mixture of good and evil, and we must learn to receive these vicissitudes of life, so as not to be unduly exalted by the one, or depressed by the other. No cup so bitter, but what some cordial drops are mingled by a kind Providence, who knows how as Sterne says, to "temper the wind to the Shorn Lamb."[5]—But I shall insensibly run into moralizing.

You mention a pr of stockings. I left a pr for you. Betsy might [have] put them into the black trunk in the entry. You will look there for them. With a kind remembrance to all our Friends and Neighbours, I am, my dear Sister,

Your truly affectionate
A. ADAMS

When you write let me know how Pheby does.

[East Chester, New York, November 1–3, 1799][1]

MY DEAR SISTER:

Tomorrow morning I expect to leave this place, and proceed on my way to Philadelphia, where I hope soon to hear from you. Frank and family had arrived before Brisler. They had only ten days passage.

Our Envoys, I presume, are ready to sail.[2] The P[resident] writes me,

[4] On January 19, 1799, the *Columbian Centinel* of Boston announced: "Thomas B. Adams, third son of our beloved President has arrived at New York from Europe." William Cranch was the lawyer of James Greenleaf, of the North American Land Company, speculator in real estate in Washington, D.C.

[5] "But, 'God tempers the wind,' said Maria, 'to the shorn lamb.'" This is an ancient French proverb which Laurence Sterne made famous in *A Sentimental Journey Through France and Italy*. See the section called "Maria."

[1] Endorsed by Mrs. Cranch: "Received November 9, 1799." See the following letter.

[2] On February 18, 1799, Adams startled Congress and the country, and infuriated the Hamiltonians, by nominating William Vans Murray as minister to France. A committee of five from the Senate waited on Adams to persuade him to withdraw the nomination. Adams suggested a commission of three, two actually residing in the United States and not to depart until the requisite assurances were received from France. He nominated three men on February 25, 1799. Ultimately, Chief Justice Oliver Ellsworth (1745–1807) and William Richardson Davie (1756–1820) joined Vans Murray in Paris. Adams, *Works*, vol. 9, pp. 161–3, and Channing, *History of the United States*, vol. 4, pp. 203–6. Ellsworth and Davie sailed from Newport, Rhode Island, on the frigate *United States* on November 3, 1799.

that he hopes they are gone that there may no longer be room for impertinent paragraphs, fabricated by busy bodies who are forever meddling with things they understand not. I inclose you a Letter from William [Steuben Smith] to me. Be cautious however in your communications as the source will be traced. I request Mr. [Richard] Cranch to have the inclosed communication publishd, taken from the N[ew] York commercial advertizer of Nov'br 2d in the centinal, or J[ohn] Russels paper.[3] I also inclose a paper which contains an answer to Coopers address.[4] If it has not been republished in our papers, it ought to be. If you could send it to Mr. Gardner [of] Milton he will see that it is done. The writer is T[homas] B[oylston] A[dams] as I have good reason to believe.

Mrs. [William Stephens] Smith goes on with me. My Love and regards to all Friends. Mrs. [Charles] Adams and children went to N[ew] York to day. She had been in part of the last week. She returned last Evening, and went again this morning.

I read in the centinal [of] the death of Lilly Field.[5] What was her sickness? The quitting of Mrs. Foster was the ruin of that poor Girl. Adieu, your ever

Affectionate Sister
A. ADAMS

Philadelphia, Novbr. 15, 1799

MY DEAR SISTER:

I wrote to you twice from East Chester.[1] I left there the day I proposed, and had a fine passage across the North River. It was quite calm

[3] [John] Russell's Commercial Gazette.

[4] Thomas Cooper (1759–1839), agitator, scientist, and educator, was born in Westminster, England, and entered Oxford in 1779. He became a friend of Joseph Priestley, and, consequently, a Unitarian and a revolutionist. He visited Paris in 1792, and then settled at Northumberland, Pennsylvania, in 1794, where he practised law and served unofficially as a physician. On June 29, 1799, Cooper published in the *Sunbury and Northumberland Gazette* a blast against the administration of John Adams, attacking the arrogance of the executive; the "seizure" of the power to make treaties; and the Alien and Sedition Laws. See Thomas Cooper, *Political Essays Originally Inserted in the Northumberland Gazette*, Northumberland, 1799; second edition, Philadelphia, 1800. Pickering called this outburst to the attention of President Adams on August 1, 1799. Adams, *Works*, vol. 9, pp. 5–7. See, also, Dumas Malone, *The Public Life of Thomas Cooper, 1783–1839*, New Haven, 1926.

[5] Lilley Field died at Quincy, aged fourteen. *Columbian Centinel*, October 23, 1799.

[1] Mrs. Adams wrote not twice, but three times from East Chester. "The President of the United States has taken his residence at Philadelphia." *Columbian Centinel*, November 9, 1799.

& not cold. We proceeded on our journey to Newark the same day, and there finding that we could go to Brunswick as conveniently by travelling through Springfield and Scotch Plain to Plainfield, the place where Col. [William Stephens] Smith is Encampd with three Regiments, we parted with Mr. & Mrs. [Samuel Allyne] Otis, and took different directions. We reachd Plainfield about 4 oclock, and found all hands, officers and Men busily employd in cutting down Trees & building log houses for winter quarters.

We took a walk through the encampment, and then went to a House which the Col. had provided for us, where we lodgd. The next morning he accompanied us to Brunswick, where the President met us. We tarried all Night, and then sat out in [the] morning for Trenton, 32 miles, which we reachd by four oclock, and the next day proceeded to this place, but were overtaken by rain, and rode 18 miles in it. We were met about four mils out of Town by the Light Horse escorted in &c.

Ever since I have been *sitting up*—receiving visitors—which prevents me going even to take a ride—which I want for exercise—The show will be pretty well over by the next week, and then I must sit out to return them all—Drawing Rooms will not commence untill after Congress meet. News we have none but what you get first from Boston. I have not a line from any one but you since I left home and that by Mr. Brisler. I quite want to hear from you; I wrote to you twice from East Chester.

I have seen by the papers the honorable testimony of respect and Regard paid to the Birth day in Quincy, as well as in other parts of Massachusets[2]—The citizens of N[ew] York and this place were not in a situation to do it, if they had been disposed. The inhabitants were not returnd to their abodes who had been driven from them by the pestilence. I suppose they will, as they did last year give a Ball and Supper, when the winter commences after [the *cancelled*] Congress meet, and the Ladies have settled the fashions which are now canvessd, and adjusting from some late importations. Amongst the Ladies presented to me the Countess de Tilly has been of the Number, by the Appelation of Madam de Tilly. She has all the appearence and dress of a Real French woman, Rouged up to the Ears: Mrs. Bingham did not appear to feel any embarresment at introducing her, tho I cannot say she did not creat one

[2] The birthday of John Adams, who was born on October 19, 1735. See the letter of November 21, 1800.

in me; for I really felt a reluctance at addressing her.[3] So I talked to her mother and sister, and as there was much other company present I easily past her over. Mrs. Black will have a curiosity to know something of the fashions. I have heard of once a Man & twice a child, and the Ladies caps are an exact coppy of the Baby caps—those which are made with drawings, and drawn with a bobbin to a point, a quarter and Nail deep, a lace upon the border, a bow upon the point, three bows behind and one before, the Hair a little drest at the side & a few curls upon the forehead, the cap to lie flat upon the head.[4] Some tye them under the chin. Gown waists, half a yd in length. Morning dress a Gown very narrow just to reach the bottom of the skirt, a Narrow frill of half a Nail pleated round the bottom—buttond with an oval shirt button down before, two rows of the same down the back, over which a cord is crossd—the sleaves short but with cuffs pleated, buttons upon them corded in the same Manner, two large buttons on the hips—A dress Gown, made with a long train behind comeing only half way down the coat before. A Muslin coat of the same with a small flounce at bottom— So much for fashions, already exhibited.

I requested you to take charge of my pork for Bacon, but left you not the means. Inclosed is a five dollors Bill to get salt peter and Molasses.

Pray write. We all send Love, Regards &c to all friends, Neighbours &c &c.

Ever your affectionate Sister
A. A[DAMS]

Philadelphia, Novbr 26, 1799

MY DEAR SISTER:

Your kind Letter reachd me on the 20th. I began to feel very impatient to hear from you: Your Letter afforded me much pleasure: I rejoice

[3] The worst scandal of the "Republican Court" at Philadelphia during 1799 was the clandestine marriage, on April 11, of fifteen-year-old Maria Matilda Bingham, second daughter of Anne (Willing), daughter of Thomas Willing, and William Bingham, a rich banker, to Jacques-Pierre-Alexandre, Comte de Tilly (1764–1816). Tilly, a handsome and profligate Frenchman, and a poet and author, was born at Le Mans and was, at one time, a page to Marie Antoinette. Fleeing from France after the storming of the Tuileries, August 10, 1792, he wandered through England, the United States, and Germany. In 1797, he turned up in the United States, and, after his marriage to Maria, the Binghams had to buy him off with a cash settlement and an annuity, and put a bill of divorce through the Pennsylvania legislature. In 1807, Tilly returned to France, where he led a disorderly life, committing suicide at Brussels as the result of a scandal at cards. For the subsequent career of Maria, see Morison, *Harrison Gray Otis*, pp. 137–9. For Comte de Tilly, see *Memoirs of the Comte Alexandre de Tilly*, New York, 1932; and Havelock Ellis, *From Rousseau to Proust*, Boston and New York, 1935, pp. 193–251.

[4] A nail measures two and one-quarter inches.

that so worthy and amiable a Man as Mr. Kendall allways appeard to me, is like to be so soon, and agreably setled.[1] I would willingly exchange all the discourses I have heard here since I came and all I shall be like to hear, for the one half which even chance offers us at Quincy. I do not believe that a people are ever made better by always hearing of the terrors of the Lord. Gloom is no part of my Religion. To mantain [*sic*] a conscience void of offence, as far as is consistant with the imperfect State we are in, both towards God and Man, is one article of my Faith, and to do good as I have opportunity, and according to my means I would wish to make the Rule of my practise. [To *cancelled*] Do justly, walk Humbly and to Love mercy—are duties enjoind upon every Christian, and if we can attain to those graces, we may cheerfully look for our recompence and reward, where it is promised to us.[2]

Shall we be so happy at Quincy as to settle a Gentleman of Mr. [Peter] Whitneys talents? I most sincerely hope we may; but fear that so good a choice is not reserved for us.

I saw in Rusels paper the answer to Cooper.[3] I found I was Mistaken in the writer. It was not the person [Thomas Boylston Adams] I conjectured, nor is it known by him, who it was. Cooper has lately appeard in the *Aurora*, and in his former Mad democratic Stile, abused the President, and I presume subjected himself to the penalty of the Sedition act. The greater part of [our *cancelled*] the abuse leveld at the Government is from foreigners. Every Jacobin paper in the United States is Edited by a Foreigner, and John Fenno is become a coppiest of them. What a disgrace to our Country.

[1] Probably James Kendall, Harvard, 1796; S.T.D., 1825; died in 1859.

[2] "He hath shewed thee, O man, what is good; and what doth the Lord require of thee, but to do justly, and to love mercy, and to walk humbly with thy God?" *Micah*, VI, 8.

[3] For the answer to Thomas Cooper's attack on the administration of John Adams, see *J. Russell's Gazette*, November 18 and 21, 1799, in which "A True American" points out the constitutional power of the executive branch to negotiate treaties, and defends the exclusion from the United States of aliens from Europe, both "Aristocrats" and "Democrats." The author of this answer observes that, according to British law of the time, no subject of Great Britain was permitted to renounce his status to become a citizen of the United States—or of any other country. In May, 1800, Cooper was convicted under the Sedition Law, and sentenced to serve six months in prison and pay a fine of four hundred dollars. Throughout the rest of his life he sought the repayment of this fine, which, after his death, was refunded to his heirs, with interest. From 1821 to 1834 Cooper was president of the University of South Carolina. In his later years, this rebel supported the Bank of the United States against Andrew Jackson, defended slavery, and argued for nullification of the federal tariff acts. See Malone, *Thomas Cooper*. See, also, the letter of November 1–3, 1799.

On thursday next [the *cancelled*] four of our N[ew] England States keep thanksgiving. I would not suffer the day to pass without noticeing it here by the Symbols of the festival as commemorated by us. I have invited a chosen set to dine upon that day, and whilst we share in & are plentifully supplied with the good things of this world, I hope we shall not be unmindfull of the many blessing[s] of the past year, which we have abundant cause to be thankfull for.

Thomas has had a Letter from your son. He appears I think much more tranquil in mind, and is quite witty in his Letter.

There is a Letter from Mr. Pitcarn in Hamburgh to Thomas [Boylston Adams] dated in Sepbr, in which he says that he heard from Mr. [John Quincy] Adams three days before, and that he was well. He makes no mention of Mrs. Adams. He would I think, if she had not recoverd or was so dangerous as she had been represented.

Mrs. Smith and Louissa desire to be rememberd to you and all our Friends. I do not get a line from Sister [Mrs. Stephen Peabody] or the Children. Mrs. Smith is anxious to hear from them. William [Smith Shaw] is well. Thomas will get into buisness in time I hope. He is very attentive to his office.

Next week Congress meet. I expect it will be a stormy Session. Electionering is already began. There will be more things aimed at than will be carried either by Jacobins or Federalists—but the Jacobins are always more subtle and industerous than there opponents.

My Love to Mrs. Norton and Greenleaf.[4] I hope if my Health remains to be with you early again in the Spring. My best regards and the Presidents to Mr. [Richard] Cranch. Accept the affectionate Regard and Love of

Your Sister
A. A[DAMS]

Philadelphia, December 4th, 1799

MY DEAR SISTER:

Mrs. Smith, Louissa, Mrs. Otis, [Dr.] Rush, Peters & a number of young Ladies are just gone to Congress to hear the speech which is deliverd at 12 oclock to day.[1] I should have liked well enough to have

[4] Elizabeth Cranch, wife of the Reverend Jacob Norton, and Lucy Cranch, wife of John Greenleaf, the daughters of Richard and Mary (Smith) Cranch.

[1] See "Speech to Both Houses of Congress," December 3, 1799, in Adams, *Works*, vol. 9, pp. 136–40. Mrs. Adams probably dated her letter incorrectly.

been of the Party, but it would not have been proper. You will see it, as soon as you will get the Letter, I presume. Some people will not be pleased, I suppose, because it will not disclose enough about the mission to France. Others will Growl, because war is not waged against England, in words at least. They will grumble at all events, and under all circumstances, and so let them. But their brightest, best, and most peacefull days they now see: Such at least are my predictions.

I have to request you, my dear Sister, to look in my large Hair cloaths Trunk which stands in the Garret for my white Lutestring Gown & coat which is trimd with silver, and for a Napkin in which is a plain Muslin Gown Embrodered with silk, which belongs to Mrs. [William Stephens] Smith. Indeed all that is pind in the Napkin belongs to Mrs. Smith. These dresses I request you to have done up in the safest manner and take them to Mr. [William] Smiths, with a request to send them to me if possible by some private conveyance; I sent Betsy [Howard] yesterday to my Trunk to get them and found to my great mortification that she had omitted to put them up, or rather, that she had by mistake put up what I did not want in lieu of them. Mrs. Smith is more dissapointed than I am, as she wants hers more; If they should not be in that trunk they must be in the imperial.[2] I had depended upon mine for fryday Evening next and as they wanted a little alteration, I discoverd that they were missing, by sending to my Trunk for them. It is like there will be persons comeing on from Boston who will in the course of the winter take them on for me. Gen'll Lincoln designs to come about Christmass but that may be uncertain.[3] I will trust to Mr. Smith['s] care to convey them for me. Sew them in a coars cloth as well as a Napkin, and I will give who ever brings them safe, as many good dinners as they will Eat.

I should certainly use some Red Broad cloth if I could come at it, for red cloth Cloaks are all the mode, trim'd with white furs. This is much more rational than to wear only a shawl in winter. I wish any thing would persuade the Ladies that muslin is not a proper winter dress. So far as example goes, I shall bring in the use of silks. At my Age I think I am priviledged to sit a fashion. The real truth is that Muslin is new every time it is clean, & new trimed, so that it is, they

---

[2] A luggage case for the top of a coach.

[3] Benjamin Lincoln (1733–1810), of Hingham, who suppressed Shays's Rebellion in 1787, and was Collector of the Port of Boston (1789–1809). See the letters of July 9, 1798, and January 28, 1800.

say, upon a principle of oconomy they use it, fewer changes being required.

I have not had a Letter from you for some time. I communicated to the President Mr. J[oseph] Cranchs Letter and he gave it to the Secretary of War to see what can be done. I shall ask the Secretary soon respecting it, and then will write you.[4]

I learn from some of the Essex leaders that Judge [Francis] Dana is to be sit up for Governour. He will make a very able one. The Bench will also lose a learned Judge. I Question however whether Judge Dana is sufficiently popular for that place. He wants the amiable & concilitating [sic] manners of Sumner.[5] Alass I know not where, is to be found all the qualities which he possess'd, concentered in any person who will be held up as a canditate [sic].

Mr. Sheaf the member from Portsmouth will be like to come soon. He will call at Mr. Storers no doubt, and I have been thinking if you was to buy me a small trunk just large enough to hold the articles whether Mr. Sheaf would not take charge of it for me, & bring it within the carriage.[6] The sooner you can get the things to Town the better. Mrs. Smith is very well and sends her duty to you. So does Mr. [John] Adams, Mr. [William Smith] Shaw & Louissa [Smith]. The City is now said to be very healthy. The Members of both houses have been punctual to a day, a sufficient Number to make both houses. I inclose the Speech.[7] With hopes of hearing from you this week I close, adding Love to Mrs. Norton & Greenleaf.

Affectionatly your Sister
A. ADAMS

Please to send all you find in the Napkin belonging to Mrs. Smith.

Philadelphia, December 11, 1799

MY DEAR SISTER:

I received this week your Letters of Novbr 24th and 28th, and this morning yours of Decbr. 3d, the contents of which gave me much

---

[4] James McHenry, third Secretary of War. See footnote 1 to the letter of July 3, 1798.
[5] See footnote 5 to the letter of June 23, 1798.
[6] James Sheafe (1755–1829), Harvard, 1774, merchant of Portsmouth, and Federalist representative and Senator from New Hampshire (1799–1802). "Mr. Storer" is probably Charles Storer, who was at one time private secretary to Mr. Adams. Adams, *Works*, vol. 8, p. 310.
[7] See Adams, *Works*, vol. 9, pp. 136–40.

pleasure. It will be a real subject of rejoicing to me, if we obtain Mr. [Peter] Whitney for our pastor. It will greatly add to the pleasure I anticipate upon my return to Quincy to find that we are in possession of a Gentleman of Mr. Whitneys known and acknowledged talents, so well adapted to the profession he has chosen. I hope that no root of bitterness will spring up, to injure his usefullness, or to impeed his settlement.

The season continues remarkable mild, but the late rains have prevented my riding more than through the city to return visits, of which I have a more than ordinary share, many persons visiting me now who never did before. They think, I suppose, that as it is the last season Congress will sit in this city, they will not be wanting in attention— I sometimes walk for exercise and make some visits in that way. I yesterday made one in this way to Mrs. Morris, which to both of us was painfull.[1] I had not seen her since the very great reverse of her circumstances. She received me with all that dignity of manners for which she more than any Lady I ever saw, is distinguished. I calld rather at an improper hour, (having been detain from going sooner by visitors). She was in a small neat Room and at dinner with her daughter & youngest son, who is with a merchant, and on whose account she said, she always dinned at one oclock, but instead of refusing herself, she rose and met me at the door. Her feelings were evidently strongly excited. She endeavourd to smile away the Melancholy which was evident upon her whole countanance, and enterd into conversation. When I left her, I requested her to come and take Tea with me. I took her by the Hand. She said she did not visit, but she would not refuse herself the pleasure of comeing some day when I was alone. She then turnd from me, and the tears burst forth. I most sincerely felt for her.

I have sent to Mrs. Black and Suky Adams a model of the New fashiond cap.[2] They are not such as you or I should wear. If I thought Mrs. Norton and Greenleaf would like them I would send each of them one. With the Hair drest as I have directed they look very pretty.

The politician[s] have before this, got the speech which Duane says, in his paper, was as anxiously expected, and sought for, as a speech is, from the tyrant of Britain. It has been received here, with more applause & approbation than any speech which the President has ever before deliverd, and what is very surprizing and remarkable, the answer

[1] Mary (White) Morris, wife of Robert Morris (1734–1806).
[2] Susanna (born 1777), daughter of Peter Boylston Adams (1738–1823), sole surviving brother of John Adams.

to it by the House past unanimously without a motion for alterating but one sentance, which motion did not obtain. The answer was draughted by Mr. [John] Marshall, and contains so full and unqualified an approbation of the Measures of the President in his late Mission, as not only gives him sincere pleasure, but the unanimnity [sic] with which it past the whole House, being the first instance of the kind is a proof that the Measure meets the wishes of the people at large.[3] The documents upon which the measure was founded I inclose to you in the paper. What would the people of this Country have said, if the President had neglected to meet the advances of France, and have sufferd himself to have been governd by a spirit of personal resentment because he had been ill used, and abused by some of their Rulers. Would such conduct have become the Head of a Great Nation? Should France conduct [herself] dishonorably, we shall not be to blame; and the President will have the satisfaction of knowing: that he has done every thing Encumbent upon him to preserve Peace and restore harmony. The replie of the Senate cold and Languid, fully discovers in what school they have imbibed their sentiments. The committe chosen to draught the replie, were known to be some of the most opposed to the Mission. There is a man in the cabinet, whose manners are forbiding, whose temper is sour and whose resentments are implacable, who neverless [sic] would like to dictate every Measure. He has to deal with *one*, who knows full well their respective departments—and who chuses to feel quite independant, and to act so too, but for this He is abused. But I am mistaken if this dictator does not get himself ensnared in his own toil. He would not now remain in office, if the President possesst such kind of resentments as I hear from various quarters, he permits himself to utter—From this fountain have flowed all the unpopularity of the Mission to France, which some of the federilists have been so deluded as to swallow large draughts off.[4]

Thomas [Boylston Adams] keeps so constantly at his office that I see him only at meal times. He sends his Respects. As to William [Smith Shaw], we have rubd of [sic] so many of his peculiarities that he has scarcly one left for us to laugh at. He is a good creature. I heard yesterday from Mr. [William] Cranch and Family. They were all well. Mr.

[3] For the acknowledgment of Adams, see Adams, *Works*, vol. 9, pp. 141–2.
[4] Timothy Pickering, having bitterly opposed the President's policy of peace with France, was summarily dismissed by Adams on May 12, 1800. Adams, *Works*, vol. 9, p. 55. Peace with France was concluded at Mortefontaine, September 30–October 1, 1800, and was, with the exception of one article, accepted by the Senate. See *Proc. Mass. Hist. Soc.*, vol. 44 (1911), pp. 377–429: Brooks Adams, "The Convention of 1800 with France."

Wainright has been there, and will see you as soon as he returns. Mrs. [William Stephens] Smith sends her Love. My paper reminds me to close. I will write to Dr. [Cotton] Tufts by the next Mail. Love &c
Your affectionate
A. A[dams]

Philadelphia, Sunday Eve'ng, Decbr. 22, 1799

My dear Sister:

I wrote to you the day after we received the account of the death of Gen'll Washington.[1] This Event so important to our Country at this period, will be universally deplored. No Man ever lived, more deservedly beloved and Respected. The praise and I may say addulation which followed his administration for several years, never made him forget that he was a Man, subject to the weakness and frailty attached to humane Nature. He never grew giddy, but ever mantaind a modest diffidence of his own talents, and if that was an error, it was of the amiable and engageing kind, tho it might lead sometimes to a want of decisions in some great Emergencys. Possesst of power, posest of an extensive influence, he never used it but for the benifit of his Country. Witness his retirement to private Life when Peace closed the scenes of War; When call'd by the unanimous suffrages of the People to the chief Majestracy of the Nation, he acquitted himself to the satisfaction and applause of all Good Men. When assailed by faction, when reviled by Party, he sufferd with dignity, and Retired from his exalted station with a Character which malice could not wound, nor envy tarnish. If we look through the whole tennor of his Life, History will not produce to us a Parrallel. Heaven has seen fit to take him from us. Our Mourning is sincere, in the midst of which, we ought not to lose sight of the Blessings we have enjoy'd and still partake of, that he was spaired to us, untill he saw a successor filling his place, persueing the same system which he had adopted, and that in times which have been equally dangerous and Critical. It becomes not me to say more upon this Head.

I inclose to you a News paper which contains all that has yet been done in commemoration of the late dispensation. Tomorrow the Senate come in a Body with a sympathetic address, and on thursday a Eulogy is to be deliverd by Genll. Lee, in the Dutch Church in this city, to which we are all invited.[2]

[1] George Washington died on Saturday, December 14, 1799. The letter to which Mrs. Adams refers was lost in the mail. See the letter of January 7, 1800.

[2] Henry Lee (1756–1818), "Light-Horse Harry" of Virginia, soldier of the Revolution, Governor of Virginia (1792–1795), and father of Robert E. Lee. In 1799 Lee entered

Monday, [December] 23, [1799]

Company comeing in last Evening, I was prevented finishing my Letter. This morning I received yours of December 15. It is unhappy that what is liked by one should for that very reason, be the object of aversion to an other, but when a spirit of private animosity is permitted to influence the mind, it always produces an illiberal conduct. The two B[lack]'s who are now opposed to Mr. Whitney, are pretty nearly upon a footing in point of talants and capacity, taking into view the comparative advantages they have had.[3] But their influence will not be very extensive. I am sorry you had such a cold time in looking for my Gown. I shall not have occasion now for any thing but Black, untill Spring. Then I shall put on half mourning. I shall be glad to have it, if it can be conveniently sent. Mrs. Smith wants her white, as she will after a certain period appear in white trimd with black. At Present the whole Family are in full mourning.

I hope Mrs. Black has received her Cap safe. Mr. Wainright did not go so soon as I expected, and Betsy Howard got a Mr. Whitney, with whom she was acquainted, to take it. It was to be left at Mr. Lambs.

Mrs. Smith has worked you a Crown of a Cap & Band, which I request you to accept of. I will send a Border the next time I write.

We all desire to be kindly rememberd to all Friends.

Your affectionate Sister
A. Adams

I send a paper containing the speech of Mr. Hopkins[on] upon the trial of Peter Porcupine for defamation. The Jury brought in five thousand dollors damages and the court confirmed the verdict.[4]

Congress, and drew up the resolutions offered by John Marshall on the death of Washington. These contained the famous description of Washington as "first in war, first in peace, and first in the hearts of his countrymen." Lee repeated the words in his memorial oration to the Congress in Philadelphia on December 26, 1799.

[3] Mr. and Mrs. Moses Black, of Quincy, who tried to prevent the appointment of the Reverend Peter Whitney as assistant to the Reverend Anthony Wibird in the parish. See footnote 5 to the letter of May 16, 1797, and footnote 3 to the letter of November 15, 1797.

[4] During the yellow-fever epidemic of 1797, Dr. Benjamin Rush treated his patients with violent purges and copious bleeding, and William Cobbett, on politico-medical grounds, made a terrific onslaught on him. Rush sued for libel, and, after a delay of two years, the case came to trial, and Cobbett was ordered to pay $5000. Rush was libelled, and deserved to be libelled, but the trial was unfair. Joseph Hopkinson, author of "Hail Columbia," represented Rush in court. Cobbett retreated to New York, where he published a new paper, the *Rush-Light*, in which (February 28, 1800), he described Dr. Rush's system as "one of the great discoveries . . . which have contributed to the depopulation of the earth." Adams thought of deporting Cobbett under the Alien Act, but Cobbett returned to England in June, 1800.

Philadelphia, December 30th, 1799

My dear Sister:

I received your Letter of the 23d this morning. I should be glad you would inform me from time to time the state Mrs. Mears is in. I have told Mrs. Brisler that she was ill, but as [she *cancelled*] it can not be of any service to Mrs. Mears, I think best not to let her know of her relapse tho I fear it will finally be fatal to Mrs. Mears—Mrs. Brisler would so distress herself as very probably to bring on her fits and render her wholy useless in the Family.[1]

I think every days experience must convince the people of the propriety of sending the Envoys at the time they went. After the President had received the Letter from Tallyrand containing the assureances from the Directory which he requir'd, he would not allow it, to be made a question whether they should proceed tho he knew certain persons set their faces against it as far as they dared. Gen'll. Hamilton made no secret of his opinion. He made the P[residen]t a visit at Trenton, and was perfectly sanguine in the opinion that the Stateholder would be reinstated before Christmass and Louis the 18th upon the Throne of France[2]. I should as soon expect, replied the P[resident], that the sun, moon & stars will fall from their orbits, as events of that kind take place in any such period, but suppose such an event possible, can it be any injury to our Country to have envoys there? It will be only necessary for them to wait for new commissions. And if France is disposed to accomodate our differences, will she be less so under a Royall than a Directorial Government? Have not the Directory Humbled themselves to us more than to any Nation or Power in contest with her? If she proves faithless, if she will not receive our Envoys, does the disgrace fall upon her, or upon us? We shall not be worse off than at Present. The people of our own Country will be satisfyed that every honorable method has been try'd to accommodate our differences. At the period the envoys went, France was loosing ground. She was defeated, and the combined powers appeard to be carrying victory with them. If they had been detained untill now, how mean and despicable should we have appeared? Reports have been circulated that the British Minister remonstrated: However

[1] Mrs. Mears was a sister of the wife of John Briesler, major-domo to John Adams. See the letter of January 7, 1800.

[2] It was fifteen years before Louis XVIII entered Paris. William V (1748–1802), Stadholder of the Netherlands (1751–1795), never regained his position. Louis Bonaparte was King of Holland from 1806 to 1810, when Holland was incorporated with France as an integral part of the empire. The son of William V became William I, King of the Netherlands, in 1815.

dissagreable the measure might be to him, he is too old a minister, and understands the nature of his Mission too well, to have ventured upon any such step. As an independant Nation, no other has a Right to complain, or dictate to us, with whom we shall form connections, provided those connections are not contrary to treaties already made.

Last frydays drawing Room was the most crowded of any I ever had. Upwards of a hundred Ladies, and near as many Gentlemen attended, all in mourning. The Ladies Grief did not deprive them of taste in ornamenting their white dresses: 2 yds of Black mode in length, of the narrow kind pleated upon one shoulder, crossd the Back in the form of a Military sash tyed at the side, crosd the peticoat & hung to the bottom of it, were worn by many. Others wore black Epulets of Black silk trimd with fring[e] upon each shoulder, black Ribbon in points upon the Gown & coat some plain Ribbon, some black Snail &c.[3] Their caps were crape with black plumes or black flowers. Black Gloves & fans. The Gentlemen all in Black. The Ladies many of them wanted me to fix the time for wearing mourning, but I declined, and left them to Govern themselves by the periods prescribed by the Gentlemen. The assembly Room is burnt down, and they have not any place to display their gay attire but the drawing Room and private parties, and as they expect it will be the last winter they will have the opportunity, they intended shining.

Mr. [William Smith] Shaw is gone to Mount Vernon the Bearer of Letters from the President & the Resolutions of congress, to Mrs. Washington. It was thought most respectfull to send a special Messenger. He sit out last Saturday. I wrote to your son by him, and he will be able on his return to give a particuliar account of their health and welfare. I expect he will be absent 10 days.

Tweseday, [December] 31 [1799]

We have a report here that the plague is in Boston, brought by a ship from the Levant. I hope it is without foundation, but let me know the Truth. The weather here has been so mild, foggy, and thawey that colds universally prevail. Dr. Rush says there is a procession fever. I do not wonder at it, for the processions was an hour and quarter from congress Hall to the churrch & an hour & half in church. The Gentlemen say they walkd over shoes in Mud. I went at Eleven & did not get home till 20 minuts before four oclock. I then had to dress and sit

---

[3] "Snail," obsolete for "chenille," in use from 1741 to 1773: *Oxford English Dictionary*.

down to dinner with 30 Gentlemen & Ladies. I went to Bed the moment the company left me, which was not till nine oclock. I felt sick enough & expected to pay for my exertions, but the next morning I was quite smart, and went through the drawing Room ceremonies in the Evening. You [will *cancelled*] may be assured that my Health is much firmer than the last winter. I was at the Theater last night to hear the Monody performd—I think sufficient has been done to express the gratefull feelings of a people towards the Character of even a Washington. The danger is, least the enthusiastic disposition of some should proceed too far. Some things are requested of the P[resident] which really appear improper, and may tend to turn what is designd as respect, into Ridicule. He will withstand it if he can without giving umbrage to the Representatives *of the People*. If the thing is done, you will know what it is.

I inclose the Border I promised, and am

Your affectionate Sister
A. ADAMS

Philadelphia, Janry 7th, 1800

MY DEAR SISTER:

I know not what could have become of a Letter written to you upon the 18 of December, that upon the 30th you should not have received it.[1] I have written you more than once since that period, but do not recollect the dates. I forget whether it was before or since then, that I inclosed to you a crown of a Cap & Band. Since that, I have sent the Border and a Cap for Mrs. Norton, which I think you could not yet have got. I have not learnt whether Mrs. Black has got my Letter & the cap sent to her by a Mr. Whitney. I should greatly regret that any obstical should prevent the settlement of Mr. Whitney with us. I would most certainly accommodate him if it was in my power, but my sons whole Library is at the House in which Mr. Clark lives, beside some cumbersome furniture which I have not yet any place for.

Thom[p]son Baxter once offerd his House and place to the President for a thousand pounds. That is a large sum for a Clergyman, yet if it could be had for that, would it not prove much Cheeper than building? 40 acres of land belongd to it. The poor old incumbent might be had into the Bargain I suppose. But who knows but if Mr. Whitney could

---

[1] See the letter of December 22, 1799.

get the place, and marry a woman kind and attentive to the old Gentleman who would clean & brush him up, but that it might prove advantageous to them. I only suggest the Idea. I received my Gown & Mrs. [William Stephens] Smith['s] safe, by Mr. Sheaff [James Sheafe] yesterday.[2] I thank you for your care & Mr. & Mrs. [William] Smith for theres.

Our Boston Printers are great blunderers. In the answer to the Senates address of condolance, they make him say a *Trojan* instead of [Traygain *cancelled*] "Trajan found a Pliny" and in an paper they say the Senate sent a Letter of condolance, whereas the truth is, the Senate came in a Body and pressented the address, which address is said to have been drawn by Mr. Dexter, a New England Man certain.[3] No Southern Man quotes Scripture—Mr. [William Smith] Shaw returnd yesterday from Mount Vernon. He was much gratified by his tour, tho regreeted that he did not see Mrs. Washington. She strove the whole time he was there, which was two days, to get resolution sufficient to see him, but finally excused herself. She had the painfull task to perform, to bring her mind to comply with the request of Congress, which she has done in the handsomest manner possible in a Letter to the President which will this day be communicated to congress. She wrote me in replie to my Letter an answer repleat with a sense of my sympathy, and expressive of her own personal Grief and anguish of mind. Mr. [Tobias] Lear told Mr. Shaw that she had not been able to shed a tear since the Genlls. death, untill she received the Presidents and my Letters when she was two hours getting through them, tho they were not Lengthy[4]—On his return he visited your son, who he says, is in good Health & spirits, as is Mrs. [William] Cranch. Richard [1797–1824] he says is not well, tho not confined. Mr. Greenleaf was with them. I fear Mr. Greenleaf is not a wise counsellor. Mr. Cranch would, a year before he did, have taken the step of relinquishing his Property if it had not been for Mr. Greenleafs advice. He certainly would have been better off, as his friends say. I am glad he had resolution enough at last to decide for himself. I have just closed a Letter to Mrs. Cranch of West Point, having obtained a promise from the Secretary of War that he shall have a place at Harpers ferry which he expects will be vacant in

---

[2] See footnote 6 to the letter of December 4, 1799.

[3] Samuel Dexter (1761–1816), of Boston, Harvard, 1781, Federalist representative (1793–1795) and Senator (1799–1800) from Massachusetts. Adams appointed him Secretary of War, May 13, 1800; and Secretary of the Treasury, January 1, 1801.

[4] See footnote 8 to the letter of June 28, 1789, and Adams, *Works*, vol. 9, pp. 45 and 164-5.

the Spring and that in the mean time he shall be employd where he is.[5]

I made Mrs. Brisler happy yesterday by your Letter containing the information that Mrs. Mears was better. She had burried her in her own mind, and when I went to tell her, she was so overcome expecting the news was fatal that she shook so I thought she would have gone into fits. No two sisters were ever fonder of each other. I hope Mrs. Mears will recover.

Inclosed is Genll. Lees oration.[6] It is a handsome performance. I will send you the pamphlet when it is out. We have charming weather. Adieu my dear Sister. I am going to take Mrs. [Samuel Allyne] Otis out to Ride. She has been very unwell with one of her old hoars colds & coughs which still hangs about her.[7]

Philadelphia, Janry 28, 1800

My dear Sister:

I yesterday received your Letter of the 19th. I think you have testified your proportion of Respect in a handsome manner to the Memory of the good and virtuous Washington. That he ought to live in our Memories, and be transmitted to posterity as a Character truly worthy Imitation is Right, but some Eulogyst[s] have ascribed to him solely, what was the joint effort & concert of Many. To no one Man in America, belongs the Epithet of *Saviour* of his Country. That Washingtons Character, when we take into view, his Education, the place of his Birth, and the various scenes in which he was call'd to act, exhibits a

[5] In spite of the declaration of John Adams to the contrary (see the letter of July 12, 1789), no one can accuse him of not having done his utmost to further the interests of his children and his relatives. Two Cranch cousins are referred to in this letter: William Cranch (1769-1855), the son of the sister of Mrs. John Adams, and Joseph Cranch, the son of the Reverend John Cranch, who died in England in 1746, the year that Richard and his sister, Mary Cranch, emigrated to America in the *Wilmington*, landing in Boston on November 13, 1746. This Joseph Cranch was given a post at West Point, New York, as early as 1790 (see the letters of April 3, 21, and 28, 1790). Ten years later he was using his influence to get a place at Harpers Ferry. His Cousin William, son of Richard (who was a close friend of John Adams), was a classmate of John Quincy Adams at Harvard. Having studied law, he entered the employment of James Greenleaf, the promoter of Washington, D.C., in 1794, and married Greenleaf's sister in 1795. Having failed to obtain the clerkship of the Supreme Court (see the letter of January 30, 1800), William Cranch was, in December, 1800, made one of the commissioners of Washington by John Adams. Two months later, March 3, 1801, Adams appointed him assistant judge of the Circuit Court of the District of Columbia, where he sat for the extraordinary term of fifty-four years. For a cool account of the career of William Cranch, see Clark, *Greenleaf and Law in the Federal City*, pp. 47-66. For a sketch of the Cranch family, see the *New-England Historical and Genealogical Register*, vol. 27, pp. 40-1: "Richard Cranch and His Family."

[6] See footnote 2 to the letter of December 22, 1799.
[7] The remaining third of the page is cut off.

most uncommon assemblage of Modesty, Moderation, Magninimity, fortititud [*sic*], perseverence and disinterestedness, will be most readily allowed, but at no time, did the fate of America rest upon the Breath of even a Washington, and those who assert these things, are Ignorant of the spirit of their countrymen, and whilst they strive to exalt one character, degrade that of their Country. These reflections have arrisen in my mind from reading Mr. Paynes oration,[1] and a Mad Rant of Bombast in a Boston centinal of a Mr. Messenger.[2] Judge [George Richards] Minots oration is exempt from these reflections. [It is the cool mild and *cancelled*] Wise and judicious observations upon his Character are those only which will out live the badges of mourning. Simple Truth is his best his greatest Eulogy. She alone can render his Fame immortal.[3]

[1] "Mr. Payne's oration" refers to the Reverend Thomas Paine's "An Eulogy on the Life of General George Washington. Written at the Request of the Citizens of Newburyport, and Delivered at the First Presbyterian Meeting-House in that town, January 2, 1800," the first paragraph of which follows:
Americans, The saviour of your country has obtained his last victory. Having reached the summit of human perfection, he has quitted the region of human glory. Conqueror of Time, he has triumphed over mortality; Legate of Heaven, he has returned with the tidings of his mission; Father of his People, he has ascended to advocate their cause in the bosom of his God. Solemn, "as it were a pause in nature," was his transit to eternity; thronged by the shades of heroes, his approach to the confines of bliss; pæaned by the song of angels, his journey beyond the stars!
Eulogies and Orations on the Life and Death of General George Washington, Boston, 1800, p. 55.
This Reverend Thomas Paine is not to be confused with "Tom" Paine (1737–1809), who did not return from France until October, 1802.

[2] Rosewell Messinger (1776–1844). See his *An Oration, Delivered at Old York on the Death of George Washington*, Charlestown, Massachusetts, 1800. Messinger's oration fills twelve pages, and contains twenty-three paragraphs. The portions quoted below will explain the contempt of Mrs. Adams:
The sun of the firmament is not darkened! The foundations of the earth do not tremble! Rocks have not fallen to dust! The mountains have not melted away! But the veil of liberty's temple is rent in twain. Her spotless high-priest hath retired to rest, through the portals of everlasting fame.
If our tongue were an angels it would falter; if our hearts were marble they would bleed; if our eyes were flint they would swell with tears; if the world were a Zembla it would melt and mourn, for Washington is no more . . . .
O, Adams, thy grief must pierce the centre of thy heart. More momentous than ever are the cares that devolve upon thee. The prophet with whom thou hast walked hand and hand, is now departed. Receive the mantle of thy brother. If the waters of death threaten to flood our country, divide them asunder; bid them roll on the right and the left, till they are lost in the desert. God will make thee Columbia's second Saviour . . . .
Though they said he [Washington] was a God, he died as a man: let us not murmur, but rather wonder, that his great and immortal soul should be contented to reside in a human form so long.

[3] George Richards Minot (1752–1802), of Boston, jurist and historian, delivered a speech on the occasion of the death of Washington, a whole edition of which sold in one day.

The News from France, is not that the Royall Standard is raised, but that a Triumvirate exists—Buonaparta is an adventerous Man. He is upon a Pinacle and with one foot only. We are yet all together in the dark respecting his views. Time must develope them. But one volcano burst[s] forth after an other, and what current the lava will take, we must wait to learn.[4]

I send you the report upon citizen Randolphs Letter. The Young Man is like to cost the Country more money in the debate by the time it will take up, than all his services will be worth tho he lived to the age of an Antideluvian. I have not a doubt that it was all a contrived buisness, by the Antifeds to raise a ferment to spread amongst their constituents. See says the fly upon the wheel, what a dust I raise.[5]

I have had Letters from Berlin and the pleasure of hearing that both Mr. & Mrs. [J. Q.] Adams were in good health. The latest date to 30 October.

When I wrote you last, I had had a sleepless Night. I then have no spirits to spair—I have had a turn of loosing my sleep, but am not otherways sick. I have for the last three Night[s] been very fortunate. Genll. Lincoln is about to return home. By him I send a little packet which I request my sister to accept. Pray desire Mrs. Porter to look to the Beds frequently. I shall have much to request your care and attention to, as soon as you get through the ordination.[6] If the spring is not more of winter than the winter itself, I hope the Building will go up early in

[4] On October 8, 1799, Bonaparte returned unannounced from Egypt to France, landing at Fréjus. Effecting an alliance with two of the Directors, Emanuel Joseph Siéyès (1748–1836) and Pierre Roger Ducos (1747–1816), and enlisting the aid of his only able brother, Lucien (1775–1840), who was President of the Council of Five Hundred, Bonaparte overthrew the Directory on November 9 (18 Brumaire), and broke up the Council of Five Hundred on the following day. The Corsican became First Consul for a term of ten years, assisted by two other Consuls, Jean Jacques Régis Cambacérès (1753–1824) and Charles François Lebrun (1739–1824), both of whom were appointed by him and had only consultative powers. A "popular" vote of December 24, 1799, "ratified" the establishment of this disastrous dictatorship.

[5] Hardly had John Randolph of Roanoke (1773–1833) got himself elected to the House of Representatives when, in advocating the reduction of the Army, he referred to the regular soldiers as "mercenaries" and "ragamuffins." After a couple of officers had tried to insult him, he wrote President Adams, demanding that notice be taken of this attack on the independence of the legislature. His letters were transmitted to the House (Adams, *Works*, vol. 9, pp. 46 and 165), and they led to a heated debate. The story of the fly upon the wheel comes from Aesop. See Francis Bacon, *Essays*: "Of Vain Glory"; and La Fontaine, *Fables*, Book 7, Fable 9: "Le Coche et la Mouche."

[6] See footnote 3 to the letter of December 4, 1799. The "ordination" refers to the Reverend Peter Whitney, who became the assistant to Anthony Wibird, minister in Quincy, and was ordained on Wednesday, February 5, 1800. Whitney's father, pastor at Northboro, delivered the ordination sermon. *Massachusetts Mercury*, February 11, 1800.

March. The doors which must be cut through the Room & chamber will require the Removal of all the furniture, and the painting of Both, which they now want. The glaseing of the front I would have done one of the first things—and the alteration in the kitchin which I contemplated I should like to have done, but the floor must be coverd, or painted again afterwards. When the new building goes up the kitchin will be so darkned that I must let the closset into it & take off a partition where the dressers now are. I think it would be best to run the partition along so as to take the Chamber door, the cellar & parlour door into the entry. This will make the kitchin much warmer & screne the [porch *cancelled*] kitchin from the view of the parlour. But more of this soon.

Mrs. [William Stephens] Smith is very unwell with a voilent cold, Soar Throat, & some fever. She has kept her Chamber ever since Saturday. I hope she is getting better—Caroline [Amelia] is well. The rest of us in pretty good Health—Adieu my dear Sister. I will write to Mrs. [Moses] Black soon.

Yours
A. A[DAMS]

Philadelphia, Jan'ry 30, 1800

MY DEAR SISTER:

I have only time this morning to write you a line, to inclose a Letter from Mrs. Brisler to her sister. It is company day. New Hampshire, Conneticut & Massachusetts delegation[s] dine with us to day: I am sure we have never had half so many Congress Ladies since I first came here. They do not expect any accommodations at the new city for them, and they seem determined to take their turn now. We have had large companies twice every week besides the drawing Rooms; and I have not got near through. Next week the Court & Bar are to dine with us. I have no time for work, and not much for writing. But I have much better health than last winter, or I could not get along. Congress have been for five or six days employd in discussing Randolphs folly. It is not yet finishd.[1]

The weather is now very cold. I hope it will be more moderate for ordination. Pray let me know how Pheby is this winter, and whether she is well supplied.

Love, Regard[s] & respects to all Friends from your

Affectionate Sister
A. A[DAMS]

[1] John Randolph's letter to John Adams. See footnote 5 to the letter of January 28, 1800.

Philadelphia, Feb'ry 12th, 1800

My dear Sister:

I did not write to you the last week. I supposed you must be much occupied by the ordination, which I hope is happily over and that I may congratulate you as well as myself upon again having a setled Pastor, in whose society I promise myself much pleasure, please God to continue my Life. I cannot entertain you with any thing new. I have the pleasure of Mrs. Cushings company frequently. She will call and see you upon her return and tell you how we are. I have sent by her a little Jockey for my Little Thomas B[oylston] A[dams] Norton, which I hope will fit him, and of which I request his mammas acceptance.[1] Since I wrote you I have received a Letter from Sister [Stephen] Peabody, who I was rejoiced to learn, was well and in pretty good spirits. I have also had a Letter from your son, who writes like the Man of sense he always was. I ventured to mention him myself to Judge Patterson, and Judge Cushing has said every thing proper upon the occasion. Judge Chase, Mr. T[homas] B[oylston] A[dams] went himself to, and ask'd him if he had been informd that Mr. Cranch was a candidate for the office of Clerk to the Supreme Court.[2] Yes Sir, I do. Do you know his Character Sir? Yes Sir, I do. Then Sir, I have nothing further to add. Judge Cushing mentiond to Judge Chase that Mr. Cranch was a Nephew of mine, to which he replied, that Mrs. Adams wish should be his Law. This tho very polite in the Judge, I am far from wishing should influence him or any of the other Gentlemen. If I did not think Mr. Cranch a person well qualified for the office, I would not recomend him if he was

[1] Thomas Boylston Adams Norton was the son of Elizabeth Cranch and the Reverend Jacob Norton, and the grandson of Mrs. Richard Cranch. A "jockey" coat was an overcoat, especially one of broadcloth, with wide sleeves.

[2] William Paterson (1745–1806), William Cushing (1732–1810), and Samuel Chase (1741–1811), associate justices of the Supreme Court of the United States. See footnote 2 to the letter of November 21, 1800. The first clerk of the Supreme Court was John Tucker (1753–1825), Harvard, 1774, who served for one year. Samuel Bayard (1767–1840), of Philadelphia, Princeton, 1784, was the second clerk. Bayard resigned his office in 1800 rather than go to Washington, D.C. Elias Boudinot Caldwell, of New Jersey, Princeton, 1796, became the third clerk of the Supreme Court, and died at Washington in May, 1825. This Caldwell was the son of the Reverend James Caldwell (1734–1781), pastor of the First Presbyterian Church in Elizabeth, New Jersey, and a militant clergyman during the Revolution. Although a chaplain, Caldwell carried arms, and rewards were offered by the British for his capture. This "soldier parson" was shot and killed by an American sentry, who was subsequently tried and hanged for murder. Charles Warren, *The Supreme Court in United States History*, Boston, 1935, vol. I, p. 158n.; John W. Barber and Henry Howe, *Historical Collections of the State of New Jersey*, New York, 1844, p. 169; and *Proc. Mass. Hist. Soc.*, vol. 50 (1917), p. 118.

my own son. To Judge Washington no application from [an]y one of the Family has been made.³ He holds his appointment as Judge from the President, and I had some scruples upon that account whether in point of delicacy I ought to say any thing to him. Judge Cushing advised that Mr. Cranch should himself write to the Judges, and I wrote to him requesting him to do so, and yesterday just before the Court rose having finished their Buisness, Mr. Cranch's Letters arrived and Mr. T. B. A. deliverd them. There is an other candidate who has made considerable interest belonging to New Jersey, the state in which Judge Paterson lives; so that I presume Judge Paterson will be silent, if Mr. Cranch should be nominated. The Gentlemans name is Colwill [Caldwell], whose father fell in Battle in the American Revolution. He is said to be a Gentleman of Merrit. A Gentleman applied yesterday morning to Judge Cushing in his behalf. The Judge replied that he could not give any encouragement, because he was interested for an other Gentleman. To this the Gentleman who applied, said that he had heard that there was an application from a Carpenter in the city of Washington. The Judge replied that Solomon who built the Temple might be as well calld a carpenter. The Gentleman who would have his vote had received a liberal Education, was regularly Bred to the Law, and had been several years a practitioner, early setled in Washington, had a fair and honorable Character, and tho he wishd well to the other Gentleman, he could not give him his interest. Thus the matter now stands. The result I presume my next Letter will inform you of.⁴

I want to hear from you. It is a long time now since I had that pleasure. Remember me kindly to all Friends.

Your ever affectionate Sister
A. A[DAMS]

³ Bushrod Washington (1762–1829), nephew of George Washington, was confirmed as associate justice of the Supreme Court on December 20, 1798.

⁴ Elias Boudinot Caldwell, of New Jersey, was the successful applicant for this position, and became third clerk of the Supreme Court in 1800. The slur in calling William Cranch a "carpenter" arose from the fact that he was confused with his cousin, Joseph Cranch, who, through the influence of Secretary of War Henry Knox, was appointed, in 1790, a supervisor of the construction which the federal government was carrying on at West Point, New York. See the letter of April 21, 1790.

Philadelphia, Febry 27th, [1800]

My dear Sister:

I have not written to you since I received your Letter giving me an account of the ordination, the fatigues of which I should have been glad to have shared with you, and I could not but blame myself, that I did not write to request Mrs. Porter to have opend our House, and Stables, and to have accomodated as many persons as they could. It is now happily over and I congratulate the Town in having made so wise, and as I think, judicious a choice. The President frequently expresses his satisfaction that we are once more a setled people not as for a long time past, sheep without a sheapard. I hope we shall live in union and harmony. The next thing will be the marriage of Mr. Whitney, I presume. If it were proper to wish a Gentlemans happiness deferd, I should like to be at Quincy when the Lady is introduced as our Madam. For the last fortnight we have had delightfull weather through the whole of it. Clear sun shine, cold enough to be pleasent without being urksome, the snow all melted, the Rivers open and the weeping willow, which is a great ornament to this City, putting on its first appearance of veg[et]ation, a yellow aspect, which changes to a beautifull Green in a few week's and is the first Harbinger of that Season, in which all nature is renovated. This appearance as I ride out brings to my view the few weeks longer which I have to remain here, and then I shall bid, very probably a final adieu to this City. There is something always melancholy, in the Idea of leaving a place for the last time. It is like burying a Friend. I could have wished that the period of the first Election might have closed in this city; It is a very unpleasent thing to break up all the establishments, and remove to a place so little at present, and probably for years to come, so ill calculated for the residence of such a Body as Congress. The houses which are built are so distant, the streets so miry, and the markets so ill supplied.

In my last I wrote you that Mr. [Samuel] Bayard, the present Clerk of the Court, intended resigning this session, but there is a revision of the judiciary system contemplated. It will soon be reported to the House. If it should pass, many alterations will take place. This I believe was the reason of Mr. Bayards determining not to resign at present.[1] You will see Judge Cushing soon, if not before this reaches you, and he will inform you more than I can. The Judge & Mrs. Cushing left here near a fortnight ago, and have had fine weather ever since. I trust they have improved it.

[1] See footnote 2 to the letter of February 12, 1800.

On Saturday the 22d [of February] I went to hear Major [William] Jackson deliver his oration.² It was a very handsome one, and much better deliverd than I had any Idea he could perform—It is not yet printed, but when it is, I think it will not suffer by any comparison with any I have yet Seen. Two months have chiefly been appropriated to funeral honours to the memory of Gen'll. Washington. I know not that in any modern Times, either Kings or Princess have received equal honors. History does not record any so deserving or so meritorious [of *cancelled*]—

Mrs. [William Stephens] Smith I expect will leave me in a week or ten days. I expect a visit from Mrs. [Joshua] Johnson & her son, the middle of next month. Mrs. Black I hope has received a Letter I wrote to her inclosing the certificate of Ann Halls baptism.³ I fear she thought me unmindfull of it, but I was not. It was oweing to the sickness of Dr. Green that I could not sooner obtain it.⁴ My Letter must have reachd her about the same time that a renewal of her request did me.

How are all our Neighbours and Friends? I have inquired once or twice concerning Pheby. I hope she is comfortable in her marriage and well provided for. We all send Love, respect &c to all our Friends. I want to know how your cold is, and whether Mr. Cranch's is better. I have great cause for thankfullness. I know not when I have past a winter with so little sickness, or a Febry without being confined upon the Birthday of Gen'll. Washington. Three years ago, I was well enough upon that day to celebrate it in Boston, but it has generally been a month of sickness to me. Except the loss of sleep which I have several times experienced, I have had more Health than for many years. I hope it may be continued to me, for without Health Life has few enjoyments.

Adieu my dear Sister. I would desire you to remember me to Miss Gannet, with whose increasing years I hope and trust wisdom, Prudence, and every female virtue will grow and increase. Where much is given, much is required. This should impress her mind and influence

---

[2] William Jackson (1759–1828), soldier and secretary, was born in England and brought up in South Carolina. From 1788 to 1791 he served as aide-de-camp to George Washington. He formed a business partnership with William Bingham, and married (1795) Elizabeth Willing, of Philadelphia, daughter of Thomas Willing, the president of the Bank of North America. Jackson's "Eulogium on the Character of General Washington" will be found in *Eulogies and Orations on the Life and Death of General Washington*, pp. 243–60.

[3] See footnote 2 to the letter of January 5, 1798.

[4] Ashbel Green (1762–1848), eighth president of Princeton, was assistant and then minister of the Second Presbyterian Church in Philadelphia from 1787 to 1812. From 1792 to 1800 he was chaplain to the Congress.

her conduct. She will I trust receive this as the admonition of a Friend. Let her think what she owes to one of the kindest [&] tenderest of Parents, and she can never wander from the path of Rectitude.[5] Once more I bid you adieu assureing you of the

         Love and affection of
           A. ADAMS

         Philadelphia, March 5, 1800

MY DEAR SISTER:

I received your Letter of Febry 23 and was glad to learn that you were well, for from not hearing from you from the time of ordination I was fearfull that the fatigue had made you sick. We have now arrived to the 5th of March with a small quantity of snow upon the ground and the weather mild. With you I suppose there is much more. Congress might easily accomplish the buisness necessary for the benifit of the Nation, but I must say their is a most shamefull waste of time. The Antifeds have brought before the House the delivering up to Justice, Thomas Nash, which in strict conformity with the Treaty with G[reat] Britain was done.[1] The Anti party have by every subterfuge, mean art & declamation wasted the time of the House upon that subject more than a week, and I dare answer will keep the buisness more than a week more before them. The Jacobins are a very wicked unprincipeld set of Beings. This whole affair is brought up not from a Love of Justice, or apprehension that a fellow creature was unjustly punished, but merely to hold out to their Party that the President had Encroached upon the Judiciary, and assumed an influence which was unconstitutional. The

[5] Miss Gannett was the daughter of Caleb Gannett. See footnote 5 to the letter of March 5, 1800.

[1] In February, 1800, the House of Representatives, under the goading of John Randolph of Roanoke, wasted a lot of time and breath over the case of a seaman, Jonathan Robbins, alias Thomas Nash, who was in jail at Charleston, South Carolina. Robbins was accused of murder and piracy on H.M.S. *Hermione*, and Admiral Sir Hyde Parker had sent a cutter to Charleston to carry him back to the West Indies for trial. Robbins first "confessed himself to be an Irishman," and then declared that he was a citizen of Danbury, Connecticut. The selectmen of Danbury denied this, under oath. Thomas Bee, judge of the district court of the United States for South Carolina, refused to surrender Robbins to the British on his own authority. When the case was referred to Pickering and Adams, Robbins was given up, according to the terms of Jay's Treaty: See the Boston *Independent Chronicle and Universal Advertiser*, February 17–27, 1800. John Marshall was the chief, and successful, defender of the action of Adams in the House of Representatives. See the letter of March 15–18, 1800. The French spy who befriended Nash, or Robbins, and who advised him to swear that he was an American citizen, was hanged at Kingston, Jamaica: *J. Russell's Gazette*, February 27, 1800.

whole correspondence is before the public and every candid person must see, that the delivering the Rascal up, was in conformity to the Treaty which is the Law of the Land, and the President is sworn to see the Laws executed. But Electioneering purposes are answerd by the gloss put upon the transaction by the Jacos, which is carefully retaild in all the democratic papers. The replies and confutation of their arguments are carefully conceald from the party whom these people wish to lead blind fold. I have not a doubt but their will be a majority in the House who will approve the conduct of the Executive. One or two more Elections will be quite sufficient I believe to convince this people that no engine can be more fatally employd than frequent popular Elections, to corrupt and destroy the morals of the people—3 years are now past, and we have enjoyd as much peace, quiet, Security and happiness as any people can boast of in the same period of time, much more than for the three years which preceeded. Our National Character has risen in the public estimation, and the public confidence has in no ways been diminished. Faction has not been so turbulent nor malice so active. The Electioneering campaign I presume will bring all their forces into action.

I send you an oration of Major [William] Jacksons, with which I think you will be pleased[2]—And now as you observe, I hope the good mans spirit may rest in quiet, for America has testified her gratitude & her Grief in the fullest manner, and I firmly believe with more sincerity than any people ever before felt for any Man—But when the collection of Sermons, Eulogiums, Poems &c are collected, more than two thirds of them will be found to have originated in N[ew] England. From thence, did he derive his chief aid in War, and his chief and principle support, in the administration of the Government. At a late festival in Kentucky, amongst a number of Jacobin toasts is one to the memory of Genll. Washington to the year 1779 [1787], and no longer, by which they mean to cast a slur upon the whole of his administration of the Government. But Hence, wretches, to your native dens—the bogs of Ireland, the dens of Scotland, and the outcasts of Britain.[3]

[2] See footnote 2 to the letter of February 27, 1800.

[3] The festival to which Mrs. Adams refers was a barbecue held by the Jeffersonians at Thomas Stephenson's Spring on the North Elkhorn, in Fayette County, Kentucky, "in order to celebrate the recent successes of our allies the French." Sixteen toasts were "drank," of which the fourth, the ninth, and the fourteenth probably annoyed John Adams and his wife:

"Thomas Jefferson; the pride of republicans, and terror of aristocrats; may he be soon raised to the seat, to which his unfortunate country has been too long in elevating

Mrs. [William Stephens] Smith and my little Caroline [Amelia Smith] left me yesterday to go to Scotch Plain's. I was very loth they should go, but could detain them no longer. I hope Dr. [Cotton] Tufts will send us his performance. I dare say it was a very judicious one.[4] I have written to the Dr. I hope the Building will go on with all speed. Mr. Porter, the Dr. writes, inclines to leave us this spring. I had rather they should remain untill the fall of the year, but if he determines to go, can you think of a man and woman to take their place untill the fall? I hope to return by the time their year expires, or that at all events they will stay untill I do.

Louissa is very well and desires me to present her duty to you. Remember me affectionately to all my Friends. I see by the late papers that Mr. Gannet is married again.[5] I hope Miss Gannet will strive to obtain and preserve the regard of her [step-] Mother, whose Character stands high and who will do justice to the charge she has taken upon her, from what I have heard of her.

Adieu my dear Sister. My best regards to Brother Cranch, in which I am always joind by the President.

Ever your affectionate Sister
A. ADAMS

Philadelphia, March 15, 1800

MY DEAR SISTER:

I find the best time for writing, is to rise about an hour earlier than the rest of the family; go into the Presidents Room, and apply myself to my pen. Now the weather grows warmer I can do it. His Room in

---

him."

"The memory of Gen. Washington, may his illustrious actions and services be faithfully recorded down to the year 1787, but no farther."

"The President of the U. States; may he soon retire to Quincy, by general consent, accompanied by his 'Defence of the American Constitutions.'"

In commenting on this "barbacue," John Ward Fenno wrote: "I would not be thought to magnify dangers, or exaggerate alarms. If the whole of this drunken Republic of Kentucky had avowed the above infamous sentiments on this occasion (as indeed they have very often done) instead of a crew whom perhaps a single work house or a single Jail will contain, I should still view them as contemptible, in respect of numbers or specific force." *Gazette of the United States*, March 3, 1800, quoting the *Kentucky Gazette*, "printed at Lexington, by one Bradford, whether a member of our illustrious family, or not, we cannot determine."

[4] Cotton Tufts, *Oration at Weymouth, February 22, 1800, on the Death of George Washington*, Boston, 1800. See also, Franklin B. Hough, *Washingtoniana: or Memorials of the Death of George Washington . . . with a List of Tracts and Volumes Printed upon the Occasion*, Roxbury, Massachusetts, 1865.

[5] Caleb Gannett, Esq., was married to Ruth Stiles, "daughter of the late President Stiles," January 19, 1800. *Massachusetts Mercury*, January 24, 1800.

which I now write has three larg[e] windows to the South. The sun visits it with his earliest beams at the East window, and Cheers it the whole day in winter. All my keeping Rooms are North, but my forenoons are generally spent in my own Chamber tho a dark one, and I often think of my sun shine Cottage at Quincy.

March 18th, [1800]

I was calld from writing on the 15 by a summons below stairs, and have not been able to reassume my pen untill this morning. Yesterday the 17th I received your kind Letter of March 9th. I hope Mr. Cranch will be able to obtain the appointment he has so much at Heart, but I know not what will be the result of the judiciary Bill which is not yet reported to the House. Congress seem loth to enter upon buisness of the most concequence. Some are for postponing this Bill untill the next Sessions, which has already Cost much time, and labour of the Committe. They will find themselves much less agreably situated the next session I presume, besides its being a short one. But they have spent much time, and I fear always will upon very trifling buisness. Jacky Randolph & Thomas Nash, or [Jonathan] Robbins, have occupied a whole Month.[1]— But whilst there is so great a disposition in the House to let the Jacobins through [throw] obsticales in the way of every measure usefull and benificial to the public, and prate whole days, least it should be said that they were affraid to contend with them, much time must & will be waisted.

I do not regreet that my Nephew is dissapointed, if so he is. I am sure the family connextion could never have proved happy, however amiable Ann was, or is. She will be better the wife of any other Man. I never thought it a judicious connextion. Oil & water might as well mix, as the Fathers harmonize. Then Boylstone always despiced the ignorance, selfishness & want of Breeding in Beals, how was it possible for him to respect or treat him, as a son ought to treat a Father? Many other things I could add why it was unequal. Ann had been Educated in a different stile from what she might expect to live. I shall wish her joy more cordially the wife of Mr. Prince if they like, or any other man they chuse. I never want any nearer relationship than that of Neighbour or [even though] I know there was a time I might have had it.[2]

I communicated to the President Mr. [Peter] Whitneys desire, and the President says Mr. Whitney shall have the House and that it shall

[1] See footnote 1 to the letter of March 5, 1800.

[2] Mrs. Adams refers to the projected marriage between Boylston Adams (born 1771), son of her husband's brother, Peter Boylston Adams, and Ann Beal (born 1774), daughter of Abijah and Ann (Canterbury) Beal, of Weymouth.

be put into decent repair. I have directions to write to Dr. Tufts upon the subject. The House is to be painted, the Garden fence new sit, and every proper repair made to render it decent & comfortable—But I am at a loss to know what to do with Mr. [J. Q.] Adams's Books. The furniture belonging to me, I can take away as soon as I can get Room to place it at home, but as the rest part of the House wants the most done to it, that may be accomplishd first. Mr. Brisler would have his furniture which remains there removed to Mr. Mears's. Mrs. Mears knows what it is. I heard from Mrs. [William Stephens] Smith yesterday. She says, as her happiness did not consist in the size of the House in which she lived, it is not essentially diminishd by Removing, from that where she has past the winter to a Log Hut, that her disposition is accommodating, that she has always found that she can support herself against the *Present*, but that in anticipating the future she has much more anxiety. She says there are 13 Hundred Men all in Huts, but so perfectly quiet both by Night and day that no Noise but that of the drum & fife is heard amongst them.

I intend to propose to her passing the summer at Quincy with me. I have not mentiond it to her. I am sorry for the [distresses *cancelled*] misfortunes of my Neighbours, particularly so for Dr. Phips, whose situation must be very distressing, with a large young family.[3] Present me kindly to Mr. & Mrs. Greenleaf when you see them. Their Brother James [Greenleaf] is here; and has been to see us a number of time. I saw him yesterday walking with Miss Allyne, as I was going to return some visits. She is a beautifull figure, and with the assistance of a little Rouge, a beautifull face, which however I think she does not need. He appears as easy, and looks as happy, as tho neither care or sorrow ever approachd his Heart.[4]

[3] Thomas Phipps, son of Samuel and Eleanor (Gardner) Phipps, was born at Cambridge on March 15, 1737/8, and died at Quincy on April 4, 1817. He was graduated at Harvard College in 1757, became a physician at Quincy, and married (1761) Mary Brackett, daughter of James and Abigail (Belcher) Brackett. Phipps was a prominent citizen, and seems to have been connected first with the First Church, and later with the Episcopal Church in Braintree. His eighth child, a son named Samuel, was born on May 13, 1801. Apparently Dr. Phipps was one of the unfortunate persons from New England who lost money through the speculations of James Greenleaf. Personal information supplied by the Reverend Frederick L. Weis, of Lancaster, Massachusetts, author of *The Ancestors and Descendants of John Phipps, of Sherborn*, 1924.

[4] After being discharged from bankruptcy, and having divorced his Dutch wife, Antonia Cornelia Albertine Schotten, James Greenleaf married, April 26, 1800, Ann Penn Allen, daughter and heiress of James Allen, the founder of Allentown, Pennsylvania, who was the son of William Allen, Chief Justice of the Province of Pennsylvania. Greenleaf, *Genealogy of the Greenleaf Family*, Boston, 1896, pp. 217–8. For reproductions of portraits of the two wives of James Greenleaf, see Clark, *Greenleaf and Law in the Federal City*, pp. 87 and 201.

My Dear Sister   Philadelphia April 17th 1800

Inclosed is a Letter for the Doctor as the contents are valuable you will be so kind as to deliver it yourself and give me notice that you have received it and done so by the first post I shall want to hear very often from you and to know how our affairs progress. I am most ansceous about the painting and having the rooms of the old House in order. Mrs porter must have help she will have such a family that she cannot do without. I would have mrs Burrel have some potts to lay me down some more butter, she has some which I desired her to put up for me last fall, but we are an Army of ourselves and shall want a good deal I am affraid I may not be in season to provide that article

please to tell mrs porter that I have got a new Coachman, and that James will not be with us this Summer — I thinke I have a decent civil sober man, and a native American — a Cook I shall want, and she must be a woman. I will have no more men cooks, Richard has just got through the small Pox, which he has had so favorable as to keep him but three days from his buismess — —

we are all well. Congress thinks of rising by the middle of May, our furniture must then all be packed and sent to the Federal city — but I mean to get out of the way of that —   affectionatly your Sister

                            Abigail Adams —

LETTER OF ABIGAIL ADAMS, 1800

Tell Miss Hazel that she is in so good Hands that I cannot think she wants any advise of mine, as I believe her to be modest, diffident & tracktable. It was oweing to a different opinion that I offerd to an other an admonition. The Lay Preacher of Pensilvana who has publishd a peice in Fennos Gazzet of the last week thinks there are some Ladies in this city, who stand in need of admonition, & I fully agree with him. His text was, "In like Manner also, that women adorn themselves in modest apparel." He observes that where the semblance of modesty is wanting, there is strong ground to presume the absence of the virtue itself. What shall we say then? Is there virtue in the woman who artfully seeks to display the rich luxuriance of natur's Charms, at the hazard and expence of sporting with all claim to Chaste appearence?[5]

The stile of dress which the preacher attacks is really an outrage upon all decency. I will describe it as it has appeard even at the drawing Room—A sattin peticoat of certainly not more than three breadths gored at the top, nothing beneath but a chemise. Over this thin coat, a Muslin sometimes, sometimes a crape made so strait before as perfectly to show the whole form. The arm naked almost to the shoulder and without stays or Bodice. A tight girdle round the waist, and the "rich Luxurience of naturs Charms" without a hankerchief fully displayd.

[5] The essay to which Mrs. Adams refers appeared in Fenno's *Gazette* for Saturday, March 15, 1800, and occupied a column and a half. In it "The Lay Preacher of Pennsylvania" denounces the notorious style of female dress under the Directory, as well as the habit of using rouge. The author took as his text part of verses 9 and 10 of the second chapter of the *First Epistle of St. Paul to Timothy:*
"In like manner also, that women adorn themselves in modest apparel, with shamefacedness and sobriety; not with broided hair, or gold, or pearls, or costly array;
But (which becometh women professing godliness) with good works."
Two samples will suffice to give the drift of this denunciation:
"It is a subject of no small astonishment, that modes and fashions should be so readily and indiscriminately adopted, without regard to their origin or use. A despicable courtezan, who commands the gallantries of a vitiated capital, is often known to lead one half the female world by her fantastic whimsies. Generated by the artifice or fancy of a wanton, to subserve the views of sensual conquest, a *new fashion* speedily obtains extensive currency, is transported to a distant land, and by a blind adoption, ensured by novelty, degrades the form and comliness [*sic*] of virtue. It cannot but create surprise, that 'we are such stuff,' as to pride ourselves in habiliments, whose only excellence is recency of invention, and whose origin is from no higher source than a harlot's brain.
"... The mischiefs of *face painting* have been amply experienced, and its evil consequences have been repeatedly detailed, but the custom extends with an alarming progress. Still do the dupes of fashion continue this unseemly practice, by which the rosy cheek of health is wasted to the paleness of disease; and nature's fairest red is defiled or counterfeited, by a daubed covering of *rouge*.... And the world at once sets down a *painted woman* either as a hag, who thus seeks to conceal her deformity, or as a fool, sporting with real charms and sacrificing a rich possession."

The face, a la mode de Paris, Red as a Brick hearth. When this Lady has been led up to make her curtzey, which she does most gracefully, it is true, every Eye in the Room has been fixd upon her her [sic], and you might litterally see through her. But in this stile of dress, she has danced nor regarded the splitting out of her scanty coat, upon the occasion. I askd a young Gentleman, if Miss. — was at the dance last Evening. The replie was: yes, most wickedly. To do justice to the other Ladies, I cannot accuse them of such departures from female decorum, but they most of them wear their Cloaths too scant upon the body and too full upon the Bosom for my fancy. Not content with the *show which* nature bestows, they borrow from art, and litterally look like Nursing Mothers. To disguise the strait appearance of the Gowns before, those Aprons, which you say look like fig leaves, were adopted. The Mother of the Lady described & sister, being fine women and in the first Rank, are leaders of the fashion, but they show more of the [bosom] than the decent Matron, or the modest woman.[6]

I am glad to learn that Sister [Elizabeth] Peabody has recoverd her spirits. She must not be too hard upon Betsy nor forget that she herself was once young, and possesst a heart as liable to impressions, and as susceptable of the tender passions as any body I can recollect. Betsy has a heridatary spice of the Romantic in her constitution. Guide her right. Her heart is good. A cold youth, would be a frozen Age. If she has more pangs in concequence of her disposition she has more pleasures.[7] Adieu my dear Sister.

I must write to Dr. Tufts before the post goes out.
Affectionatly your Sister
A. A[DAMS]

[Philadelphia], March 22, 1800

MY DEAR SISTER:

I received your Letter yesterday. I know from what I saw and heard whilst I was at home that there was pains taken to make Mr. & Mrs. Porter uneasy, and that they were too apt to listen to stories which were

---

[6] Anne Willing, that is, Mrs. William Bingham, of "The Mansion House," Philadelphia, and her two daughters, Anne, who married Alexander Baring, of the celebrated family of London bankers, and Maria Matilda, divorced wife of the Comte de Tilly.

[7] Elizabeth Smith, one of the daughters of William Smith, the brother of Abigail Adams, Mrs. Cranch, and Mrs. Peabody (formerly Mrs. Shaw). Mrs. Peabody eked out the slender emoluments of her ministerial husband by taking college students and young relatives as paying guests.

in themselves Idle, and raised from Envy. Many would be glad to get into their hands such a charge as is left with Mr. & Mrs. Porter, who would not be so honest in their care and attention of our Property. I feel a safety in leaving my things to their care, because as I know it is their duty faithfully to fulfill the trust. I consider them conscientious people, and having a principle of honesty, that they will not betray the confidence reposed in them. I would have you say to them that I had much rather they should continue upon the place than make the exchange for any other persons, and the President would not have them go this season. If I remain through the winter at Quincy, I may not think it necessary to continue a Family through the winter, but in that case, I have mentiond my terms for Mr. Porter, which I think generous ones. As to any persons who may offer, I do not know any whom I should like. I cannot think of taking any person with Children, or who may be like to have any. I hope every exertion will be made by Mr. Bates to get forward the building, that it may be compleated by the last of May at furtherst.

I intended giving Mrs. Porter a Muff this winter. If she has not one, will you get one for her of about four dollors value and give it her in my Name. If Mr. Cary should come with flax be so good as to get me 30 weight. I inclose ten dollors for these purposes.

We have had two days severe rain. I hope it has not been snow with you. I must depend upon you to visit our House and with Mrs. Porter see the things removed, when the Carpenters begin to work; Mrs. Porter will want help. I understand Zube is with Mrs. Tufts. I presume it is only conditionally, for I expressly engaged her to return to me in the spring.

Do you know whether Mrs. Brigs, who lived with Mrs. Black, would go out again & what she is for a Cook? I must get a woman somewhere who will undertake that buisness. Do be upon the inquiry for me. I shall not encumber myself with Frank & family, nor shall I have more than three or four men servants this season.

Adieu my dear Sister. Send the inclosed Letter to [the *cancelled*] Dr. Tufts as soon as you can. With Love to you all, I am, my dear Sister,

Your affectionate

A. ADAMS

Philadelphia, April 7th, 1800

My dear Sister:

Yesterday Mr. Johnson and his Mamma [Mrs. Joshua Johnson] arrived here, in good Health. By her I heard from Mr. & Mrs. Cranch. She, poor thing, has had a mishap. I rather think it good than ill luck however, for it is sad slavery to have children as fast as she has. She has recoverd tho she is thin & weak. Your son is rising, Rising in his own estimation, which was the place where he most wanted it. He plead a cause, spoke three hours against Mr. Mason & an other Gentleman, and obtain his cause.[1] He gaind much applause & Reputation, I am informd. Having broken the Ice, I hope he will gain courage and be yet successfull and prosperous. He has been born down by his circumstances, & deprest beyond measure. He is now rising above them, I hope.

The weather is remarkable fine. The verdure of the feilds and the bursting of the Buds, with the beautifull foilage [sic] of the weeping willow, which you have often heard me admire and which is the first tree to vegitate in the spring, all remind me of Quincy, my building, my Garden, &c. I would have gardning commence upon a large scale that we may be provided with vegatables sufficient for a large family. I know we want a skilfull gardner. Peas I would have put in & of the sort which Stutson [Stetson] procured of Major Millar. I am informd here of what is said to be a fact, that the Peas which are first planted bear much the longest and best, taking deeper Root into the Ground. I must request you to see Mr. Porter and desire him to have due attention by Stutson to all the vines &c which George planted last year.

I am dissapointed in not getting a Letter from you this morning. Monday usually brought me one. You will have received several from me all requesting your attention to something or other for me. I shall want you to see Bates & hurry him as much as possible. The painting must be done in the Room & chamber this Month. The closset in the keeping parlour wants it too, the floor I mean.

Major Tousard, the Gentleman you have seen with one Arm, requested me the other day to inquire if there was any Family in Quincy where Mrs. Tousard could be Boarded. He is going to superintend the fortifications at fort Independance, and wants to have Mrs. Tousard near him, where he can occasionally be with her. I thought of Capt. James Brackets. She is a pretty little woman, and received here into

---

[1] Probably Jonathan Mason, Jr., of Boston, who was appointed Senator from Massachusetts in the autumn of 1800. Mr. Mason went to Washington, D.C., as the legal representative of certain creditors of James Greenleaf in his disastrous speculations in real estate.

the first circles. She is an American, has no Family. He is much of a Gentleman. Will you inquire & write me by the first opportunity.[2]

I must close, not having more time this morning than to assure you of
My sincere affection
A. ADAMS

Philadelphia, April 15, 1800

MY DEAR SISTER:

I received a few lines from you yesterday in replie to Mr. Bates queries. I would have the Room above finishd off the same size with the lower Room, the North clossets to remain in the Room and chamber, the stairs to be one flight, a portico with a flat Top which I would have leaded, and a smilar [sic] one built over the front door of the House, the two trees cut down. But I do not wish to have the window to open to the floor, because the window in the other entry does not, and cannot easily be made to, and I wish to preserve as much uniformity in appearence as possible. The fence in front will be made to conform with the other, the side fence I would not have at present removed: I wish to have the length & Breadth of the Hearths as soon as may be, intending to get Marble cut for them as well as for the sides and front of the the chimney without. I would have a chimny made in the upper Chamber or Garret, windows to the North as well as South & 2 upon the side of the chimny if they can be admitted, and the chamber made as convenient & handsome as it will admit.

I hope workman [sic] will be employd so as to get along as fast as possible. I shall have many a schooling for the sound of the hammer &c and for not having the buisness finished sooner than I fear it will be accomplishd—the painting in the old part I hope will be done directly.

Mrs. Porter must have help. If Zuby chuses to stay & Mrs. [Cotton] Tufts to keep her, I certainly will not say a word. Mrs. Porter must look out & get other help—Mrs. [Joshua] Johnson desires to be rememberd. I must send this directly to the post or miss it.

Yours
A. ADAMS

I am very well & sleep soundly—when I am not vexed.

[2] Anne Louis de Tousard (1749–1817), soldier, was born in Paris and served in America as an aide to Lafayette. In Santo Domingo, in 1788, Tousard married Maria Francisca Regina (Joubert) St. Martin, widow of a rich planter. In 1793 Tousard joined his wife and children in the United States, where his wife died in July, 1794. In 1795 he married Anna Maria Geddes. Reinstated in the United States Army, he became a colonel, and superintended the building of fortifications at West Point, New York; Newport, Rhode Island; and Fort Independence, Boston.

Philadelphia, April 17th, 1800

MY DEAR SISTER:

Inclosed is a Letter for the Doctor [Cotton Tufts]. As the contents are valuable you will be so kind as to deliver it yourself, and give me notice that you have received it and done so by the first post.

I shall want to hear very often from you and to know how our affairs progress. I am most anxious about the painting and having the Rooms of the old House in order. Mrs. Porter must have help. She will have such a family that she cannot do without. I would have Mrs. Burrel have some pots to lay me down some more butter. She has some which I desired her to put up for me last fall, but we are an Army of ourselves, and shall want a good deal. I am affraid I may not be in season to provide that article.

Please to tell Mrs. Porter that I have got a new Coachman and that James will not be with us this summer. I think I have a decent, civil, sober Man, and a Native American—A Cook I shall want, and she must be a woman. I will have no more men cooks. Richard has just got through the small pox, which he has had so favorable as to keep him but three days from his buisness.

We are all well. Congress think of rising by the middle of May. Our furniture must then all be packd and sent to the Federal city—but I mean to get out of the way of that.

Affectionatly your Sister
ABIGAIL ADAMS

Philadelphia, April 24th, 1800

MY DEAR SISTER:

It is with great pleasure, my dear Sister, that I can say to you, your son has recoveid from a dangerous complaint, which threw us all here into great distress and anxiety upon his account. He returnd from Court sick. It proved to be a Billious Cholic. Mr. [Joshua] Johnson wrote Mrs. Johnson that he had been to see him, but that he was so ill that he could not be seen. The Children too were all sick, and she poor creature just recovering from a late illness so that it was a House of distress. You may be sure what we all sufferd untill the pleasing news of his restoration reachd us. I wrote to her, but have not yet received an answer. Mr. [James] Greenleaf also wrote & waited only to hear to have sit off to her, if Mr. [William] Cranchs illness had required him. When I wrote last to you, I dared not hint the subject to you. To [be] so far distant and know that a dear child is ill, and that we cannot render any aid to them is painfull in the extreem. Mrs. Johnson says he often rides late at Night in order to get back to his family. This he should avoid. I know his last years low spirits was in some measure occasiond by a slow aguish intermitting. He has lately obtaind a cause of considerable concequence in which he spoke near two hours, and did himself much honour. Mr. Mason too his opponent.[1] He will do very well if he will but think himself the most sensible & capable Man with whom he is acquainted. I think I can be reconciled to go to the city [Washington], if I can aid and serve him by any means. He has been crampt, hurt & wounded by his situation. Mrs. Johnson says Col. Forrest has been a very sincere Friend to him.[2]

April 26th, [1800]

Since writing the above I have heard twice from Washington. Mr. [James] Greenleaf, who lodges at the next door, sent me in a Letter to read from his sister. She writes Mr. Cranch had been very ill but was then so much recoverd as to have gone again to Court to finish his buisness there. Yesterday Mr. G[reenlea]f informd me that he had a Letter from Eliot who wrote him that Mr. Cranch was quite recoverd.

Mrs. [Joshua] Johnson is still with me. She will return next week, when I shall seriously sit about getting away. My last drawing Room is notified for the 2d of May. On thursday we had 28 young or rather unmarried Ladies and Gentlemen to dine with us. They were from Families with which our young people have been most intimate, and who had shewn them many attentions & civilities. Just before I rose from table, Thomas [Boylston Adams] came round to me and whisperd me, have you any objection to my having a dance this Evening? None in the world, provided it comes thus accidental. The company soon came up to the drawing Room to Tea, and in an hours time, the tables were removed, the lights light & the Room all in order. At 8 the dancing commenced. At 12, it finishd. More pleasure, ease and enjoyment I have rarely witnessd. The President went down about an hour & then retired. I tarried it out, but was obliged to go to Bed at 8 oclock last night in concequence. Several of the company declared that they should always remember the Evening as one of the pleasentesst of their lives— Amongst the company was Miss B. M. with manners perfectly affable, polite and agreable, without affectation, or any haughtyness of demeanour, but really fassinating. I could not but lament, that the un-

[1] See footnote 1 to the letter of April 7, 1800.
[2] Possibly Uriah Forrest, with whom John Adams was acquainted as early as 1797. See Adams, *Works*, vol. 8, p. 546.

coverd bosom should display, what ought to have been veild, or that the well turnd, and finely proportiond form, should not have been less conspicuous in the dance, from the thin drapery which coverd it.[3] I wishd that more had been left to the imagination, and less to the Eye. She dances elegantly. "Grace was in all her steps."[4] She is not yet 17, and tho she cannot be said to have regular features, she has fine teeth, and Eyes, and the winning graces, far superiour to inanimate symetry: I never could endure a clod, yet it has been my lot—to have met *with them*. In the first instanc[e] Education and example may do allmost any thing. In the last, who can make an impression. But wither runs my pen?

I must stop it to talk about domestic affairs. Has Mrs. Porter got any help? And do you know where I can get a steady body? A cook is of the most concequence. I must not have one who will be put out of humour by company comeing in unexpectedly. She must be willing upon washing & Ironing days to assist in the after part of the day to fold cloaths & to help Iron if necessary, to keep every thing clean and neat in her department. She will be assisted when necessary. If Mrs. Briggs will comply with these terms, and an other, which is indispensable, to have no concern or interference with Mrs. Porters Family, I shall like to have you engage her for me; With respect to the building, will you tell Mr. Bates that I think there ought to be a portico over the back entry door as well as front. It will serve to keep off the Rains & cold in winter—I am quite impatient to get a Letter from you—We have had such fine weather that I should suppose our people may go on rapidly. I left word for Mr. Beal to paint the floor of the chamber over the wash house & the stairs. If it was not done in the fall, I would have it done as soon as the Painters come. And pray, my Sister, tell them to lay out for Garden enough. Peas had best be bought for seed beside those which we have. I inclose you ten dollors to lay out such part as is necessary for

---

[3] "Miss B. M." was Betsy, or Elizabeth Mason, one of the five daughters and seven children of Jonathan Mason, Jr. (1756–1831), United States Senator from Massachusetts (1800–1803), and close friend and business associate of Harrison Gray Otis. Mason made a fortune in Boston real estate, and all his five daughters married well. Elizabeth became the wife of Samuel Dunn Parker on December 12, 1807. Her sisters, Susan, Anna, Miriam, and Mary, became Mrs. J. Collins Warren, Mrs. Patrick Grant, Mrs. David Sears, and Mrs. Samuel Parkman. See *Columbian Centinel*, November 5, 1831; Robert Grant, *Fourscore: An Autobiography*, Boston and New York, 1934; *Boston Marriages: 1752–1809*, Boston, 1903, p. 266; and Abner Forbes, *Our First Men: A Calendar of Wealth, Fashion and Gentility* . . . , Boston, 1846, p. 34.

[4] Grace was in all her steps, Heav'n in her Eye,
In every gesture dignitie and love.
Paradise Lost, Book 8, lines 488–9.

the Garden. Do not let my flowers be neglected. Pray, if you can, get me some stursion seed, double Larks spur and the Marble perue.[5]

Mr. Gore is here just arrived from England.[6] Our Envoys were not arrived at Paris when he le[f]t England. They were hastning on. Great Britain as surly as John Bull, tho he dare not Growl loud, hating our Prosperity most cordially, and swelling to see our Navy rising in power and respectability. We have quite as much to Gaurd against from that quarter, as from the Great nation [France].

Adieu my dear Sister. Let me hear from you as soon as you can.

Affectionatly yours
A. ADAMS

Philadelphia, [May 3d, 1800]

MY DEAR SISTER:

I think you have been exercised in deeds of Charity to that poor, forlorn Man who would once have said, is thy Servant a dog, that he should become a living prey to worms, or what is worse?[1] He is a most striking instance of Indolence, and having no stimulous to action? none of those tender endearing ties of wife, child, sister, or Brother, Indolence Created first an apathy, and apathy Crept on untill all that was estimable and praise worthy in Man, was sunk into torpor, like waters that stagnate when they cease to flow. [The very *cancelled*] It ought to be a warning to every man not to contract habits of sloth, and inaction, to consider that no Man liveth for himself. Mr. [Anthony] Wibird is punished in this Life, not for sins of commission but of omission. Talents have been committed to him, which from the same source of indo-

[5] Marvel of Peru, one of the popular names for *mirabilis jalapa*, commonly called "four o'clocks." See Miller, *Gardeners Dictionary*, Eighth Edition, London, 1768, and E.L.D. Seymour, *The Garden Encyclopedia*, New York, 1936, p. 782.

[6] Christopher Gore (1758–1827). He was graduated from Harvard in 1776, was appointed United States district attorney in 1789, and a commissioner under Jay's Treaty in 1796. Rufus King left him as *chargé d'affaires* in London in 1803. Gore was Governor of Massachusetts (1809–1810) and United States Senator (1814–1817). He was a Fellow of Harvard, and president of the Massachusetts Historical Society (1806–1818). Gore Hall, the Harvard College Library from 1841 to 1912, was named for him. See 3 *Coll. Mass. Hist. Soc.*, vol. 3, pp. 191–204. Oddly enough, no life of Gore is to be found in the great *Dictionary of American Biography*, nor was this oversight corrected in the first Supplement.

[1] Mrs. Adams seems to have made a conflation of two kings—Hazael, of the Old Testament, and Herod, of the New.

"And Hazael said, But what, is thy servant a dog, that he should do this great thing? And Elisha answered, The Lord hath shewed me that thou shalt be king over Syria." 2 *Kings*, VIII, 13.

"And immediately the angel of the Lord smote him [Herod], because he gave not God the glory: and he was eaten of worms, and gave up the ghost." *Acts*, XII, 23.

lence, have not been improved to the best use and advantage. For the Good he has done, may the Lord reward him, and for what he has neglected to do, pardon him. We all have much to be forgiven, and as we hope for mercy, so may we extend it to others.

But to quit moralizing—Last Eveng was my Last Drawing Room. Both Rooms were so crowded as to render the Air very oppressive. It was judged that about 200 Gentlemen & Ladies were present: We got through, some what fatigued you may easily suppose, but I got sleep, which I did not expect, and to day feel bright enough to dine between 20 & thirty persons. On thursday next will be the last dinner of a formal nature. Mrs. [Joshua] Johnson & son leave me on Monday. Mr. Cranch and family were well this week. I heard from him.—Yesterday I sent some Trunks on Board a vessel with my Hearths and Jams. When they arrive and are to be put up, I will thank Mr. [Richard] Cranch to be present with his advice. I would have the chimneys made to conform to them. I am much affraid of having the Chimneys contracted too small, which in a Room so large would look bad. I have mentiond to the Doctor [Cotton Tufts] the method in which I am told the Hearths & fronts must be put up. I will thank you when the Rooms new painted, are quite dry to have the furniture replaced. I expect to leave here the week after next. It will bring it near the last of May before I can get home, so that I hope there will be time enough for the paint to dry.

I will thankfully accept Mr. Blacks offer for Mr. [J. Q.] Adams's Books.

Congress persist in saying they shall rise the week after next. The weather is fine indeed, as growing and Luxurient a season as I ever knew. With Love regards &c

Affectionatly your Sister
A. Adams

Love to Mrs. Norton & thanks for her Letter.

[Philadelphia, May 5th, 1800]

My dear Sister:

After I had closed my Letter yesterday, I received yours of the 28th. The Garden seeds are in a small wooden Box in the garret Chamber over the best Chamber, made for the purpose of securing them from the mice. The Box is lockd and Mrs. Porter has the key, tho she may have forgotten it. It is a long Box unpainted.

I should like much to have a passage to the kitchin from the entry; My intention was to have a closset taken of where the dressers now are, & to have taken in the other closset into the kitchin. I care very little about the North window, which must be darkned by the other building, but as you observe a window may be made opposite. The cellar door might be removed if necessary, and my Liquors were removed, but that is not practicable at Present. If Mr. Cranch, Dr. Tufts or Mr. Bates can contrive such a communication, it would be very desirable.

Major Tousard was with Mrs. Tousard at the drawing Room, and he inquired of Louissa if there was any Prospect of procuring Lodgings. She is a little tight looking *fashionable* Native America, made french by her marriage. She is pretty & much younger than he is. She is a second wife, has not any children.[1]

You need not write to me after the present week. It is my present intention to leave here some time next week. I will give you notice— My Coachman is a stranger to the Roads. Richard I shall take with me— Mrs. [William Stephens] Smith goes on fryday to N[ew] York. I wish it was so, that we could be in company.

I shall have a very buisy week the next; It is the last time that I shall reside in this city, and as present appearences indicate, the last time I shall visit it; The people are led blind fold by those who will ride them without saddle, but well curbed and bitted. It is generally supposed that N[ew] York would be the balance in the [scaile, scale, *cancelled*] skaill, scaill, (is it right now? it does not look so). N[ew] York by an effort to bring into their assembly antifederal Men, will make also an antifederal ticket for President; and this will give all the power sought by that Party, which at the sacrifice of all that Good men hold dear and sacred, they are determined upon—To this purpose was Randolph['s] Letter, Livingstones Resolutions, and Coopers libels—with all the host of Callenders lies.[2]—Much animosity is springing up between South & North & East;

[1] See footnote 2 to the letter of April 7, 1800.

[2] For Randolph's letter, see footnote 5 to the letter of January 28, 1800. Edward Livingston (1764–1836), while a member of the House of Representatives from New York in 1795, introduced a resolution calling for all the papers from the President concerning Jay's Treaty with England. Livingston settled in New Orleans in 1804. For Thomas Cooper, see footnote 3 to the letter of November 1–3, 1799, and footnote 2 to the letter of November 26, 1799. James Thomson Callender (1758–1803), political writer, was born in Scotland, and settled in Pennsylvania in 1796. His *History of the United States for 1796* forced Hamilton publicly to confess his adultery with the so-called Mrs. James W. Reynolds. Because of his notorious pamphlet, *The Prospect before Us*, 1800, containing criticism of John Adams, Callender was tried under the Sedition Law in May and June of that year, and fined two hundred dollars and sentenced to nine months' imprisonment. By 1802, Callender was attacking the private life of Thomas Jefferson.

A whole year we shall hear nothing else, but abuse and scandel, enough to ruin & corrupt the minds and morals of the best people in the world. Out of all this will arise, something which tho we may be no more, our Children may live to Rue—I hope we may be preserved from confusion, but it is much to be dreaded. Adieu, my dear Sister,

Affectionatly yours
A. ADAMS

Norwalk, State of Conneticut,
Monday, 26 May, 1800

MY DEAR SISTER:

Detained here by a cold North east rain, I write to inform you I am thus far on my journey to Quincy 100 [and] 44 miles from Philadelphia, which I left this day week in the afternoon; I tarried one day in N[ew] York and have taken Little Susan [Adams] on with me. I went to the incampment upon Scotch Plains [New Jersey] and lodged one night in the Col's Log House, which I found quite a comfortable habitation. Mrs. Smith was there, tho she soon must quit it, as the Army is disbanded. I should have taken her with me, but she was not quite ready. I brought Caroline [Amelia Smith] on to her Grandmamma [Margaret (Stephens)] Smiths. She has taken a House at Newark in the Jersies. The Col. [William Stephens Smith] talks of going up with his Brother to the Miami. In that case Mrs. [Abigail (Adams)] Smith and Caroline will spend the summer with me. I was present at the Review of the Troops by Gen[era]ll Hamilton, who had come on for the purpose.[1] They did great honor to their officers and to themselves. The Col. has been the Principle hand in forming and disciplining them. They need not be ashamed of appearing before regular troops. The officers & men Respect and Love him, and it is with much pain that they seperate. There is a very general feeling exprest for Col. Smiths situation, and a wish that he might receive some appointment. This is a very delicate subject. I hope however that he will get into some buisness. You may be sure that I have my feelings on this subject, and that they are not of the most consolatary kind. Every soul knows its own bitterness. I wish I had no other source of sorrow than that which I have just named—

[1] At the time of the danger of war with France, and following the passage of a law for raising a provisional army, Hamilton, at the suggestion of Washington, was appointed Inspector-General, with the rank of Major-General, by John Adams. He was commissioned July 25, 1798, after a long wrangle over precedence. See footnote 2 to the letter of July 17, 1798.

My mind is not in the most cheerfull state. Trials of various kinds seem to be reserved for our gray Hairs, for our declining years. Shall I receive good and not evil? I will not forget the blessings which sweeten Life. One of those is the prospect I have before me of meeting my dear sister soon, I hope in health and spirits. A strong immagination is said to be a refuge from sorrow, and a kindly solace for a feeling Heart. Upon this principle it was that Pope founded his observation, that "hope springs eternal in the human breast."[2]

My intention was to reach Home on fryday next [May 30], but the Election Storm as we term it with us, may continue and prevent my making the progress I hope to. I will request you to have the House open and aired, the Beds shook up. If there was time and a fine day, I should like to have them sun'd, as they have not been slept in for a long time. I have not heard from Philadelphia but once since I left it. I do not yet know whether the President has left it. I have heard of so many lies and falshoods propagated to answer electioneering purposes since I left Philadelphia and for the last three weeks that I was there, that I am disgusted with the world, and the chief of its inhabitants do not appear worth the trouble and pains they cost to save them from destruction— You see I am in an ill humour. When the rain subsides and the sun shines, it will dispell some of the gloom which hangs heavey at my heart. I heard a sermon yesterday upon the subject of Humility. I believe I do not yet possess enough of that negative quality to make me believe that I deserve all that can be inflicted upon me by the tongues of falshood— I must share in what is said reproachfull or malicious of my better half— yet I know his measures are all meant to promote the best interest of his Country—Sure I have enough of public and Private anxiety to humble a prouder Heart than mine. Adieu, my dear Sister, and believe me ever

Your affectionate Sister
[ABIGAIL ADAMS][3]

[2] Hope springs eternal in the human breast;
Man never is, but always to be blessed.
An Essay on Man: Epistle 1, lines 95–6.

[3] The gap of five months which follows is explained by Mrs. Adams's residence in Quincy. John Adams arrived in the District of Columbia on June 3, 1800. Georgetown *Centinel of Liberty*, June 6, 1800. See the following letter.

New Haven, Sunday, 2d Nov'br, [1800]

MY DEAR SISTER:

You will forgive me, my dear Sister, that I spaired both you and myself the pain of a formal leave, and that I left you without bidding you an adieu. I never was so divided between duty, and affection, the desire I had to remain with you, and the necessity I was under to commence a long and tedious journey at this late season of the year. My Heart was rent with the distrest situation of yourself and family; I could not be with you as I wished. I saw Mrs. [Moses] Black, and requested of her sisterly kindness and attention. I have no doubt of the fullfillment of her kind promise. To the great Physician both of body and soul I committed you and yours, and sit out with an anxious mind and heavey Heart. I reachd this place last Evening, and as usual put up at my old quarters, Mrs. Smiths, where I shall remain this day.[1] We got on without any accident and had a fair week for travelling. The weather to day is rainy, but promises to clear up. By Wednesday [November 5] I hope to reach New York and there to hear from you as my good Brother promised I should. The President left Philadelphia for Washington the day I left Quincy.[2]

Mrs. Smith desires to be affectionatly rememberd to you. With Love to Mrs. Greenleaf and Norton I am

Your affectionate Sister
A. ADAMS

Philadelphia, Novbr. 10, 1800

MY DEAR SISTER:

I arrived in this City last Evening & came to the old House now occupied by Francis as a Hotel. Tho the furniture and arrangment of

---

[1] Probably Mrs. Margaret (Stephens) Smith, widow of John Smith, and mother of Colonel William Stephens Smith.

[2] President Adams left Philadelphia on May 27, 1800, accompanied by his secretary and nephew by marriage, William Smith Shaw. In a carriage drawn by four horses, he proceeded to Georgetown by way of Lancaster and York, Pennsylvania, and Frederick, Maryland. On June 3, 1800, he entered the District of Columbia, and was escorted to the Union Tavern, where he stayed over night. The next day he crossed the Rock Creek Bridge into Washington, inspected the White House and the Treasury Building, and put up at Tunnicliff's Hotel. Tristram Dalton made the speech of welcome in the capitol building on June 5, after which Adams dined with Joshua Johnson, the father of the wife of John Quincy Adams. On June 9, Adams went to "Mount Vernon" to call on the widow of Washington, and spent the next day there. On June 13 he left Washington for Quincy, by way of Baltimore. For full details of Adams's visit, see Bryan, *History of the National Capital*, vol. 1, pp. 347–50.

the House is changed I feel more at home here than I should any where else in the city, and when sitting with my son [Thomas Boylston Adams] & other friends who call to see me, I can scarcly persuade myself, that tomorrow I must quit it, for an unknown & an unseen abode.[1] My Journey has hetherto been as propitious as I could have expected at this season. Hearing by Louissa [Smith] & from my worthy Brother Cranch that you & yours were regaining your strength & gradually advancing I hope to Health, has given a new spring to my spirits, and I shall go on my way rejoicing. Mercy & judgment are the mingled cup allotted me. Shall I receive good and not evil? At N[ew] York I found my poor unhappy son [Charles Adams], for so I must still call him, laid upon a Bed of sickness, destitute of a home. The kindness of a friend afforded him an assylum. A distressing cough, an affection of the liver and a dropsy will soon terminate a Life, which might have been made valuable to himself and others. You will easily suppose that this scene was too powerfull and distressing to me. Sally [Sarah (Smith) Adams] was with him, but his Physician says, he is past recovery—I shall carry a melancholy report to the President, who, passing through New York without stoping, knew not his situation.[2]

I shall not say any thing to you upon political subjects, no not upon the little Gen'll['s] Letter but reserve it for a future Letter when I arrive at Washington and you have more health to laugh at the folly, and pitty the weakness, vanity and ambitious views of, as very a sparrow as Sterne commented upon, in his Sentimental Journey, or More describes in his fables.[3]

With my best wishes for your perfect restoration to Health and that of your Family, I am, my ever Dear Sister,

Your affectionate
A. ADAMS

[1] Mrs. Adams refers to the residence in Philadelphia, which Washington and Adams had used as the Executive Mansion. The "unseen abode" is Washington, D.C., to which the capital of the United States was moved in the autumn of 1800.

[2] This was the last time which Mrs. Adams saw her son Charles, who died about three weeks later, on November 30, 1800.

[3] See Laurence Sterne, *A Sentimental Journey Through France and Italy:* "The Passport: Versailles," for the sparrow which interrupted the "grave and learned Bevoriskius" in his "commentary upon the generations from Adam." "More" is Edward Moore (1712–1757), a popular author and playwright, whose *Fables for the Female Sex*, 1744, went through many editions. See *The Cambridge Bibliography of English Literature*, 1940, vol. 2, p. 323. For the election pamphlet of "little" General Alexander Hamilton, see the following letter.

Thank Mr. [Richard] Cranch for his kind Letters & Mrs. [Moses] Black for her sisterly attention. Heaven reward her. May she never know the want of a Friend.

Washington, Nov'br 21, 1800

My dear Sister:

I arrived in this city on Sunday the 16th ult. Having lost my way in the woods on Saturday in going from Baltimore, we took the road to Frederick and got nine miles out of our road. You find nothing but a Forest & woods on the way, for 16 and 18 miles not a village. Here and there a thatchd cottage without a single pane of glass, inhabited by Blacks. My intention was to have reachd Washington on Saturday. Last winter there was a Gentleman and Lady in Philadelphia by the Name of Snowden whose hospitality I heard much of. They visited me and were invited to dine with us, but did not, as they left the city before the day for dinner. They belong to Maryland, and live on the road to this place 21 miles distant.[1] I was advised at Baltimore to make their House my stage for the night; the only Inn at which I could put up being 36 miles ride from Baltimore. Judge [Samuel] Chase who visited me, at Baltimore, gave Mr. T[homas Boylston] Adams a Letter to Major Snowden, but I who have never been accustomed to quarter myself and servants upon private houses, could not think of it, particuliarly as I expected the chariot & 5 more Horses with two servants to meet me.[2] I sit out early, intending to make my 36 miles if possible: no travelling however but by day light; We took a direction as we supposed right, but in the first turn, went wrong, and were wandering more than two hours in the woods in different paths, holding down & breaking bows of trees which we could not pass, untill we met a solitary black fellow with a

---

[1] Major Thomas Snowden, descendant of a Welshman who came to Maryland before 1675, married Ann Ridgely, and built for her a magnificent colonial manor-house which she named "Montpelier," after her birthplace in Anne Arundel County, Maryland. The house stands a short distance southeast of Laurel, Maryland, on the Great Northern and Southern Post Road which connects Annapolis and Washington. Major Snowden's house was a favorite stopping-place for George Washington on his trips north from "Mount Vernon" to New York, or to Philadelphia. J. D. Warfield, *The Founders of Anne Arundel and Howard Counties, Maryland*, Baltimore, 1905, pp. 362–3.

[2] Samuel Chase (1741–1811), of Maryland, signer of the Declaration of Independence, was appointed to the Supreme Court on January 26, 1796, by George Washington. In March, 1804, he was impeached by the House of Representatives, but in June, 1805, in spite of secret, and improper, pressure by Jefferson, the effort to have him removed failed in the Senate, although 25 of the 34 members were of Jefferson's party.

horse and cart. We inquired of him our way, and he kindly offerd to conduct us, which he did two miles, and then gave us such a clue as led us out to the post road and the Inn, where we got some dinner. Soon after we left it, we met the chariot then 30 miles from Washington, and 20 from our destination. We road as fast as the roads would allow of, but the sun was near set when we came in sight of the Majors. I halted but could not get courage to go to his House with ten Horses and nine persons. I therefore orderd the coach man to proceed, and we drove rapidly on. We had got about a mile when we were stoped by the Major in full speed, who had learnt that I was comeing on; & had kept watch for me, with his Horse at the door; as he was at a distance from the road. In the kindest, and politest manner he urged my return to his House, represented the danger of the road, and the impossibility of my being accomodated at any Inn I could reach: A mere hovel was all I should find. I plead my numbers. That was no objection. He could accomodate double the number. There was no saying nay and I returnd to a large, Handsome, Elegant House, where I was received with my Family, with what we might term true English Hospitality, Friendship without ostentation, and kindness without painfull ceremony. Mrs. Snowden is a charming woman of about 45. She has a lovely daughter of 16 & one of 6, a son whom I had seen often in Philadelphia and who had several times dinned with us. I need not add that they are all true federal Characters. Every attention possible was shown me and the next morning I took my departure, having shared in the common bounty of Major Snowdens hospitality, for which he is universally celebrated—I arrived about one oclock at this place known by the *name* of *the city*, and the Name is all that you can call so. As I expected to find it a new country, with Houses scatterd over a space of ten miles, and trees & stumps in plenty with, a castle of a House—so I found it—The Presidents House is in a beautifull situation in front of which is the Potomac with a view of Alexandr[i]a. The country around is romantic but a wild, a wilderness at present.

I have been to George Town and felt all that Mrs. [William] Cranch described when she was a resident there. It is the very dirtyest Hole I ever saw for a place of any trade, or respectability of inhabitants. It is only one mile from me but a quagmire after every rain. Here we are obliged to send daily for marketting; The capital is near two miles from us. As to roads we shall make them by the frequent passing before winter, but I am determined to be satisfied and content, to say nothing of inconvenience &c. That must be a worse place than even George Town, that I would not reside in for three Months [in *cancelled*].

I found your dear son [William Cranch] here at the House to receive me. He is well and grows much like his Father. He dinned with us on Sunday & yesterday, and yesterday I went to see Nancy and your dear little modest Boys. Richard is a fine Boy. William is more bashfull, and Nancy is a fat little doe. They are all pretty children, and Mrs. Cranch tho thin is handsomer than she was as a Girl.[3]

When I arrived here I found a Boston News paper, which containd the celebration of the Birthday [October 19] at Quincy. It was truly gratifying to find in a world of calumny and falshood, that a Prophet could meet with honour in his own native soil. I hope the benidiction prounounced upon those who are reviled and persecuted falsly, may be his, who conscious of his own pure views and intentions; walks steadfastly on, tho the shafts and arrows of dissapointed ambition are hurled at him from every quarter. The Letter of Hamilton, which you have no doubt seen, can never be answerd properly but by the person to whom it is addrest, because no one else knows all the circumstances, or can deny what he has published for facts; many of which are as grose lies as Duane has told in the Aurora—Such a replie may one day appear, when the [modern *cancelled*] Man may appear still more odious than he now does. I have heard from every quarter, but one voice. It is Hamilton has done his own buisness.[4] Pray can you inform me by whom those pas-

---

[3] Children of William and Nancy (Greenleaf) Cranch: William Greenleaf (1796–1872), Richard (1797–1824), and Anne Allen (1799–1822).

[4] On August 1 and October 1, 1800, Hamilton wrote to Adams asking for an explanation of rumors as to certain charges which the President was said to have brought against his character and conduct. Adams did not answer either letter. In October, Hamilton prepared his strange paper, "The Public Conduct and Character of John Adams, Esq., President of the United States," for circulation among leading Federalists: Hamilton, *Works*, vol. 6, pp. 391–444. Burr got hold of a copy of this untimely attack, and had it published. Hamilton put himself in the ridiculous position of telling Federalists that the best they could do was to vote for Adams, although he was not fit for the office of chief executive. Adams did not answer Hamilton until 1809, when he published eighteen letters in the Boston *Patriot*, the last one dated "June 10, 1809." Adams, *Works*, vol. 9, pp. 241–311.

For a remarkably charitable letter written by Adams on the subject of Hamilton, on December 3, 1800, see Adams, *Works*, vol. 9, p. 576: "This last pamphlet I regret more on account of its author than on my own, because I am confident it will do him more harm than me. I am not his enemy, and never was..." *et seq*. Yet as late as July 12, 1813, in writing to Jefferson, Adams was so bitter as to refer to Hamilton as "a bastard Bratt of a Scotch Pedlar." *Historical Magazine*, July, 1870, pp. 50–1. This last sentiment recalls the spirit in which John Quincy Adams refused to witness the granting of an honorary degree by Harvard to Andrew Jackson in 1833, a spirit which casts suspicion on many of the judgments in that son's famous *Memoirs*. Jefferson, it is interesting to remember, placed a bust of Hamilton in the hall of "Monticello."

sages were selected from Shakespear[e] which composed the Quincy toasts? The President says if his Friends intended to flatter him, they have succeeded, for he would not exchange the Quincy celebration for any other that he has heard off.[5]

My dear Sister the few lines in your own hand writing were a cordial to my spirits. I pray most sincerely for your perfect restoration to health and my dear Mrs. Norton. I have received all the kind Letters of my Brother Cranch and thank him for them. If my future peace & tranquility were all that I considered, a release from public life would be the most desirable event of it—I feel perfectly tranquil upon the subject, hoping and trusting that, the Being in whose Hands are the Hearts of all Men, will guide and direct our national counsels for the peace & prosperity of this great people.

Remember me affectionatly to all my Friend[s], never omitting Mrs. Black.

I have the pleasure to say we are all at present well, tho the news papers very kindly gave the President the Ague and fever. I am rejoiced that it was only in the paper that he had it.

This day the President meets the two Houses to deliver the speech. There has not been a House untill yesterday—We have had some very cold weather and we feel it keenly. This House is twice as large as our meeting House. I believe the great Hall is as Bigg. I am sure tis twice as long. Cut your coat according to your Cloth. But this House is built for ages to come. The establishment necessary is a tax which cannot be born by the present sallery: No body can form an Idea of it but those who come into it. I had much rather live in the house at Philadelphia. Not one room or chamber is finished of the whole. It is habitable by fires in

[5] An account of the celebration of the birthday of John Adams, at Quincy, October 19, 1800, appeared in the *Columbian Centinel* for Saturday, November 1, 1800. Moses Black was in the Chair, and there were sixteen toasts, in all. The second was drunk to the President, and the fifteenth to John Quincy Adams, "our Minister at Berlin." Only one of the passages to which Mrs. Adams refers comes from Shakespeare. Cardinal Wolsey's words to Henry VIII were quoted in offering the toast to the President:

> ... though perils did
> Abound as thick as thought could make 'em and
> Appear in forms more horrid—yet my duty,
> As doth a rock against the chiding flood,
> Should the approach of this wild river break
> And stand unshaken.

William Shakespeare and John Fletcher, *Henry VIII*, Act 3, Scene 2, lines 194-9. The first 203 lines of this scene are attributed to Shakespeare, rather than to Fletcher.

every part, thirteen of which we are obliged to keep daily, or sleep in wet & damp places.[6]

Yours as ever
A. A[DAMS]

Washington, December 1st, 1800

MY DEAR SISTER:

I have written to you, my dear Sister, twice since my arrival here. I know not but one of the Letters was in the lost mail.[1] I miss your pen, which used to detail to me both public and private affairs. I have reason to bless God, that your Life is spared to your family, and Friends. I hope you will not be induced by any means to over exert yourself, or try your strength beyond its bearing, a relapse being often more fatal than an original disease. If you can recover your strength and appetite, I hope your Health will be benifitted. Poor Mrs. [Joshua] Johnsons eldest unmarried daughter has been sick ever since I came with the same kind of fever. She is much reduced, and her complaints have been very similar to those who have been sick with us. She has been twice bled. I am not however satisfied that it was the best practise; The fever has run to 21 days—We have hetherto [sic] been very well, untill last night Susan [Adams] was threatned with the Quincy, which allarmd me very much as she went well to bed. I was waked in the night by a strange noise. She sleeps in a little chamber near to mine. I went in, and found her labouring with that dreadfull hoars cough, and sound which indicated immediate medical aid. We sent for the Physician nearest to us, who gave her calomil, put her feet in warm water, and steamed her with warm vinigar. She puked, and that semd to relieve her. She has coughed all day, but not with so much hoarsness. I think she has woorms. I saw Mr. [William] Cranch on fryday. He is well. Little Nancy had a return of the Ague. Mr. [William] Cranch is going to remove to Capitol Hill, which will bring him half a mile nearer to me, and is I believe a much healthier spot.

My dear Sister, I beg you would not trouble yourself about my Bacon this year, only be so kind as to give the proper directions to Mr. &

---

[6] "Before I end my letter, I pray heaven to bestow the best of blessings on this house, and on all that shall hereafter inhabit it. May none but honest and wise men ever rule under this roof!" John to Abigail Adams, November 2, 1800: *Letters of John Adams, Addressed to his Wife*, Charles Francis Adams, Editor, Boston, 1841, vol. 2, p. 113.

[1] Of the two letters to which Mrs. Adams refers, only that of November 21 has been found.

Mrs. Porter. I was rejoiced to learn by your son in a Letter from his Father, that Mrs. [Jacob] Norton was on the recovery, and able to walk her Room. Poor creature. What has she not Suffered? I have not got a line from my much honord and respected Friend Dr. Tufts since I left home. I hope bad health is not the cause. Pray tell him I am only one hundred and 50 miles, further off than formerly, tho the winter communication is 14 days instead of 7.

As to politicks; they are at present such a mere turn penny, that I believe it is best to leave all calculations to those who daily occupy themselves with them, and say what from the Sincerity of my Heart I do: that I hope the termination of the present contests will be such as will be most productive of the Peace, Liberty and happiness of our common Country, let who will be at the Head of the Government.—

Inclosed are some Letter[s] which you will be so kind as to have deliverd—

With the sincerest regard to all my Friends and my dear Sister, in particuliar, I am

Ever Yours
A. ADAMS

Washington, [Monday], 8 December, 1800

MY DEAR SISTER:

I know, my much loved Sister, that you will mingle in my sorrow, and weep with me over the Grave of a poor unhappy child who cannot now add an other pang to those which have peirced my Heart for several years past; Cut off in the midst of his days, his years are numberd and finished; I hope my supplications to heaven for him, that he might find mercy from his maker, may not have been in vain: His constitution was so shaken, that his disease was rapid, and through the last period of his Life dreadfully painfull and distressing; He bore with patience & submission his sufferings and heard the prayers for him with composure; His mind at times was much deranged thro his sufferings, and through a total want of rest; He finally expired without a groan on Sunday week. Mrs. [Margaret (Stephens)] Smith & Sally [Sarah (Smith) Adams] have had a distressing scene to pass through, yet I cannot be thankful enough that Mrs. Smith got home when she did, and that she took him into her care. She has a satisfaction in knowing that she spared no pains to render his last moments less distressing to his Parents and relatives than they could have been else where. I was satisfied I had seen him for the last time when I left him. Three weeks only has he been really confined, but his constitution was broken down. Food has not been his sustanance, yet he did not look like an intemperate Man—He was bloted, but not red—He was no mans Enemy but his own—He was beloved, in spight of his Errors, and all spoke with grief and sorrow for his habits.[1]

Afflictions of this kind are a two Edged sword. The Scripture expresses it as a mitigation of sorrow [that *cancelled*] when we do not sorrow as those who have no hope—The Mercy of the almighty is not limited; To his sovereign will I desire humbly to submit.

Mr. [Richard] Cranch in the cover of his Letter refered me to one written to his son for the state of your Health. Mr. [William] Cranch did not get the Letter, so I have not heard, but I know I should see your own hand writeing if you were able. I have not been well myself for the week past. I have been afflicted with a loss of voice & a sad cough— It is not worse—I hope [it] is going off. The President is well and has been so ever since we have been here. Your son [William Cranch] dinned with us yesterday. He and family were well—Pray remember me kindly to all our Friends and let me hear of or from you as often as possible. I am, my dear Sister,

Your truly affectionate but afflicted Sister
A. ADAMS

Washington, Janry 15, 1801

MY DEAR SISTER:

I received from you two kind Letters which I have not yet acknowledged; I am surprized to find that the frost & cold have not yet put a stop to the fever. I hope it will not be permitted to make a renewed visit, at the approach of the summer with a severity never before experienced in our healthy and delightfull village. I cannot say that I have enjoy'd so much health this winter as the last. I am very frequently shut up, tho but for a few days at a time; I fancy we have too much damp here for Rhumatick Constitutions, but my constitution appears to have sufferd severely from the Ague and fever, and to be much broken by repeated attacks of an intermitting kind. I patch up, but it is hard work. Heretofore I have had spirits which would surmount & rise above bodily

---

[1] Charles Adams (1770–1800) died in New York on Sunday, November 30, 1800. The death of this unhappy son is the conventional and dishonest excuse usually offered for the last-minute departure of John Adams from Washington at sunrise on March 4, 1801!

infirmity; whether they will be continued to me, I know not; I hope they may, for a groaning, whineing, complaining temper I deprecate.

I have no disposition to seclude myself from society, because I have met with unkind or ungratefull returns from some; I would strive to act my part well and [resign *cancelled*] Retire with that dignity which is unconscious of doing or wishing ill to any, with a temper disposed to forgive injuries, as I would myself hope to be forgiven, if any I have committed. I wish for the preservation of the Government, and a wise administration of it. In the best situation, with the wisest head and firmest Heart, it will be surrounded with perplexities, dangers and troubles, that are little conceived of by those into whose Hands it is like to fall. The President had frequently contemplated resigning: I thought it would be best for him to leave to the people to act for themselves, and take no responsibility upon himself. I do not regreet that he has done so. He has had the pleasure of appointing your son to the office of commisoner for the city, in the place of Mr. Scott, who dyed a few weeks since, and tho this will be sit down by the Antis, as a promotion on account of Relationship, we care not now what they say.[1] The Senate had nothing to do with this appointment, and therefore could not quibble as they have done upon some former occasions. The principle proprieters in the city came forward in a recommendation of Mr. [William] Cranch to the President, and I trust the appointment will give general satisfaction—I think Mr. Cranch is rising fast and will be one of the first Men in the city in a short time—The duties of his office will be arduous, and delicate to give satisfaction to the contending interests, but I hope he will act impartially, tho it may sometimes be difficult to persuade interested people to believe that he is so. The sallery I think is sixteen hundred dollors a year.

I hope I shall return to Quincy sometime in Feb'ry but I own it is a mountain before me, so many horrid Rivers to cross and such Roads to traverse—my health very delicate.

I feel most sensibly for our dear Respected and venerable uncle.[2] I

---

[1] Gustavus Scott (1753–1800), of Maryland, lawyer and patriot, was appointed a commissioner for the Federal City by George Washington in 1794. He died at "Rock Hill," Washington, D. C., December 25, 1800. Adams appointed his wife's nephew, William Cranch, to the vacancy, and then, on February 27, 1800, placed him on the Circuit Court of the District of Columbia as junior assistant judge. Jefferson made Cranch chief judge of the Circuit Court in which office he served for fifty years, until his death, in 1855. See Clark, *Greenleaf and Law in the Federal City*, pp. 52–3.

[2] Norton Quincy (1716–1801), Harvard, 1736, the brother of Elizabeth (Quincy) Smith (1722–1775), the mother of Mrs. Richard Cranch, Mrs. John Adams, and Mrs. Stephen Peabody.

know not, nor do I think it possible to supply to him the loss he has sustaind. Tho Mrs. Pope's temper was not pleasent, she was attentive towards him, knew all his wants and wishes. She was prudent and saveing of his interest, and had many excellent qualities. To a person of his years it is peculiarly urksome to have new faces, new habits, new fancies to conform to—It will probably shorten the period of his existance—but it would seem as if there remained but little desirable in this world to him—Yet we must live all the days of our appointed time, and when our change commeth, may it be happy to us.

I thank you, my dear Sister. I have not any thing yet to ask for. I rejoice you are in such health as to be able to assist your Friends, and I rejoice that our dear Mrs. [Jacob] Norton is spaired to her family and Friends. Surely we may sing of mercy as well as judgment.

We all send Love. The President has enjoyed very good health ever since he has been here, and hopes to be a good Farmer yet. He some times says he would go to the Bar again if he had the powers of speech, but of public Life he takes a final farewell.

Betsy Howard and her Lover have chosen to signilize their marriage by having it performed whilst in the Family of the President. I did not much oppose it, tho I thought they had better have waited untill they returnd, as I supposed it would subject them to reports wholy groundless & unfounded, but they, conscious of their innocence, disregarded such rumours and last Sunday Evening were married. Richard and Becky have not yet proposed a similar subject to me. I trust they think themselves young enough yet.

Adieu my dear Sister. It is my large dinner party to day and I must dress to sit at table as I have Ladies, tho I have not been below for three days. I make an exertion as it is the last time I expect the pleasure of dinning them.

Affectionatly your Sister
Abigail Adams

Washington, Febry. 7th, 1801

My dear Sister:

I suppose the reason why I have not had a Letter from you for a long time, arises from your expectation that I am upon my Journey; The Roads have been represented to me as so intolerable bad, and I know them to be so, that I have been prevaild upon to remain longer than I designd. I now think I shall stay untill after the 13th of Febry, the great important day, which may in its concequences deside [*sic*] the fate of our Country.[1] I feel as it is so near at hand, as tho I could not quit the city untill I know what, or rather who is to be our future Ruler. Never were a people placed in more difficult circumstances than the virtuous part of our Countrymen are at the present Crisis. I have turnd, & turnd, and overturned in my mind at various times the merits & demerits of the two candidates. Long acquaintance, private friendship and the full belief that the private Character of one is much purer than the other, inclines me to him who has certainly from Age, succession and public employments the prior Right. Yet when I reflect upon the visonary system of Government which will undoubtedly be adopted, the Evils which must result from it to the Country, I am sometimes inclined to believe that, the more bold, daring and decisive Character would succeed in supporting the Government for a longer time.

> A Sceptre, snatch'd with an unruly hand
> Must be as boistrously mantain'd as gain'd;
> And he that stands upon a slipp'ry place
> Makes nice of no vile hold to stay him up.[2]

What a lesson upon Elective Governments have we in our young Republic of 12 years old? What is the difference of Character between

[1] The whole number of electoral votes in 1801 was 138; necessary to the choice of a President, 70. Jefferson and Burr each had 73; therefore, the election went into the House of Representatives. The balloting continued from February 11 to 17, inclusive. Nine states were necessary to a choice. On the first ballot, Jefferson had 8, Burr 6, and two states were divided. On the thirty-sixth ballot, Jefferson received the vote of ten states and was declared elected President. On the decisive ballot, the states were divided as follows: Jefferson: New York, New Jersey, Pennsylvania, Virginia, North Carolina, Kentucky, Georgia, Tennessee, Maryland, and Vermont; Burr: Massachusetts, Connecticut, Rhode Island, and New Hampshire. Delaware and South Carolina cast blanks. Matthew L. Davis, *Memoirs of Aaron Burr*, New York, 1837, vol. 2, pp. 73–4.

In writing to Elbridge Gerry from Washington, December 30, 1800, President Adams commented on the results of the election of that year as follows:

"Your anxiety for the issue of the election is, by this time, allayed. How mighty a power is the spirit of party! How decisive and unanimous it is! Seventy-three for Mr. Jefferson and seventy-three for Mr. Burr. May the peace and welfare of the country be promoted by this result! But I see not the way as yet. In the case of Mr. Jefferson, there is nothing wonderful; but Mr. Burr's good fortune surpasses all ordinary rules, and exceeds that of Bonaparte. All the old patriots, all the splendid talents, the long experience, both of federalists and antifederalists, must be subjected to the humiliation of seeing this dexterous gentleman rise, like a balloon, filled with inflammable air, over their heads. And this is not the worst. What a discouragement to all virtuous exertion, and what an encouragement to party intrigue, and corruption! What course is it we steer, and to what harbor are we bound? Say, man of wisdom and experience, for I am wholly at a loss." Adams, *Works*, vol. 9, pp. 577–8.

[2] *King John*, Act 3, Scene 4, lines 135–8.

a Prince of Wales, & a Burr? Have we any claim to the favour or protection of Providence, when we have against warning admonition and advise [sic] Chosen as our chief Majestrate a man who makes no pretentions to the belief of an all wise and suprem Governour of the World, ordering or directing or overruling the events which take place in it? I do not mean that he is an Atheist, for I do not think that he is—but he believes Religion only usefull as it may be made a political Engine, and that the outward forms are only, as I once heard him express himself—mere [Mumery *cancelled*] Mummery. In short, he is not a believer in the Christian system—The other if he is more of a believer, has more to answer for, because he has grosely offended against those doctrines by his practise.

Such are the Men whom we are like to have as our Rulers. Whether they are given us in wrath to punish us for our sins and transgressions, the Events will disclose—But if ever we saw a day of darkness, I fear this is one which will be visible untill kindled into flame's.

My Health is better than it was the first part of the winter: I hope I shall be able to encounter this dreadfull journey, but it is very formidable to me, not only upon account of the Roads, but the Runs of water which have not any Bridges over them, and must be forded—Mr. and Mrs. [William] Cranch are very well and dinned with me last Sunday, as did William and Richard. To day the Judges and many others with the heads of departments & Ladies dine with me for the last time—My best Regards to all my Friends and acquiantance. With the hope of seeing them e'er long, I am,

Your truly affectionate Sister
A. ADAMS

Susan [Adams] sends her duty. She has had the hooping cough, but is getting better.

Bibliography

Letters of Mrs. Adams, the Wife of John Adams. With an Introductory Memoir by Her Grandson, Charles Francis Adams (Boston, 1840).

Letters of Mrs. Adams, the Wife of John Adams. Charles Francis Adams (Boston, 1841). I (1761–1784); II (1784–1816).

Letters of John Adams, Addressed to His Wife. Edited by . . . Charles Francis Adams (Boston, 1841). I (1774–1777); II (1777–1801).

Letters of Mrs. Adams, the Wife of John Adams. Charles Francis Adams (Boston, 1848).

Familiar Letters of John Adams and His Wife Abigail Adams, During the Revolution. Charles Francis Adams (New York, 1876).

Warren-Adams Letters (Boston, 1917–1925). I (1743–1777); II (1778–1814).

"Abigail Adams, Commentator." Massachusetts Historical Society, *Proceedings*, 66 (Boston, 1942).

Journal and Correspondence of Miss Adams, Daughter of John Adams. Edited by Her Daughter, [Caroline Amelia (Smith) DeWindt] (New York and London, 1841).

Correspondence of Miss Adams, Daughter of John Adams. Edited by . . . [Caroline Amelia (Smith) DeWindt] (New York and London, 1842).

Henry Adams of Somersetshire, England, and Braintree, Mass. His English Ancestry and Some of His Descendants. Compiled by J. Gardner Bartlett (New York, 1927).

John Adams's Book: Being Notes on a Record of the Births, Marriages, and Deaths of Three Generations of the Adams Family, 1734–1807. By Henry Adams, Jr. (Boston, 1934).

Abigail Adams, The Second First Lady. By Dorothie Bobbé (New York, 1929).

"Abigail Smith Adams": *Portraits of American Women.* By Gamaliel Bradford (Boston and New York, 1919).

"Abigail Adams": *Some American Ladies: Seven Informal Biographies.* By Meade Minnigerode (New York and London, 1926).

Abigail Adams and Her Times. By Laura E. Richards (New York and London, 1917).

Abigail Adams. By Janet Whitney (Boston, 1947).

3: THE QUINCY-SMITH FAMILY OF NEW ENGLAND

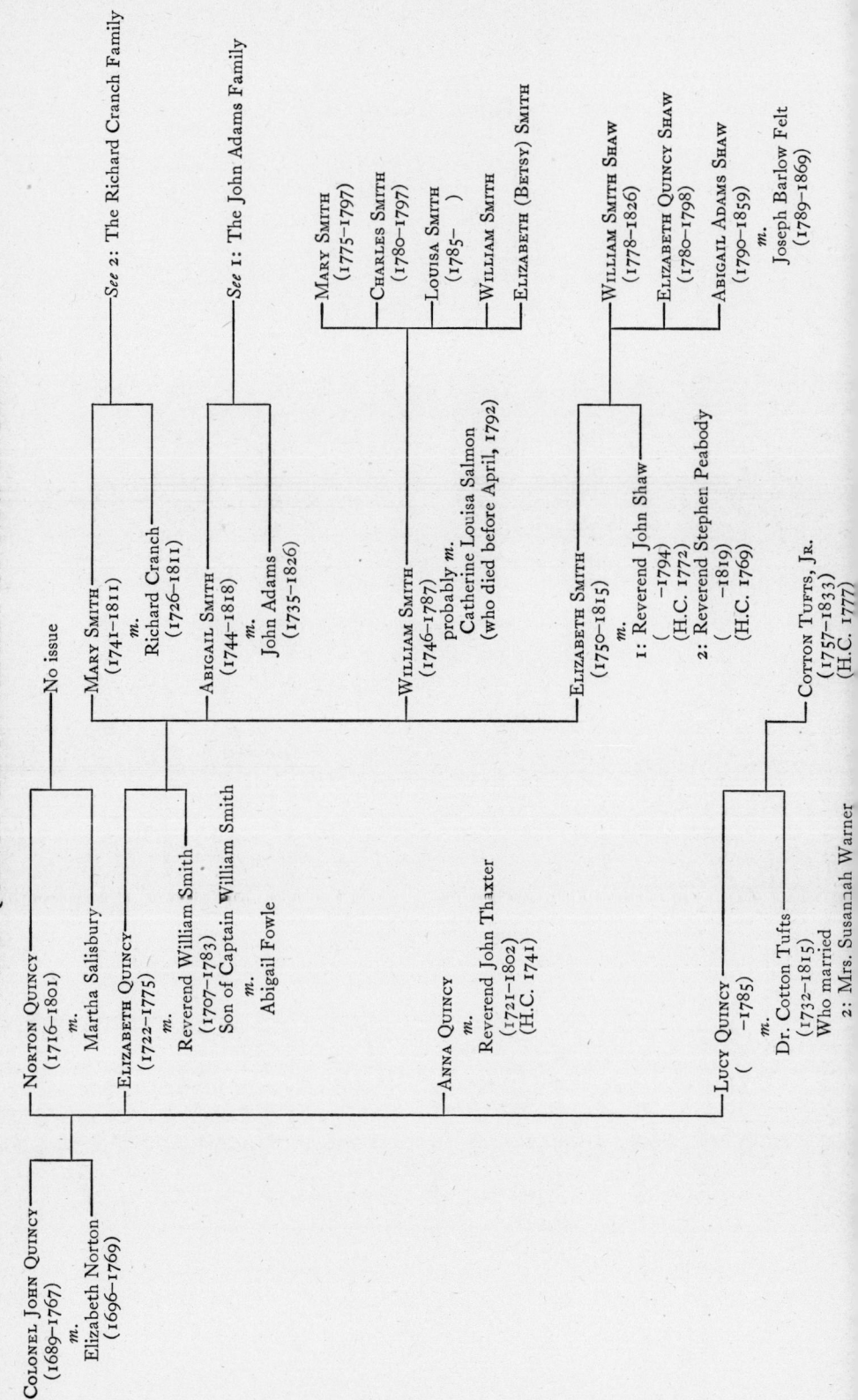

Colonel John Quincy (1689–1767)
m.
Elizabeth Norton (1696–1769)

Children:

- **Norton Quincy** (1716–1801)
  m. Martha Salisbury
  — No issue

- **Elizabeth Quincy** (1722–1775)
  m. Reverend William Smith (1707–1783), Son of Captain William Smith m. Abigail Fowle
  Children:
  - **Mary Smith** (1741–1811) m. Richard Cranch (1726–1811) — *See 2:* The Richard Cranch Family
  - **Abigail Smith** (1744–1818) m. John Adams (1735–1826) — *See 1:* The John Adams Family
  - **William Smith** (1746–1787) probably m. Catherine Louisa Salmon (who died before April, 1792)
    Children:
    - Mary Smith (1775–1797)
    - Charles Smith (1780–1797)
    - Louisa Smith (1785–)
    - William Smith
    - Elizabeth (Betsy) Smith
  - **Elizabeth Smith** (1750–1815)
    m. 1: Reverend John Shaw (–1794) (H.C. 1772)
    m. 2: Reverend Stephen Peabody (–1819) (H.C. 1769)
    Children:
    - William Smith Shaw (1778–1826)
    - Elizabeth Quincy Shaw (1780–1798)
    - Abigail Adams Shaw (1790–1859) m. Joseph Barlow Felt (1789–1869)

- **Anna Quincy**
  m. Reverend John Thaxter (1721–1802) (H.C. 1741)

- **Lucy Quincy** (–1785)
  m. Dr. Cotton Tufts (1732–1815)
  Who married 2: Mrs. Susannah Warner
  Child:
  - **Cotton Tufts, Jr.** (1757–1833) (H.C. 1777)

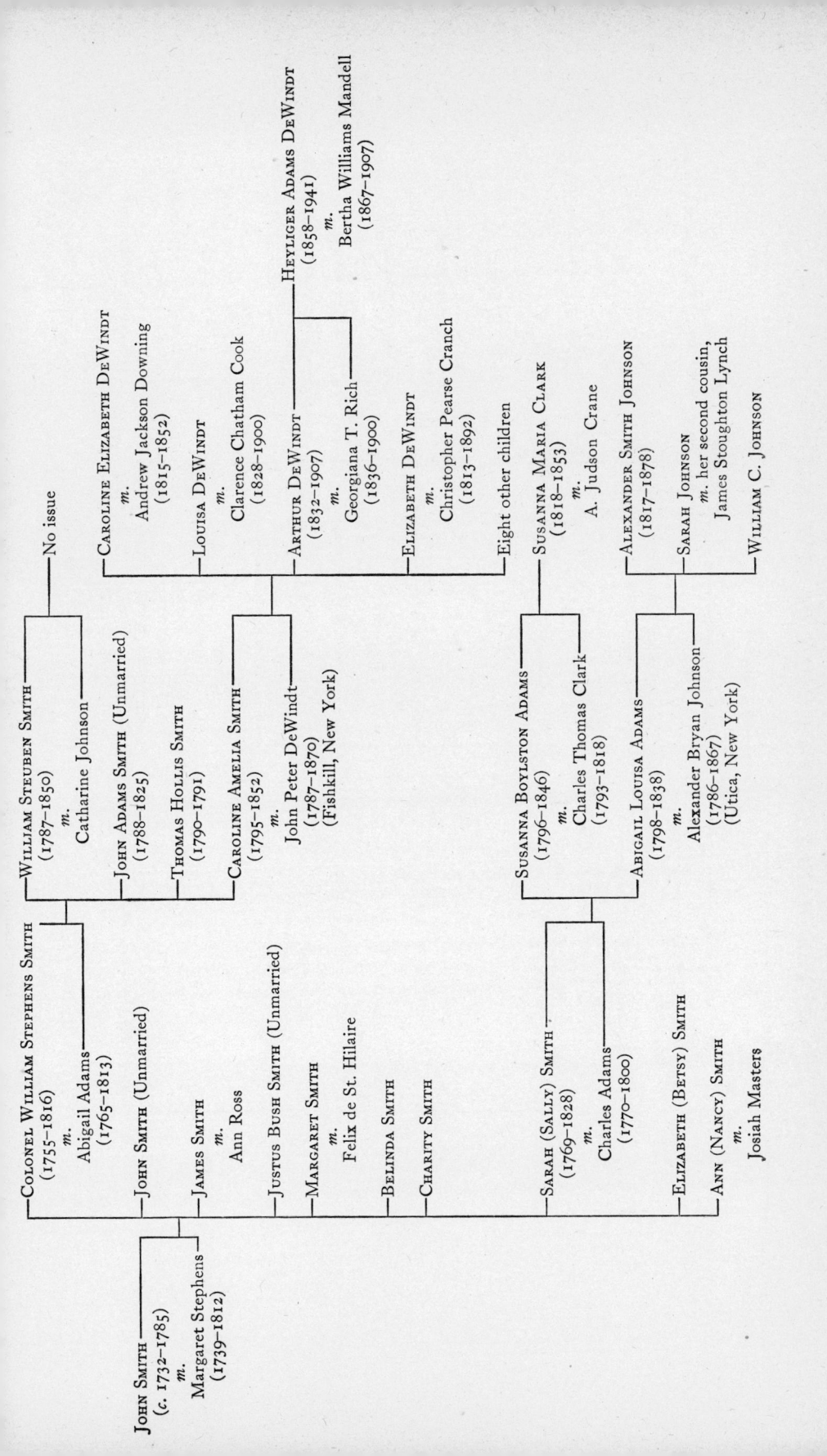

Smith Family Genealogy

- **John Smith** (c. 1732–1785) m. **Margaret Stephens** (1739–1812)
  - **Colonel William Stephens Smith** (1755–1816) m. **Abigail Adams** (1765–1813)
    - **William Steuben Smith** (1787–1850) m. Catharine Johnson — No issue
    - **John Adams Smith** (1788–1825) (Unmarried)
    - **Thomas Hollis Smith** (1790–1791)
    - **Caroline Amelia Smith** (1795–1852) m. **John Peter DeWindt** (1787–1870) (Fishkill, New York)
      - **Caroline Elizabeth DeWindt** m. Andrew Jackson Downing (1815–1852)
      - **Louisa DeWindt** m. Clarence Chatham Cook (1828–1900)
      - **Arthur DeWindt** (1832–1907) m. Georgiana T. Rich (1836–1900)
        - **Heyliger Adams DeWindt** (1858–1941) m. Bertha Williams Mandell (1867–1907)
      - **Elizabeth DeWindt** m. Christopher Pearse Cranch (1813–1892)
      - Eight other children
  - **John Smith** (Unmarried)
  - **James Smith** m. Ann Ross
  - **Justus Bush Smith** (Unmarried)
  - **Margaret Smith** m. Felix de St. Hilaire
  - **Belinda Smith**
  - **Charity Smith**
  - **Sarah (Sally) Smith** (1769–1828) m. **Charles Adams** (1770–1800)
    - **Susanna Boylston Adams** (1796–1846) m. **Charles Thomas Clark** (1793–1818)
      - **Susanna Maria Clark** (1818–1853) m. A. Judson Crane
    - **Abigail Louisa Adams** (1798–1838) m. **Alexander Bryan Johnson** (1786–1867) (Utica, New York)
      - **Alexander Smith Johnson** (1817–1878)
      - **Sarah Johnson** m. her second cousin, James Stoughton Lynch
      - **William C. Johnson**
  - **Elizabeth (Betsy) Smith**
  - **Ann (Nancy) Smith** m. Josiah Masters

Additions and Corrections

In preparing these letters for the press, the editor confused two obscure persons of the same name: William Smith (1755–1816), merchant of Boston, a kinsman of Mrs. John Adams, and William Smith, Jr. (1746–1787), younger brother of Mrs. Adams. This William Smith, Jr., married Catherine Louisa Salmon, and seems to have had five children: Mary (1775–1797), Charles (1780–1797), Louisa (1785)—who lived with President and Mrs. John Adams—William, and Elizabeth. He settled in Lincoln, and died of black jaundice, September 3 or 10, 1787—the letters of his sisters, Mary Cranch and Elizabeth Shaw, do not agree on the date. The kinsman, William Smith, merchant of Boston, married Hannah Carter in 1787, and was the father of Mary Carter Smith (1791–1798). Thus, four William Smiths appear in the index and notes: the Reverend William Smith (1707–1783), father of Mrs. Adams; his son, William Smith, Jr.; his son, William Smith, 3rd; and William Smith, merchant of Boston. Therefore, footnotes on pages 4, 40, 46, 129, and 130 should be read with this correction in mind. This information was supplied by Henry Adams, Jr.

Page 8, footnote 5: delete statement as to Richmond Hill.

Page 9, line 23: "Mr. Mason" is Jonathan Mason, Jr. (1756–1831), of Boston, who married Susannah Powell.

Page 40, footnote 3: "Brother" refers not to William Smith, Jr. (1746–1787), but to Peter Boylston Adams (1738–1823), who married Mary Crosby (1749–1823).

Page 67, lines 26–27: Mrs. Adams, in comparing Bush Hill, Philadelphia, with Richmond Hill, New York, refers to Edmund Burke's essay, *On the Sublime and the Beautiful* (1756).

Page 108, footnote 4, line 2: *for* 1799 *read* 1790.

Page 137, footnote 5 should read: See footnote 7 to the letter of November 15, 1797.

Page 220, line 33, a lost footnote should read: Benjamin Franklin Bache, proprietor of the *Aurora*, died of yellow fever in Philadelphia, September 10, 1798. His widow married the associate editor, William Duane, who continued the paper, and with great success. William Duane (1760–1835) was born near Lake Champlain, New York, taken to Ireland as a child, and went out to India in 1787, from which country he was deported without trial. Leaving England in disgust, he settled in Philadelphia and helped Bache edit the *Aurora*. In the autumn of 1799, he was indicted under the Sedition Law, but his trial was postponed twice, and President Jefferson dismissed the charges. To Jefferson alone Duane remained a faithful follower and devoted friend. Jefferson thought that his "passions" were "stronger than his prudence," and described him as an "honest" but "intolerant" man.

Page 224, last line, a lost footnote should read: The "British Minister" to whom Mrs. Adams refers as having been accused of protesting, in 1799, against the proposed peace with France was Sir Robert Liston (1742–1836), of Edinburgh, "ambassador extraordinary and minister plenipotentiary" to the United States (1796–1802). Liston, then H.B.M. ambassador to Constantinople, was appointed on February 17, 1796, and arrived in Philadelphia on May 12.

Page 251, line 11: *for* America *read* American.

Page 263, footnote 1, line 4: *for* 1800 *read* 1801.

Index

A.

Adams, Abigail. *See* Abigail (Adams) Smith.

Adams, Abigail (Smith), opinion of New York, 7; receptions and dinners of, 8, 19-20, 75, 90, 91, 98-99, 100, 107, 114, 119, 129, 134, 167, 169, 183, 196, 214, 217, 220, 225, 226, 231, 247-248, 250, 264, 266; character, 6, 14-15, 16, 22, 26, 28, 32, 36, 37, 41-42, 43, 58, 62, 67, 71, 72, 76, 79, 80-81, 83, 87-88, 89, 96-97, 110-111, 112, 116, 117, 120, 125, 133, 134, 135, 137, 139-140, 142, 144, 147-148, 154, 159-160, 166, 168, 174-175, 176, 181, 183, 185, 186, 187, 193, 194, 198, 208, 211, 212, 214-215, 216, 217-218, 220, 225, 232-233, 234, 241-242, 243, 245, 247-248, 249-250, 252-253, 254-255, 257, 259, 261-262, 263, 266; health, 63, 65, 77, 78-79, 80, 81-82, 90, 113, 134, 152, 178, 230, 231, 235, 245, 262, 266; daily routine, 91, 238-239.

Adams, Abigail Louisa. *See* Abigail Louisa (Adams) Johnson.

Adams, Boylston, 187, 239.

Adams, Charles, 12, 17, 19, 20, 21, 35-36, 43, 46, 49, 59, 64, 67, 70, 77, 89, 93, 183, 184, 211, 255, 261-262.

Adams, John, 4, 6, 7, 12, 13, 30, 31, 32, 35, 39, 40, 41, 42, 44, 58, 61, 79, 89, 103, 120, 144, 151-152, 160, 170, 174, 183, 187, 188, 192, 198, 201, 209, 211, 214, 219, 243, 247, 253, 254, 255; political patronage, 16-17, 66, 127, 189; as Vice-President, 20-21, 29, 54, 83, 118; attacks on, 25, 126, 159-160, 236-237, 258; character, 21, 25, 28, 29, 91, 94, 99, 110-111, 115, 123, 133, 136-137, 167, 183, 189, 195, 199, 212-213, 224, 259; visit to New England, 29, 34; health, 49, 50, 62, 74, 75, 82, 96, 98, 113-114, 152, 172-173, 178, 209, 210, 262, 264; land poor, 61; speech on France, 90, 92, 93, 151, 156, 190, 217-218, 219, 220-221; birthday, 108, 258-259; opens letter to wife, 110-111, 120; respect for, 112-113, 118, 143, 161, 165, 167, 169, 171, 173, 175, 176, 214; Duke of Braintree, 116; messages and speeches, 146, 153-154, 227; French hatred of, 147; hopes for peace with France, 148, 220-221, 224-225; thoughts of resigning Presidency, 263.

Adams, John Quincy, 4, 6, 28, 30, 31, 52, 64, 65, 67, 69, 82, 90, 95, 97, 110, 116, 129, 131, 144, 146, 147, 155-156, 157, 159-160, 162, 169, 175, 180, 181, 183, 185, 190, 191, 194, 208, 211, 212, 217, 226, 230, 240, 250; character, 70, 138.

Adams, Louisa Catherine (Johnson), 110, 157-158, 208, 212, 217, 230; character, 116, 190-191.

Adams, Peter Boylston, 7, 40, 64, 73, 74, 76, 131, 136, 187, 239, 254.

Adams, Sarah (Smith), 5, 89, 209, 211, 213, 255, 261.

Adams, Susanna, 187, 220.

Adams, Susanna (Boylston). *See* Susanna (Boylston) [Adams] Hall.

Adams, Susanna Boylston. *See* Susanna Boylston (Adams) Clark.

Adams, Thomas, 159, 165.

Adams, Thomas Boylston, 21, 34, 35, 36, 39, 41, 42, 49, 50, 52, 55, 56, 58, 59, 63, 66, 67, 68, 69, 70, 71, 74, 75, 82, 95, 110, 116, 131, 144, 157-158, 169, 175, 185, 211-212, 213, 216, 217, 221, 232, 247, 255, 256.

Aesop, Fables of, 48, 230.

Ague, 65, 82, 85, 183, 260, 262.

Algerines, 151, 154.

Alien and Sedition Laws, 165, 172, 179, 193, 196, 216.

American Biography, Belknap's, 198.

Americans, vexation with, 124, 150, 154, 159, 165, 168-169, 177, 179, 186, 216, 218, 237, 251-252, 261, 265.

Ames, Fisher, 38, 64.

Ames, Frances (Worthington), 65.

271

Anetseed, 93.
Annapolis College, 189.
Apoplexy, 197, 200.
Assembly Room, Philadelphia, 225.
Assumption of state debts, 38.
As You Like It, 24.
Atheism, 168, 266.
Atwood, Sarah, 122.
Aurora, Philadelphia, 92, 94, 95, 96, 97, 112, 116, 117, 118, 120, 128, 137, 143–144, 150, 154, 159, 165, 166, 167, 171, 172, 216, 258.

B.

Bache, Benjamin F., 92, 94, 95, 96, 97, 112, 116, 117, 118, 120, 128, 137, 143–144, 146, 150, 154, 159, 165, 166, 167, 171, 172, 189, 193, 200.
Baker, Hilary, 171.
Baltimore, Md., 51, 256.
Bankruptcy, 97, 117, 128–129, 134, 142, 143, 155, 169, 203–204, 247.
Barbary Coast pirates, 151.
Baring, Anne (Bingham), 242.
Barnard, Moses, 10, 23, 30, 34, 46, 47, 50, 51, 54, 56, 59.
Barras, Paul F. J. N., Director, 92.
Bartlett, Bailey, 114.
Bastille, The, Paris, 125.
Bathing machine, 93.
Baths, use of cold, 196.
Battle of the Kegs, The, 153.
Baxter, Mary, 100.
Baxter, Thompson, 46, 115, 134, 226.
Baxter, Mrs. Thompson, 107, 134.
Bayard, Samuel, 234.
Beal, Abijah, 239.
Beal, Ann, 239.
Beal, Richard, 61, 141, 193.
Belknap, Jeremy, 180, 197, 198.
Bellamy, ———, 94, 99, 103, 123, 125, 128, 139, 140–141, 143, 146, 148, 150–152, 153, 154, 156, 161, 166, 175, 177, 178, 185–186, 192–193, 205.
Belmont, Pa., 187–188.
Berlin, 138, 157, 158; royal court at, 191.
Berne, capture of, 192.
Bingham, Anne (Willing), 171, 214–215, 242.
Bingham, Maria Matilda. *See* Maria Matilda (Bingham) Tilly.

Birthday of John Adams, 214, 258–259.
Birthday Ball for Washington (1798), 133, 137.
Black, Moses, 112, 114, 115–116, 120, 121, 131, 167, 168, 172, 173, 174, 179, 181, 185, 198, 223, 250.
Black, Mrs. Moses, 79, 112, 116, 120, 121, 124, 129, 131, 137, 141, 155, 162–163, 167, 176, 184, 185, 187, 198, 215, 220, 223, 226, 231, 235, 243, 254, 256, 259.
Blair, Rev. Samuel, Jr., 101, 142, 144.
Bleeding and blistering, 63, 65, 66, 78, 79, 105, 119, 143, 194, 195, 201, 205, 210, 260.
Blount, Thomas, 101.
Blount, William, 100, 101.
Bonaparte, Napoleon, 230.
Bond, William Cranch, 21, 28.
Boston, Mass., plague in, 225; printers, 227.
Boston Mall, 54.
Boston Post Road, 108.
Bourne, Sylvanus, 177.
Bowen, Ann, 12.
Bowen, Elizabeth, 12.
Bowen, Jabez, 10, 11, 12.
Bowen, Mrs. Jabez, 12.
Bowen, Mary, 10.
Brackett, James, 244.
Braintree, address from, 186.
"Braintree, Duke of," 116.
Brehan, Comtesse de, 13.
Briesler, Abigail, 60.
Briesler, Elizabeth, 47, 60, 141.
Briesler, John, Sr., 14, 20, 28, 30, 31, 33, 34, 46, 47, 48, 55, 64, 65, 68, 70, 71, 72, 73, 86, 87, 88, 110, 111, 130, 209, 210, 212, 240.
Briesler, Mrs. John, Sr., 10, 11, 18, 30, 32, 43, 50, 52, 63, 64, 65, 71, 74, 75, 78, 87, 88, 105, 109, 111, 121, 141, 184, 190, 224, 228, 231.
Briesler, John, Jr., 95, 120, 210.
Briesler, Lucy, 65.
Brookfield, Mass., 73, 87, 208–209.
Brown, John, 10, 11.
Brown, Sarah (Smith), 11.
Buck, Daniel, 164.
Buck, Mrs. Daniel, 164.
Burk, John Daly, 200.
Burke, Edmund, 67, 161, 181.
Burr, Aaron, 156; character, 265–266.
Bush Hill, Philadelphia, 65, 67, 187.

272

C.

Cabot, George, 178.
Caillard, Antoine-Bernard, 162.
"Ça ira," 164.
Calamanco (calimanco), 6.
Caldwell, Elias Boudinot, 233.
Callender, James Thomson, 251.
Calvinism, 117, 119.
Cambridge, address from, 186.
Campbell, George W., 117.
Campo Formio, Treaty of, 123.
Canterbury, Archbishop of. *See* Charles Manners-Sutton, Bishop of Norwich.
Carroll, Daniel, 176.
Census and reapportionment, 80–81.
Ceres, 73.
Chase, Samuel, 232, 256.
Childbirth, treatment for, 45.
China tea, 206.
Cholera morbis, 105.
Christianity, Jefferson's disbelief in, 266.
Chronicle, Boston, 91–92, 94, 95, 96, 172.
Church, Benjamin, 25.
Church, Edward, 24, 25, 26, 189, 190.
Church's Cough Drops, 143.
Cincinnati, Society of the, 20.
Civil War, fear of, 172.
Clark, Susanna Boylston (Adams), 89, 209, 211, 213, 252, 260, 266.
Clarke, Rev. John, 45, 174, 197.
Clarkson, Belinda (Smith), 3, 5, 6.
Clergymen, superiority of New England, 26–27, 216; dullness of New York, 27, 53, 117, 119; compared with lawyers, 126.
Clinton, Cornelia (Tappen), 13.
Clinton, George, 13.
Cobbett, William, 95, 101, 132, 143–144, 169, 183, 223.
Cockades, brawl over, 171–172, 176.
Collins, John, 10.
Columbian Centinel, 116, 131, 136, 159, 176, 182, 183, 200, 213, 229, 258.
Conechigo waggons, 188.
Congress, 7; comments on, 15, 28, 29, 39, 44, 54, 83, 92, 93, 94–95, 100–101, 102, 124–125, 127, 132, 135, 139, 140, 142, 143, 145, 146, 148, 149, 153, 154, 155, 161, 162, 173, 178, 193, 194, 201, 207, 217, 219, 221, 227, 230, 231, 236, 239, 263.
Congress Hall, Philadelphia, 225.

Constitution of the United States, comments on, 20–21, 29, 135, 139.
Consulate, French, 230.
Consumption, 41, 192, 193, 201.
Continental Congress (1774–1775), 118, 146.
Convoys, use of, 162.
Cooper, Thomas, 213, 216, 251.
Cost of living, 33, 34, 43, 44, 58, 67–68, 75, 97, 141.
Coxe, Tench, 126, 127.
Craigie, Dr. Andrew, 18.
Cranch, Ann Allen, 258, 260.
Cranch, Anna (Greenleaf), 8–9, 86, 110, 115, 134, 137, 140, 176, 202, 204, 205, 227, 244, 266.
Cranch, Elizabeth. *See* Elizabeth (Cranch) Norton.
Cranch, Elizabeth (Palmer), 36, 40, 42, 45, 49, 112, 227.
Cranch, Joseph, 41, 42, 44, 45, 47, 112, 219.
Cranch, Lucy. *See* Lucy (Cranch) Greenleaf.
Cranch, Mary (Smith), 173, 183, 257, 260; domestic difficulties, 15–16, 67.
Cranch, Richard, Sr., 7, 9, 16, 21, 31, 34, 39, 45, 46, 50, 54, 58, 60 61, 63, 65, 67, 71, 73, 88, 93, 97, 99, 108, 117, 122, 130, 133, 136, 141, 155, 157, 172, 180, 195, 202, 209, 213, 217, 235, 238, 250, 251, 255, 256, 259, 261, 262.
Cranch, Richard, Jr., 102, 115, 227, 258, 266.
Cranch, William, 16, 39, 64, 67, 71, 85, 98, 102, 104, 105, 106, 110, 115, 134, 137, 139, 140, 142, 149, 157, 169, 175–176, 185, 190, 192, 202, 203–204, 205, 211, 217, 221, 225, 227, 232, 233, 239, 244, 246–247, 250, 258, 260, 261, 262, 263, 266.
Cranch, William G., 115, 149, 258, 266.
Crosby, Dr. Ebenezer, 7.
Crosby, Elizabeth, 7, 40.
Cushing, Hannah (Phillips), 9, 37, 40, 62, 119, 129, 144, 232, 234.
Cushing, William, 144, 232, 233, 234.
Custis, Eliza Parke. *See* Eliza Parke (Custis) Law.

D.

Dacca Muslin, 173.
Daggett's Inn, 9.

Dalton, Tristram, 203-204.
Dalton, Mrs. Tristram, 37, 46, 78, 82.
Dana, Francis, 94, 99, 219.
"Dangerous Vice, The," by Edward Church, 24-25.
Daniel, 114.
Darby and Joan, 118, 119, 120.
Davie, William Richardson, 212-213, 249.
Dawes, Lucy (Greenleaf), 173.
Dawes, Thomas, 175.
Deakins, William, Jr., 149, 169.
Debts of the United States, funding of, 22-23, 37, 38, 83; bonds a good investment, 136.
Decatur, Stephen, Sr., 200.
Dejanira, 147.
Delaware, 200.
Delaware River, 188.
Democrats. See Republicans.
DeWindt, Caroline Amelia (Smith), 85, 106, 109, 183, 197, 208, 209, 210-211, 231, 238, 252.
Dexter, Samuel, 227.
Directory, French, 92, 114, 123, 151-152, 156, 158-159, 161, 175, 178, 186, 190, 194, 224.
Draco of Athens, 124.
Duane, William, 220, 258. See Additions and Corrections.
Duncanson, William Mayne, 203-204.
DuPont, Victor Marie, 180-181.
Durant, John Waldo, 64, 68.
Dutch Church, New York, 53; Philadelphia, 222.
Dutch customs, in New York, 35.
Dysentery, 104, 194.

E.

Eastchester, N. Y., 108.
Election of 1800-1801, 217, 237, 251-252, 253, 261, 263, 264-265.
Eliot, Elizabeth, 134, 140.
Elisha, arrogance of, 167, 249.
Ellsworth, Oliver, 212-213, 249.
England, rumored invasion of, 123, 159, 186; comments on, 162, 225, 249.
Episcopal Church, Eastchester, N. Y., 108.
Essay on Man, An, 253.
Essex Junto, 219.
Evans, Thomas, 95.

F.

Fables for the Female Sex, 255.
Farrar's Tavern. See Pease's Inn.
Fashions, 145, 173, 214-215, 218-219, 220, 223, 225, 226, 241-242, 247-248.
Fast Day (May 9, 1798), 171.
Federalists, comments on, 125, 132, 135, 161, 217, 221, 257.
Felt, Abigail Adams (Shaw), 36, 42.
Fenno's *Gazette*, 99-100, 116, 131, 154, 216, 241.
Field, Abigail, 60, 121, 125.
Field, Lilley, 213.
Field, Lucy, 60.
Field, Phoebe (Trask), 104, 114, 115, 120, 121, 125, 131, 163, 212, 231.
Field, Rebecca, 30, 59, 60, 105, 111.
Findley, William, 159-160.
Flagg's Inn, Weston, 107.
Flint, Rev. Jacob, 90, 112, 115.
Foreigners, objections to, 48, 69, 216, 237, 246.
Foreign Intercourse Bill, 127, 139, 142, 149.
Forrest, Uriah, 247.
Fort Stanwix, 116.
Foster, Dwight, 188.
Fourth of July, 20, 98-99, 100, 102, 192-193, 199.
Fox, Gilbert, 165.
France, trouble with, 94, 101-102, 140-141, 145, 146, 148, 151-152, 177, 188, 190, 192, 196, 221; opinion of, 114, 153, 154, 230, 249; denunciation of, 124, 131, 148, 150, 151, 155, 156, 162, 168, 179-180, 181, 186, 193, 205-206; emissaries from, 159.
Francis, Abby (Brown), 10, 12.
Francis, John, 10, 12.
Francis I., of Austria, 123.
Francis Hotel, Philadelphia, 254.
Franking of letters, 58-59.
Franklin, Benjamin, 146.
Frederick William II, of Prussia, 138, 156.
Frederick William III, of Prussia, 138, 145, 156, 158, 191.
Freeman, Nathaniel, Jr., 92, 93, 95, 124.
Freemasons, plots of, 179-180.
French, influence and manners in U.S.A. 120, 161; cockade, 156; conspiracy against U.S.A., 170.

G.

Gallatin, Albert, 139, 151, 161, 162, 175.
Gannett, Caleb, 238.
Gannett, Ruth (Stiles), 238.
Gardiner, John, 38, 40.
George III, 15, 19, 220.
George IV, 266.
Georgetown, D. C., 203, 257–258.
Gerry, Ann (Thompson), 154, 192, 196.
Gerry, Elbridge, 15, 16–17, 38, 81, 99, 103, 186, 192, 193, 196, 205.
Giles, William B., 94, 145, 149, 151.
Giles Gingerbread, 211.
Gill, Mrs. Rebecca, 152.
Gore, Christopher, 249.
Gout, 131.
Governor's House, Boston, 54.
Green, Rev. Ashbel, 235.
Greenleaf, Ann Penn (Allen), 117, 240.
Greenleaf, Anna. *See* Anna (Greenleaf) Cranch.
Greenleaf, Antonia C. A. (Schotten), 86.
Greenleaf, James, 85–86, 97, 117, 128–129, 134, 140, 142, 169, 183, 204, 227, 247; character, 155, 240, 246.
Greenleaf, John, 86, 174, 240.
Greenleaf, Lucy. *See* Lucy (Greenleaf) Dawes.
Greenleaf, Lucy (Cranch), 7, 8, 9, 14, 16, 18, 21, 23, 31, 32, 34, 39, 40, 43, 49, 56, 62, 69, 71, 97, 103, 115, 117, 120, 132, 139, 144, 157, 217, 219, 220, 240; letter to, 173–174.
Gustavus IV, of Sweden, 146.

H.

"Hail Columbia," 164–165, 166, 171.
Hall, Anna, 116, 120, 121, 129, 133, 137, 141, 155, 162–163, 164, 167, 174, 176, 184, 185, 235.
Hall, Susanna (Boylston) [Adams], 6, 14, 18, 21, 24, 31, 34, 51, 55, 60, 67, 164; character, 168.
Hamburg, 157, 180, 181, 185.
Hamilton, Alexander, 21, 37, 81, 83, 126, 252, 255; character, 224; *Public Character ... of John Adams*, 258.
Hamlet, 24.
Hancock, 12.
Hare, Robert, 171.
Harlem, N. Y., 30.
Harper, Robert Goodloe, 139, 163.
Harpers Ferry, 227.
Harvard Commencement, 51, 54, 57, 205.
Hauteval, Lucien, 94, 99, 103, 123, 125, 128, 139, 140–141, 143, 146, 148, 150–152, 153, 154, 156, 161, 166, 175, 177, 178, 185–186, 192–193, 205.
Heath, William, 166.
Hebrews, 88.
Henry VIII, 259.
Hesse-Darmstadt, Louisa of, 156.
Hingham, Mass., Academy at, 198.
Hohenzollern, Prince Ferdinand, 191.
Hohenzollern, Princess Henry, 191.
Hopkinson, Francis, 153.
Hopkinson, Joseph, 164–165, 223.
Hottinguer, Baron, Jean-Conrad, 94, 99, 103, 123, 125, 128, 139, 140–141, 143, 146, 148, 150–152, 153, 154, 156, 161, 166, 175, 177, 178, 185–186, 192–193, 205.
Howard, Elizabeth, 88, 98, 100, 105, 121, 212, 218, 223, 264.
Howell, Richard, 179.
Hudson River, N. Y., 54, 213.
Humphreys, David, 13, 19.
Hunt, Abigail, 60, 98, 99, 105, 111, 172, 184, 206.
Hunt, Ann, 104.
Hunt, Elizabeth, 60, 99, 104.
Hutchinson, Shrimpton, 10.

I.

Ice cream, 19, 55, 98.
Independent Chronicle, Boston, 159, 165.
Indians, visits of, 56, 57, 145–146.
Indian War, 75–76, 77, 81.
Indigence, in old age, 136.
Influenza, 49, 50, 134.
Irish, character of, 132.
Isabella, 82.
Isaiah, 101.
Israel, Children of, 154.
Italian Monk, The, 165.
Izard, Ralph, 30, 37.

J.

Jackson, William, 30, 235, 237.
Jacobins, 91–92, 96, 101, 112, 117, 127, 147, 152, 153, 171, 181, 182, 205, 217, 236–237, 239.

Jamaica, Long Island, 3–7, 43, 44.
James's Powders, 63.
Jarvis, Dr. Charles, 94.
Jarvis, William, 127.
Jay, Sarah Van Brugh (Livingston), 8, 37.
Jay's Treaty, 85, 236–237.
Jefferson, Thomas, 83, 94, 117, 126, 156; character, 44, 137, 265–266; French support of, 147; danger of succession of, 178.
Jeffersonians, spite of, 230, 236, 237, 251–252, 263.
Jeffries, Dr. John, 57, 76, 188.
Jeffries, Mrs. John, 74.
Jeremiah, 127, 159.
Jesuit's Bark, 62, 63, 78.
Johnson, Abigail Louisa (Adams), 209, 211, 213.
Johnson, Joshua, 110, 115, 169, 185, 246.
Johnson, Mrs. Joshua, 169, 175–176, 185, 190, 191, 202, 203, 204, 205, 235, 244, 246, 247, 250, 260.
Jones, Lucy, 42.
Judiciary system, revision of, 1801, 234, 239.
Jugurtha, 153.
Julius Caesar, 69, 94.

K.

Kegs, The Battle of the, 153.
Kendall, Rev. James, 216.
Kentucky, Jeffersonian barbecue in, 237.
King, Mary (Alsop), 46.
King, Rufus, 123, 144–145, 155, 177, 186.
King John, 265.
Kings, Second Book of, 167.
Kings Bridge, New York, 118.
King's Pantheon, 157.
Knox, Henry, 41, 42, 44, 45, 83.
Knox, Lucy (Flucker), 8, 13.

L.

Lafayette, Marquis de, 181.
La Fontaine, 190.
Lamb, John, 127, 189.
Land, as an investment, 136.
Langdon, John, 92.
La Rochefoucauld-Liancourt, Duc de, 114.
Laurance, John, 64.
Law, Eliza Parke (Custis), 30, 134, 140, 149.

Law, Thomas, 140, 149, 203–204.
Lawyers, 38–39, 126.
Lay Preacher of Pennsylvania, 241.
Lear, Tobias, 13, 19, 227.
Le Croyable, 200.
Lee, Henry, 222, 228.
Leoben, Treaty of, 123.
Létombe, Joseph Philippe, 181, 205.
Letter to General Heath, 166.
Letters on the Regicide Peace, 161.
Levant, The, 225.
Liancourt, Duc de. *See* La Rochefoucauld-Liancourt.
Lincoln, Benjamin, 218, 230.
Linn, Rev. William, 27, 53.
Lisbon, Portugal, 95, 138.
Liston, Sir Robert, 224–225. *See* Additions and Corrections.
Livermore, Samuel, 104.
Livingston, Edward, 251.
Livingston, Rev. John Henry, 53.
Louis XVIII., 224.
Louisa of Hesse-Darmstadt, 156.
Louise of Mecklenburg-Strelitz, character, 191.
Lowell, John, 78.
Lowell, Susanna (Cabot), 78.
Ludden, Ruth, 30, 46, 47, 48, 50.
Lyon, Matthew, 132, 135, 146, 194.
Lyons, cloaks from, 158–159.

Mc.

McCormick, Daniel, 4, 12.
McGillivray, Alexander, 57.
McHenry, James, 199, 201, 204, 205, 207, 219, 227.

M.

Madiera Island, 76.
Madison, James, 94, 156.
Mails, tampering with, 104.
Malcom, Samuel B., 100, 155.
Mammea, Creek name for Mrs. John Adams, 56.
Manners-Sutton, Charles, Bishop of Norwich, 116–117.
Man's Inn, Wrentham, 9.
Marchant, Henry, 12.
Marchant, Mrs. Henry, 12.
Maria, 82.
Marriage, sanctity of, 181.

Marshall, John, 94, 125, 193, 195, 196, 221.
Marshall, Thomas, 209.
Marshall, Mrs. Thomas, 208–209.
Marvel of Peru, four o'clocks, 249.
Mason, Elizabeth, 247–248.
Mason, Jonathan, Jr., 9, 244, 247.
Mason, Stevens T., 92.
Mason, Susannah (Powell), 9.
Massachusetts, politics of, 23, 38–39, 124, 195–196, 219.
Massachusetts Mercury, Boston, 116, 117, 183.
Masters, Ann (Smith), 6, 210, 211.
Measles, 37, 39, 41.
Medford, Mass., address from, 186.
Medical Society, Boston, 41.
Merchantmen, Arming of, 146.
Messinger, Rev. Rosewell, 229.
Micah, 216.
Mico Maco, 56.
Mifflin, Thomas, 171.
Milton, John, 46, 153, 157, 248.
Milton, Mass., petition, 150, 152.
Minot, George Richards, 229.
Monroe, James, 189.
Montpelier, Md., 257.
Moore, Edward, 255.
Morris, Gouverneur, 189.
Morris, Mary (White), 134–135, 220.
Morris, Robert, 97, 134, 142, 143.
Mortefontaine, Peace of, 212–213, 218, 221, 224, 249.
Morton, Eliza Susan, 211.
Morton, John, 211.
Mount Vernon, 57, 201, 204, 205, 225, 227.
Mulmull, 103.
Mumps, 210.
Murray, William Vans, 125, 129, 177, 192.

N.

Nash, Thomas, 236, 239.
Negroes, 3, 20, 48, 70, 72, 73, 75, 91, 99, 125, 256.
Nemours, Pierre Samuel Dupont de, 180.
Netherlands, The, 157, 224.
Neutrality, American theory of, 148, 162, 186.
New England, preference for, 140, 142, 227, 237.
Newspapers, malice of, 19, 25, 28, 55, 95, 96–97, 117, 146–147, 159, 160, 165, 176, 213, 237, 253.

New Theatre, Philadelphia, 164–166.
New Year's Day, in New York, 34–35; in Philadelphia, 119.
New York, N. Y., climate of, 18, 32, 46, 64; yellow fever, 209–210; and election of 1800, 251.
New York *Commercial Advertiser*, 213.
Nicholas, John, 142.
Nicholas Amendment, 142.
Nicholson, John, 143.
Nighthawks, 72.
Night Thoughts, 87.
Non-Intercourse Bill (1798), 188.
North American Land Company, 97, 102.
Norton, Elizabeth (Cranch), 4, 7, 8, 16, 17, 21, 23, 31, 32, 34, 36, 39, 41, 42, 43, 44, 45, 47, 49, 50, 52, 56, 60, 69, 71, 76, 77, 88, 90, 93, 103, 108, 115, 117, 120, 124, 132, 139, 144, 157, 163, 164, 166–167, 170, 178, 181, 217, 219, 220, 226, 250, 259, 261, 264.
Norton, Rev. Jacob, 71, 169.
Norton, Richard Cranch, 43, 45, 49, 56, 59, 69, 71.
Norton, T. B. Adams, 232.
Norton, William Smith, 77.
Norwich, Bishop of. *See* Charles Manners-Sutton.

O.

Old Colony (Plymouth), 188.
On the Sublime and the Beautiful, 67. *See* Additions and Corrections.
Otis, Harrison Gray, 92, 95, 139, 166.
Otis, Mary (Smith) [Gray], 75, 79, 129, 144, 152, 163, 164, 190, 202, 204, 208, 214, 217, 228.
Otis, Sally (Foster), 103.
Otis, Samuel Allyne, 12, 41, 164, 170, 210, 214.

P.

Packard, Ann (Quincy), 57.
Packard, Rev. Asa, 108.
Paine, Mrs. Eunice (Treat), 64, 76.
Paine, Thomas, 189.
Paine, Rev. Thomas, 229.
Palmer, Elizabeth. *See* Elizabeth (Palmer) Cranch.
Palmer, Joseph Porter, 37.
Palmer, Mary, 36, 40, 45, 49.

277

Palmer, Mary (Cranch), 18, 22, 34, 36–37, 39.
Paper money, 16.
Paradise Lost, 153, 157, 248.
Parisian girl, story of, 42–43.
Paterson, William, 232, 233.
Paulus Hook, N. J., 17.
Peabody, Elizabeth (Smith) [Shaw], 21, 31, 36, 41, 42, 60, 104, 109, 112, 113, 122, 125, 192, 201, 217, 232, 242.
Peabody, Rev. Stephen, 192.
Peace Field. *See* Quincy, Adams houses at.
Pease's Inn, Shrewsbury, 107, 209.
Penn's Hill, Braintree, memories of, 28.
Peruvian Bark, 62, 63, 78.
"Peter Porcupine." *See* William Cobbett.
Peters, Richard, 187–188.
Peters, Sarah (Robinson), 188.
Pharaoh, and the Red Sea, 186.
Philadelphia, climate of, 23, 68, 81, 103, 104, 105–106, 113, 121, 124, 128, 143, 147, 152, 167, 170, 182, 192, 194, 195, 199, 204, 208, 220, 225, 231, 234, 236, 238–239, 243, 244, 250; as capital, 49, 51, 58, 59, 60, 220; house in, 74, 188, 238, 239, 254–255, 259; social life in, 77; yellow fever in, 111, 194, 210; manners in, 133, 140.
Phillipse' Bridge. *See* Kings Bridge, New York.
Phipps, Dr. Thomas, 240.
Pickering, Timothy, 128, 138, 156; character, 221.
Pinckney, C. C., 92, 186, 193.
Piozzi, Hester Lynch (Salusbury) [Thrale], 168.
Plainfield, N. J., 214.
Pleurisy, 65.
Pliny, 227.
Pope, Alexander, 253.
Popery, 168.
Popular government, 83; danger of, 237, 251, 253, 263, 265–266.
"Porcupine, Peter." *See* William Cobbett.
Portugal, 95, 189.
"President's March," 164.
Price, Rev. Richard, 21, 45, 53.
Princes Gardens, 29.
Privateers, French, 178.
Proofs of a Conspiracy . . . of Freemasons, 180.
Proverbs, 22, 26, 181.

Prussia, Treaty with, 156.
Prussia, mission to, 1797. *See* J. Q. Adams.

Q.

Quakers, 5, 112, 132.
Quincy, Abigail (Phillips), 152.
Quincy, Josiah (1772–1864), 95.
Quincy, Josiah, Jr., 152.
Quincy, Martha (Salisbury), 9.
Quincy, Nancy. *See* Ann (Quincy) Packard.
Quincy, Norton, 32, 53, 67, 104, 263–264.
Quincy, Adams houses at, 22, 28, 41, 44–45, 50, 52, 54, 55, 58, 60–61, 72, 73, 74, 76, 80, 82, 85, 88, 89, 96, 99, 101, 103, 104, 106, 107, 110, 114, 119, 122, 130, 141, 144, 148–149, 160, 163, 166, 167, 170, 183, 184, 195, 199, 206–207, 230–231, 234, 240, 246; praise of, 262.
Quinsy, 115, 208, 260.

R.

Randolph, Edmund, 189.
Randolph, John, of Roanoke, 208, 230, 231, 239, 251.
Ray, James, 202–203.
Real estate, burden of, 49–50, 51, 52, 54–55, 58, 60–61, 122, 141.
Reed, John, 149.
Religion, 53; plot against, 179–180; importance of, 124, 148, 150, 155, 181, 186, 197–198, 216, 266.
Republicans, spite of, 55, 161, 230, 236, 251–252, 263.
Reynolds, Dr. James, 128.
Rheumatism, 46, 66, 75, 78, 119, 131, 158, 178, 262.
Rhode Island, politics of, 1789, 11.
Richmond Hill, N. Y., beauty of, 14, 17–18, 23, 33, 44, 49; life at, 19, 22; picture of, 54.
Rip Van Dam Church, 53.
Robbins, Jonathan, 236, 239.
Robison, John, 179–180, 181.
Rodgers, Rev. John, 26.
Rodgers, Mary [Grant], 3, 40, 44, 50, 54, 122.
Rome, Jugurtha's opinion of, 153.
Rosina, 165.
Roxbury, Mass., petition, 150, 152.
Rum, strange use of, 163.
Rush, Dr. Benjamin, 66, 69, 78, 131, 140, 201, 217, 225; libel suit, 223.

Russell, Benjamin, 94, 182, 183.
Russell's *Commercial Gazette*, Boston, 213, 216.
Russia sheeting, 206.

S.

St. Anthony's Fire, 47.
St. Clair's Defeat, 75-76, 77, 81.
St. Croix, 68.
St. Hilaire, Margaret (Smith), 5, 61.
St. James's, Court of, 35.
St. Paul's Church, New York, 27.
Salaries and wages, 28, 47-48, 51, 97, 138, 139, 147, 159, 172, 184, 259, 263.
Sally and Polly, 178, 184.
Santo Domingo, 182.
Schuylkill River, Pa., 188.
Scotch Plains, N. J., 238, 240, 252.
Scott, Gustavus, 102, 263.
Search and seizure, 156, 162, 175, 177, 186.
Sectionalism, growth of, 251-252.
Sedan, English goods at, 158.
Sedgwick, Theodore, 38.
Sentimental Journey, A, 212, 255.
Servants, comments on, 17, 20, 30, 33, 35, 43, 46, 47-48, 68-69, 73, 76, 82, 91, 111, 121, 194, 243, 246, 248, 251.
Sewall, Samuel, 95.
Shakespeare, 24, 69, 94, 142, 259, 265.
Shaw, Abigail Adams. *See* Abigail Adams (Shaw) Felt.
Shaw, Elizabeth Quincy, 112, 113, 117, 137, 143, 145, 155, 167, 176, 178, 184, 192, 195, 197, 201, 205.
Shaw, Elizabeth (Smith). *See* Elizabeth (Smith) [Shaw] Peabody.
Shaw, William Smith, 74, 195, 202, 204, 217, 219, 221, 225, 227.
Sheafe, James, 219, 227.
Shenango, Pa., 111.
Shepard, William, 99.
Simplicity cap, 157.
Sisyphus, labors of, 125.
Skinner, Thomson J., 93, 95, 124.
Slaves, negro, the best servants, 48.
Small pox, 23, 30, 31, 47, 60, 61, 63, 65, 95, 155, 163, 164, 246.
Smith, Abigail. *See* Abigail (Smith) Adams.
Smith, Abigail (Adams), 3, 4, 5, 7, 13, 16, 17, 19, 25, 30, 32, 33, 41, 43, 44, 46, 50, 51, 52, 56, 57, 59, 60, 61, 63, 64, 65, 66, 68, 69, 72, 73, 76, 77, 78, 79, 80, 84, 85, 88, 89, 93, 103, 106, 108, 109, 110, 111, 112, 113, 114, 116, 119, 122, 125, 129, 130-131, 139, 144, 195, 197, 209, 210, 211, 213, 217, 218, 219, 222, 223, 227, 231, 235, 238, 251, 252; character, 240.
Smith, Ann. *See* Ann (Smith) Masters.
Smith, Belinda. *See* Belinda (Smith) Clarkson.
Smith, Caroline Amelia. *See* Caroline Amelia (Smith) DeWindt.
Smith, Catherine Louisa (Salmon), 21, 23, 82.
Smith, Charity, 5.
Smith, Charles, 112, 122, 123, 195.
Smith, Elizabeth. *See* Elizabeth (Smith) [Shaw] Peabody.
Smith, Elizabeth, niece of Mrs. Adams, 75, 79, 82, 122, 130, 132, 152, 182, 187, 195, 242.
Smith, Elizabeth, 6.
Smith, James, 6.
Smith, John, 6.
Smith, John Adams, 3, 5, 13, 17, 20, 30, 31, 36, 43, 44, 66, 68, 85, 105, 107, 109, 113, 120, 187, 217.
Smith, Justus Bush, 6, 111.
Smith, Louisa, 12, 17, 20, 21, 23, 30, 31, 32, 41, 50, 63, 65, 73, 74, 78, 105, 134, 141, 149, 174, 187, 189, 190, 210, 217, 219, 238, 251, 255.
Smith, Margaret. *See* Margaret (Smith) St. Hilaire.
Smith, Margaret (Stephens), 3, 6, 23, 43, 119, 197, 210, 252, 254, 261.
Smith, Mary. *See* Mary (Smith) Cranch.
Smith, Mary, 88, 122, 129-130, 131, 132.
Smith, Mary Carter, 168, 174, 195.
Smith, Sarah. *See* Sarah (Smith) Adams.
Smith, Thomas Hollis, 56, 59, 65.
Smith, William, Jr., (1746-1787), 51.
Smith, Mrs. William, Jr., 84, 85, 109, 129, 131, 155, 163, 174, 197.
Smith, William, III., 23, 43, 123.
Smith, William, merchant, 4, 46, 52, 88-89, 93, 99, 106, 107, 136, 168, 169, 174, 178, 183, 184, 185, 218, 227.
Smith, William Loughton, 37, 194.
Smith, William Stephens, 3, 6, 13, 17, 30, 46, 59, 61, 66, 69, 77, 79, 80, 88, 89, 105,

113, 116, 129, 203, 211, 214, 252; character, 69–70, 109, 110, 111, 119, 120, 130–131, 252–253.
Smith, William Steuben, 3, 5, 13, 20, 23, 32, 36, 43, 44, 46, 77, 84, 107, 109, 113, 120, 187, 213, 217.
Snowden, Ann (Ridgeley), 256–257.
Snowden, Thomas, 256–257.
Solomon, as carpenter, 233.
Spain, foreign policy of, 177–178.
Speculation, mania for, 81, 82, 84, 89, 91, 109, 129, 134–135, 142, 143, 169, 183, 202–204, 220.
Stage coaches, 4.
State debts, assumption of, 38.
Sterne, Laurence, 76, 147, 212, 255.
Stoddert, Benjamin, 204.
Storer, Ann, 211.
Storer, Charles, 61.
Storer, Ebenezer, 61, 219.
Storer, George, 21, 61.
Storer, Hannah (Quincy), 11, 61.
Storer, Mary, 61.
Strong, Caleb, 83.
Suicide, 42.
Sullivan, James, 87.
Sumner, Increase, 195–196, 219.
Supreme Court, clerkship, 232–233, 234.
Sweden, treaty with, 146.
Swift, Jonathan, 47.
Switzerland, 123; conquest of, 192.

T.

Tailor, Polly, 10, 11, 12, 20, 30, 33, 47, 48, 50, 52, 65, 66, 70, 73, 74, 76, 77, 86.
Talleyrand, Charles Maurice, 151 152, 190, 193, 224.
Tartar Emetic, 50.
Temple, "Lady" Elizabeth (Bowdoin), 8, 13, 46.
Thacher, George, 101.
Thacher, Rev. Peter, 45.
Thanksgiving, in New England, 217.
Thaxter, Rev. John, 61.
Thayer, Atherton, 200.
Theophilanthropy, 180.
Thrale, Hester Lynch (Salusbury). *See* Piozzi.
Three Warnings, The, 168.
Tilly, Comtesse de, Maria Matilda (Bingham), 214–215, 242.

Timon of Athens, 142.
Tirril, Nathan, 68, 141.
Tousard, Anna Maria (Geddes), 244–245, 251.
Tousard, Anne Louis de, 244–245, 251.
Trajan, 227.
Trenton, N. J., 210, 211, 224.
Trumbull, John, 56.
Tudor, William, 108.
Tufts, Dr. Cotton, 14, 22, 32, 36, 40, 41, 42, 53, 58, 59, 61, 70, 71, 72, 76, 79, 80, 82, 93, 98, 122, 130, 133, 141, 144, 145, 160, 166, 167, 170, 175, 178, 183, 184, 190, 199, 201, 222, 238, 240, 242, 246, 250, 251, 261.
Tufts, Mrs. Cotton, Jr., 42.
Tufts, Susannah [Warner], 32, 42, 90, 144, 243, 245.
Turner, Mrs. George, 49.

U.

United States, 182.
United States, Funding of debts of. *See* Debts.

V.

Varnum, Joseph B., 93, 124, 175.
Vendues, 72.
Vermin, 106.
"Virginia Declamation," 127–128.
Virginia manners, 133, 142, 149, 208, 227.
Volney, Comte de, 189.
Voltaire, prediction about Popery, 168.
Volunteers, for Army, 175, 179.

W.

Washington, Martha [Custis], 8, 19, 46, 134, 225; appearance and character, 13, 15, 29–30, 32, 57, 140, 227; receptions of, 35, 55; trip with, 51.
Washington, D.C., 102; as new capital, 234, 247, 254, 257; commissioner of, 263.
Welsh, Dr. Thomas, 183, 185, 187, 198.
Welsh, Mrs. Thomas, 93, 102, 117, 132, 155, 157, 190, 197.
Welsh, Thomas, Jr., 185.
West Point, N. Y., 227.
Whist, 55.
White House, Washington, D.C., 257, 259–260.

280

Whitman, Rev. Kilborn, 111, 112, 115–116, 117, 119, 185.
Whitney, Rev. Peter, 90, 125, 126, 208, 216, 220, 223, 226, 232, 234, 239.
Whooping cough, 266.
Wibird, Rev. Anthony, 26, 104, 120, 125, 226–227, 249–250.
William V., of Holland, 224.
Williams's Inn, Marlborough, 87, 107.
Wine cellar, at Quincy, 55, 107, 129–130.
Wolcott, Elizabeth (Stoughton), 101.
Wolcott, Oliver, Jr., 125, 127; advises John Adams against leaving Philadelphia, 1797, 101.
Warner, Susannah, 139, 143, 164, 168, 195.
Warren, James, 188.
Warren, Mercy (Otis), 16–17, 188.
Washington, Bushrod, 233.
Washington, George, 83, 97, 126; illness, 13; appearance and character, 15, 19, 20, 26, 29–30, 32, 35, 222, 228–229; visit to New England, 29, 34; dread of his death, 49; tour of the South, 71; coinage and statue, 81; criticism of, 98–99, 189; political patronage, 127; birthday, 133, 137, 235; courtesy of, 197; nominated commander-in-chief (1798), 199, 201, 204, 207; death of, 222, 225, 226, 227; tributes to, 226, 227, 228–229, 235, 237, 238.

X.

"X Y Z Mission," 94, 99, 103, 123, 125, 128, 139, 140–141, 143, 146, 148, 150–152, 153, 154, 156, 161, 166, 175, 177, 178, 185–186, 192–193, 205.

Y.

"Yankee Doodle," 164.
Yellow fever, Philadelphia, 111, 194, 210, 214; New York, 209–210.
Young, Edward, *Night Thoughts*, 87.

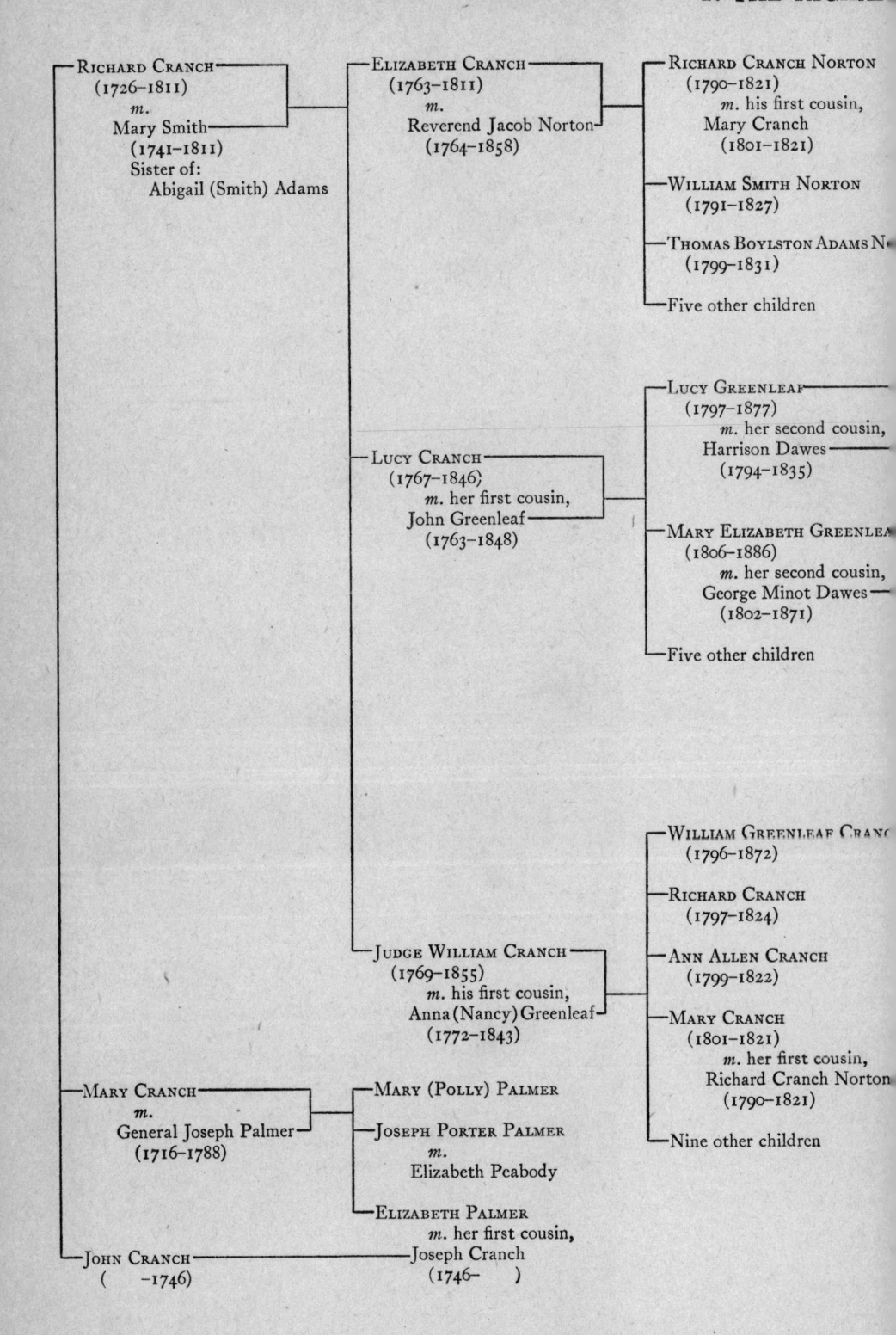

2: THE RICHAR[D]

- RICHARD CRANCH
  (1726–1811)
  m.
  Mary Smith
  (1741–1811)
  Sister of:
  Abigail (Smith) Adams
  - ELIZABETH CRANCH
    (1763–1811)
    m.
    Reverend Jacob Norton
    (1764–1858)
    - RICHARD CRANCH NORTON
      (1790–1821)
      m. his first cousin,
      Mary Cranch
      (1801–1821)
    - WILLIAM SMITH NORTON
      (1791–1827)
    - THOMAS BOYLSTON ADAMS N[ORTON]
      (1799–1831)
    - Five other children
  - LUCY CRANCH
    (1767–1846)
    m. her first cousin,
    John Greenleaf
    (1763–1848)
    - LUCY GREENLEAF
      (1797–1877)
      m. her second cousin,
      Harrison Dawes
      (1794–1835)
    - MARY ELIZABETH GREENLEA[F]
      (1806–1886)
      m. her second cousin,
      George Minot Dawes
      (1802–1871)
    - Five other children
  - JUDGE WILLIAM CRANCH
    (1769–1855)
    m. his first cousin,
    Anna (Nancy) Greenleaf
    (1772–1843)
    - WILLIAM GREENLEAF CRANC[H]
      (1796–1872)
    - RICHARD CRANCH
      (1797–1824)
    - ANN ALLEN CRANCH
      (1799–1822)
    - MARY CRANCH
      (1801–1821)
      m. her first cousin,
      Richard Cranch Norton
      (1790–1821)
    - Nine other children
- MARY CRANCH
  m.
  General Joseph Palmer
  (1716–1788)
  - MARY (POLLY) PALMER
  - JOSEPH PORTER PALMER
    m.
    Elizabeth Peabody
  - ELIZABETH PALMER
    m. her first cousin,
    Joseph Cranch
    (1746–   )
- JOHN CRANCH
  (–1746)